THIS VAST
SOUTHERN EMPIRE

THIS VAST
SOUTHERN EMPIRE

Slaveholders at the Helm
of American Foreign Policy

Matthew Karp

Harvard University Press

Cambridge, Massachusetts, and London, England

2016

Second printing

Names: Karp, Matthew, 1981– author.
Title: This vast southern empire : slaveholders at the helm of
American foreign policy / Matthew Karp.
Description: Cambridge, Massachusetts : Harvard University Press, 2016. |
Includes bibliographical references and index.
Identifiers: LCCN 2016009232 | ISBN 9780674737259 (alk. paper)
Subjects: LCSH: Slavery—Government policy—United States—History. |
Slavery—Political aspects—United States—History. | United States—Foreign
relations—1783–1865. | United States—Politics and government—1783–1865. |
Power (Social sciences)—United States—History.
Classification: LCC E183.7 .K345 2016 | DDC 306.3 / 62097309033—dc23
LC record available at http://lccn.loc.gov/2016009232

For my mother, Freddi Karp

Contents

Introduction: The World the Slaveholders Craved   1

1. Confronting the Great Apostle of Emancipation   10

2. The Strongest Naval Power on Earth   32

3. A Hemispheric Defense of Slavery   50

4. Slavery's Dominoes: Brazil and Texas   70

5. The Young Hercules of America   103

6. King Cotton, Emperor Slavery   125

7. Slaveholding Visions of Modernity   150

8. Foreign Policy amid Domestic Crisis   173

9. The Military South   199

10. American Slavery, Global Power   226

Epilogue: The Rod of Empire   251

Notes   259
Acknowledgments   345
Credits   349
Index   351

In the foreign, as in the domestic,
policy of the United States,
the interest of the slaveholders
served as the guiding star.

—Karl Marx, 1861

Introduction

The World the Slaveholders Craved

THE STRUGGLE OVER THE FUTURE OF SLAVERY spanned the nineteenth-century world. For centuries the toil of enslaved African workers had formed the backbone of a colonial economy that stretched across the Atlantic Ocean. Then the great revolutions at the close of the eighteenth century—American, French, Haitian—unleashed social forces and political ideas that offered a sweeping challenge to slave labor. Over the next several decades, slavery's wide-ranging opponents—republican lawmakers, liberal reformers, rebellious bondspeople themselves—achieved a number of major victories. Some New World states and provinces, from Chile to Vermont, abolished slavery altogether; others, like Pennsylvania and Peru, took measures that aimed at gradual emancipation. In 1833 abolitionists claimed a further triumph when the greatest power in the world, Great Britain, passed a law that announced the end of slavery in its remaining American colonies.[1]

Yet for all the momentum of antislavery politics, the three largest slaveholding societies in the world—the Spanish colony of Cuba, the Empire of Brazil, and the United States of America—remained firmly committed to black servitude. At the midpoint of the nineteenth century all three flourished as never before, exporting unprecedented quantities of cotton, sugar, and coffee to the industrializing economies of the North Atlantic. British emancipation notwithstanding, the total value of trade in slave-produced goods nearly doubled between 1820 and 1860. By the start of the American Civil War, six million men, women, and children toiled in bondage, the largest number in the history of the Western Hemisphere.[2]

Although the transatlantic abolitionist movement declared with increasing vehemence that human bondage had no rightful place in modern life, the planters and politicians who presided over slavery's boom saw no reason to abandon the field. On the contrary, slaveholders grew increasingly confident about the strength of their position within the mid-nineteenth-century world order. In an era marked by global economic expansion and fierce political collision, the fate of chattel slavery remained very much undecided. As both proslavery and antislavery forces scrambled for advantage, the shock waves of their struggle spread far beyond the traditional nodes of the Atlantic basin. Farmers, migrants, merchants, and soldiers from Ottoman Turkey, Qing China, British India, and Mexican California found their worlds affected by the international contest over slavery.

No wonder American abolitionists believed that national arguments about bondage had global consequences. "This question of Slavery does not concern America alone," proclaimed the Massachusetts minister Theodore Parker in 1856. "[A]ll Christendom is likewise party to the contest."[3] American slaveholders agreed. By the middle of the century southern masters ruled over the wealthiest and most dynamic slave society the world had ever known. If slave labor had an international future, they would certainly command it. Far from isolated reactionaries, crying out against the transformations of the age, proslavery leaders warmly embraced the global dimensions of their struggle. A chief instrument in their endeavors was the foreign policy of the United States. Throughout the antebellum decades, it was through the operation of U.S. foreign policy that southern statesmen mounted some of their most daring efforts to advance the international cause of slavery. The partial success and ultimate failure of these ventures—including the boldest foreign policy project of all, the founding of the Confederate States of America—played no small part in determining the future of the nineteenth-century world.[4]

————

Not so long ago, it seemed self-evident that human bondage could not survive the mid-nineteenth century. "Of course slave societies, including that of the South, were doomed," sighed Eric Hobsbawm as he settled in to consider the subject in *The Age of Capital*. By the 1850s, slavery as a factor in world history was "patently on the decline," its economic muscle amputated by the spread of free labor, its social logic repudiated by bourgeois values.[5] Twenty-first century scholarship, however, has turned this verdict almost upside down. Slavery's massive midcentury expansion, its dynamic integration into the world market, and its brutal assimilation of modern economic practices have all received new and powerful emphasis.[6] Older assumptions about the provincialism of the antebellum South have been demolished as historians have rediscovered the intellectual sophistication of the slaveholding elite.[7]

Few mid-nineteenth-century Americans were more deeply engaged with international politics than southern slaveholders. A class whose main source of income derived from the global marketplace could not afford to isolate itself from the rest of the world. Compared with Maine dairy farmers, Michigan lumber dealers, or Pennsylvania iron makers, whose goods were consumed within national borders, cotton planters from Georgia to Texas were almost inescapably cosmopolitan in outlook.[8] Yet the most powerful American slaveholders paid close attention to developments all around the globe in ways that went far beyond a desire to market their plantation exports.

Southern elites kept the international politics of slavery under constant surveillance, tracking threats to slave property across the hemisphere and monitoring oscillations in global attitudes toward emancipation. They carefully followed the course of world affairs—not only the storms of revolution and reaction in Europe, but also the steady growth of imperial influence in Africa and Asia. They stayed abreast of the latest developments in military technology and administration, from British naval armaments to French infantry deployments in Algeria. Above all, slaveholding leaders sought to keep pace with the constant strivings of the mid-nineteenth-century world—the expansion of commerce, the march of empire, the advance of science, and the reshaping of state power.[9]

Neither flaming hotheads nor desiccated reactionaries, America's most powerful slaveholders were earthbound and waterbound men of the world—practical visionaries who, in Hobsbawm's phrase, "thought in continents and in oceans." This does not mean that antebellum southerners were no different from the other bourgeois elites whose ambition and imagination gave shape to the Age of Capital. Unlike London financiers or New York railway executives, the leading men of the South could not envision a global future without the fundamental institution of African slavery. Their continents were to be civilized with the enforced toil of dark-skinned workers, and their oceans were to be opened as highways to the rich produce of bound labor.[10]

But in the evolving world of the mid-nineteenth century, the South's commitment to bondage made it distinctive, not irrelevant or obsolete. If there was little that was "domestic" about southern slave institutions, there was less that was "peculiar." Enslaved Cuba and Brazil were also booming, and by 1850 even antislavery European powers had begun to experiment with new systems of racialized and coerced labor, from Dutch Java to the British West Indies. For the southern masters who celebrated it, slavery could claim a distinguished history, a flourishing present, and a glorious future. In both the American world they made and the global order they craved, southern elites understood the growth of slavery as no more and no less than "the true progress of civilization."[11]

During the middle decades of the nineteenth century, southern statesmen not only imagined an alternative slaveholding "history of the future": they worked actively to construct it.[12] The ideological confidence and worldly sophistication of American slaveholders cannot be separated from their control of American state power. The name Hegel was first pronounced in the U.S. Congress by a Mississippi representative who quoted the *Philosophy of History* on the benefits of slavery to the African race. One of the earliest congressional citations of Auguste Comte came from a Texan as part of an argument that slave labor was a necessary feature of global development.[13] Slaveholding statesmen in Washington reached for these transatlantic intellectual authorities not merely to show off their learning— although that was surely a consideration—but because they intended to advance their theoretical reflections with the material power of the U.S. government. To fathom their intentions and to take an accurate measure of their strength, we need not only an ideological but also an institutional account of proslavery internationalism.[14]

That account must begin with the blunt fact of southern power within the American state. In the two decades before the Civil War, proslavery elites and their largely compliant northern allies maintained a vise-like grip on the executive branch of the U.S. national government, including the presidency, the cabinet, and important lower levels of federal administration. This much we know both from abolitionist litanies about the scope of the "Slave Power" and from careful modern scholarship on the proslavery bias of the early American republic.[15] Nevertheless, those old antislavery invocations may still have new things left to teach us. "Since the slavery agitation," Iowa congressman Josiah Grinnell observed in 1865, slaveholders "have had the Secretaryship of State for two thirds of the time; and . . . for four fifths of the time have the Secretary of War and the Secretary of the Navy been from the South." W. E. B. Du Bois later calculated that before the Civil War 80 out of 134 U.S. ministers abroad hailed from the slaveholding states.[16] Relative to its free population, the South held disproportionate influence in virtually every branch of the antebellum U.S. government. But slaveholders maintained especially firm control over what might be called the "outward state"—the sector of the federal government responsible for foreign relations, military policy, and the larger role that American power assumed outside American borders.[17]

Looking back after years of brutal civil war, Grinnell saw a whiff of separatist menace surrounding the South's domination of antebellum military affairs. But in the 1840s and 1850s slaveholding leaders did not assume cabinet posts to prepare for a coming conflict of arms, or even to augment their sectional strength in a divided union. Instead they sought with terrific ambition to command the power of the entire United States—and then, crucially, to use that power in world politics. International in aspiration, slaveholding leaders were profoundly national in operation.

As early as 1922 Arthur Schlesinger dismissed the notion that the South's antebellum commitment to limited government had meaning beyond the necessarily defensive tactics of a political minority. Throughout American history, he wrote, "the group advocating state rights at any period have sought its shelter in much the same spirit that a western pioneer seeks his storm-cellar when a tornado is raging." Plenty of issues in antebellum politics sent southerners rushing to the storm cellar of states' rights. The power of the central government in domestic affairs, many believed, could threaten the sovereignty of masters over the enslaved people they held as property.[18]

But when the question involved the national government's direct relationship to slavery, southern elites were more tornado than pioneer. In debates over the congressional gag rule on abolitionist petitions, fugitive slave laws, and other issues, slaveholders eagerly embraced the proslavery clout of the federal government.[19] "Between the slave power and states' rights there was no necessary connection," argued Henry Adams in 1882. "Whenever a question arose of extending or protecting slavery, the slave-holders became friends of centralized power, and used that dangerous weapon with a kind of frenzy."[20]

Nowhere did slaveholders wield their power with more energy or commitment than in the realm of foreign and military policy. As executive

officers, legislators, diplomats, military commanders, and journalists, influential southern elites worked to build a vigorous U.S. government that
could pursue significant objectives abroad. The two warmest friends of
centralized power in all antebellum foreign affairs were Secretary of State
John C. Calhoun of South Carolina and President James K. Polk of Tennessee. The two most ambitious reformers of the antebellum armed forces
were Secretary of the Navy Abel Upshur of Virginia and Secretary of War
Jefferson Davis of Mississippi.

It may be tempting to regard this embrace of federal power as a clear
proof that all southern political ideas were no more than hypocritical justifications for slave property. "Mr. Calhoun," as one Richmond editor wrote
of the famous states' rights champion, "was the master and not the slave of
theories."[21] But the proslavery effort to build a strong outward state differed from the South's parallel support for the gag rule or fugitive slave
laws. In foreign and military policy slaveholders summoned federal authority not only to secure their immediate property rights, but also to extend the power of the United States on an international stage. This was not
hypocrisy; it was ideology, and strategy, too. The master theorists of the
master class did not demand a rigid or slavish obedience to the principle of
local sovereignty. Rather, they sought to consolidate proslavery forces for a
larger struggle that spanned the Atlantic world.

The wealth and power of the United States counted among slavery's
most important strategic assets, especially in the Western Hemisphere, where
the growing North American union loomed over the younger and smaller
republics to its south. Traditionally, historians have tended to assume that
slaveholders' chief interest in Latin America lay in gobbling it up. Southern
hunger for more slave territory, whether in the Caribbean basin or in the
continental southwest, has long figured as the centerpiece of proslavery
foreign policy. From the perspective of domestic politics, this makes perfect
sense: the Civil War emerged from a conflict over the extension of slavery.[22]
But as an interpretation of the way slaveholding leaders viewed the world, it
leaves something to be desired.

The most pronounced characteristic of proslavery foreign policy was
neither a ravenous quest for fresh slave territory nor a desperate search for
possible new slave states. Over and above these desires stood the need to
protect systems of slave property across the hemisphere. After all, American
soil was not the only slave soil; the United States was not the only slave
state. Southern elites showed special concern for their fellow slaveholding

societies in the hemisphere, especially Cuba, Brazil, and the independent republic of Texas. Sometimes, as with Texas in 1845, protecting slavery required annexing new territory. On other occasions, as in Cuba in 1843 or 1854, it involved a more restrained policy of proslavery solidarity and cooperation. In virtually every situation, however, the preservation of slave institutions took priority over the acquisition of new land. Territorial expansion was only one tactical option on a larger strategic menu—a more comprehensive foreign policy agenda that contemporary opponents of bondage, including Karl Marx, rightly identified as "armed propaganda for slavery abroad."[23]

The most spectacular examples of this armed propaganda were the filibuster invasions of Latin America. Between 1848 and 1860 a handful of lone commandos in the United States raised private armies to attack Cuba, Mexico, and Nicaragua, often with the stated goal of expanding the domain of slavery.[24] These swashbuckling imperialists have claimed a large share of historical attention even though their efforts universally ended in disaster. This book takes a different approach; it concentrates not on private filibusters but on the much more powerful and only occasionally less flamboyant southern elites in charge of the U.S. government. It was these slaveholders, after all—weighty statesmen, not wild-eyed soldiers of fortune—who acquired Texas, protected slavery in Cuba, and oversaw the conquest of Mexico.

For nearly two full decades, these men organized U.S. foreign relations around what might fairly be called a foreign policy of slavery. To be sure, slaveholding leaders did not always agree on their objectives abroad; frequently, on questions of national politics, they quarrelled among themselves at home. Yet for all the political fault lines that divided the antebellum southern elite, it would be misleading to view master class foreign policy as a chaos of colliding egos, regional splits, and partisan feuds. In fact, a broad and powerful combination of southern elites, from Andrew Jackson and John Tyler to Jefferson Davis and Alexander Stephens, insisted on the centrality of slavery in American international relations.[25]

Equally important, these elites insisted on an essential unity between the slave South and the rest of the nation. Amid the 1844 debates over Texas annexation, the *Richmond Enquirer* published a letter from a particularly hot-tempered central Virginia correspondent. C. R. Fontaine had just organized a pro-Texas public meeting in Buckingham County, and he wrote to denounce the anti-slavery opponents of annexation as "base and villainous" agitators. Former President John Quincy Adams, the most outspoken national critic of

Texas and slavery, provoked Fontaine's special fury: this "Hyena in human shape," he alleged, hoped to trigger a civil war and spread "butchery, murder and rapine" across the land. Yet Fontaine was assured that such "disunionist" fanatics would not succeed in bringing about the ruin of "this vast Southern Empire." To thwart this terrible fate, he predicted, "plenty of Americans, North, South, and West," would leap to defend the nation by rescuing Texas from "the unhallowed hands of England."[26]

Throughout the antebellum period, the slaveholding statesmen at the helm of U.S. foreign policy generally shared Fontaine's worldview. (Very often, they also shared his opinion of John Quincy Adams.) Their imperial imagination was not narrowly sectional or separatist; their proslavery zeal did not diminish their national patriotism. As leaders like Calhoun and Davis worked to strengthen bondage both at home and abroad, they understood themselves in command not of a mere region or a section, but a mighty world power. From their international perspective, "this vast Southern Empire" was, quite simply, the United States.[27]

———

The midcentury struggle between bondage and freedom began in earnest with the emancipation of the British West Indies in 1833. The world's leading economic and naval power, American slaveholding leaders now believed, had determined to wage a global war on servitude. Chapter 1 recounts how slaveholders came to see a vigorous and assertive U.S. foreign policy as necessary to combat Great Britain's imperial abolitionism. Southern-led efforts to reform and expand the U.S. Navy, chronicled in Chapter 2, make sense only when they are viewed in the light of this emerging foreign policy of slavery. And although historians have long understood antebellum expansion in terms of the sectional struggle over the balance of power in Congress, Chapters 3 and 4 explore the ways in which southerners were often equally concerned with the balance of power in the Western Hemisphere. Identifying the United States as the chief hemispheric champion of slavery, southerners sought to defend the security of vulnerable slaveholding regimes across the Americas, from Brazil to Cuba. Their struggle to protect slavery in the Republic of Texas led to the U.S. war with Mexico, which, as Chapter 5 describes, brought about the massive enlargement and consolidation of an effectively proslavery American continental empire.

After the triumphant war with Mexico, slaveholding leaders assumed a confident posture in foreign affairs: the antislavery energies of Great Britain appeared to be receding, while the proslavery imperialism of the United States grew stronger than ever. Yet in these same years, a surging domestic reaction against possible spread of slavery threatened slaveholders' power in Washington. This contradiction of the 1850s—slaveholders growing more confident abroad but becoming more beleaguered at home—frames the second half of the book. Chapters 6 and 7 explore slaveholders' deep conviction that the world economy depended on slave-grown staple agriculture: not just "King Cotton," as they famously boasted, but the other vassals of Emperor Slavery, including Cuban sugar and Brazilian coffee. European states, slaveholders argued, had become disillusioned by the experience of slave emancipation. The global spread of colonial empires and "coolie" labor systems reflected a general acceptance that racial hierarchy and bound labor were necessary elements of modern civilization. Chapters 8 and 9 examine how this broader proslavery worldview informed the actual workings of American foreign policy in the 1850s, which sought continually to protect slave institutions across the hemisphere. And even as sectional arguments corroded domestic politics, proslavery leaders worked as hard as ever to enhance the power of the U.S. military.

Southern secession itself, Chapter 10 argues, was a kind of foreign policy decision. The election of an antislavery president snapped the last and strongest bonds connecting the South to the Union—access, through the executive branch, to foreign affairs, the army, and the navy. Deprived of any further investment in the United States' international clout, southern elites found the appeal of an independent career irresistible. In the Civil War that followed, their slaveholding Confederacy was utterly defeated. Yet in some ways, as W. E. B. Du Bois argued a full generation later, American slaveholders bequeathed a legacy that outlived even the destruction of slavery, and found echoes far beyond the American South. Selected to give a lecture at Harvard's 1890 commencement ceremonies, Du Bois titled his address "Jefferson Davis as a Representative of Civilization." Davis and the antebellum master class were long gone, but key elements of the global order they envisioned—based on white supremacy, coerced labor, and aggressive state power—continued to shape world politics at the turn of the twentieth century.

1

Confronting the Great Apostle of Emancipation

IN THE SUMMER OF 1836 Nathaniel Beverley Tucker had every reason to be delighted with his budding literary career. After fifteen years as a circuit court judge in Missouri, in 1833 Tucker returned to his native Virginia to accept an academic post at the College of William and Mary. Thus comfortably installed in Williamsburg, the fifty-year-old law professor turned his attention to the writing of novels. First he published *George Balcombe*, a frontier romance whose vigorous plotting and shrewd characterizations impressed critics more than its delicacy of style. ("With the mere English, some occasional and trivial faults may be found. Perhaps it would have been better to avoid such pure technicalities as '*anastomozing*,'" noted Edgar Allan Poe, who nevertheless praised the book as "the best American novel" yet written.)[1]

Now Tucker had completed his second novel, a work of much greater formal ambition. *The Partisan Leader* was set thirteen years in the future and reflected Tucker's lifelong immersion in southern separatist politics. Equal parts cautionary tale and wish-fulfillment fantasy, the novel imagined a civil war between an independent southern confederacy and a despotic northern rump state ruled by Martin Van Buren. In Tucker's vision of 1849, Virginia finds itself caught between the sovereign Lower South and the power-mad Van Buren regime, which has imposed an "odious tariff" on all agricultural exports. Pushed to their limits by "northern cupidity and northern fanaticism," a heroic band of Virginia partisans fights off Van Buren's invading army and averts "the plunder and desolation of the South."[2]

Tucker's first novel had been published by Harper and Brothers in New York, but for *The Partisan Leader* he turned to the veteran journalist and

Washington insider Duff Green. Like Tucker, Green emerged from family roots in Virginia, went on to a public career in Missouri, and maintained a firm devotion to the interests of slaveholders throughout the Union. But while Tucker cultivated the style of an independent intellectual—conservative scholar, jurist, and man of letters—Green was a thoroughly political animal. As editor of the *United States Telegraph,* Green had masterminded media strategy during Andrew Jackson's 1828 presidential campaign. Bound by intimate ideological and marital ties to South Carolina's John C. Calhoun—his daughter married Calhoun's son—he later broke with Jackson but remained one of the most influential proslavery operators in Washington.[3]

In September 1836, Green wrote Tucker to notify him of the book's forthcoming appearance in print, chiding his author on one major point: "[T]he defect in your plot is that you have made the tariff the prominent idea when I think you should make the slave question the basis of your supposed separation." Green recommended adding "a chapter showing the interest which Great Britain has in substituting the cotton of the East Indies for the cotton of our South Atlantic states." This international threat to southern slavery and southern produce, Green believed, represented a far greater danger than the merely domestic wickedness of Martin Van Buren and his allies in the North. Certainly it warranted a mention in Tucker's story. Great Britain's larger "scheme of mercantile and mechanical cupidity might [be] demonstrated in a commentary by some character either from the north or the south," Green suggested, helpfully referring Tucker to a series of recent British parliamentary debates in case the author wanted original source material to cite.[4]

The publisher's attempt at criticism revealed, somewhat comically, the limits of his artistic imagination: like his patron Calhoun, Green might well have tried to begin a poem with "Whereas" and then stopped.[5] But this literary dispute also contained a world of political meaning. After the South actually seceded from the Union twenty-five years later, a New York publishing house reprinted *The Partisan Leader* with the subtitle *A Key to the Disunion Conspiracy.* But perhaps the novel's most visionary achievement was not its prophecy of secession but its portrait of a South that could secede for purely domestic and economic reasons. By emphasizing "the tariff" rather than "the slave question," Tucker presented a version of the sectional crisis that anticipated the South's post–Civil War justification of its antebellum history. *The Partisan Leader*'s melodrama of commercial rivalry, sectional rancor, and local patriotism foreshadowed the southern imagination of 1881, not 1861.

In fact, as Duff Green's criticism made clear, this perspective struck important southern contemporaries as oddly incomplete. During much of the antebellum period it was Green rather than Tucker who best captured the dominant political orientation of the elite South. This southern leadership was ambitious and cosmopolitan, not defensive and provincial; it was explicit rather than implicit about the importance of slave labor both at home and abroad. While Tucker could see Great Britain only as a possible commercial ally of an independent South, Green's keen and roving eye kept close watch not only on foreign tariff rates but also on the larger international politics of slavery. For many powerful antebellum slaveholders, British imperialism and antislavery were as dangerous to the South as national tariff policy or northern abolitionism.

In his revisions of *The Partisan Leader*, Tucker declined to take Green's literary advice. Even the author of *George Balcombe* was reluctant to reshape his novel around a character who specialized in the extended quotation of parliamentary debates. But other and more influential southern elites soon came to share Green's interpretation of British foreign policy. Within a decade nearly all the dominant figures in the South's national political leadership, from Jackson to Calhoun, understood British motives in a similar light. Britain's ambition to control the global market for cotton, these leaders believed, had spawned a crusade for slave abolition throughout the Western Hemisphere and represented a direct threat to slavery in the United States.

This Modern Black Crusade

After years of public agitation and parliamentary debate, in August 1833 the British government outlawed slavery in its West Indian possessions.[6] For U.S. abolitionists, this act of emancipation, which eventually freed over 800,000 people, represented a watershed victory in the global struggle against bondage. But opponents of slavery were not the only Americans paying attention; southern slaveholders, too, followed the news from London. Ultimately, British emancipation would transform the way southern elites thought about foreign affairs more forcefully than any other global event between the American Revolution and the Civil War.[7]

To be sure, southern statesmen had drawn connections between slavery and U.S. foreign relations long before 1833. A marked concern for slave property shaped American diplomacy in the negotiations that ended the Revolutionary War and the War of 1812.[8] Southern fears about slave insurrection and race war strongly influenced U.S. policy toward the rebellious French colony of Saint Domingue and later the independent black nation of Haiti.[9] In the 1810s Presidents James Madison and James Monroe, along with General Andrew Jackson, used overwhelming force to destroy black maroon settlements in Spanish Florida, extending the area for secure slaveholding settlement. Indeed, the rapid spread of slave-labor plantations into the North American continental interior, from Alabama to Missouri, was achieved equally through the lure of agricultural profits and the firm protections of state power.[10]

All this federal support for slavery, however, did not imply a coherent strategic worldview. Southern leaders in the early republic were concerned with the security of slave property on the southwestern frontier and anxious about the prospect of another Haitian revolution spreading to American shores, but they saw no reason to organize all U.S. foreign policy around the defense of bondage.[11] From the disputed presidential election of 1800 to the Missouri crisis of 1819–1821, the question of slavery was seldom far from center stage in national politics. But in the major foreign policy debates of the era, slavery played a more ambiguous role. Few southern leaders applied a consistent proslavery framework to transatlantic or hemispheric affairs. When Spain's Latin American provinces revolted in the 1810s and 1820s, U.S. slaveholding elites generally embraced their struggles for independence and republican government even when those struggles involved the emancipation of slaves.[12]

The Panama Congress of 1826 marked a turning point in both southern and national attitudes toward international slavery. President John Quincy Adams endorsed U.S. participation in the conference, which had been organized by Simón Bolívar to encourage political and economic goodwill across the newly independent hemisphere. But a bloc of mostly southern legislators objected to any direct engagement with the racially mixed Latin American governments. Virginia senator John Randolph shrank from the horror of a U.S. diplomat taking his seat in the Congress "beside the native African, their American descendants, the mixed breeds, the Indians, and the half breeds, without any offense or scandal at so motley a mixture." Worse yet, the new regimes in Colombia, Mexico, and elsewhere manifested too much sympathy for free black Haiti and too much hostility toward slaveholding Spanish Cuba. A Haitian-aided invasion of Cuba and

Puerto Rico, rumored to be under discussion at the meeting in Panama City, might bring the nightmare of race war even closer to American shores. "With a due regard to the safety of the Southern States," Georgia's John Berrien asked rhetorically, "can you suffer these Islands to pass into the hands of bucaniers, drunk with their new born liberty?" The United States, Randolph reminded the Senate, "could be invaded from Cuba in rowboats."[13]

The debate over the Panama Congress announced the breakdown of the Monroe Doctrine consensus in foreign policy, the rise of aggressive white supremacist rhetoric in national politics, and, perhaps most important, the arrival of an organized opposition that would grow into the Jacksonian Democratic Party.[14] In foreign affairs the southern leadership of this new coalition demonstrated a greater sensitivity to hemispheric slavery, and perhaps a greater willingness to muster U.S. power on its behalf, than the Jeffersonians before them. Virginia's John Floyd was not the only southern legislator willing to "take up arms" to prevent Cuban emancipation. But most anti-Panama Congress southerners did not think that arms would be necessary. Protecting slavery in Cuba required little more than a firm stand against a few small and divided nations in Latin America. It did not entail a collision with a major European power, let alone a larger reorganization of U.S. foreign policy.[15]

In fact, slaveholding leaders in the 1820s generally expressed satisfaction with the existing balance of power in the Western Hemisphere. With the final defeat of Napoleon and the disintegration of the Spanish Empire, the Atlantic world was dominated more than ever by the power of Great Britain. Like other Americans, southerners expressed their share of hostility toward Britain, the nation that Thomas Jefferson had famously called "our only natural enemies." Yet in the two decades after the War of 1812, there were many reasons for southern statesmen to view British power with acceptance rather than alarm.[16] After all, Britain had become by far America's most important trading partner and most generous foreign investor. The cotton boom that was remaking the American Southwest in slavery's image depended heavily on the growth of the British textile industry: by 1830 over two-thirds of U.S. cotton exports went to Britain. Although some southerners followed Henry Clay in hoping that the United States might escape the "commercial dominion of Great Britain" through tariff protections, most planter elites looked agreeably on the Anglo-American economic relationship. If anything, they sought fewer trade restrictions and a more intimate commercial exchange with Britain.[17]

Under these circumstances, it was no surprise that the logic of Anglo-American strategic cooperation often appealed to southern leaders. In 1823, when British foreign secretary George Canning proposed a united declaration against possible European interference in Latin America, Secretary of War Calhoun and other influential southerners urged President Monroe to accept the offer. Jefferson put aside his lifelong distrust of Britain in hopes of building an Anglo-American partnership that might defend "free government" from Greece to Argentina. "With the British fleets and fiscal resources associated with our own," declared Madison, "we should be safe against the rest of the World." It was Secretary of State John Quincy Adams, a Massachusetts man, who persuaded Monroe to forgo Canning's joint declaration and issue the unilateral state paper that would become known as the Monroe Doctrine.[18]

During the Panama debates three years later, many slaveholding elites still looked to Great Britain as a helpfully conservative force in a turbulent region. For South Carolina congressman James Hamilton, a French or British seizure of Cuba would be "inconvenient," but unlike a Mexican or Colombian invasion, "it would be attended with no violent concussion. . . . Either European Power would have the naval and military means to coerce the brigands and blacks into peace and submission." The key to this comforting calculus, as John Floyd noted, was Britain's ongoing commitment to slavery. The British West Indies contained "six to seven hundred thousand of slaves, which, if the doctrine inculcated by these new Republics prevail, will be incited to rebellion. . . . It would be nothing short of folly to believe, that [Britain] would jeopardise these territories, or permit them to be torn from her by revolution."[19]

Less than a decade later, a political revolution in London ended slavery in the British West Indies for good. John Randolph, perhaps alone among the anti-Panama southerners, had seen this coming as early as 1826. Over the past several years, he told Congress during the Panama debates, a "total change has taken place in public opinion, in Great Britain." The progress of antislavery sentiment in "Old England" worried Randolph as much as any Caribbean uprising or New World emancipation. There could be no end to "this modern *black crusade*," as he called it, but a war against slavery throughout the Americas.[20] Seven years later, in May 1833, Parliament passed the Slavery Abolition Act. Great Britain's decision to free its Caribbean slaves changed the basic order of things in the Western Hemisphere. The world's most powerful nation had now begun to organize its considerable economic, diplomatic, and military resources in opposition to one of American society's most fundamental institutions. The modern black crusade had reached its Jerusalem. What would the United States do about it?

———————

The Abolition Act of 1833 softened its blow to West Indian planters in a number of ways. Britain's approximately 800,000 slaves were not freed all at once; they would remain "apprentices," formally bound to their masters, for a term of four to six years. Meanwhile, three thousand British planters received £20 million in compensation—an enormous sum, roughly equivalent to four times the annual budget of the Royal Navy.[21] For American slaveholders, however, none of these concessions outweighed the essential fact of emancipation itself. An aggressive antislavery lobby in Britain had won control of Parliament and had ended bondage through legislative fiat. From an American perspective, one political lesson of the British experience was clear: the security of slavery depended on proximity to national power.[22]

On this score South Carolina and Louisiana planters maintained a much stronger position than their counterparts in Jamaica or Barbados. By 1833 slaveholding elites had occupied the U.S. presidency for all but eight of the past forty-five years. Even more important, the evolution of the second party system in the 1820s, in which both Whigs and Democrats competed for votes in the North and the South, effectively removed antislavery voices from the national political debate.[23] Nevertheless, the precedent of British emancipation left a significant imprint on American politics. Over the course of the next decade it set the tone for the South's emerging defense of slavery while stiffening southern resistance to even the faintest hint of antislavery activity in Congress.[24]

The international implications of British emancipation were even more profound. The specter of freedom in the West Indies, southern elites feared, would come to haunt slavery in the United States. Between Haiti and the British islands, the South Carolina intellectual Hugh Swinton Legaré calculated, the Caribbean was now home to "a *black* population of some 2,000,000, free from all restraint and ready for any mischief." The simple presence of so many freed people in the West Indies represented an intrinsic threat to the American system of bondage.[25] Southern slaveholders, one Charleston newspaper urged, must "counteract the influence which it is supposed the English project will necessarily have." Two years after Nat Turner's bloody rebellion in Virginia and just over a decade after Denmark

Vesey's conspiracy in Charleston, American slaveholders well understood the mischief that could result when enslaved people encountered the influence of freedom.[26]

Just as fundamentally, British emancipation transformed the geopolitical struggle over slavery throughout the Atlantic world. Across the Western Hemisphere in the Age of Revolution, the greatest victories for abolition were generally won by shifting alliances of local actors: bondspeople themselves, free people of color, and sympathetic Creole elites. This combination of forces, as slaveholders like Hugh Legaré understood, was potent enough. Certainly, colonial pressure from below had played an important role in British emancipation.[27]

Yet with the partial and temporary exception of revolutionary France, until 1833 the opponents of slavery had not received the support of any great Atlantic power. As a result, they had often lacked the economic resources, military might, and naval capacity that only a major state could provide. The Abolition Act thus represented a literal sea change in the balance of power between slavery and freedom in the Atlantic World. To be sure, after 1833 Great Britain did not immediately reorganize its entire overseas policy around the destruction of slavery in the Western Hemisphere. But when questions involving bondage bled into international relations, the representatives of British power—colonial officials, consular agents, and Royal Navy commanders—now generally lined up on the side of the slaves. Inevitably this put Great Britain on a collision course with the most powerful slaveholding society in the hemisphere, the United States.[28]

The first major postemancipation clash between the two nations involved three American slave ships that ventured into British waters in the early 1830s. The *Comet*, the *Encomium*, and the *Enterprise* were engaged in the coastwise slave trade that stretched from Virginia to Louisiana; all three were either stranded by storms or wrecked near Bermuda. In each case local British authorities freed the enslaved people on board. For years, U.S. officials remonstrated with the British government in London, demanding compensation for the slave property they believed had been unlawfully taken from American owners.[29]

In January 1837 British foreign secretary Lord Palmerston at last issued a formal response. While hinting that he might compromise on the *Comet* and *Encomium* cases, Palmerston declared that Britain would not compensate the owners of the slaves aboard the *Enterprise*. Palmerston contended that since the ship docked in Bermuda after August 1, 1834, when the Abolition

Act took effect, slavery was illegal in the West Indies, and there could be no reimbursement for illegal property. Naturally, this verdict did not sit well with American leaders, least of all the U.S. minister in London, Andrew Stevenson. A prominent lawyer and planter in tidewater Virginia, Stevenson had represented a Richmond district in Congress and had served as Speaker of the House from 1827 to 1834. In London he would also become ante-bellum America's first major proslavery diplomat.[30]

Before Palmerston announced the British position on the shipwrecked slaves, Stevenson had written the foreign secretary with his government's views. There could be "no distinction in principle between property in persons and property in things," he argued. Any British attempt to impose such a distinction in the *Comet, Encomium,* and *Enterprise* cases would be understood by the American government as a violation of international law. "When or where has the doctrine ever been established," Stevenson asked with rhetorical confidence, "that slavery . . . was prohibited or contrary to the law of nations?" Freedom was still the exception; slavery remained the norm. U.S. secretary of state John Forsyth, a former governor of Georgia, took the same position: British emancipation had altered the municipal law of the West Indies, not the status of slavery in an international context.[31]

In fact, both U.S. officials argued, the celebrated Abolition Act had not really ended bondage at all. By law, adult West Indian slaves were to become "apprentices," bound to their masters until 1838 or 1840. Forsyth argued that this scheme could not be "distinguished from slavery itself." Many northern states, after all, had passed laws of gradual emancipation, but none of them were so audacious as to pretend that bound laborers, as long as they were not yet free, were anything but slaves.[32]

These slaveholding American diplomats had begun to feel the international reverberations produced by Great Britain's turn against bondage. For Stevenson, the "principles and doctrines" asserted by Lord Palmerston raised "matters of higher and deeper importances, connected with the national interest and institutions of [the] whole [United States]." Forsyth felt especially concerned about Palmerston's affirmation that slavery, under any circumstances, could never exist on British colonial territory; this gave American slaves "the strongest inducement to flight, or abduction." The U.S. government had no choice but to see this position as "evidence of a spirit hostile to the repose and security of the United States." British antislavery, in other words, threatened the safety of American slaveholders and thus the very foundation of Anglo-American peace.[33]

Stevenson delved even deeper into the troubling legal implications of Britain's statement on the *Enterprise* case. Palmerston's ruling presupposed "not merely that *slavery for life* has been abolished within the British dominions, but that human beings cannot be the subject of property, *any where*, or to *any extent.*" Stevenson declared that this proposition could not be maintained by a British government whose laws were "founded on the previous right of property in slaves for life." The American minister verged on declaring British abolition itself a violation of international law: the denial of a right to slavery anywhere, he implied, was a denial of a right to slavery everywhere. Although Stevenson did not lean hard on this proslavery principle—a kind of international precursor to the logic of the *Dred Scott* ruling in 1857—the fact that he even transmitted it to Palmerston reflected his concern with the implications of the British turn against slavery.[34]

But although Forsyth and Stevenson had effectively constructed a proslavery interpretation of international law, they did not formulate a proslavery interpretation of Atlantic geopolitics. Despite their warnings that British abolitionism would threaten the "national interest and institutions" of the United States, neither the minister in London nor the secretary of state proposed directing American foreign policy to safeguard those vital institutions.[35] The correspondence over the *Enterprise* constituted the beginning of the South's confrontation with British antislavery, but only the beginning. It required a genuine war scare for slaveholders to grapple with the new alignment of forces across the hemisphere.

In 1837 British colonial officials decided to act against American traders who were supplying arms to Canadian rebels against the Crown. The British seized and burned the ship *Caroline* in a western New York harbor, killing one American and provoking a demand for reparations from President Martin Van Buren. Later, the 1838–39 Aroostook War erupted on the disputed boundary line between Maine and New Brunswick. No Americans were killed in these informal hostilities, but northeastern representatives in Washington demanded that the government act to secure the Maine frontier. In February 1839 Congress approved a bill that gave President Van Buren "additional powers for the defence of the United States," including funds for a volunteer army of up to fifty thousand men.[36]

The tensions along the northeastern boundary were soothed before any serious military collision could occur, but the prospect of an Anglo-American war was real enough for slaveholders to contemplate its implications. "We are on the eve of hostilities with that very country which is the center and source of antislavery fanaticism," warned a contributor to the *Richmond Enquirer* in 1840. "In such an event, will not an appeal be made to our slaves, and arms put in their hands?" The entire country between Maryland and Louisiana, implied South Carolina congressman Francis Pickens, could be turned into "a howling wilderness . . . wrapt in conflagration." War with Britain now involved not merely the risk of battlefield defeat, but the nightmarish possibility of slave rebellion and mass emancipation.[37]

No wonder southern leaders often took dovish positions on the northeastern border feuds. In the aftermath of the *Caroline* affair, John C. Calhoun urged Congress to avoid aggravating tensions with London; in 1840 Virginia congressman Henry Wise mocked the idea of waging war over "a few old pine logs in Maine."[38] The United States was simply not prepared to enter an armed conflict with a major antislavery power, and the social consequences of such a conflict were almost too terrifying to imagine. But if many southerners agreed that it was critical to avoid war with Britain in the short term, the broader strategic implications were less certain. After 1840 southern leaders increasingly began to view all global politics through the lens of America's commitment to slavery and Great Britain's commitment to abolition.

In these years there was plenty of British global activity on view. Between 1839 and 1841 Britain fought significant war in Afghanistan, launched a major naval expedition against Qing China, and intervened in the Turkish-Egyptian conflict in Syria. American slaveholding elites noted all these distant confrontations and accumulations of the expanding British Empire.[39] In a letter to Calhoun, the South Carolina planter-politician James Henry Hammond blasted Britain's Opium War in China, expressing the somewhat quixotic hope that the United States would "send a strong squadron there under a firm officer" to protect American interests in the area. Few regions of the globe were too remote to warrant attention from southern leaders: at his post in London, Andrew Stevenson worried about "extension of the authority of the British Govt to New Zealand," which might affect American commercial interests in the Pacific.[40]

A strong distaste for British imperialism was hardly unique to southern slaveholders. New England whalers feared British control over the Pacific; New York merchants hoped for an increasing American share of the China trade; and many Americans in different regions criticized British empire building in Asia. What distinguished elite southerners in this period was their tendency to connect British imperialism to British antislavery. In southern eyes the philanthropic motive for West Indian emancipation was belied, or at least outweighed, by Britain's *"grasping disposition"* in world affairs. The humanitarian pretensions of British abolitionists rang hollow in a world dominated by British imperial power. "The Queen of England," snapped one southern editor with defiant irony, "is the largest slaveholder in the world."[41]

In March 1840 Calhoun gave a speech in the Senate that crystallized some themes of the evolving southern critique. The South Carolinian observed that Britain's antislavery position in international law could be justified only by one of two larger premises, both dangerously grandiose. Either Britain asserted "that her municipal laws [against slavery] are paramount to the laws of nations . . . or that slavery—the right of man to hold property in man—is against the law of nations." In the former case, the British government would be "virtually abolishing the entire system of international laws." More likely, however, Britain had chosen the latter course and, flouting centuries of legal precedent and established custom, now sought to destroy the property rights of slaveholders all across the Atlantic world.[42]

Moving beyond international law, Calhoun attempted to take stock of Great Britain's bizarre conduct around the globe. On the one hand, British politicians boasted about slave abolition in the West Indies; on the other, they organized a brutal invasion of Afghanistan and violently forced Indian opium into the Chinese market. For Calhoun, the scale of British hypocrisy was simply staggering:

> There never before existed on this globe a nation that presented such a spectacle as Great Britain does at this moment. She seems to be actuated under the most opposite and conflicting motives. While apparently actuated by so much zeal on this side of the Cape of Good Hope in the cause of humanity and liberty, she appears to be actuated on the other side by a spirit of conquest and domination not surpassed by Rome in the haughtiest days of the republic.[43]

Leaving aside the question of how such an eccentric policy had developed, Calhoun predicted that it could end only in ruin. If it was "contrary to the laws of nature or of nations for man to hold man in subjection," how could the British government justify its rule over Ireland? Britain could not forever promote a principle—the emancipation and liberation of enslaved peoples—that struck so directly "at the foundation of [its] mighty power." Even within England itself, the rising Chartist movement showed that a struggle against "social or political slavery," once begun, could not easily be

contained. Calhoun urged Britain to abandon its abolitionist crusade before it resulted in "the utter overthrow of the present political system of
Great Britain and the rest of Europe."[44]

Calhoun's political warning joined other southern arguments about the
immediate dangers of militarized British imperialism in North America.
As the Virginia-born U.S. consul in Jamaica, Robert Monroe Harrison,
wrote to Secretary of State Daniel Webster, Britain had recently "crushed
Muhamet Ali, frightened 'John Chinaman' out of his wits and put down
insurrection in her India possessions." What was to prevent this hostile
abolitionist empire from landing "upwards of 200,000 blacks" from the
West Indies on the southern coast?[45] A range of southern political leaders
began to link British imperial antislavery and American strategic vulnerability. In August 1840 Secretary of State Forsyth told a Georgia audience
that only President Van Buren and the Democratic Party could defend
southern slaveholders from the menace of political abolitionism. Such
recourse to "the politics of slavery" was not new during a presidential
campaign, but Forsyth's speech took special pains to emphasize the international threat to bound labor. He accused Great Britain of converting all
the West Indies into "places of refuge" for escaped slaves, dispatching commissioners to Havana to "scrutiniz[e]" American commerce, and organizing
antislavery "black regiments" through "the enlistment of recaptured Africans." Van Buren and the Democrats, Forsyth promised, would protect the
slave South from British interference far more energetically than the An-
glophile elites in the Whig Party.[46]

In a domestic setting where the second party system had successfully
barred antislavery voices from mainstream politics, the most fearsome enemies of bondage came from outside American borders. The tiny and mar-
ginalized community of New England abolitionists loomed large in
southern imaginations after 1833 precisely because its radical program had
an ally in the world's most powerful empire. Whatever their numbers, declared the *Richmond Enquirer*, the abolitionists could not be a "'contemptible
sect,' either at home or abroad. They have emancipated, against the will
of their owners, slaves of the West Indies and the Mauritius." Now, through
the formidable mechanism of British power, they aimed a blow at the
United States.[47]

This line of thought did not wither away after the 1840 election. In
February 1841 Francis Pickens, now chairman of the House Committee
on Foreign Affairs, delivered a comprehensive report on the state of

Anglo-American relations. Imperial Britain's forward march appeared unstoppable, from its naval victory in Syria, which gave Britain "ascendancy on the Mediterranean and the Levant," to its "recent movements in the China seas and islands," indicating a British disposition to subjugate the whole of Asia. Pickens pointed ominously to Britain's considerable holdings in the Western Hemisphere, tracing an arc all the way from "Falkland island" through the Caribbean and up to Nova Scotia. Considering Britain's antislavery zeal, "her growing power in the West Indies" represented a real threat to American security. The danger was especially grave for "near one-half the states of this Confederacy," the slaveholding South. Pickens still dreaded the prospect of a war with Britain, but since the Maine crisis in 1839 he had grown much more concerned about the urgency of the British threat and much more willing to use American power to repel it. Two years earlier he had opposed a twenty-thousand-man provisional army to defend the northeastern border. Now he urged Congress to begin a "wise preparation" of the armed forces and to establish "an enlightened system of national defence suited to the exigencies of the times."[48]

In November 1841 Great Britain and the United States again butted heads over a wayward American slave ship. This time the culprit was not a storm in the Bermuda Triangle but the enslaved passengers themselves. On October 31 the American brig *Creole* left Hampton Roads, Virginia, bound for New Orleans with a cargo of 135 slaves. Just one week into the voyage, 19 slaves on board rebelled, seized control of the ship, and forced the surviving crew to pilot it into Nassau harbor in the Bahamas. British officials freed most of the slaves immediately and, after consulting with London, released the mutineers a few months later.[49]

When word of the revolt news reached American shores, southern outrage at British abolitionism rose to new heights. The Mississippi state legislature knew exactly where to place the blame: "[T]he doctrine of universal emancipation, now so acceptable to the rulers and the ruled of Great Britain, certainly stirred up these rebellious slaves to mutiny and murder."[50] In Congress prominent southerners reacted with differing degrees of belligerence. But virtually all of them agreed with Calhoun, who declared that Britain's current antislavery policy was "the most dangerous innovation on national rights and national honor ever claimed by one independent power of another."[51]

Between 1836 and 1841 leading southern editors and politicians had gradually come to reckon with the geopolitical consequences of British emancipation. "Philanthropy," Virginia senator John Tyler had declared in 1838, "when separated from policy, is the most dangerous agent in human affairs." For Calhoun, Pickens, and other southerners in 1840, the reverse was proving to be the case. Abolitionist "philanthropy," when joined to policy—especially British imperial foreign policy—was proving an even more dangerous agent.[52]

Many southern critics, however, still ceded to Great Britain a sort of perverse moral high ground: West Indian emancipation, however irresponsible and dangerous, at least grew out of a genuine philanthropic impulse. Calhoun himself granted that in the Western Hemisphere, at least, Britain's rulers sincerely believed that they were serving "the cause of humanity and liberty." Of course, Britain's ruthless exploitation of Asia cast doubt on its inherent benevolence, but here Calhoun charged hypocrisy, not deception. As yet, neither he nor most other leading southern statesmen claimed to understand why Britain had embraced Western emancipation and Eastern imperialism at the same time. The brutality of the latter mocked the supposed altruism of the former, but the relationship between the two remained obscure. A satisfactory explanation for Britain's "opposite and conflicting motives" awaited the intervention of Duff Green.

Imperial Abolitionism

Perhaps if Nathaniel Beverley Tucker had taken his publisher's advice while revising *The Partisan Leader*, Calhoun and other southern leaders would not have remained in the dark for so long. In 1836, after all, Green had urged Tucker to bring light to "the slave question" by emphasizing "the interest which Great Britain has in substituting the cotton of the East Indies for the cotton of our South Atlantic states." Six years later this general idea would become the core of a new explanation for British hostility to American slavery. Yet it is doubtful whether Green fathomed the full implications of his suggestion in 1836. Nor can we be sure whether its insertion into *The Partisan Leader* would have had much impact on southern opinion. Green's questionable management as publisher meant that the novel was soon out of print; by 1837 Tucker's Virginia friend Abel Upshur complained that even in Charleston, the capital of southern separatism, there was not a single copy available for purchase.[53]

In the meantime Green moved on; other business ventures had proven more lucrative than the marketing of futuristic secessionist fiction. In the late 1830s he briefly left politics to concentrate on land speculation, canal building, and coal mining in Maryland and Virginia. Yet Green was a man of diverse talents but singular focus: throughout his long career in business and journalism he never lost sight of the politics of slavery. During the 1840 election he helped lobby for John Tyler's inclusion on the Whig presidential ticket. When President William Henry Harrison died shortly after his election, and Tyler entered the White House, Green found himself in a position to shape U.S. foreign policy.[54] That fall he sailed to Europe. Although he was nominally traveling on private business, Green operated as a not-altogether-secret envoy for the Tyler administration. As befitted his wide-ranging business interests, he sought to negotiate a number of commercial arrangements—a possible direct mail route from Brest to New York, a French loan for the U.S. Navy, and plans for railroad construction in Russia. Green's most important objective, however, was to report on the economic and foreign policy of Great Britain.[55]

As powerful southerners grew increasingly wary of British designs on slavery, some wondered whether Andrew Stevenson's replacement as minister in London, Edward Everett of Massachusetts, would adequately defend southern interests. "The present condition of the country imperiously requires that a southern man & a slaveholder should represent us at that court," fumed Abel Upshur. "And yet a Boston man is appointed, half school-master, half-priest, and whole abolitionist!" Green's trip to Europe may well have reflected Tyler's desire to place a "southern man" in a position to report on the direction of British foreign policy. John Quincy Adams, for one, thought so: when Green returned to London two years later, Adams dubbed him America's roving "ambassador of slavery."[56]

Disembarking in Britain in December 1841, Green immersed himself in the latest Anglo-American controversy, this time over the "right of search" at sea. For years British leaders had insisted, accurately enough, that much of the illegal African slave trade took place under the American flag. Both Lord Palmerston and Lord Aberdeen, his successor as foreign minister, argued that the only effective way to crack down on this trade was to allow the Royal Navy to stop and search suspected slave ships, even when they flew foreign colors. The United States vociferously rejected this procedure, declaring that it infringed on American sovereignty at sea. Matters came to a head in December 1841, when Britain persuaded French, Prussian, Austrian, and Russian diplomats to sign a joint agreement granting the right of search. This so-called Quintuple Treaty represented a major victory for

British antislavery diplomacy—if the other great powers ratified the pact, it might have a major impact on the politics of slavery across the Atlantic Ocean.[57]

With the French Chamber of Deputies about to begin debating the treaty, Green quickly made his way to Paris. There he joined U.S. minister Lewis Cass and other American diplomats in an energetic propaganda campaign against the British-led pact. In early 1842 Green published several letters in different Parisian journals, warning French readers that the demand for "the right of search" was really part of Britain's quest for "dominion of the seas." It is not clear what impact the U.S. propaganda effort had on the French debate, but in the Chamber of Deputies the Quintuple Treaty soon ran into trouble. By the end of the summer the French government retreated from its efforts to ratify the agreement.[58]

Before he crossed the Atlantic, Green had hoped that the new Tory government in London would be friendlier to the United States than the Whigs had been under the pugnacious Lord Palmerston.[59] But amid the hubbub over the Quintuple Treaty, the "ambassador of slavery" evidently changed his mind. In January 1842, while working on his essays for the Parisian press, Green struck upon a new explanation for Britain's antislavery foreign policy. It must have come over him like a fever. During a single week in late January he wrote long letters on the true state of Anglo-American relations to virtually everyone he knew in the U.S. government, including Tyler, Webster, Upshur, Everett, and Calhoun.

Green argued that the British government now sought to monopolize global commerce by crushing its slave-labor competition. Britain, he wrote President Tyler, "believes that we cannot raise cotton & sugar but by slave labor—that if she can destroy the culture of these staples in the United States, Cuba & Brazil all the world will be dependent upon her East Indian Colonies for the supply of the raw material." This effective monopoly on cotton and sugar would put the survival of "all other manufacturing nations" in the hands of the British government.[60] Under a "pretense of benevolence," then, Britain sought to make merciless economic war on the rest of humankind. British antislavery was not contradicted by British imperialism; British antislavery was, in a real sense, British imperialism. The international "war on slavery and the slave trade" simply served as one arm of a larger British project to "command the markets of the world."[61]

Uncharacteristically, Green did not take sole credit for developing this interpretation of British policy. "Many intelligent men in the South," he informed Everett, had long believed that West Indian emancipation was part of a ploy to control global markets. He was not entirely making this up: besides his editorial advice to Nathaniel Beverley Tucker, a smattering of southern commentators after 1833 had accused Britain of pursuing West Indian emancipation in order to benefit "her own East India possessions."[62] But this interpretation of British motives had not yet gained wide currency in elite circles. Only after Green's frenzied Paris dispatches did the argument come to dominate proslavery political discourse. Calhoun wrote back to Green promptly:

> I have read your letter with interest, and am disposed to concur in most of the views you have expressed, as to the designs of England. It is surprising to me, that the State[s]men of the Continent do not see, that the policy of England is to get control of the commerce of the world, by controlling the labour, which produces the articles by which it is principally put in motion. Humanity is but the flimsy pretext—too flimsy, one would suppose, to deceive any but the most shallow and inexperienced at this late day. The United States are the principal obstacle in the way of accomplishing this great scheme of ambition, and hence the hostility towards her.[63]

This was in April 1842. Over the next several weeks similar assessments of Britain's imperial abolitionism began to pop up all across the landscape of southern politics—in newspapers, periodicals, and private correspondence. The Washington *Madisonian,* the official organ of the Tyler administration, declared that Britain sought "the destruction of slave labor in America" as a means to eliminate "the cotton culture to which this country is the successful rival of her East India possessions."[64] That same month the *Southern Quarterly Review* published a forty-seven-page essay that examined the influence of the East India Company on British foreign policy. "New Orleans and Calcutta are the two great rival cities in the world," the anonymous author contended, "whose imports and exports are similar." Recognizing this, the East India Company had long sought to "break up . . . negro slavery every where" and destroy India's competition in the Western Hemisphere. The *Southern Quarterly* author saw the company's hand in the origins of the Haitian Revolution, Britain's domestic antislavery movement, and, of course, West Indian emancipation. "There is no hope of peace to the South," he warned, "while this company, thirsting for gold and universal dominion, with all the wealth of India at its feet and all the power of the British Empire at its back, is permitted to pursue its machinations unseen, unnoticed, and unmolested."[65]

With its murmur of false pretenses, dark machinations, and ambitious schemes, this southern explanation for British abolitionism reflected the anxious, if not paranoid, temper of slaveholding classes across the Age of Revolution. The economic depression that set in after the panics of 1837–1839 may have further encouraged American slaveholders to question the security of their position, while feverishly exaggerating the determination of their enemies.[66] There can be little doubt that they overstated the nature of the British threat. Increasingly after 1830 British textile manufacturers did seek to develop India as an alternative source of raw cotton; certainly after 1833 the British government often acted against the interests of slave-holders in the Atlantic basin. But historians have uncovered no nefarious conspiracy that linked the two policies, unless, perhaps, it was the nefar-ious conspiracy of global capitalism itself. In any case, in the early 1840s it was far from clear that capitalism could do without the labor of American slaves. British efforts to promote Indian cotton had so far failed to dent the South's commanding share of the global export market.[67]

Nevertheless, there was much for slaveholders to be concerned about. Even if the connection between Eastern cotton and Western abolitionism was neither as direct nor as conscious as Duff Green believed, it was true that after 1833 British leaders began to regard opposition to slavery as a critical component of Britain's world mission. This opposition was circumscribed and counterbalanced in a number of ways. The Royal Navy generally con-centrated its efforts on suppressing the African slave trade, rather than undermining domestic bondage; the Foreign Office applied diplomatic pressure on other slaveholding societies, but not at the risk of triggering a major armed conflict. Yet if actual British policy did not quite amount to Green's imperial "war on slavery," it nevertheless reflected a sincere and ap-parently growing belief that slave labor was an obstacle to global progress.[68] In the mouths of abolitionist agitators, this was a dangerous but repressible heresy. As a principle guiding the policy of the world's most powerful state, slaveholders now understood, it had transformed the geopolitical landscape of the Western Hemisphere.

How should American slaveholders respond? Two years earlier a South Carolina newspaper had proffered one possible answer. If Great Britain had determined "to become the great Apostle of emancipation," declared the Charleston *Southern Patriot*, let those countries largely interested in Slave property know the fact that they may be prepared to resist a preten-sion so extravagant."[69] In 1842 those countries included France, Spain, the

Slavery and emancipation in the Western Hemisphere, c. 1842

Netherlands, and Brazil, a formidable set of potential partners for an anti-abolitionist coalition. Southern slaveholders increasingly came to view the whole of the Atlantic world as a strategic checkerboard of free and slave societies. Duff Green's struggle against French ratification of the Quintuple Treaty represented only the first of many U.S. efforts to coordinate its diplomacy with other slaveholding powers.

Other southern elites argued that the United States must act forcefully to match the British threat all across the globe. James Henry Hammond had wanted the navy to "send a strong squadron" to defend American rights against British colonialism in China. The *Southern Quarterly Review* essayist went even further. If East India cotton was indeed the driving force behind abolitionism in the Western Hemisphere, it might be necessary to uproot the danger at its source: "[T]he question of abolition we will never discuss or entertain; but the question by which we shall stand or fall, the ill-got power of Britain in India . . . is the one which America should always be ready to debate, either at home or on the Ganges, with sword and with cannon."[70]

The likelihood of the United States outfitting a major marine expedition to Canton or Calcutta was remote, but even these rhetorical flights of fancy sprang from a sturdier truth about how slaveholding leaders saw the wider world. Their faith in the future of American power was nearly boundless. "England cannot close her eyes to the fact that America is destined to become the first of civilized nations," Duff Green declared in 1842. "Her extent of fertile territory . . . her inexhaustible material wealth . . . are all elements of wealth and power, placing in her hands the destiny of mankind."[71]

And for elite southerners, American power was grounded not only in vast territory and abundant natural resources but also in the indispensable system of slavery. African servitude, according to Green, "unites the interests of the several states, furnishes the basis of foreign commerce . . . [and] constitutes an element of their common prosperity." It was the marvelous productivity of slave labor, after all, that had forced Britain to adopt abolitionism as a means of promoting East India cotton. As Calhoun told Congress, the most important American advantage over British imperial production was the slave system: "[A]bove all, we have a cheap and efficient body of laborers, the best fed, clothed, trained, and provided for, of any in the whole cotton growing region, for whose labor we have paid in advance. . . . With these advantages we may bid defiance to Hindoo or Egyptian labor, at its two or three cents a day."[72]

In this important sense, slaveholders understood the looming conflict with Great Britain as a clash of ideologies, not interests. From a structural economic perspective, the slave South and industrial Britain were not competitive but compatible: "There is nothing in our institutions," Abel Upshur observed in 1843, "unfriendly to England's prosperity. We produce what she wishes to buy, and we buy what she wishes to sell."[73] In fact, Britain was the world's largest consumer of goods produced by American slaves. The problem was that British leaders had become captive to the moral ideas of the antislavery movement, which now (slaveholders believed) had locked arms with the imperial ambitions of the British state. In the short term, this presented a great danger to American slavery, but in the longer term, it offered hope that Britain might again change course. The crucial thing was to convince the British government—by force, persuasion, or enticement—that its own interests, and the future of the world economy, lay not with emancipation but slavery. It was here that American foreign policy could play a critical role.

Challenged by the imperial abolitionism of Great Britain, powerful southerners in the early 1840s began to formulate a comprehensive American rebuttal—a U.S. foreign policy that would preserve slavery's strength in the Western Hemisphere while pushing Britain to recognize its enormous strategic error. Not all slaveholding statesmen participated in or even supported this effort. But over the next decade the most powerful and most influential of them—in the Tyler administration, in Calhoun's clique, and in the Jackson-Polk wing of the southern democracy—pursued it with alacrity.

For these southerners, it was critical that the United States stand up to the British challenge. War was a perilous prospect, but so was conciliation with the international forces of antislavery. Instead, the United States should act boldly and forcefully on the international stage, strengthen its military and strategic capacity at home, and work to defend the interests of fellow slaveholding nations throughout the Atlantic world. These were the main tenets of the foreign policy of slavery. Together, they provided the blueprint for an assertive or even aggressive U.S. role in the world—a blueprint that was followed with great precision by American leaders over the next decade. One of the first areas in which this new foreign policy of slavery made itself felt was in the effort to reform the U.S. Navy.

2

The Strongest Naval Power on Earth

On December 4, 1841, President John Tyler's new secretary of the navy, Abel Parker Upshur, submitted his first annual report to Congress. The fifty-one-year-old Upshur was not a prominent national figure. Thrown out of Princeton University for leading a student rebellion in 1807, Upshur had retreated to his tobacco plantation on Virginia's Eastern Shore, where he built a modest regional reputation as a jurist, constitutional scholar, and intellectual champion of slavery. Appointed to Tyler's cabinet in September, Upshur's naval credentials were uncertain. Wrongly identifying him as the author of Nathaniel Beverley Tucker's novel *The Partisan Leader*, one New Orleans newspaper scoffed: "Novel-writing, of late, seems to qualify a man for the office of the Secretary of the Navy."[1]

Upshur's political views were much easier to place. An "ardent admirer of Mr. Calhoun," the new secretary was said to combine "ultra-Jeffersonian" states'-rights views with a deep conservatism on social questions. Upshur was "a political metaphysician of the Virginia school," reported another paper, and perhaps "*the greatest man at splitting a hair in the Old Dominion.*" In short, Upshur seemed a fastidious defender of state sovereignty, an outspoken advocate for southern rights, and a determined critic of federal power in all its guises. It was precisely this ideological background that made his December report so striking.[2]

Uphsur's message to Congress betrayed no uneasiness about the concentration or sweep of national military power. On the contrary, its expansive vision of American sea power far exceeded the recommendations of any previous naval secretary. Most important, Upshur demanded a "very large increase of our naval force." Although he declined to give exact numbers, his projected naval expansion would not stop until U.S. forces equaled half the size of the largest navy in the world, Great Britain, effectively quadrupling overall American naval capacity.[3] Upshur further recommended an ambitious program of modernization: a universal "code of laws and rules" for the entire navy, a reorganized system of naval administration, a new emphasis on technology and steam-powered warships, the introduction of the European rank of admiral, a marine corps tripled in size, and a naval academy comparable to West Point. As Upshur boasted privately to a friend in October 1841, if Congress could be rallied around his report, "the Navy will soon be, what it has never been before."[4]

Upshur's blizzard of innovation, along with the crusading, centralizing attitude behind it, would suffice to strike a dissonant note in the context of his political career as a states'-rights hair-splitter. But Upshur's particular recommendations were not half as interesting as the larger strategic vision that informed them. The secretary called for not only an expanded navy but also a globally active American sea power—a maritime force that could take on a major European power at full strength. "Ranking in the first class of nations," Upshur declared, the United States could not afford to fall behind in the international arms race at sea. "All the considerable maritime Powers have, within late years, added greatly to their naval forces. . . . This fact alone would seem to render it absolutely necessary that we should make similar preparation on our part."[5] In his premises, as in his conclusions, the new secretary rejected the older notion that the United States could and should remain aloof from the doings of belligerent European empires. The era of expansion had replaced the era of isolation, both on land and at sea.

That was only the beginning. Anticipating classical republican arguments against a large standing military power, Upshur simply inverted the traditional paradigm: "Free Governments, which are necessarily more embarrassed in their councils, and slower in their action, than those which are not bound to observe the necessary *forms* of free government, have a peculiar interest to guard their soil from invasion. The nature of our institutions presents a very strong appeal upon this point." Virginia metaphysics this may have been, but Jeffersonian republicanism it surely was not. Upshur effortlessly maneuvered around the republican idea that the greatest danger to liberty was not its opponents abroad but corruption and militarized consolidation at home. Instead, he drew the opposite conclusion: since its free "institutions" made the United States uniquely vulnerable to outside attack, the federal government must take even stronger measures to build a military power capable of defending its shores.[6]

Only later in the report did the secretary hint at an explanation for this apparent ideological about-face. In a war against "any considerable maritime power," Upshur warned, "the first blow would be struck at us through our own institutions." This time, the dual identity of the institutions involved was unmistakable: not only the republican principles that upheld the American government, but the legal and social structures that upheld American slavery. Enemy "attempts to subvert our social systems," Upshur wrote, "would be terrible every where, but in the southern portion of our country, they might, and probably would, be disastrous in the extreme."[7]

A series of "incursions" by abolitionist British armies could wreak "disastrous" havoc all across the slaveholding southern coast. As Upshur saw it, a conflict with Britain was nearly unavoidable. The only question was "where and by whom shall these battles be fought.... Shall we meet the enemy upon the ocean, with men trained and disciplined for the contest, or suffer him to land upon our shores, trusting to a scattered and harassed people to expel him from their farms and their firesides?" This was a crucial reason that the United States must build up its oceangoing navy: to relocate the inevitable clash to the open sea, hundreds of miles from American farms and firesides—and American slaves.[8]

Upshur never once used the word "slavery" in his report, but the connection between his long-standing commitment to bound labor and his newfound enthusiasm for an imperial navy was drawn by at least one contemporary observer. Congressman John Quincy Adams, America's foremost antislavery politician in the early 1840s and a longtime advocate of naval expansion, was initially baffled by the secretary's report. "This newborn passion of the South for the increase of the navy," he noted in his diary in February 1842, "is one of the most curious phenomena in our national history. From Jefferson's dry-docks and gunboats, to admirals, three-deckers, and war-steamers equal to half the navy of Great Britain, is more than a stride—there is a flying-fish's leap." By April, however, Adams began to put the pieces together: "This sudden Virginian overflow of zeal for the patronage of the navy comes reeking hot from the furnace of slavery. 'Tis a wholesome stream from a polluted fountain."[9]

Why was a states'-rights reactionary now leading the charge for enhanced federal power? In truth, Upshur's December 1841 report was not the product of an idiosyncratic imagination but a coherent worldview. His anxiety about hostile British abolitionism; his faith that concentrated American military power could defend American slavery; his presupposition that the entire Western Hemisphere should be an American domain— none of these features of the report were unique to the secretary of the navy. Upshur was only one member of a loosely connected group of southern military officers, politicians, and editors who, in the late 1830s and early 1840s, led the charge for expanded American sea power.[10]

To be sure, not all antebellum navalists were southerners, and not all southerners were navalists. The cohort of southern naval advocates who backed Upshur's audacious reforms in the 1840s, and who continued to promote naval expansion for the next two decades, frequently relied on the support of like-minded naval spokesmen from New England and the Mid-Atlantic. Their dream of a large, oceangoing U.S. Navy—at once a safeguard for southern slavery and a projection of American imperial power—did not always command majority support within the South. But there is no question that the navalist program, in its inception and its execution, represented a vigorous military wing of the southern foreign policy of slavery.

The navalists' strategic calculus emerged directly out of southern concerns about slavery and the balance of power in the Gulf of Mexico, the Caribbean, and the near Atlantic. Their eagerness to enfold those areas within the proslavery power of the United States reflected a maritime dimension of the continental imperialism that profoundly shaped American foreign policy throughout the early republic. Above all, as Upshur's report made clear, the South's leading naval reformers drew heavily on a new and audacious vision of national military force as a vital tool in the international struggle to protect slavery. For southern navalists, the defense of the seaboard and the command of the oceans overrode potential qualms about national consolidation or the trampling of states' rights. At sea, at least, federal power was not a danger to be feared but a force to be utilized.[11]

Our Sword and Shield

The central figure in the development of southern navalism was Lieutenant Matthew Fontaine Maury. Born to a genteel Virginia family in 1806, Maury won a lasting reputation as an oceanographer and naval scientist whose career spanned the middle fifty years of the nineteenth century. As the superintendent of the Depot of Charts and Instruments in Washington from 1842 to 1860, Maury produced a systematic analysis of wind and current charts that dramatically reduced sailing times throughout the Western Hemisphere. His pioneering work in oceanography during the 1850s, especially his 1855 book *The Physical Geography of the Sea,* earned him the acclaim of European and American scientific societies.[12]

Maury's status as an internationally recognized man of science did not compromise his dedication to slavery and the South. Alongside his better-known oceanographic endeavors, he pursued an equally notable career as a defender of slavery and spokesman for an assertive American foreign and military policy. In the 1850s and 1860s Maury went on to advocate southern slave colonization of the Amazon, to serve as a Confederate naval officer and diplomat in Europe, and finally to encourage ex-Confederate migration to Maximilian's Mexican empire.[13] But his career as a political and military actor commenced in the 1830s, when he began to write regularly on behalf of wide-ranging naval reform.

Maury's first efforts came in a series of articles on the navy published in the *Richmond Whig* during the summer of 1838. Writing under the pseudonym Harry Bluff, the young officer offered a bracing critique of the navy's clumsy organizational structure. In the current navy, he argued, too many subordinates had too much power—"clerks, friends, and politicians" hampered the decision-making power of the secretary; ship commanders selected their own officers without oversight from Washington; and junior officers used political influence to subvert the orders of their seniors. Concentrating the department's executive power in the person of the secretary would solve such problems. After cleaning up the navy's bureaucracy, Maury hoped, the newly empowered secretary could begin working toward more significant reform. He would establish a clear code of laws, punish or remove recalcitrant subordinates, and create a system of naval instruction comparable to the education received by naval officers in France and England. Maury's program of centralized reform, in other words, directly prefigured the innovations demanded by Abel Upshur three years later.[14]

In the winter of 1838 a debilitating stagecoach accident permanently disrupted Maury's active naval career. Denied his lifelong dream of ocean-going service, Maury turned back to his formidable skills as a naval propagandist.[15] Writing in the *Southern Literary Messenger,* again under the name Harry Bluff, he published a new series of articles that both broadened and sharpened his call for sweeping naval reform. His point of departure was simple enough: the United States should become a great naval power. "The interest of American citizens," he insisted, "and the dignity and honor of the American nation all require, and are urgent in their demands, that a larger force than is now maintained, should be kept in commission."[16] Maury called for an American navy that could challenge the supremacy of British fleets all around the world. Such a navy would require considerable enlargement of U.S. squadrons in the East Indies (to balance British power in China), in the North Pacific (to prevent Britain from seizing Oregon), and in Africa (both to police the slave trade and to protect innocent American merchants from overzealous British policing).[17]

In their emphasis on bureaucratic centralization and aggressive expansion, Maury's arguments resembled those of northern naval advocates like Captains Matthew C. Perry and Robert F. Stockton.[18] But although he shared northeastern concerns about protecting American overseas commerce, Maury's larger strategic vision for the navy was distinctively southern. His most pressing anxiety was the "nakedness" of the southern coast, especially in light of what he saw as a coming military confrontation in the Caribbean Sea. The West Indies, he argued, would eventually "be the scene of our great Naval engagements—the vast slaughter-house of maritime nations at war." While Great Britain and France possessed island ports and naval harbors in the Caribbean and the Gulf of Mexico, the American naval presence in the region was completely inadequate. "In a war with either of these two powers," he warned, "all the rich outpourings of the Mississippi would be at their mercy."[19]

Maury's concerns about the helplessness of the Gulf Coast reflected the historic intimacy between the American armed forces and the region's slave economy. The Lower South was largely the creation of U.S. military power: the Creek War of 1813–14, the Battle of New Orleans in 1815, and the acquisition of Florida in 1819 all established the conditions for a flourishing economy based on slave labor and staple-crop exports. But the booming plantation districts of Alabama, Mississippi, and Louisiana also required protection at sea. In 1829 Captain William Henry Chase, the army's chief engineer in the region, argued that the United States should establish "a great Naval Arsenal" at Pensacola, Florida, with the goal of providing naval security for the entire Gulf Coast.[20]

British emancipation in 1833 only heightened southern interest in Gulf Coast defenses. Throughout the 1830s southern newspapers, congressional representatives, and even naval squadron commanders occasionally referred to British abolitionists, West Indian "picaroons and bucaniers," and the combined danger they posed to southern shores. Even when the threat of abolitionism was not mentioned explicitly, it seems to have influenced southern calls to extend American strategic dominance over the Gulf region.[21]

The writings of William Henry Chase offer an instructive example. Born and raised in Massachusetts, Chase had served along the Gulf since 1822; by the 1830s he was a settled southern slaveholder, well on his way to a future career in the Confederate navy.[22] Coastal fortifications alone, Chase insisted in 1836, could not guarantee U.S. dominance in the Gulf region. Sea power was necessary: "The immense commercial interests in the Gulf of Mexico would require that we should always maintain a decided superiority in our naval forces in that sea."[23] Although Chase's reports did not specifically refer to a British abolitionist threat, his 1839 editorial in the *Pensacola Gazette* made the point with admirable clarity. "[T]he policy of England and the abolitionists," he wrote, was dead set on the emancipation of Cuba and the rest of "the slave islands of West Indies." Like Matthew Maury, Chase foresaw "a great naval battle in the Gulf of Mexico or the Caribbean Sea." To fight and win this battle—and to protect slavery across the Gulf region—Chase again stressed the supreme importance of U.S. naval power. The navy should occupy Key West, deploy a fleet of "armed steamers" to guard the coast, and construct a large base in the Gulf, capable of reinforcing a powerful American squadron in the West Indies.[24]

With Anglo-American diplomatic tensions mounting, southern arguments on behalf of the navy found a more receptive audience than ever. In early 1840 John C. Calhoun took up the cause of naval expansion. As Congress debated the proposed extension of the Cumberland Road in Illinois, Calhoun appeared first in his familiar garb as a critic of Whiggish internal improvements, denouncing the project as a "wasteful and thoughtless expenditure." But the great South Carolinian did not speak on behalf of austerity for austerity's sake. Instead, he offered a vigorous defense of naval spending: government resources squandered on "this internal bleeding," Calhoun urged, should be directed toward "the great objects for which the Government was really instituted. . . . We must look to the ocean. That is the exposed side—the side of danger. . . . [I]t is on the Navy we must rely. It [is]our cheapest and our safest defense—at once our sword and shield."[25]

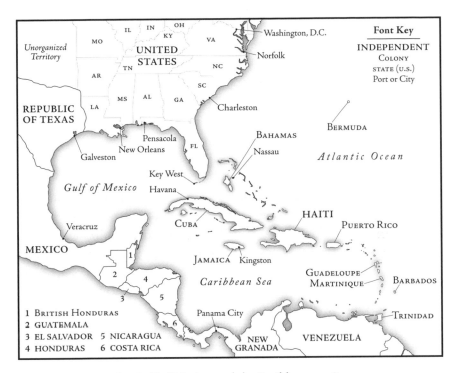

The Gulf of Mexico and the Caribbean, c. 1840

The most important of these seas, Calhoun made clear in subsequent speeches, were those that abutted slaveholding country. He wanted a dry dock at Pensacola "for the protection of southern interests" in the Gulf of Mexico and, not unnaturally for a South Carolinian, believed that "the most exposed and vulnerable part of the Union" was the Atlantic coast between Virginia and Florida. Yet Calhoun's naval interest transcended mere coastal defense; he saw the navy as equally a "shield" and a "sword." Gaining "habitual command of the adjacent seas" required something more than dry docks and harbor fortifications.[26] Although he insisted that the navy was "the right arm of *defense,—not as an instrument of conquest or aggrandizement,*" Calhoun nevertheless proposed to build a navy somewhere between "one third" and just "less than half" the size of Great Britain. The best naval defense, his arguments implied, was a strong offense.[27]

Calhoun's brief for naval expansion exemplified the ways in which southern navalism distorted traditional partisan divisions in the early 1840s. While most naval advocates (both northern and southern) throughout the antebellum period were high-tariff, big-spending Whigs, Calhoun fused standard Democratic fiscal conservatism in domestic policy with a "most liberal support" for a muscular military establishment. Without giving up either his southern or Democratic commitments to free trade and states' rights at home, Calhoun happily joined the navalist call for a radically expanded maritime force.[28]

War to the Knife

John Tyler's inauguration as president in April 1841 presented southern navalists with their first real opportunity to translate advocacy into policy. Whether out of caution, lethargy, or fiscal restraint, Martin Van Buren's administration had mostly stood in the way of large-scale naval reform. In John Tyler, however, the navalists found a firm friend and champion.

A planter from eastern Virginia, Tyler was both personally and ideologically committed to black servitude.[29] The Whig credentials that earned him a place on the 1840 presidential ticket as William Henry Harrison's running mate stemmed in large part from Tyler's defense of South Carolina during the nullification crisis. When Harrison died in April 1841, Tyler became president; only months later the new chief executive quarreled with Whig leader Henry Clay and watched Harrison's entire cabinet resign from office. As a president now without a party, Tyler was no longer fully bound by the partisan imperatives that constrained American politics during the second party system.[30] He was, moreover, exquisitely sensitive to the Anglophobic and proslavery anxieties of men like Duff Green and Matthew Maury. The Tyler administration acted almost at once to advance a bold and distinctly southern-flavored naval program.

In June 1841 a young Whig congressman from Georgia, Thomas Butler King, delivered the Committee on Naval Affairs' official report on a home squadron. "[T]he introduction of steam power," King declared, had revolutionized "the naval armaments of the maritime powers of Europe." In this brave new world of steam navies, the United States could no longer trust its protection to the mere width of the Atlantic Ocean. King reviewed American coastal defenses, especially in the South, and found them lacking: there was not a single substantial cannon between Charleston and Mobile. "Our unprotected harbors might be entered by fleets of armed steamers, loaded with black troops from the West Indies, to annoy and plunder the country." But since building coastal fortifications was expensive and slow, the United States must develop a "Home Squadron"—a battle-ready naval unit, including steamships, that could patrol the whole of the American coastline and swing into action rapidly in case of an attack.[31]

On the floor of Congress, King connected naval reform to his reading of international politics—in particular, the international politics of slavery and abolition. Great Britain, he alleged, "was gradually and silently, yet surely, altering her whole system." The British government now sought to eliminate its dependence on American "raw material"—in other words, slave-produced American cotton. This larger plan explained both Britain's naval expansion and its stern diplomatic posture. Thus "while she had emancipated her slaves in the West Indies, she still retained millions in slavery in India" in an attempt to cultivate cotton there. If Britain succeeded in developing a viable alternative to American cotton, "we might expect war—war to the knife—war with all her thunder." King closed by urging Congress to create the Home Squadron and rebuild the navy before British armies made a deadly first strike on American soil.[32]

Months after Congress passed the Home Squadron bill, Upshur delivered his annual report. The secretary's avalanche of proposed reforms and expansions was easily the fullest statement of southern navalism yet on record, fusing the various arguments for centralization, modernization, coastal defense, and expansion. And in his repeated comparisons of American and British naval strength and his oblique references to enemy attacks on "our social systems," Upshur hit on another important theme.[33] His language remained implicit where King had been explicit, but both men's arguments reflected the increasingly bipolar worldview of southern political elites. Like Calhoun, Duff Green, and others who in the early 1840s divided the world—or at least the Western Hemisphere—between the slaveholding United States and abolitionist Britain, southern navalists saw American sea power as both a defensive and an offensive weapon against the British Empire.[34]

News of the slave revolt on the *Creole* arrived in Washington in the same month in which Upshur presented his report. Predictably, Britain's decision to free the ship's rebellious slaves threw southern politicians into an uproar. Senator Alexander Barrow of Louisiana declared that if Britain's antislavery crusade continued, "the South would be compelled to fit out armaments and destroy Nassau." Others resisted a rush to war, worrying, as Calhoun wrote to James Henry Hammond, that "the Government is in no condition to make an issue of arms at this time. . . . We must get things right at home, & begin seriously to prepare." This preparation, leading southerners understood, must involve an expanded navy. "What then are we to do?" asked one Georgia newspaper. "The practical and significant answer . . . is 'increase and strengthen the American Navy without a moment's delay!'"[35]

Britain's ongoing claim to the right of search only heightened Anglo-American discord. For southern elites, the Quintuple Treaty of 1841 had supplied crucial evidence that the world was now divided into strategically and ideologically opposing power blocs. Were it not for France's unwilling-ness to ratify the treaty, Matthew Maury warned, "this most Christian alliance would have made the green sea red." In the *Madisonian,* one contributor asserted a fundamental difference between the guiding principles of American and British policy: "SLAVERY is one of ours—UNIVERSAL EMANCIPA-TION is one of theirs—and each is right *within the limits only* of their respec-tive dominions."[36]

Defining those limits and dominions, then, became a critical task for the U.S. Navy—and for southern navalists. Maury argued that the Quin-tuple Treaty exemplified Britain's "systematic efforts" to destroy "the pro-duce of slave labor" throughout the Western Hemisphere. The United States could not remain inactive while Britain sought to impose its antislavery will on the rest of the world:

> So long as [England] sought to carry out her schemes of aggrandizement, not upon us, and was content to plot her alliances against European Sover-eigns and Asiatic Despots, we had not one word to say against them. But when, in her dark designs, she attempts to push her plans across the "great waters;" and, under the *black* flag, preaches a crusade against the rights of neutrality and American principles, it is high time the country should be waked up from its slumbers, should examine its arms, and look to its defenses.[37]

Like Upshur and others, Maury saw an antislavery Royal Navy as little better than a pirate fleet—a force that promised to unleash a dangerous new wave of abolitionist activism and, perhaps, empowered black resis-tance. The only force capable of opposing these "dark designs" was the U.S. Navy.[38]

Responding to the threat posed by an abolitionist empire, southerners proposed to build a proslavery naval empire of their own. This was a pro-cess that involved both the fears and the hopes of the slaveholding elite. Deeply concerned about the South's vulnerability to an invasion of "Jamaica recruits," these slaveholders nevertheless envisioned the United States as a "young giant," able to stand up as Britain's "most powerful rival upon the Ocean."[39] In both their strutting and their fretting, southerners remained consistent in one critical respect: the identification of American naval policy with the aggressive championship of slavery and slaveholding throughout the Atlantic world.

While Maury beat the drum in the press, Upshur continued to work hard for tangible reform. The secretary's remarkable report of December 1841 was followed in the early months of 1842 by repeated efforts to win congressional support for expanding the American naval presence in the Gulf of Mexico. In two separate reports to Congress, Upshur emphasized the strategic primacy of this cotton-exporting region, while seeking a major increase in funds for the naval base at Pensacola. No stationary base, of course, could provide adequate protection if it were not matched by "an adequate naval force" patrolling the Gulf. As evidence, he submitted to Congress an extensive survey of the southern coast, composed by Lieutenant Levin M. Powell of Virginia, that emphasized the importance of naval superiority in the defense of the Gulf region. Recent naval conflicts in the Mediterranean and the Caribbean, the report argued, showed that even the most formidable coastal batteries could not stand up to well-armed modern fleets. For Powell and Upshur, as Calhoun and Captain Chase, the only way to defend the Gulf was to establish firm naval command over it.[40]

As Congress debated the requested appropriations, Upshur did everything in his power to reinforce the American naval presence in the Gulf. In late 1841 and throughout 1842 he directed additional ships from other squadrons to cruise through the West Indies with a special view to "the protection of American interests in that quarter."[41] In the winter of 1842 he folded the existing West India Squadron into the Home Squadron and made the combined force responsible for both squadrons' duties, a maneuver that effectually advanced the U.S. maritime frontier by several hundred miles. As he reported to Congress, "[T]he cruising ground of the home squadron now extends from the Banks of Newfoundland to the river Amazon, including the Caribbean sea and Gulf of Mexico." The consolidation made sense on both a practical and a symbolic level. The Home Squadron was now guaranteed to spend most of its time south of the Mason-Dixon Line; and the United States had formally asserted that the Gulf and the Caribbean were both, in some sense, American home waters.[42]

Even beyond the Gulf of Mexico, Upshur's Navy Department formulated American naval policy in terms of continuous strategic competition with Great Britain, often from a recognizably southern perspective. The case of Commodore Thomas ap Catesby Jones and his twenty-four-hour seizure of Monterey, California, affords a revealing example of southern Anglophobia at work in Upshur's navy. In September 1842 Jones, the Virginian commander of the Pacific Squadron, received erroneous intelligence from the American chargé d'affaires in Peru that the United States and Mexico were at war. The sudden departure of the British fleet confirmed Jones's suspicions that Great Britain and Mexico had signed a secret treaty, and that the British were moving immediately to seize control of California. The commodore called an urgent meeting with his squadron captains and American diplomats in Peru. He determined to sail north at once and "possess ourselves of every point and port in California" before the British could arrive.[43]

In late October Jones reached Monterey and demanded that Mexican authorities surrender the town to his occupying force. The surprised Mexicans capitulated without a fight; by the following morning the American flag was raised over Monterey harbor. It was not until the next day that Americans on shore located more recent newspapers that showed that the United States and Mexico were not at war. Jones admitted his blunder and withdrew from the town at once, but the incident prompted such outrage in Mexico that the Tyler administration was practically compelled to relieve the commodore of his command.[44]

Upshur's role in the vest-pocket war at Monterey remains somewhat murky. But the decisiveness of Jones's actions suggests he believed that his superiors would uphold his course.[45] And although American concern over British activities in California crossed sectional lines, the language of Jones's correspondence indicated a sympathy with the larger project of proslavery navalism. Recounting the international tensions that could explode into war, Jones referred to "the *Creole* affair" and "the question of the right of search," but not to any of the northeastern boundary tensions that had inflamed Anglo-American relations for years.[46]

When the British fleet left suddenly from Peru, Jones feared that it was "on its way to Panama, where it will be reinforced by troops from the West Indies, destined for the occupation of California." The elaborate detail of this scheme is especially suggestive because it had precedent in the hyperactive proslavery imagination of the early 1840s. "Let Great Britain succeed in planting her colored battalions in the Californias," warned one New Orleans writer in an 1840 piece reprinted in the *Army and Navy Chronicle*, "and . . . the unscrupulous fanatics of England would [then] find argument for all of their abolition doctrines."[47] Whether Jones acted explicitly to counteract such an imagined horror is impossible to know; but it is not unlikely that he shared some of these anxieties. For southern navalists, the specter of Britain's "colored battalions" loomed over the entire hemisphere, from the Straits of Florida to Monterey Bay.

In his instructions to the officer who replaced Jones in the Pacific, Upshur continued to agonize about British designs in California: "[T]here is some reason to apprehend that the policy of England contemplates one or more permanent settlements on the borders of the Pacific Ocean which may seriously affect our interests." The secretary ordered the Pacific Squadron to cruise the California coast actively, scout out potential naval bases, and "take prompt measures" in the event that "other powers" acted first.[48] Whatever Upshur's complicity in the Monterey affair, it seems clear that he and Jones shared a fundamentally similar strategic worldview. Both the secretary and the commodore were slaveholding Virginians. Both worried about an Anglo-Mexican alliance and the prospect of British West Indian mischief in the Gulf of Mexico and the Pacific. And both, finally, saw an expanded and modernized U.S. Navy as critical to American strategic goals across the Western Hemisphere.[49]

As the Monterey episode suggests, many of the navalists' fears were exaggerated. Although Great Britain had outlawed slavery in all its possessions and was working diligently to halt the African slave trade, the actual course of British North American foreign policy in the 1840s—contested, uncertain, and at best a third priority after Europe and Asia—bore little resemblance to the picture of implacable antislavery imperialism drawn up by southern navalists.[50] Britain did not try to force Mexico to surrender California, as Jones and his officers dreaded; there were no plans for the construction of a free black colony on the Pacific coast. British mail steamers on the Cunard line were not, as innumerable Anglophobes claimed, scouting out the southern shoreline in preparation for an imminent attack. Southern navalists, as often as not, were simply scaring themselves.[51]

Yet the very unreality of their nightmares underlines the grandeur of their dreams. Even if southern navalists' panic was illusory—or consciously propagandistic—they manifestly shared a commitment to aggressive armament, regardless of immediate threats. The British menace served as both a goad and a license for the navalists; the military expansion they proposed was conceived in desire as well as fear. An 1842 article in the *New*

Orleans Commercial Bulletin captured something of this spirit. The paper boasted that Samuel Colt's experiments had yielded "a shell constructed upon a new principle, and capable of a destructive agency exceeding all that was ever imagined before." The *Bulletin* reported breathlessly that "a single vessel armed with the weapon might be more than a match for the largest fleet." The United States could at last "bid defiance to the navy of England. . . . The possession of the secret will . . . put us on an equality with the strongest naval power on earth."[52]

Nothing came of this supposed secret weapon, but southern fantasies about such a technological breakthrough should not be dismissed as idle braggadocio. They conform to a larger tendency of the southern navalist project: the consolidation and expansion of American military power, partly as a response to Great Britain, but partly for the sake of power itself. Upshur, Maury, and their allies expended much energy arguing for shipyards at Pensacola, steamers in the Gulf of Mexico, and other primarily defensive measures, but the offensive implications of the southern navalist world-view were never far below the surface. From enhanced squadrons in the North Pacific to the construction of a "terrible engine" to win an international arms race, these southerners' strategic imaginations recognized few limits. To realize their vision, they sought nothing less than the transformation of the American navy.[53]

In this regard, what appeared to be Uphsur's most mundane undertaking as secretary of the navy—the reorganization of the department's bureaucratic structure—became, in the end, his most far-reaching achievement. Although his new administrative system did not immediately strengthen the American presence in the Gulf of Mexico or defy British power on the high seas, it significantly enhanced the navy's capacity for strategic growth. The navy's bureaucracy that Upshur inherited in 1841 had remained largely unchanged since the War of 1812. The secretary of the navy shared power with the Board of Navy Commissioners—three senior captains appointed directly by the president—who were authorized to manage large sections of the naval establishment, including most matters relating to ship construction, armament, equipment, and docking. The secretary, meanwhile, maintained executive responsibility for squadron organization and personnel decisions.

Although this structure had constituted an improvement over the skeletal bureaucracy before 1815, by the 1840s many naval advocates agreed that it was a tangled mess. The board's administrative independence from the secretary meant that its aged commanders could, and did, block the adoption of new technology and other innovations. Upshur's report of December 1841 built on suggestions by Maury and other naval writers that the board should be abolished in favor of specialized bureaus, each directly responsible to the secretary. In August 1842 Congress passed and President Tyler signed a bill mandating just such a reorganization; the bureau system formally replaced the board and continued to serve as the Navy's basic administrative apparatus for the next hundred years.[54]

This reorganization was not a wholly southern measure: it won broad support from both northern and southern men in Congress. But its main proponents and decisive sponsors hailed from the slaveholding states. Maury raised the issue in the press; Upshur demanded it in his report; Naval Affairs chairman King shepherded it through the House; Henry Wise called for a floor vote; and Tyler signed it into law.[55] Although the new scheme entailed a considerable centralization of power in the hands of the secretary of the navy—and therefore a consolidation of executive power—for the southern navalists, this aspect of the plan was an advantage, not a defect. As so often occurred in the early 1840s, the military and foreign policy vision of the southern navalists trumped whatever conservative or antigovernment prejudices might have obstructed the reforms.

Upshur's bid for naval expansion, however, fared less well in the halls of Congress. In May 1842, when the House finally got around to debating the secretary's request for a navy fully half the size of Great Britain's, a coalition of antinavy westerners and Democrats mounted strong opposition to Upshur's proposals. Congress eventually voted to slash $1 million from Upshur's proposed appropriation, blocked his proposal to enlarge the marine corps, and voted down extra money for the naval base at Pensacola. Although the final funding could have been even skimpier, considering the depressed Treasury, the secretary's grand plans to quadruple the U.S. Navy were effectively halted.[56]

By the fall of 1843, after Upshur had left the navy to become secretary of state, Lieutenant Maury pronounced the navalist project dead. "As for reform in the Navy," he wrote his cousin, "there is no such thing. U. [Upshur] utterly failed." Maury had a point. Certainly, the southern navalist revival of the early 1840s fell far short of its grandest aspirations. No mighty fleets flaunted American power in distant seas; no new naval technologies threatened British superiority on the ocean; and closer to home, American hegemony over the near Atlantic and the Gulf remained a statement of government policy rather than a description of strategic reality. Harry Bluff's disillusionment was real.[57]

By 1843, however, Maury could afford to complain about the failure of naval reform quite comfortably from his new perch as superintendent of the navy's Depot of Charts and Instruments, deep within the newly created Bureau of Ordnance and Hydrography. In 1844 he also became the head of the new Naval Observatory.[58] His own career path provided tangible evidence that the navy had changed under Upshur's tenure. The bureau arrangement, beyond its concentration of power in the person of the secretary, allowed far more flexibility and specialization than the old board structure. Maury's subsequent breakthroughs in oceanography—along with other technological advances in steam power, gunnery, and iron armor—certainly found a friendlier audience in the post-Upshur navy than they would have in the pre-1842 system. Slaveholding elites like Maury would remain heavily involved in efforts to modernize and expand the U.S. Navy across the antebellum decades.[59]

The emergence of southern navalism encouraged even some of the most dogmatic southern conservatives to broaden their view of federal powers. In September 1841 Upshur wrote his Virginia friend Nathaniel Beverley Tucker to berate the Tyler administration for its inadequate commitment to states' rights. Three months later Upshur was trying to persuade Congress to fund the largest peacetime expansion and centralization of military power yet seen in American history—while Tucker, the most ultra of southern ultraists, cheered him on.[60]

Southern navalists were seldom troubled by the constitutional implications of their views on foreign policy and military power. In Upshur's most strident defense of limited government, his 1840 review of Massachusetts judge Joseph Story's *Commentaries on the Constitution*, he carefully divided domestic from international politics. While chastising "consolidationists" like Story for trampling on the Constitution in search of "grandeur, power, and splendor" at home, he nevertheless recognized the "ample and unquestioned" power of the federal government in foreign affairs. Upshur could "scarcely" imagine a case in which "any serious doubt would arise" about the central authority's ability to conduct an unfettered foreign policy. Coming out of a treatise in which nearly every other sentence sought to clamp or shrink federal power, this was a marvelously forceful statement.

As his annual naval reports made clear, Upshur perceived no problem with the pursuit of "grandeur, power, and splendor" through foreign or military policy.[61]

He did not even oppose "consolidation," federal agglomeration, or plain old government spending, so long as it enhanced American power abroad. As his 1842 report argued, "[T]he expenses of the navy . . . are not to be considered a dead tax upon the Treasury." Because such military spending gave "employment to industry, encouragement to enterprise, and patronage to genius," while also boosting national strength, "the navy can be made to return to the country twice the wealth which is expended in support of it." Like Calhoun arguing for naval warships instead of western canals, Upshur suspended his ordinary opposition to federal spending when it related to overseas military power.[62]

An 1842 essay in the Savannah magazine *Magnolia; or, Southern Monthly* caught a hint of this contradiction. Denouncing the Quintuple Treaty and British antislavery imperialism, the anonymous author called for a spirited American response:

> Let the present feeble policy which governs our affairs with foreign nations be done away with . . . and our naval marine will be made to correspond, as it should, with that of our commerce. The only centralism which will ever be popular in the United States, will be that which is made to exhibit itself in the eyes of foreign nations.

In domestic politics, the ideological commitment to slavery often drove southerners toward a defensive emphasis on states' rights. In foreign and military policy, the same commitment led to the unapologetic centralism of the southern navalists. Men like Upshur and Calhoun willingly embraced the power of the federal government as they pursued, in effect, a proslavery arms race across the Western Hemisphere.[63]

3

A Hemispheric Defense of Slavery

JOHN QUINCY ADAMS HAD NO ILLUSIONS about John Tyler's foreign policy. "The support, the perpetuation, and the propagation of slavery," he wrote in 1842, "was at the root of the whole system of policy of the present Administration." Two years later, after Tyler had attempted and failed to annex the independent slaveholding republic of Texas, the old New Englander expanded on his theme: "A self styled President of the United States, and two successive Secretaries of State of his appointment, have with shameless effrontery avowed, to the scorn and indignation of civilized man, that their project of wholesale treachery, robbery, and murder was undertaken for the deliberate purpose of overreaching, overturning, and destroying the system of the British nation to promote the abolition of Slavery throughout the world."[1]

Adams was characteristically grandiose, but he was not wrong. In their management of U.S. foreign policy during the early 1840s, Tyler and his "two successive Secretaries," Abel P. Upshur and John C. Calhoun, identified British abolitionism as the most dangerous international threat to American sovereign power. Equally important, they identified American sovereign power as the most potent weapon in slavery's international arsenal. Their bold and unprecedented advocacy of naval expansion was just one element of a larger strategic program. Historians have understandably concentrated on the annexation of Texas as the centerpiece of Tyler's "slave-mongering diplomacy," but the foreign policy of slavery reached well beyond the Rio Grande.[2]

Understanding the United States to be the chief defender of bound labor in the Western Hemisphere, the most powerful slaveholders in Washington pursued a vigorous strategic program that often overrode whatever states'-rights or small-government principles they officially espoused. For Tyler, Upshur, and Calhoun—and for a broad swath of southern leaders, from the dying Andrew Jackson to the youthful Jefferson Davis—the foreign policy of slavery was too important to be governed by the restrictive code of conservative republicanism. For these men, as for many southerners during the antebellum and Confederate years, extremism in the international defense of slavery was no vice, and moderation in the pursuit of hemispheric slave power was no virtue.

Peace Is Indeed Our Policy

During his first two years in office, President Tyler showed a keen sensitivity to the dangers of British antislavery. The deepest impulse behind the president's push for naval expansion, in the words of his secretary of the navy, was the fear that a "considerable maritime power" might attempt to "subvert our social systems" in "the southern portion of our country."[3] Tyler's official newspaper organ borrowed freely from Duff Green's proslavery theory of international relations, which explained British antislavery as an adjunct of British imperialism. There could be no doubt, the *Madisonian* warned, that Great Britain was "aiming an insidious blow at the domestic institutions and the perpetuity of our Union." Given this very real danger, the United States must expand its navy, secure its borders, and resist the pretensions of British abolitionism at every possible turn.[4]

Yet despite all this Anglophobic angst, the first major diplomatic success of the Tyler administration was a comprehensive Anglo-American peace pact. The Treaty of Washington, signed in August 1842, emerged after a summer of negotiations between Secretary of State Daniel Webster and British envoy Lord Ashburton. Under the terms of the agreement, Great Britain and the United States resolved their ongoing quarrel over the Maine–New Brunswick boundary, established a final borderline in the disputed Lake Superior region, and agreed to form a joint naval squadron to police the illegal slave trade off the coast of Africa.[5] Later in August the Senate ratified the final Webster-Ashburton Treaty by an overwhelming vote of 39–9. "Peace," proclaimed John C. Calhoun, "is indeed our policy." Tyler's annual message in December 1842 hoped that the treaty "may be the means of preserving for an indefinite period the amicable relations happily existing between the two Governments." Secretary Upshur was scarcely less optimistic, writing to a friend that the agreement was a "very felicitous settlement of a very old dispute. It removes every possible source of dispute with England, for years to come."[6]

How can we reconcile such pacific deeds with the belligerent Anglophobia that seemed to predominate among the southern foreign policy elite in the same period? The most concrete explanation is that Tyler, Calhoun, and other leading southerners in Washington saw the Webster-Ashburton Treaty as a good bargain for the United States as a whole and the slave South in particular. Despite loud protests from a few northeastern Jacksonians, most observers did not believe that Webster's treaty surrendered any vital land along the Canadian border. In purely territorial terms, the settlement was more favorable than several compromises Jackson and Van Buren had been willing to accept. From a southern point of view, "a narrow strip of wild and desolate highlands" in northern Maine was a small thing to sacrifice for a reprieve from panics about an imminent British landing on the Gulf coast. And given that Webster-Ashburton settled the northeastern boundary dispute but remained conspicuously silent about Oregon and the Southwest, it was not unreasonable for some continental expansionists to see it as a favorable arrangement in the short term.[7]

More important, Tyler and his southern coterie endorsed Webster-Ashburton because they believed that the treaty forced Great Britain to abandon its claim to the right of search. This claim, of course, was what had so inflamed Duff Green, Matthew Maury and other leading southern opponents of the Quintuple Treaty. Britain's announced intention to stop and search all U.S. ships suspected of participating in the African slave trade, they had argued, represented yet another sinister aspect of its larger plan to gain "dominion of the seas" and "destroy the produce of slave labor" across the Americas. For these proslavery elites, a British withdrawal of the right of search was no paltry strategic victory.[8] Years before the ratification of the Webster-Ashburton Treaty, Maury had expressed his willingness to equip a joint Anglo-American anti-slave-trade naval squadron if Britain would abandon the right of search. When the final text of the treaty contained a similar arrangement, proslavery navalists understood this as a triumph, not a concession, for both slavery and American sea power.[9]

For Calhoun, Britain's "surrender" of the claim to the right of search constituted one of the Webster-Ashburton Treaty's chief merits. Some southerners in the press were more explicit: "England abandons all right of search now and forever," declared the *New Orleans Commercial Bulletin* in its editorial supporting the treaty. "Had not that point been fully and cheerfully conceded . . . the entire mission of Lord Ashburton would have been fruitless."[10] In his December 1842 message to Congress, Tyler insisted that with the ratification of the treaty, "all pretense is removed for interference with our commerce for any purpose whatever by a foreign government." When it later became clear that the British government did not share this interpretation, Tyler felt the need to submit another message to Congress. The president asserted once more his official belief that the Webster-Ashburton Treaty had, in fact, removed "all possible pretext . . . to visit or detain our ships upon the African coast because of any alleged abuse of our flag by slave traders of other nations."[11]

Yet one may suspect that for most of the southern foreign policy elite, the specific virtues of the treaty mattered less than the substantial fact of its existence. "The question," Calhoun observed, "was not whether it was all we could desire . . . but whether it was such a one that, under all the circumstances of the case, it would be most advisable to adopt or reject." By settling the irksome questions of the northeastern boundary and the African slave trade, the treaty removed two possible triggers for war while pointing the way to a more lasting Anglo-American accord. And peace, for Calhoun, was "the first of our wants." Only with peace could the United States reach its formidable potential as both a free, prosperous nation and a mighty world power. "A kind Providence," said Calhoun, "has cast our lot on a portion of the globe sufficiently vast to satisfy the most grasping ambition, and abounding in resources beyond all others, which only require to be fully developed to make us the greatest and most prosperous people on earth." By avoiding conflict with Great Britain, the most dangerous of all possible rivals, the United States could best attain that greatness and that prosperity—and, by implication, that continental empire.[12]

Peace, indeed, was good proslavery policy. Without surrendering their imperial dreams, key southerners nevertheless worked assiduously to avoid war. Although southern elites believed that slavery was a crucial key to American power, they also understood the unique danger that war presented for a slave society. As William Harper of South Carolina had observed in his formative proslavery treatise, "[I]f our country should at any time come into hostile collision, we shall be selected for the point of attack." Although Harper and other defenders of slavery rejected the popular view that "this institution will prove a source of weakness in relation to

John C. Calhoun. "When speaking in the Senate, he is a very startling looking man. The skin lies loose on the bold frame of his face . . . and his eyes, bright as coals, move with jumps, as if he thought in electric leaps from one idea to another." N. Parker Willis, *Hurry-Graphs; or, Sketches of Scenery, Celebrities, and Society* (New York: Charles Scribner, 1851), 180–81. This undated engraving by Alexander Hay Ritchie is based on a daguerrotype by Matthew Brady.

military defence," they nonetheless realized that a slave society possessed both extraordinary strengths and extraordinary vulnerabilities in wartime.[13] From Francis Pickens's hawkish congressional report to Upshur's naval advocacy, this vulnerability figured explicitly in southern urgings to strengthen the national defense. All the paranoid rhetoric about "raven colored troopers with their sable banners" and Britain's intent to "foment servile war" existed for a reason. Leading slaveholders were quick to demand a vigorous foreign policy and a strong military establishment but slow to clamor for an actual war.[14]

The evolution of Upshur's opinions between 1841 and 1842 provides a useful window into the southern foreign policy elite's complex attitude toward war, peace, and Anglo-American relations. In early 1841, when Pickens urged Congress to respond to British encroachments with "a wise preparation" of the armed forces, Upshur registered a fierce dissent. "I see no sufficient ground for war" with Britain, he told Nathaniel Beverley Tucker. Pickens was "a small man" to make "such a great noise" about Anglo-American conflict. But that same December Upshur justified his own call for a gargantuan naval enlargement on the very same basis, laying great stress on the plausible danger of a war between the United States and "the strongest maritime power in the world," which might well "strike its first blow through our institutions."[15]

In early 1842 the newly aggressive Upshur lambasted Congress's sluggish response to the British threat: "They know how delicate & precious our relations are with England," he told Tucker, "yet they will not put the country in a posture of defence." When the British government announced Ashburton's peaceful mission to the United States, the secretary hoped that Britain was genuinely "desirous of peace," but he kept his guard up. The "Creole affair," he worried, raised "new & delicate questions"—questions presumably relating to Britain's imperial abolitionism—and represented a "serious difficulty" to any peaceful settlement.[16]

Yet even while Upshur worried about British antislavery and worked to build a powerful American navy, he retained his sincere desire for Anglo-American peace. Britain and the United States, he wrote Duff Green, possessed "all the inducements of peace: common blood, common language, and their mutual interest." Ashburton's arrival in Washington in the spring of 1842 further lifted his hope that war could be avoided. Tyler's cabinet, he believed, was united by a "very strong desire for peace, & no honorable means of pursuing it, will be left untried." When the final treaty was signed in August, the dedicated navalist gave the "felicitous settlement" his hearty endorsement.[17]

For all their apparent volatility, Upshur's actions reflected a basic consistency: he simultaneously advocated the maximum possible military firepower and the minimum possible risk of having to use it. And like other influential southerners, he supported the most forceful possible diplomacy short of actual war. Thus while Upshur concurred with Calhoun that an Anglo-American conflict "would be the greatest of calamities," he agreed also that the United States must act energetically to combat British antislavery. The two objectives reinforced each other: American firmness behind slavery encouraged British concessions. Upshur noted that French rejection of the Quintuple Treaty—a development facilitated by Duff Green and U.S. diplomats in Paris—had taken the teeth out of Britain's insistence on the right of search. The British government, he believed, was not prepared to sustain a war without the complete support of the continental powers; "I think therefore, that she will not be very strenuous in her demands upon us."[18]

Despite their very real fear of British abolitionism, Upshur, Calhoun, and Tyler rejected the idea of aggressive war in defense of slavery. It was too dangerous and its outcome too uncertain. But they did not reject aggressive diplomacy. The Webster-Ashburton Treaty worked as a complement, not a contradiction, of their larger foreign policy of slavery. After the agreement was signed, the Tyler administration could return to its more fundamental project of building the navy, stewarding continental expansion, and monitoring the state of slave property throughout the hemisphere. Not all southerners agreed with this view, and several, including Missouri Senator Thomas Hart Benton, denounced Webster's "ominous conjunction" with London, the world "headquarters of abolition."[19] But the great majority were eager for Anglo-American peace. Only four of the twenty-two senators who represented slaveholding states voted against ratification of the final agreement between Britain and the United States.[20]

The Webster-Ashburton Treaty, however, did not signal any slackening of southern energies in the larger battle against British abolitionism. Less than three weeks after the treaty's ratification, the *Madisonian* rebuked Great Britain for "spreading her dominions by force and wrong and bloodshed"; in the next few months the paper repeatedly referred to Britain's "meddlesome zeal of abolitionism" and the continued vulnerability of the southern coast.[21] There would be no respite from the Tyler administration's foreign policy of slavery. If anything, after 1842 southern leaders proved more attentive to the threats facing slave property, not just within the borders of the United States but across North and South America. The danger of war with Great Britain had temporarily receded, but the pursuit of a hemispheric defense of slavery was only beginning.

Cuban Slavery, American Power

The most influential southern defenders of bondage had long evinced great concern for the international pedigree of chattel slavery. The Virginia professor Thomas Roderick Dew and the South Carolina jurist William Harper, often identified as the antebellum South's first major proslavery thinkers, ventured all the way back to classical antiquity in order to establish the primordial bonds between Western civilization and property in human beings. But these early proslavery *philosophes* also displayed an interest in the contemporary history of servitude—especially in the Americas. Both Dew and Harper sought to distinguish between the successful New World societies that had embraced bondage, principally Brazil and Cuba, and the unsuccessful ones, nearly everywhere else.[22]

In 1832 Dew worked up an extended comparison between the British West Indies and Cuba. Although some "British philanthropists" blamed slavery for the "depressed condition" of the West Indies, he wrote, "they are refuted at once by the fact, that never has an island flourished more rapidly than Cuba, in their immediate neighborhood." The Cuban population, Dew observed, "has, for the last thirty years, kept pace with that of Pennsylvania ... and her wealth has increased in a still greater ratio." Brazil, meanwhile, with "her slaves three times more numerous than the freedmen," had become "the most prosperous state of South America." Even Cayenne, in French Guiana, "never flourished as long as she was scantily supplied with slaves, but her prosperity commenced the moment she was supplied with an abundance of this ... labor." Slavery, in short, was an inherently dynamic economic institution; only the destructive action of the central government could threaten its productivity. British obstruction of the slave trade in the West Indies thus appeared as an analogue to abusive tariff policies in the United States. Both were strategies, Dew claimed, by which free-labor interests in government expropriated the wealth of productive slaveholders.[23]

Six years later William Harper echoed these arguments in his influential "Memoir on Slavery." Less concerned than Dew with relating British abolitionism to American domestic politics, Harper presented African slavery as a kind of development strategy for the beleaguered nations of Latin America. Nowhere in the tropical or subtropical world, Harper asserted, had a nonslaveholding society attained "a state of high civilization." "Mexico and the South American republics . . . having gone through a farce of abolishing slavery, are rapidly degenerating, even from semi-barbarism." The black republic of Haiti, he continued, "is struck out of the map of civilized existence, and the British West Indies will shortly be so." The flourishing nations of Latin America, meanwhile, shared a common social ingredient: "The only portion of the South American continent which seems to be making any favorable progress, in spite of a rich and arbitrary civil government, is Brazil, in which slavery has been retained. Cuba . . . is daily and rapidly increasing the industry of her civilization; and this is owing exclusively to her slaves."[24]

A more direct concern with hemispheric slavery also manifested itself intermittently in the foreign policy of the early republic. The South Carolina politician Joel Poinsett, later secretary of war in the Van Buren administration, stopped in Cuba during a diplomatic journey to Mexico in 1822. In the 1820s the threat to Cuban slavery seemed to come most pointedly from the new independent states of Mexico and Colombia, where anticolonial forces plotted against Spanish rule on the island. Poinsett was grateful, however, that Colombia's slave emancipation seemed unlikely to influence "the Creoles of Cuba," and that the Spanish government took an active role in protecting the island. Slavery in Cuba, he observed, was "a subject highly important to our southern Atlantic States, and I am glad to find, that every precaution will be used to prevent the black population from gaining an ascendancy."[25]

During the 1820s and 1830s the diplomats who represented the United States in Havana and Mexico City occasionally responded to similar alarms. But it was not until the early 1840s that larger anxieties about the fate of hemispheric slavery began to transform U.S. foreign relations from the inside out. In these years influential southerners in and around the Tyler administration fused Dew and Harper's ideological sympathy for Cuba and Brazil with Poinsett's pragmatic concerns about the security of American slavery. To this they added a belief in the capacity of the United States to wield power over the whole of the Caribbean basin. These ideas cohered into a critical element of the developing foreign policy of slavery: a determination to defend slave labor across the New World, not merely as a

direct means to protect bondage in the South, but as part of a larger hemispheric struggle between slavery and abolition. In the 1840s Cuba, Brazil,
and Texas were the brightest flashpoints in that struggle.

———————

Fewer than one hundred miles from the Florida Keys, and only about a
week's voyage from Charleston, the Spanish colony of Cuba long commanded the fascination of U.S. expansionists. Thomas Jefferson considered
the island "the most interesting addition which could ever be made to our
system of states," and he was hardly the only American whose curiosity
bore a striking resemblance to appetite. In the early nineteenth century the
favorite metaphor imagined Cuba as a ripe fruit, primed to tumble from the
frail tree of the Spanish Empire. Even northerners like John Quincy Adams
looked forward to the day when the Caribbean's largest island would obey
the laws of "physical gravitation" and land gently in the waiting arms of the
United States.[26]

It stands to reason, then, that our understanding of the nineteenth-
century relationship between Cuba and the United States has revolved
around the very real prospect of American annexation.[27] Yet what is at
least as striking, across the entire antebellum period, is the continual and
ardent American interest in the perpetuation of Cuban slavery. For American slaveholders, the question of Cuba's political allegiance—whether it
would be a colony of Spain, an independent nation, or a part of the United
States—remained subordinate to the question of Cuba's social structure,
that is, whether it would be a free or a slave society.[28] The "Government of
the United States," the *Richmond Enquirer* declared in 1837, "could not remain
indifferent to [Cuba's] political condition." This strategic concern grew out
of a deeper ideological imperative: the island's "social institutions . . . are
analogous to our southern States. This portion of our Confederacy, as well
as the Republic of Texas, must ever have a deep interest in the question of
slavery in Cuba."[29]

The most serious threat to Cuban slavery now came from the imperial
and abolitionist power of Great Britain. As recently as 1826 Virginians and
South Carolinians contemplated the British acquisition of Cuba with a degree
of complacency.[30] But in the altered atmosphere of the early 1840s, southern
observers looked at Great Britain's designs on Cuba with extreme suspicion, if
not horror. British efforts to pressure Spain into abolishing slavery, feared the
New Orleans Commercial Bulletin, might result in the mass emancipation of

Cuba's slaves—a development "too painful to be entertained for a moment" and a disaster for "our southern institutions."[31]

It was not that the *Bulletin* objected to all forms of European colonization in the Americas: "We do not know any reason why the United States should object to a reassertion of the French title to Hayti. On the contrary, we think it desirable that that island should come again under the control of an established Government." Cuba, however, was a different story "[I]f it conclude to throw off the dominion of Spain, there is no reason why it should be a province of any other European state . . . least of all England, whose hostility to our institutions is so bitter and active." The basis of this distinction between free black Haiti and slaveholding Cuba was clear. So too was the *Bulletin's* evident interest in the maintenance of Cuban slavery—an interest that existed independently of any hunger for American annexation.[32]

Cuba's booming sugar economy had begun to attract the interest of American slaveholders—not just intellectuals like Thomas Dew and William Harper, but practical and powerful men of affairs. Between 1827 and 1840 the island's total sugarcane output doubled, and its exports now claimed over a fifth of the global market in sugar. Cuba's impressive productivity, as Harper had put it, was "owing exclusively to her slaves." While the British West India islands had abolished slavery and watched their sugar output stagnate as former plantation workers withdrew from the plantation fields, Cuba's slave population grew by leaps and bounds. Despite Britain's mounting effort to crack down on the Atlantic slave trade, over 180,000 enslaved Africans arrived in Cuba in the decade before 1840. The island on which they landed had begun to transform itself from a sleepy colonial afterthought to an aggressively developing society centered on the mass production and transport of slave-produced sugar. Steam-powered cane mills now dotted the sugar-growing countryside; in 1837 Cuba's first railway reached out of Havana to collect their rich produce, well before rail tracks were laid anywhere else in Latin America, the Caribbean, or even Spain.[33]

By the early 1840s the prosperous colony had become a popular destination for American slaveholders on the make. Both John C. Calhoun and Georgia naval advocate Thomas Butler King, among other southern politicians, had close relatives with business interests in Cuba. Calhoun even compared the island's "flourishing condition" favorably with the somewhat slower progress of Alabama and Mississippi—by 1840 Cuba's slave population surpassed that of every U.S. state except Virginia.[34] The most extensive southern depiction of Cuban slave society came from the Charleston physician J. G. F. Wurdemann, who published a travel guide to the island in 1844. Contrary to abolitionist slanders, the doctor wrote, "the crowds of cheerful black laborers on the quay of Havana, and even those of the much belied sugar-plantation" would convince any "unprejudiced person" that "the Cuba slave ... has been much bettered by his transportation across the Atlantic." In addition to such picturesque reportage, Wurdemann's book offered potential American tourists a striking commentary on British abolitionism, the future prospects of Cuban slavery, and the high U.S. interests at stake in the Caribbean. "The present policy of England," he wrote, "is evidently to form around our southern shores a cordon of free negroes." As proof of Britain's intentions, Wurdemann cited Britain's "refusal to acknowledge the independence of Texas, while a slave-holding country, and her repeated attempts to abolish slavery in Cuba." The doctor painted a grim picture of the consequences of Cuban abolition: "Our southern seas would swarm with pirates. . . . [T]housands would be immolated on the altar of the abolitionist, for the war would then necessarily become one of 'the knive to the hilt.' "[35]

Perhaps it was no surprise, then, that the record of U.S. foreign policy in this period forms little more than a chronicle of anxieties about Cuban slave emancipation. The publicly announced and assiduously repeated American policy toward Cuba was simple: the island should remain Spanish, and it should continue to hold slaves.[36] Yet especially in the early 1840s threats to Cuban slavery seemed to emerge everywhere. At least three distinct panics at the possibility of Cuban emancipation afflicted the State Department during the Tyler administration. In the fall of 1841 South Carolina congressman Waddy Thompson, an outspoken Tyler ally, heard from a Spaniard traveling in the South that "there is a deeply laid scheme of insurrection in Cuba—stimulated and fomented by the British Government through the agency of the British Consul and emissaries from Jamaica." For Thompson, this news confirmed his belief that "Great Brittain is anxious to extirpate slavery in the West Indies and everywhere else." Through another South Carolina intermediary, he passed the information on to President Tyler, who personally instructed the State Department to keep its eyes on a British plot to destroy Cuban slavery.[37]

A year later a new set of rumors bubbled forth from another private source. Domingo Del Monte, a prominent Cuban planter, wrote his American friend Alexander Hill Everett with disturbing intelligence. Del Monte reported that British agents had scattered throughout the Cuban country-side and were now offering independence to creole farmers in return for the abolition of slavery. Meanwhile, an invading force of Jamaican and British antislavery instigators, working in tandem with a Venezuelan general, planned to land on Cuban shores and provoke an island-wide slave insurrection. Noting the disastrous consequences for the United States if such a scheme succeeded, Del Monte urged Everett to inform the American government of the impending danger.[38] Everett hastened to pass the news on to Washington. In January 1843 Secretary of State Webster sent letters to American representatives in Havana and Madrid that contained a detailed summary of Del Monte's nightmare scenario. The secretary of state faithfully reported the Cuban's claim that Great Britain intended to compel a general emancipation in Cuba and convert the island "into a *black Military Republic*, under British protection." He even passed on Del Monte's conclusion about the dangerous implications of the project for the American South: "If the scheme should succeed, the influence of Britain in this quarter . . . will be unlimited. With 600,000 blacks in Cuba, and 800,000 in her West India Islands, she will, it is said, strike a death blow at the existence of slavery in the United States."[39]

Once again, these fears came to nothing.[40] Nevertheless, the summer of 1843 proved a tense time for southern politicians with their eyes on Cuba. Tyler, Calhoun, and Abel Upshur—newly installed as secretary of state—were then working overtime to protect another endangered slave society in the Caribbean basin, the Republic of Texas. Yet as Calhoun wrote Upshur in August, "Cuba deserves attention. Great Britain is at work there, as well as in Texas; and both are equally important to our safety."[41] In July 1843 the liberal, pro-British regime of Baldomero Espartero in Madrid fell to the more conservative, French-oriented Partido Moderado. In one sense, this was cheering news for American slaveholders: "The interests of the West Indies and of the southern States of this Union," opined the *New Orleans Commercial Bulletin*, preferred "French rather than English politics in the Home Government of Cuba." The new regime in Madrid, backed by France, was more likely to resist British efforts either to purchase Cuba or threaten "its existing institutions."[42]

In the short term, however, a change of power in the Spanish metropolis might destabilize the politics of its most valuable colony. Spain's minister in Washington, Pedro Alcantara de Argaiz, feared that the deposed Espartero would flee to Cuba and bring abolitionist British influences with him. The prospect was worrisome enough for Argaiz to bring his concerns directly to Secretary of State Upshur, requesting "armed assistance" from "the government of the United States" in the event that an antislavery threat surfaced in Cuba. Upshur, for his part, willingly agreed to form what amounted to a temporary Spanish-American military alliance.[43]

Espartero did not materialize, but in the meantime both Upshur and Argaiz received the troubling news that the former British consul in Havana, David Turnbull, was returning to the West Indies to fill an official post in Jamaica. Turnbull had served in Cuba until Spanish authorities, believing him to be the "avowed and unblushing tool of the British Society of Abolitionists," successfully lobbied Great Britain to remove him from his position. During the summer and fall of 1843 the reappearance of this "arch fiend" rattled U.S. representatives across the Caribbean basin.[44] Most alarmed was the American consul in Kingston, Jamaica, a sixty-three-year-old Virginian named Robert Monroe Harrison. Tolerance and equanimity were not common qualities among the anxious southerners who manned the ranks of Tyler's diplomatic service, but even in the company of his fellow proslavery dogmatists and obsessive Anglophobes, Harrison stood out. The Kingston consul had spent the better half of the past decade flooding the State Department with frantic reports about British abolitionist designs against slavery in Cuba, Texas, and the United States. Until the early 1840s officials in Washington largely ignored Harrison's hysterical dispatches, but in Abel Upshur the consul found a kindred spirit. In July 1843 the new secretary of state replied to Harrison at once, requesting more information on David Turnbull and the British threat to Cuba. The main current of elite proslavery opinion had finally caught up with Harrison's gushing paranoia.[45]

Turnbull's arrival in the West Indies, Harrison believed, portended a new and more "villainous" British effort to destroy Cuban slavery, whether through diplomatic pressure, the distribution of insurrectionary pamphlets, or a direct invasion with help from Haiti. Harrison's consular counterpart in Havana, the former South Carolina congressman Robert Blair Campbell, was less impressed by the threat to Cuba's slaveholders. Campbell dismissed Turnbull as a "Glasgow bankrupt" whose plans to foment revolution could be handled with ease by the Spanish authorities and their "standing army of 18,000 men." Nevertheless, he suggested that the U.S. Navy "send a force here which would give an adequate idea of our power, for good, or evil."[46] The collective impact of Harrison's and Campbell's reports proved decisive. The Tyler administration determined to act on the informal Upshur-Argaiz agreement, and within weeks three American warships arrived in Havana harbor. Campbell immediately informed Cuban authorities of "the rediness and alacrity in which the American residents and the Naval force now here would cooperate in defending the City against any foreign armed intervention."[47]

Leopoldo O'Donnell, the new Spanish captain general of Cuba, officially declined to accept the cooperation of the U.S. forces. But in his correspondence with Argaiz and the government in Madrid, O'Donnell reported that "the appearance of the American fleet in the waters of Cuba, had through its moral as well as actual force, imparted, as if by magic, a feeling of security to the Island, and at once allayed the feverish excitement which had existed."[48] U.S. naval officers in Havana, David Turnbull noted in the late 1830s, were seldom shy about proclaiming their fidelity to the "glorious inheritance" of American slavery, or their support for fellow slaveholders in Cuba.[49] By 1843 Upshur's reformed, expanded, and Gulf-focused navy had begun to demonstrate its value as the chief military arm and first line of defense for the increasingly interconnected slave societies of the Americas.

As it happened, O'Donnell's confidence in the restoration of calm was premature. All may have been quiet in Havana, but that November a significant slave uprising broke out in Matanzas Province, the heart of Cuban sugar country. It remains uncertain whether this insurrection, or a similar revolt in Cárdenas Province the following March, had links to any of the elaborate Anglo-Caribbean abolitionist schemes feared by Cuban and American slaveholders alike. Whatever the case, O'Donnell claimed that he had uncovered a larger, island-wide plot. In the first months of 1844 the Spanish government in Cuba established a military commission both to punish the accused conspirators and to renew masters' grip on their evidently restive slaves. Hundreds of slaves and free blacks died, and thousands were arrested in the course of the official proceedings, described by one visiting spectator from New York as "most sordid, brutal and sanguinary." In Cuba 1844 was known as "the Year of the Lash."[50]

In Havana and in Washington the U.S. government stood firmly behind O'Donnell's crackdown. Cuban slavery, Campbell informed the captain general, was "a salutary institution. . . . [N]o punishment can be too severe for the intermeddling fanatic who attempts to arm the slave against the master."[51] Meanwhile, Upshur fired off new instructions to Washington Irving, the celebrated writer, then serving as Tyler's minister in Madrid. The author of "Rip Van Winkle" was ordered to exercise "sleepless vigilance" in regard to "every movement which England may make with reference to Cuba." Upshur directed Irving to give special attention to anything that might "affect the institution of African slavery now existing there."[52]

Irving had accepted the appointment to Madrid with the hope of renewing his lifelong interest in Spanish culture, while devoting his idle hours to a biography of George Washington. Once installed as minister, however, the New Yorker proved an alert and willing agent of Tyler's transatlantic campaign to defend slavery. In March 1844 Irving promised the new government in Madrid that the United States would "maintain Spain in the possession of Cuba by force of arms, if necessary." Spain's new foreign secretary, he reassured Upshur, was "much gratified" by this avowal and even went out of his way to inform the U.S. minister that "the interests and feelings of the Spanish and United States Governments were identical on most subjects connected with negro slavery."[53]

Later that year Upshur's successor as secretary of state, John C. Calhoun, returned even more systematically to the problem of "the recent insurrectionary movements in Cuba." He directed Campbell to make a "minute and detailed" investigation of their origins. Calhoun felt particularly concerned about the "agents who are known or supposed to have been employed in exciting the blacks to rise on their masters," "[t]he part which Foreigners may have taken in these disturbances," and "what countenance they may have received, if any, from the English." Campbell's reply did not make it into the consular archives, and at least one diplomatic historian has speculated that the report was too confidential to file in an ordinary fashion.[54] Whatever the case, by late 1844 the immediate danger of a slave insurrection seemed to have receded. Cuba's colonial administrators, aided by the diplomatic and naval power of the United States, had repulsed a threat to the largest slaveholding society in the West Indies. Tyler's foreign policy of slavery had achieved its first significant success.

Three striking features marked American diplomacy toward Cuba in the early 1840s. The first was a willingness on the part of official American representatives to speak candidly about the preservation of slavery as a foreign policy goal. All four secretaries of state between 1840 and 1844— John Forsyth, Webster, Upshur, and Calhoun—expressed a passionate interest in the organization of Cuban society.[55] In conversation with Spanish officials, U.S. envoys abroad wasted little effort trying to disguise the source of their concerns. "I embrace this occasion," Robert Campbell told Captain General O'Donnell, "to say to yr Excellency that I have no sickly sensibility on the subject of slavery." In Madrid Washington Irving made his meaning equally clear, although he showed a greater aptitude for innuendo. "[E]very blow to the internal quiet and safety" of Cuba, he informed the Spanish minister of war, "vibrates through the southern parts of our Union and awakens solicitude at the seat of our Government."

Within the extremely solicitous Tyler administration, even the typically heedless scramble for minor diplomatic appointments bore traces of the omnipresent foreign policy of slavery. Writing Calhoun to recommend his brother for the post of consul to Santiago de Cuba, one Ohio correspondent assured the secretary of state that the applicant "stands at the head of the anti-British and anti-abolition party." After an additional letter from the candidate himself, denouncing Britain's efforts to stir up "servile war" in Cuba, Calhoun assented to the appointment.[56]

Why were U.S. officials so frightened at the prospect of Cuban emancipation? Between 1841 and 1844 the barest wisps of rumor triggered the most frenzied reactions. Certainly, a red thread of racial panic ran through all the State Department correspondence of the period, from Webster's anguish about a "future *Ethio-Cuban Republic*" to the new Santiago consul's warning of a British plot to "revolutionize and St. Domingomize Cuba."[57] For the diplomatic officials of the antebellum American republic, little could be more horrifying than the idea of an independent nation of former slaves within a hundred miles of the southern coast. Still, the Tyler administration's hostility to Cuban emancipation amounted to something more than fear of a black polity. It was a direct consequence of a larger strategic imperative—the defense of vulnerable slave societies across the Gulf and Caribbean basin. Previous regimes in Washington likely shared Tyler's racial phobias and prejudices, but they had not dispatched a U.S. naval squadron to Havana to help subdue an abolitionist conspiracy.

Indeed, a second feature of American diplomatic interaction with Cuba was its strong and often explicit military component. In 1840 Secretary Forsyth told the American chargé in Madrid that the protection of Spanish power in Cuba was a "fixed resolution" of the United States, and that Washington pledged its "military and naval resources" to Spain in the event that another nation threatened the island.[58] Spanish power, here as elsewhere, seems to have been a useful synonym for black slavery. But Forsyth's rather cavalier commitment of unlimited "military and naval resources" was equally striking. With John Tyler as commander in chief, U.S. officials demonstrated an even greater eagerness to wield the promise, or the threat, of American military power in the Gulf. If Great Britain attempted to move on Cuba, one Democratic congressman reported in 1844, President Tyler "said he would strike her at once without even waiting for Congress."[59]

Tyler's deployment of an actual naval force to Havana, on the flimsiest of pretexts, said much about the quasi-imperial prerogative with which American leaders regarded Cuban affairs. This attitude was neither brand new nor confined exclusively to southern slaveholders.[60] Yet only the leading southerners of the 1840s combined an intense solicitude for Cuban slavery with an assumption of the United States' properly imperial oversight in the region. As they saw it, Cuba was not merely a future province or a valuable trading partner but a vital slaveholding ally—a Spanish possession, to be sure, but in an important sense a client regime under the proslavery patronage of the United States. It was the duty of the U.S. government, they believed, to sustain and defend this weaker ally from antislavery danger. For reasons not completely reducible to racist hysteria or expansionist hunger, leading slaveholders sought to turn American power into a shield for Cuban slavery—and, in fact, for slave property throughout the Caribbean basin.

In the spring of 1842 the *New Orleans Commercial Bulletin* asserted this point with extraordinary force. The "meddling spirit of Great Britain," the paper declared, stood in clear violation of the "American doctrine ... laid down with much emphasis by Mr. Monroe." It was British pressure, after all, that had induced "the Republics of Southern and Central America" to "become 'free' States—that is, to discard the system of slavery." The *Bulletin* called for the U.S. government to respond by invoking the Monroe Doctrine in defense of slave property across the hemisphere. "What degree of protection and encouragement," the paper asked rhetorically, did the United States "owe to nations struggling for liberty and existence under her shadow?" Great Britain's campaign against slavery, which spanned the whole Western Hemisphere, "ought to be resented, and prevented by this country."[61]

This stance was both revealing and representative. Although Tyler administration officials seldom articulated the point with such candor, they accepted both assumptions inherent in the *Bulletin*'s position: first, the fierce reality of a hemispheric struggle between slavery and abolition; and second, the rather nonchalant corollary that it was the duty of the United

States to exercise a kind of proslavery oversight over the entire "new world." How best to prevent Great Britain from converting slave states into free ones? The *Bulletin* suggested a series of international alliances to defend slavery. One possibility was a Cuban pact with Texas, complete with "guarantees for the permanence of the domestic institutions peculiar to the island." Another, still grander idea involved a transatlantic alliance against British abolitionism: "It is high time that a coalition was formed among civilized nations upon the plan of the Holy Alliance against Bonaparte" to check Britain's plot "to break down the agriculture of slave holding countries in this section of the world."[62]

The editors of the *Bulletin* saw little irony, and less contradiction, in their invocation of both the Holy Alliance and the Monroe Doctrine to serve the same strategic purpose. For the *Bulletin*, as for slaveholding foreign policy actors generally, the Monroe Doctrine represented not simply an ideological rejection of European monarchism but a useful umbrella for the advancement of American interests in the region. It made perfect sense that a primary national interest—the protection of slave labor across the hemisphere—might require any number of alliances, whether republican, holy, or otherwise.[63]

American participation in a range of proslavery agreements, joint activities, and quasi-alliances formed a third major characteristic of U.S.-Cuba diplomacy during the 1840s. "Both the Spaniard and the creole," wrote Dr. Wurdemann, apprehended the "obvious desire of England to ruin the prosperity of Cuba by the emancipation of its slaves"; both groups looked to the United States for protection. Across the period U.S. diplomats remained justly confident that they could rely on the support of Spanish colonial officials and Cuban slaveholders alike. As early as 1838 Spain's minister of foreign affairs stressed the "strict alliance and happy conformity of political views" between the United States and Spain, especially in their united opposition to British antislavery in the Caribbean. In Havana, meanwhile, consul Campbell affirmed that "the Creoles of this Island" were, if anything, even more favorably disposed toward American power: "To the United States alone will they ever look for aid, or alliances of any description."[64]

American diplomats, in turn, welcomed this kind of informal collaboration with their slaveholding partners on both sides of the Atlantic. Between 1841 and 1844 U.S. envoys passed along sensitive information to the Spanish government—most notably, Domingo Del Monte's warning about a British-sponsored invasion of Cuba—shared information about "naval facilities" and establishments in the Caribbean, and ultimately coordinated the arrival of a U.S. squadron in Havana in November 1843.[65] In the United States, American, Spanish, and French diplomats discussed a possible treaty that would guarantee Spain's possession of Cuba. And in Paris, where Washington Irving took his holiday in the autumn of 1844, an even larger plan was afoot. Thomas Marie Adolphe Jollivet, delegate from Martinique in the French Chamber of Deputies, had emerged as France's leading advocate for transatlantic cooperation in the defense of slavery. Irving reported to Secretary of State Calhoun that Jollivet was "earnestly prosecuting the scheme of organizing a coalition between the French and Spanish colonies, Brazil and the southern parts of the United States to protect themselves from the Abolition intrigues and machinations of England." Here was the *New Orleans Commercial Bulletin*'s grand alliance idea brought vividly to life in the French capital. Irving feared the influence of abolitionist influence in Paris, but expressed optimism that the Spanish and French governments would work together with the United States to defeat British antislavery in the Caribbean.[66]

The threads that bound these antiabolitionist allies together, from New Orleans to Old Castile, were coarse rather than fine, loose rather than rigid. The precise size, shape, and strategy of the coalition they formed remained uncertain. Nevertheless, there can be no doubt that in the early 1840s, under the ideological and geopolitical pressure of British abolitionism, the slaveholding leaders of the Atlantic world drew themselves together more closely than ever before. If Great Britain continued its effort to destroy slavery in the Americas, Calhoun warned Duff Green, "she must be prepared for universal conflict with the civilized world." The spirit of proslavery fraternity suffused the whole of American diplomacy in the 1840s. In Brazil and in Texas slave property was also under siege, and there, too, southern elites were active in its defense.[67]

4

Slavery's Dominoes: Brazil and Texas

"NEXT TO THE UNITED STATES," remarked an essayist in the *Southern Quarterly Review* in 1847, "the Empire of Brazil, is the grandest political feature of the Western World." The most populous nation in South America and the second-largest slaveholding society in the hemisphere, Brazil long held special relevance for American southerners. Since the 1830s proslavery intellectuals had made much of the distinction between rich, stable, slaveholding Brazil and its supposedly poorer and more chaotic neighbors. Commentators in Congress and the press contrasted this "flourishing" empire with the rest of Latin America, "blighted" by emancipation and social disarray. "The truth is," averred the *Southern Literary Messenger*, "that the Brazilians, both in their character and in the nature of their government, contrast most favorably with the other States of South America."[1]

To the southern diplomats in and around the presidential administration of John Tyler, it was obvious that Brazil, like Cuba, occupied a vital position in the larger hemispheric battle between freedom and slavery. Duff Green had no doubt that "the United States, Cuba & Brazil" were natural strategic and ideological allies. In his correspondence with administration officials, Green consistently yoked the three societies together as the chief targets of Great Britain's effort to destroy African slavery in the Americas. For Green, it was clear that Britain "does not expect slavery to be abolished in the United States, until you shall have first induced Cuba and Brazil to abolish it." "Let England succeed with Brazil & she will coerce emancipation in Cuba"; the United States would be next.[2] This nineteenth-century domino theory provided the strategic rationale for what Green hoped would be a vigorous U.S. foreign policy response. "I would urge upon the Government that now is that time to make common cause with Brazil & Cuba," he wrote Secretary of State Abel Upshur. "I hope you will not sleep over this question—that you will not fail to see in the position which England has assumed towards Brazil a conclusive argument why the United States & Brazil should act together."[3]

Tyler's State Department shared Green's view of the situation. In the summer of 1843 Upshur informed the U.S. minister in Rio de Janeiro that Britain was "endeavoring to abolish the institution of domestic slavery throughout the American continent." The United States could take no comfort in Brazil's mere physical distance from its borders: "Whatever affects [slavery] in a neighboring country, necessarily affects it incidentally among us." A hemispheric struggle to end slavery required a hemispheric response to save it.[4] When Calhoun replaced Upshur as secretary of state in 1844, he took Green's advice to "make common cause with Brazil" even more earnestly. In his first set of instructions to the new minister at Rio de Janeiro, Henry Wise, Calhoun emphasized Brazil's ideological and strategic affinity with the United States: "Between her and us there is a strict identity of interests on almost all subjects, without conflict, or even competition, on scarcely one."[5]

Calhoun's optimism about Brazilian-American friendship obscured several very plausible sources of tension between the two countries—a budding rivalry in cotton production, for instance, or the structure of Brazil's commercial tariffs, which tended to favor British over American imports. The secretary of state also elided the possibility of any ideological discomfort between the republican United States and imperial Brazil, the only state in the Americas ruled by a hereditary monarch.[6]

For Calhoun, all these potential concerns vanished in the light of both nations' shared commitment to black slavery. His instructions to Wise were delicate but unmistakable: Brazil had "the deepest interest" in maintaining the independence of its "domestic concerns . . . especially in reference to the important relation between the European and African races as it exists with her and in the Southern portion of our Union." Great Britain, he reminded Wise, sought to undermine "the peace and prosperity of both" while transferring the production of slave-grown staple goods to British colonies in Asia. Like Green and Upshur, Calhoun stressed that slavery's hemispheric dominoes must either stand or fall together: "To destroy [slavery] in either" the United States or Brazil, he declared, "would facilitate its destruction in the other. Hence our mutual interest in resisting her interference with the relation in either country."[7]

Slavery was indeed the tie that bound the two governments together. When Brazilian leaders expressed concern over the American effort to acquire the Republic of Texas, Calhoun urged Wise to reassure them that the policy of annexation had been conceived as a safeguard for American slaveholders. "It will be necessary," he explained, to enlighten the Brazilian court about "the views and policy of Great Britain in reference to Texas, especially as they relate to the subject of abolishing slavery there, and to point out the danger to which they would expose us." For Calhoun, it was self-evident that Brazil and the United States shared an equally overriding interest in resisting British abolitionism—not just in South Carolina cotton plantations or São Paulo coffee estates, but across the Western Hemisphere.

Slave Trade versus Slave Empire

In May 1844 the Virginia lawyer and planter Henry Alexander Wise seemed as good a candidate as any to strengthen this proslavery bond. Just thirty-seven years old, Wise had already served in Congress for eleven years, where he had forged a reputation as one of the South's most spirited critics of abolitionism. In an age where passionate oratory was commonplace, and in a climate where political eccentrics blossomed with every spring rain, Wise still impressed contemporaries with his curious manner and theatrical intensity on the floor of Congress. "He is very slovenly in his apparel," wrote one observer, with "his coat hanging like a miller's bag on his shoulders," while "his white cravat adds to [his] appearance of livid pallor." When he began to speak, "his eyes brilliant and fixed, his voice high yet sonorous," Wise exuded an almost unearthly passion: "A stranger, a few days ago, of his own party, on coming into the hall for the first time . . . compared his appearance to that of a corpse galvanized."[8]

Wise's most frequent debating foe, John Quincy Adams, found him somewhat less captivating. "Wise is the personified caricature of Virginia," Adams noted in his diary, "great conception, wild but energetic elocution—bathos of conclusion, small and pitiful result."[9] Yet few doubted Wise's commitment to slavery or his hostility to Britain's imperial abolitionism. As the "Captain of the Corporal's Guard"—the unofficial chief of Tyler's

Henry A. Wise. "All his predominant characteristics are brought out with great rapidity— firmness, impetuosity, a disdain for honeyed words . . ." "Glances at Congress," *United States Magazine and Democratic Review,* October 1837, 73. This uncredited photograph probably dates from the 1840s.

little band of supporters in Congress—Wise in his stature and loyalty, if anything, reflected the high importance with which the administration viewed the U.S. mission to Brazil. Certainly there was little reason to believe that Wise would do anything to disrupt the evolution of a proslavery friendship between the two nations.[10]

But Wise's tenure as minister to Brazil, from 1844 to 1847, confounded such easy expectations. In Rio de Janeiro, the U.S. envoy distinguished himself for his tireless battle against the ongoing Atlantic slave trade and, even more, his outrage at American participation in the illegal traffic. The importation of African slaves to Brazil, he reported to Calhoun in the fall of

1844, "has grown so bold and so bad as no longer to wear a mask even to those who reside here." Wise was astonished at "how shamefully the flag of the United States is prostituted" in the open conduct of the slave trade; the Stars and Stripes served as a useful cover to discourage antislavery search by British cruisers. "Congress ought at once be called to the amendment of our laws for the suppression of the African slave trade," Wise urged, and the federal government should take action against "the ship owners in the United States, and their American cosignees, factors, and agents abroad" who enabled the slave traders to continue their dirty work.[11]

Wise's "zeal and activity" against the slave trade eventually earned him "the gratitude of England," according to the British minister at Rio de Janeiro. Former secretary of state Calhoun was less impressed. "I fear with you," he wrote his son-in-law in 1845, "that Wise is pursuing an injudicious course in reference to the slave trade. My instructions to him were full & pointed on the necessity of preserving the most friendly relations with Brazil in every respect. It would be greatly to be regretted, if he has taken any step, calculated to have a contrary effect." In the end Wise accomplished little for Brazilian-American friendship. By 1846 the envoy himself admitted that his campaign against slave trafficking had "rendered me naturally unpopular in this country" and "obnoxious to this Govt."[12] In 1847, after a final falling-out with the imperial court at Rio, Wise returned from his post to Virginia. Anything but a faithful servant of the foreign policy of slavery, the minister seemed, on the contrary, to have done real harm to the possibility of an informal slaveholding alliance with Brazil. How had this happened?

This question has puzzled more than one historian. Wise's biographer, Craig M. Simpson, argues that his battle against the slave trade grew out of his "doubts about the efficacy of slavery as a social system." Wise, in other words, defended slavery against northern abolitionists but held mixed feelings about bondage in the abstract and may have opposed a process that would make Brazil or any nation more dependent on slave labor. Gerald Horne, meanwhile, suggests an opposing hypothesis—Wise struggled against the slave trade, not because it would make Brazil too weak, but because it might make Brazil too strong. Noting Virginia's role as a slave-exporting state to the Deep South and several later Virginia-based schemes for the slaveholding colonization of the Amazon valley, Horne speculates, Wise may have seen Brazil above all as a future market for Upper South slaves. Perhaps he sought to block the flow of slave traffic from Africa as a subtle means to open a second channel from his home state.[13]

To best understand Wise's Brazilian crusade, however, it may not be necessary to plumb the secret depths of his conscience. The Virginian may well have been a tormented slave master and a cunning slave exporter at the same time. But in Rio de Janeiro Wise was most of all an agent of the American foreign policy of slavery. Although his haughty temperament made a mockery of his diplomacy, Wise's goals in opposing Brazilian slave importation accorded very well with the strategic aspirations of Calhoun, Tyler, and other slaveholding internationalists. Wise fought against American involvement in the slave trade, but focused particularly on northern and even abolitionist participation. He called for a better international system to police the illegal traffic, but decried Britain's assumption of an imperial prerogative, claim to the right of search, and hypocritical involvement in the trade itself. Most of all, Wise denounced the Brazilian slave trade but never said a word against Brazilian slavery. Indeed, he probably believed that his battle against the former was indispensable to the preservation of the latter. To protect African slavery inside Brazil, the African slave trade had to be eliminated.

Wise's mission began auspiciously. In his first correspondence with the Brazilian foreign minister, Ernesto F. França, Wise copied Calhoun's instructions almost word for word: he explained Britain's nefarious plan to "transfer the production of tobacco, rice, cotton, sugar, and coffee" to "her possessions beyond the Cape of Good Hope"; he pointed out the danger this scheme presented for both Brazilian and American societies; and he spoke to the interest the two nations shared in the security of slave labor. Wise added detail and color to Calhoun's prose, defending the U.S. annexation of Texas as a vital measure to protect slavery and likening Britain's imperial abolitionism to "the coils of an Anaconda from which there was no escape but in death." His lurid portrait of British power at work in the Americas intended to provoke, as well as persuade, the Brazilian government to grasp the necessity of united action against this danger.[14]

Later in 1844 the ongoing civil war in Uruguay presented an opportunity for exactly this kind of collaboration. Foreign Minister França, Wise informed Calhoun, hoped to preempt European intervention in the region

by establishing "a stronger connexion with the U. States than any which
has ever yet existed." A joint Brazilian and American effort to end the war,
by diplomacy, if possible, but "force, if necessary," might be required to stave
off British or French meddling. Wise did not commit himself to any specific
plan, but he argued that the United States, working closely with Brazil,
might now "manifest a leading interest in South American affairs." During
his residence in Rio de Janeiro, the American minister helped arrange for
the Brazilian admiralty to tour visiting U.S. Navy ships. Wise boasted that
the Brazilians were so "struck by our naval excellence" that they dispatched
several junior officers to sail and study under American captains.[15]

No concrete pact emerged from these conversations, but that was not
what Wise sought: as he told Brazil's naval minister, "Brazil & the U. States
strengthened themselves, as they strengthened each other, ipso facto,
without any alliance." A preference for informal collaboration, rather than
binding covenants, was the hallmark of U.S. proslavery foreign policy
during the 1840s. And for Wise, as for Calhoun, there could be no question
that slave property formed the ultimate foundation for any U.S.-Brazilian
partnership: "[T]he understanding the U. States should have with Brazil
is, that . . . both should firmly defend their institutions from foreign interference." The security of these crucial Brazilian "institutions"—as ever, the
favorite antebellum euphemism for slavery—loomed large in Wise's strategic
thinking throughout his tenure in Rio de Janeiro.[16]

Even Wise's struggle against slave trafficking was conducted within the
distinctive mental framework of a Virginian suspicious of antislavery hypocrisy. The Americans involved in the trade, Wise reported, "are all from North
of Balt[imore]," and northern abolitionists were deeply complicit in the
cruel traffic. One notorious ship, which landed about six hundred slaves in
Brazil, "was owned by a Quaker of Delaware who would not even eat slave
sugar." Another American vessel, Wise declared, "which has made several
trips to the coast under the charter party of notorious slave traders here, is
also the owner of an abolition newspaper in Bangor, Maine."[17]

Critical as he was of American involvement in the slave trade, Wise saved
his choicest scorn for British hypocrisy—or, rather, British criminality.
Wise, like Green, Calhoun, and others, had concluded that British antislavery was not a contradiction of its imperial foreign policy but the logical
consequence. The British government, he knew, was the world's leading
opponent of the Atlantic slave trade; the patrols of the Royal Navy were

certainly the most serious obstacles facing Brazilian slave traders. And Wise appreciated that many individual citizens, such as Hamilton Hamilton, Britain's minister to Brazil, sincerely wanted to end the human traffic. But the whole of British policy toward slavery in the Western Hemisphere, as he understood it, was so fundamentally selfish and destructive that even this apparently benign effort to stop the Brazilian slave trade had become deeply compromised.

Britain's assertion of its right to search every suspected slave ship, Wise lectured Hamilton, only generated anti-imperialist hostility in the Americas. Britain's practice of "carrying every captured slave to her colonies at Demerara" made the Royal Navy's squadrons something more like labor pirates than a disinterested maritime police force. And if the British government truly wanted to end the traffic, he declared, it would punish "the offenders at home"—that is, the "vessel-owners, shippers, manufacturers, merchants and dealers" who kept the slave trade afloat. "The very lands in the Old and in the New World . . . where abolition petitions flow, are the lands where . . . there are owners of vessels to be 'chartered and sold deliverable on the coast of Africa'." As long as this wrongdoing went unpunished, Wise insisted, he would continue to doubt the motives behind Britain's opposition to the slave trade.[18]

A similar view of British policy defined President Tyler's message to Congress on the slave trade in February 1845. Tyler began by denouncing American involvement in the "inhuman traffic" and calling for the punishment of those responsible. But the president's message soon mutated into an angry condemnation of British slave-trade polices: "British factors and agents, while they supply Africa with British fabrics in exchange for slaves, are chiefly instrumental" in the continuation of the trade. Tyler echoed Wise's doubts about the practice of shipping liberated Africans to serve as apprentices in the West Indies—"in effect but a continuance of the slave trade in another and more cruel form." Finally, Tyler questioned whether Britain really even desired to end the traffic. "It seems to me," he declared, "that the policy it has adopted is calculated rather to perpetuate than to suppress the trade by enlisting very large interests in its favor."[19]

Both Wise and Tyler drew a distinction between the larger British war on slavery and the specific effort to end the African slave trade. Neither man doubted London's earnestness in the quest for "universal emancipation": Britain remained, if anything, frighteningly sincere in her desire to destroy slavery in the Americas. But the struggle against the slave trade was another matter. That illegal traffic was, in Wise's view, chiefly maintained by New Englanders and Britons, many of them involved in antislavery politics. The British government's failure to crack down on these actors suggested that its moral crusade lacked practical urgency. Was it possible, even, that Britain hoped to use the ongoing African trade as an excuse to attack established slave-labor systems across the hemisphere? Wise, Tyler, and their allies thought so. In that sense, the struggle against the Brazilian slave trade is perhaps best understood as a struggle to preserve Brazilian slavery.

Proslavery internationalists across the Caribbean basin often found themselves insisting on this distinction between slavery and the slave trade. In an 1842 Senate speech Calhoun expressed the hope that Brazil and the Spanish colonies would soon end the African trade. "Higher considerations," he noted, "connected with [Brazil's] safety, and that of the Spanish colonies, made it in their interest that the market should be closed against the traffic." What "considerations" related to "safety" could Calhoun have meant, if not a British attempt to undermine Brazilian domestic slavery by policing the slave trade or—even worse—foment an African slave revolt? This was exactly the scenario that troubled Cuba's slaveholders. Many of them, including Domingo Del Monte, even considered the ongoing African trade virtually a British plot, aimed, in the end, at slave "insurrection and emancipation."[20] In Brazil Wise sometimes described his own endeavors in similar terms. "The best defense of the lawful slavery already existing in Brazil and the United States," he told Foreign Minister França in 1845, "would be for both those powers to enforce, sternly and strictly, their own laws for the suppression of the contraband slave trade." Without the international odium attracted by the persistence of the African traffic, Wise reasoned, the British would have no "pretext for visit and search on the high seas and on the coast."[21]

For Henry Wise, the slave trade was a filthy and villainous business, managed by and organized for the benefit of Yankee capitalists, Liverpool merchants, and antislavery scoundrels generally. Little about it augured well for the sturdy domestic slaveholder, whether American or Brazilian.[22] Even the regular influx of new Africans, however necessary to perpetuate Brazilian slavery in the short term, could not offer a long-term solution for Brazilian masters. "The worst of it," Wise wrote regarding the transatlantic traffic, "is that they import so few females in comparison with the number of males, that the annual increase by propagation in Brazil is not likely, for a long period, to diminish the necessity for new slaves." The trade, in other words, prevented Brazil from becoming the slave society Wise would have liked to see: stable, healthy, and self-regenerating. This was the fondest hope of the proslavery internationalists—that the other slaveholding nations in the Americas could reconstitute themselves on the model of the southern United States. As the Charleston doctor J. G. F. Wurdemann had written of Cuba, "[W]ere the slave-trade effectually suppressed, [slaves'] increased value on the island would call for greater care from their masters, and they would then increase, as they have done in our Southern States, in population, in morals, and in usefulness."[23]

From this perspective, Henry Wise's seemingly bizarre battle against the slave trade makes sense within the context of a hemispheric defense of slavery. Wise failed to influence Brazilian policy toward the slave trade, and, in truth, did active harm to Calhoun's hope for a pan-American proslavery coalition. But the roots of this failure were perhaps more personal than ideological. The most "prominent characteristics" that defined Wise as a congressional orator—"firmness, impetuosity, a disdain for honeyed words, fierce sarcasm and invective"—spiked his diplomatic exchanges with a bitter taste that no amount of proslavery comradeship could disguise.[24] After butting heads with França throughout his first year in Brazil, Wise boasted in late 1845 that his relationship with the new minister of foreign affairs, Antonio Paulino Limpio de Abreo, was on "a more favorable and friendly footing" than ever before.[25] But within a year Wise and Abreo became embroiled in a dispute over the arrest of drunken American sailors on the streets of Rio de Janeiro. Wise aggravated the situation by instructing the U.S. naval squadron off the coast not to fire its customary cannon salute in celebration of Emperor Dom Pedro II's birthday. It was this incident, and not anything related to the slave trade, that led directly to Wise's removal from Brazil in early 1847.[26]

In some ways, these diplomatic embarrassments hinted at a structural weakness of U.S. proslavery internationalism. Its reflexively imperial imagination could envision the United States only as first among proslavery equals in the hemisphere. Brazilian and Cuban slaveholders might stand several ranks higher than what Wise called the "degraded... mongrel-Spaniards" of free Mexico and South America, but they remained, and must ever remain, junior partners within the hemispheric partnership to defend slavery. The Anglo-Saxon heritage of the United States, no less than its greater geopolitical clout, ordained a self-evident supremacy. In this respect, Wise's personal pugnacity only amplified a race problem that would haunt the foreign policy of slavery over the course of the next two decades.[27]

Condescension to the Brazilians, however, should not be confused with a lack of concern for the fate of Brazilian slavery. In all his struggles to limit the slave trade, Wise believed that he was working to save Brazil's masters from themselves. "British policy," he reminded França, "is at this moment avowedly aiming at universal emancipation throughout the world." The U.S. government, on the other hand, agreed with Brazil that "slavery, & property in slaves, do rightfully exist under their jurisdiction," and that "humanity does not require, but forbids, universal emancipation." Brazil should cooperate with the United States against the slave trade, not only to sustain high principles of natural law, but also "in defense of those peculiar institutions at home and on the high seas which they are obliged to maintain and preserve inviolate from intrusion or invasion by all foreign powers." The slave trade had to die, Wise insisted, so that domestic slavery could live.[28]

Nor is it clear that Wise's mission was a total failure. In 1849–50, when Brazil bowed to British pressure and took effective steps to stop the international slave traffic, Brazilian conservatives openly endorsed a version of Wise's basic strategy, surrendering the Atlantic slave trade in order to protect the overall security of the slave system. In the decade that followed, Brazil's ruling planters worked consciously to duplicate the thriving American model: a slave society that could reproduce itself through better slave management, the internal slave trade, and a close slaveholding grip on the power of the central government. Wise's clumsy and combative diplomacy may not have directly inspired these endeavors. But the wealth and stability of Brazil's slave empire during the 1850s and 1860s, long after the African traffic ended, offered a real, if indirect, fulfillment of his international vision.[29]

For once, John Quincy Adams probably erred when he accused Wise of "mountebank abhorrence of the African slave-trade."[30] The Virginian's campaign against U.S. involvement in Brazilian slave trafficking was well in earnest. But Adams rightly suspected Wise's larger purposes in opposing the trade—in fact, as Wise saw it, he was acting on behalf of the truest interests of slave owners from Porto Alegre all the way to Baltimore. It would probably go too far to suggest that this proslavery motivation single-handedly fueled his campaign against the slave trade; Wise's letters to a mostly indifferent State Department ring out with genuine moral indignation. Yet it seems unlikely that his outrage would have taken the form it did if Wise had not also believed that his cause was congruent with the international welfare of slavery. His tenure in Brazil must be understood within its most important context: the broader southern effort, beginning in the 1840s, to defend the hemispheric security of slave labor.[31]

A Sort of Hayti on the Continent

Brazil and Cuba, as the second- and third-largest slaveholding societies in the West, were natural theaters for the Tyler administration's struggle to protect slave labor in the Americas. But they were not the only theaters. Wherever British antislavery influence was or might be, there, too, were American slaveholders who sought to beat it back. In 1841 Tyler dispatched a covert agent to examine British fortifications and troop numbers throughout the West Indies; the ensuing report, with its keen focus on the enlistment of "Black Artillerists," underlined the thoroughness of the administration's strategic reconnaissance of the Caribbean. In 1843 Duff Green called Abel Upshur's attention to British Guiana, whose "Authorities," he had learned, planned "to induce the slaves in Dutch Guiana to emigrate to the British Colony." Once on British territory, the escaped bondspeople were "protected and made the agents of persuading others to desert their masters, thus transferring the labor from the Dutch to the British colony."[32]

All around the Caribbean basin U.S. agents kept Washington informed about the politics of race and labor, even in societies where slavery had been partly or wholly abolished. The fledgling Dominican Republic, which won its independence from Haiti in 1844, attracted proslavery attention as a vulnerable white government besieged by the forces of emancipation. In 1845 John C. Calhoun dispatched his political confidant John Hogan to Santo Domingo with special instructions to investigate the racial "character and composition of the population." Hogan returned a favorable report, noting that the island's blacks "have the utmost veneration & respect for their White masters." This only confirmed Calhoun's belief that the United States should cultivate ties with the new regime. The Dominican Republic, he wrote, was "of vast importance to us & this continent. It is a reaction against barbarism, and an important step should it succeed to maintaining the ascendancy of the more civilized portion of what may more truly be called Spanish America over the less civilized."[33]

Concern over hemispheric slavery entailed concern over hemispheric racial hierarchy. In 1844 two U.S. envoys to Venezuela, both from slave-holding states, reported "civil strife" between the white Creole government and "the coloured people, as a class." Birthed by the "evil and contagious example of Haiti" and nursed on false rumors that the United States "had *just elected an abolitionist* for their president," the popular opposition now threatened to free Venezuela's few remaining slaves, perhaps leading to "*a war between the races.*" Although the Americans in Caracas did not believe that slavery could be preserved, they still hoped that the United States might send its West Indian squadron to the Venezuelan coast. A show of naval force in restive, multiracial Venezuela, as in unsteady, enslaved Cuba, would warn "the discontented spirits of this Country" that the power of the United States stood vigorously on the side of the white elite.[34]

But although Tyler's minions stood guard all across the Americas, the most critical front in the cold war over race and labor emerged directly on U.S. borders. It concerned the effort to protect bondage in what was, by the early 1840s, the fourth-largest outpost of slavery in the hemisphere: the Republic of Texas. Historians have approached the 1845 U.S. annexation of Texas from a variety of perspectives. Some have seen it as a triumph of ex-pansionist "manifest destiny"; others, as an act of racial imperialism toward Mexico, a southern plot to add slave states to the Senate, an electioneering tactic for the Democratic Party, or simply the fruit of ravenous land specu-lation. In some measure, of course, annexation was all these things. But for influential southern leaders, Texas was above all a slaveholding republic in the Western Hemisphere. As such, it quite naturally required U.S. sup-port—and, if necessary, U.S. protection. Threatened by abolitionist forces from both Great Britain and Mexico, the Lone Star Republic represented a key arena in the larger battle over the future of slavery. In American his-tory textbooks Texas often appears in tandem with Oregon and Cali-fornia, but in the early 1840s its more natural companions were Cuba and Brazil. For the key southern leaders involved in annexation, the most crit-ical balance of power was not sectional or senatorial but international and hemispheric.

———

American statesmen had long looked to the Mexican province of Texas with an ill-concealed sense of expectation. Given its vast potential to grow sugar and cotton, Thomas Jefferson predicted, "Techas will be the richest

State of our Union." But if Jefferson's generation had assumed that Texas, like Cuba, would soon fall into the orbit of the United States, the national leaders that followed did little to speed up the process. In their 1819 treaty with Spain, President James Monroe and Secretary of State John Quincy Adams abandoned the shaky American claim to Texas in exchange for certain rights to Florida. The question of southwestern expansion then remained largely dormant for another decade or more.[35]

By the mid-1830s, however, rapid slaveholding settlement in the Mississippi valley, together with the looming specter of British abolitionism, helped produce a different set of attitudes toward the Southwest. When American settlers in Texas revolted against Mexican rule in 1835, southerners in the United States needed little prompting to identify the political stakes involved. Most American rhetorical support for the Texas revolution was either loftily republican or sordidly racist, but underneath it all were signs that southerners understood the conflict's implications for the future of slave labor. In the Senate, Robert J. Walker of Mississippi celebrated the 1836 Texan victory at San Jacinto as a triumph for both white supremacy and the security of slave property. The United States, Walker proclaimed, could never have allowed Mexico "to establish a government of Zamboes and Mestizoes, of Africans and Mulattos on the borders of Louisiana and Arkansas . . . —a people prepared . . . to unite with and instigate the people of their own colored race within our limits to deeds of bloodshed and massacre."[36] A Mexican victory in Texas, as Walker understood it, would threaten the racial and social organization of the slave states. In the decade that followed San Jacinto, this formulation came to govern all American foreign policy in the region.[37]

As Anglo-American tensions mounted in the 1840s, and as the outlines of a conscious foreign policy of slavery emerged, elite southerners kept their eyes trained toward the Southwest. The spring of 1842 saw an outpouring of anxieties about the prospect of a joint British-Mexican effort to purge slavery from the larger region. One Charleston editor worried that Mexico had received "secret assurances of support from England," prompting a renewed effort to reconquer its lost province. The *New Orleans Commercial Bulletin* trembled at the prospect of such an invasion: "The Mexican army marches into Texas as avowed abolitionists," warned its editors, citing a recent manifesto issued by Mexican president Antonio López de Santa Anna. Without Texas as a buffer state between Louisiana and Mexico, "the slave holders" of the Gulf South would face mortal danger.[38]

On the floor of Congress, Henry Wise took the lead in denouncing the Anglo-Mexican threat to continental slavery. "The tyrant of Mexico," he declared in April 1842, "was now at war with Texas, and had threatened that he would invade her territory, and 'never stop till he had driven slavery beyond the Sabine'"—the river boundary between Texas and the southern United States. His face no doubt assuming its familiar expression of livid pallor, Wise raised the horrifying prospect that "Mexican arms might drive back the slaves of Texas . . . upon Louisiana and Arkansas." But what most marked this 1842 speech was the alacrity with which he transformed the Mexican antislavery threat into an opening for American proslavery expansion. If Texas would only "proclaim a crusade against the rich States to the South of her," he declared, Americans from across the Mississippi valley would "flock to her standard," and no feeble Mexican resistance could break their advance. "And would not all this extend the bounds of slavery?" Wise asked, anticipating potential northern objections to his vision. "Yes, and the result would be that before another quarter of a century the extension of slavery would not stop short of the Western Ocean."[39]

Wise had indulged himself in a remarkably candid statement of proslavery imperialism. Although he attempted to frame his discussion in terms of old Jeffersonian arguments about the diffusion of slavery—whereby the spread of bondage abroad enabled its removal from the United States—the actual opponents of slavery in Congress did not receive the speech in this spirit.[40] John Quincy Adams mocked Wise's braggadocio, likening Wise's "heroic enterprise" to "a sort of crusade, in which the gentleman from Virginia is likely to transcend the exploits of Tamerlane and Genghis Khan."[41] His adversaries might have scoffed, but Wise's speech, delivered five years before U.S. troops occupied Mexico City, remains noteworthy as an odd example of southern grandiosity actually vindicated by future events.[42]

Wise's remarks also combined two critical elements within the foreign policy of slavery: concern for slave property beyond U.S. borders, coupled with a belief in the U.S. government's ability to protect that same slave property. In 1843 the Tyler administration began its campaign to bring the Lone Star Republic into the Union, thus keeping slaves on both sides of the U.S.-Texas border safe from British abolitionists and Mexican armies alike. In their private correspondence and public remarks, pro-annexation southerners stressed the danger to regional slavery as a major rationale for annexation. To win national support for the measure, of course, they offered other arguments—that Texas would be a boon to the national economy and a market for northern manufactures, a key addition to block British encirclement from the Gulf of Mexico all the way up to Canada, and, most disingenuously, a safety valve for the ultimate diffusion of American slavery.[43]

But for the southerners who led the annexation effort—Tyler, Upshur, and Calhoun—all these nationalistic hopes rested atop the essential foundation of slavery. Texas's gifts to the national economy, after all, would come primarily through the extension of the cotton empire to the banks of the Rio Grande. The danger of British encirclement, meanwhile, was above all a danger to southern slavery, already menaced by the black troop garrisons of the emancipated West Indies. And the central point of the famous safety-valve argument, that slaves would flock to Texas in droves, provoked no dispute from southern annexationists. The cynical corollary was that the great exodus would drain the South of its slaves—but this, of course, was intended for credulous northern audiences only. Slaveholders themselves knew better. Texas annexation was organized to defend and enlarge the field of slave labor, not to scatter it abroad uselessly.[44]

In January 1843 former Virginia governor Thomas W. Gilmer introduced the subject that would dominate the national political conversation for the next two years. In a public letter quickly reprinted by the Tyler administration's official organ, the *Madisonian*, Gilmer argued that the United States should annex the Republic of Texas. The Virginian downplayed the significance of slavery and presented a neutrally economic and geopolitical case for U.S. annexation.[45] But his letter opened a serious discussion of the real subject: the threat that British abolitionism posed to an independent but vulnerable Texas republic. In his correspondence with Gilmer, the Texas politician Memucan Hunt envisioned an antislavery strike against Texas that might, in its way, represent a greater danger than the Mexican army. It would be "easy," he wrote, "for the government of Great Britain through her *Abolition society in London* to introduce a population sufficient under the colonization contracts now existing in Texas to pass a law abolishing slavery." Transforming the Lone Star Republic into "an independent non-slaveholding state" would be "a dreadful calamity" for the United States. Only the American annexation of Texas, Hunt concluded, could prevent this nightmare from becoming reality.[46]

He was hardly the only proslavery figure to follow this logic to its conclusion. Andrew Jackson, now living out his old age at the Hermitage in

Tennessee, offered up his own nightmare scenario, thick with graphic detail: "Great Britain enters into an alience with Texas—looking forward to war with us, she sends to Texas 20 or 30,000 . . . marches thro Louisiana and Arkansa . . . excite[s] the negroes to insurrection . . . and a servile war rages all over the southern and western country." As was often the case, Old Hickory's terse misspellings seemed only to add heat and urgency to his argument. To disrupt the military threat posed by a possible Anglo-Texan alliance, and to protect the slaveholding states from ruin, the United States must acquire Texas.[47]

In Washington, President Tyler had kept Texas in the back of his mind almost since he entered the White House. Beyond his very real concerns about slave property along the Gulf of Mexico, Tyler knew that the acquisition of Texas might be the diplomatic masterstroke he needed to build support for a possible reelection campaign. Yet it was not coincidental that his administration's annexation effort began in earnest only in 1843. Political ambition played a part in the drive for Texas, but both the underlying rationale and the immediate impetus for annexation emerged from the logic of the foreign policy of slavery.[48]

The ubiquitous Duff Green was again at the center of the action. From London, Tyler's ambassador of slavery informed the president that he had uncovered fresh evidence of an abolitionist plot against Texas.[49] The British government, Green alleged, was providing secret aid for antislavery propaganda in the Lone Star Republic and might even offer the cash-strapped Texas government a direct loan in exchange for emancipation. This scheme fit perfectly with Green's interpretation of British foreign policy across the hemisphere: "[S]o long as Cuba, Brazil & the United States raise sugar coffee & cotton by slave labor they will drive the products of English East & West Indies out of the market." By emancipating the bound laborers of Texas, Green argued, Britain would "create a depot for runaway slaves," which, along with "the Indians on the Western border," could be used to threaten slavery in the United States. Here was an abomination whose horror could be suggested only by the grimmest of conceivable analogies. As a Texas government official put it in a June letter to Calhoun, Britain hoped to raise up "a negro nation, a sort of Hayti on the continent."[50]

Not for the first time, these proslavery observers radically overestimated the depth of Britain's commitment to antislavery action in the Gulf of Mexico. Although several local British agents worked intermittently to combat the extension of slavery in Texas, Sir Robert Peel's government in

London sought most of all to avoid an Anglo-American clash in the region.[51] Nevertheless, in the spring of 1843 the Tyler administration leaped into action. Secretary of State Webster resigned and was replaced first by Hugh Legaré of South Carolina and then, after Legaré's sudden death, by Abel P. Upshur. The new secretary, of course, shared Green's general view about the danger that British abolitionism posed for the entire hemispheric slave system.[52]

Within months of arriving at the State Department, Upshur received valuable new intelligence from a surprising source: the British minister in Washington, Henry S. Fox. In early August Fox approached Upshur with a problem "of some delicacy." The British West Indies, he confessed, was "suffering severely in their productive industry, from a dearth of agricultural labourers." Would the Tyler administration help encourage "labourers of the free colored class" to emigrate to the Caribbean? Upshur briskly rejected Fox's proposal. But here, from the lion's mouth, came fresh proof that the free-labor experiment in the Caribbean had failed—and thus oblique corroboration of the theory behind British imperial abolitionism. Perhaps Britain's hemispheric crusade against slavery had grown even more desperate than Upshur had previously understood. After all, this was the same summer in which the excitable Robert Monroe Harrison in Jamaica had warned Washington about a far-ranging Anglo-Caribbean plot to stir up a slave insurrection in Cuba.[53]

Well before he encountered Duff Green's reports, Henry Fox's confessions, or Harrison's alarms, Upshur believed that British abolitionism posed an existential threat to American slavery. But it was only in the summer of 1843 that he and other powerfully placed southerners grasped the immediacy of the danger. Now was the time to move. In late August Calhoun wrote Upshur with a detailed plan of action. From any other source, the letter might have sounded like an arrogant set of instructions for the sitting secretary of state, but the South Carolinian saw himself, with some justice, as a kind of presiding guru for Tyler's foreign policy team. Calhoun instructed the administration to demand an explanation from Great Britain, issue a "forcible statement" about the danger of Texas abolition, and privately reassure the Texas government of American "friendly feelings & disposition." Meanwhile, U.S. representatives in Mexico, France, and Prussia should be empowered to "baffle, as far as it may be possible," British plans in Texas.[54]

In fact, Upshur had already embarked on a similarly aggressive program. Earlier in August he had warned William S. Murphy, the U.S. chargé d'affaires in Texas, of Great Britain's "general plan ... to abolish domestic slavery throughout the entire continent and islands of America." The United States, Upshur wrote, "have a high interest to counteract this attempt," and the struggle must begin in Texas. Although it was too early to promise the Texans that they would be annexed—Upshur knew that getting congressional approval for the measure would be difficult—he made it clear to Murphy in late September that the Tyler administration had "every desire to come to the aid of Texas in the most prompt and effectual manner." By October Upshur was speaking regularly with the Texas representative in Washington about the shape of a possible annexation treaty.[55]

Fearing both British interference and domestic political uproar, administration officials kept these discussions quiet. But by the second half of 1843 they were all firmly committed to the project of annexation. The *Madisonian* spent much of that autumn sounding the alarm about British plots in Texas, whose ultimate aim could only be printed in screaming capitals: "THE ABOLITION OF SLAVERY IN AMERICA."[56] Like-minded southern newspapers blazed forth on the British threat to "slave states" in the Gulf of Mexico—a phrase that, in the *Charleston Mercury*'s telling usage, referred not to the American South but the foreign "states" of "Cuba and Texas." And in private, administration men were candid about their goals. Acquiring Texas for the United States, Upshur wrote Tucker in October, was now "the great object of my ambition. I do not care to control any measure of policy except this."[57]

As always, the principal southerners involved in the annexation effort framed their labors in a larger international context. Calhoun could not counsel Upshur on Texas policy without also proposing a transatlantic guarantee for Spanish control of Cuba; to protect slavery on one end of the Gulf of Mexico while seeing it destroyed on the other would be no victory at all. Upshur, meanwhile, could not discuss the politics of annexation without invoking the hemispheric landscape. Great Britain's inability to "compete with the slave labor of the United States, Texas, and Brazil," he reminded Murphy, was at the root of all British abolitionism.[58]

The hemispheric context mattered because the struggle over Texas was not simply about political control over valuable territory, but the fundamental relationship between free and bound labor in the Americas. Leading southern annexationists returned frequently to the language of proslavery interdependence—the idea that a threat to slavery anywhere was a threat to slavery everywhere. "If France ... should abolish slavery in her Colonies," wrote the Alabamian who represented the United States in Paris, "Spain, and Brazill, will be compelled to yield to the pressure which will be brought to bear upon them; and the United States will be left alone, with the whole civilized world against her." France's few Caribbean possessions contained just 200,000 slaves, fewer than the number of bondspeople in Alabama, and a tiny fraction of New World slavery as a whole. But such was the fragile unity of the hemispheric system, southerners feared, that even the slightest of slavery's dominoes could topple the entire institution.[59]

The precarious alignment of forces meant that in Texas, as in Cuba, the preservation of slavery sometimes seemed to overshadow the comparatively smaller question of political allegiance. For Waddy Thompson of South Carolina, the U.S. minister in Mexico City, the importance of slavery in Texas outweighed even the fate of annexation. "If Texas could be reannexed to Mexico," he suggested in 1844, "with the toleration of Slavery and a merely nominal supremacy of Mexico I do not see any cause of regret on our part."[60] But in practice the secure embrace of the American union generally seemed the best guarantee for slave property in Texas. For Upshur, the worst possible case was the establishment of Texas as "an independent government forbidding the existence of slavery," placed "in the very midst of our slave-holding States." This scenario would be even more dangerous than the existing "contiguity of slaveholding and non-slaveholding States of our Union." The U.S. Constitution, after all, "guaranties all the rights of the slave-holder and there is an act of Congress which provides the means for enforcing them." As the shipwrecked-slave cases had shown, no such overarching legal framework could protect these rights beyond U.S. borders. On the world stage American power remained the slaveholder's most trusted ally.[61]

None of this meant that Texas annexation would be simple. Between 1843 and 1845 it required southern leaders to overcome the resistance of the Whig Party, the fickleness of the Texas government, and the combined opposition of British and Mexican diplomacy. These obstacles demanded a commitment to the hemispheric defense of slavery that transcended traditional southern and Democratic principles—states' rights, a strict construction of the Constitution, and decentralized federal power. But in their furious efforts to make Texas safe for slavery, southerners in the Tyler and Polk administrations bypassed these potential ideological hurdles with impressive ease. In the mid-1840s the foreign policy of slavery proved nearly impervious to domestic political restraints.

The Imperious Duty of the Federal Government

For years, the presence of Edward Everett as the American minister to Great Britain had rankled Abel Upshur. A "Southern man & a slaveholder," not a Massachusetts "abolitionist," he complained, should represent U.S. interests in London. In the fall of 1843 his desire for an explicitly slaveholding diplomatic corps grew more insistent. "Mr. Everett," Upshur told Calhoun, "is from the wrong side of Mason & Dixon. We should be represented in England, by some one who understands domestic slavery."[62] For his part, Duff Green fretted about American representation on the continent. Since "the slave question is the question of the day," he wrote Upshur, "[n]o one north of the Potomac is suited to represent us, at London Paris or Madrid." Without proper "representation or agency," the southern-born U.S. consul in Paris argued, proslavery forces in France risked losing the diplomatic war against abolitionism. In the end, Tyler left Everett in Britain but replaced the outgoing minister to France with William R. King, a moderate in his native Alabama but unquestionably a southern man and a slaveholder on the world stage.[63]

It is tempting to see such southern insistence on slaveholding diplomats as evidence of a fiercely sectional political consciousness. Upshur and other southerners did occasionally bring such a spirit to the Texas question. Annexation, he told Calhoun, "is a *Southern* question, and not one of whiggism & democracy. The southern people are far, far too lethargic upon this vital question. They ought to be roused, & made of one mind." This was the kind of talk that has fueled historical treatments of Texas annexation as primarily or exclusively sectional in character.[64]

But despite Calhoun's commitment to a purified southern politics and Upshur's desire to energize the South, even the most sectional Texas annexationists ultimately understood the question in national terms. Their center of operations, after all, was not Charleston or New Orleans but Washington, at the State Department office on Pennsylvania Avenue. The chief threat to bondage in the 1840s came not from northern rabble-rousers but the imperial abolitionism of Great Britain. To vanquish that threat, slaveholding elites could not act as representatives of a minority regional interest. They had to wield the national power of the United States.

In his letter to the U.S. envoy in Texas, Upshur contrasted the world of international relations, hostile and dangerous to slavery, with domestic American life, where the U.S. Constitution offered the strongest possible bulwark for slave property. He even dared imagine that American politics might become more sympathetic to bondage: "[T]he slave holder of the United States has not yet lost hope that all the embarrassments which individuals or States have thrown in the way of that property, may be removed by the quiet action of our own system."[65]

Although pro-Texas southerners understood the importance of the sectional balance of power within the Union, they remained confident that slaveholding interests would come out on top. As Calhoun put it, a strong South "cannot fail to control the other and more disordered sections." His major domestic antagonist, Andrew Jackson, agreed: the "rising greatness of the South and West" would define the future of the American republic.[66]

It is this sense of confident expectation in regard to American slavery that historians have sometimes overlooked in accounts of the southern push for Texas. To be sure, Upshur and his fellow maestros of annexation had their moments of darkness and pessimism. Genuine anxiety about northern population growth and the control of Congress inflected the worldviews of the men who led the campaign for Texas. But this sectional defensiveness also mingled with a deep well of confidence in American power, and the southern ability to manipulate that power for the protection and benefit of slavery. In 1843 and 1844 that confidence encouraged Upshur, Tyler, and the others to push the boundaries of expansionist diplomacy as they had seldom been pushed before. Upshur may have believed in the Constitution as a conservative safeguard for slaveholding, but he did not intend to let its restrictions on executive power obstruct his campaign for Texas. In this he was joined by nearly all the slaveholders involved in the annexation project.

Even Upshur's old Virginia friend Nathaniel Beverley Tucker, the author of *The Partisan Leader*, set aside some ideological scruples when it came to Texas. In December 1843 Upshur wrote Tucker to seek advice on the form of a possible annexation treaty. Did the Texas leadership have a legal "right to transfer the *country*," via a diplomatic agreement, "without the consent *of the people*"? "How shall this be managed?" This legalistic fussing was more than a little disingenuous. Already deep in negotiations with the Texas chargé d'affaires in Washington, the secretary of state knew that he had little time to spare on such fine theoretical dilemmas. Without waiting for a response to his opening question, he asked Tucker to draft "the preamble of a treaty & the clauses transferring the territory." Tucker agreed to help. Constitutional and legal objections, in this context, were problems to be "managed," not seriously contemplated. The fate of slavery on the continent was too large a question to be left to philosophical timidity.[67]

By late 1843 the major obstacle to an annexation treaty was Texas president Sam Houston, who still dreamed of a glorious independent future for the Lone Star Republic. Finally, Houston agreed to begin work on a treaty, but only if the Tyler administration provided a military guarantee against a Mexican attack during negotiations. Such a formal promise would be flagrantly unconstitutional: it would commit the United States to a war with Mexico at the behest of a foreign power, without the input or consent of Congress. Even Tyler and Upshur could not go so far; beyond any principled objections, they knew that if this kind of guarantee were made public, it might put the entire annexation project in political danger. Nevertheless, Upshur assured the Texas representative in Washington that the administration would do the next-best thing. He promised to send a large armed force to the border while concentrating a U.S. naval squadron off the Texas coast. Tyler's envoy, W. S. Murphy, went a step further. "Neither Mexico nor any other power," he promised Texas officials, "will be permitted to invade Texas, on account of any negotiation which may take place." Although the administration later officially disavowed Murphy's illegitimate guarantee, in February 1844 it helped coax Houston into giving his crucial blessing for an annexation agreement.[68]

That same month, however, Abel Upshur's plans for annexation suffered a gruesomely ironic setback. On February 12 Captain Robert F. Stockton steamed into the Potomac aboard the USS *Princeton*, a new screw-propeller sloop and the pride of the navy. A tangible product of Upshur's modernizing campaign as secretary of the navy, the *Princeton* carried unusually high-powered weaponry for a sloop-of-war: twenty-four forty-two-pound cannon plus two enormous twelve-inch guns, each capable of pulverizing iron and wood targets at a distance of three miles. In its continual quest for naval funding, the Tyler administration often sought to dazzle legislators with the display of high-tech warships. Upshur, as navy secretary, had invited Congress to the Potomac in 1842 to examine two new "specimens of American naval architecture." Now Tyler and his new secretary of the navy, early Texas annexation advocate Thomas Gilmer, pulled out all the stops for the *Princeton*. A week after its arrival in Washington, Congress adjourned so that its members could visit the ship. The skeptical John Quincy Adams grumbled that the exhibition was intended primarily "to fire their souls with patriotic ardor for a naval war."[69]

On February 27 Tyler invited Stockton to a public reception in the East Room of the White House in preparation for a gala excursion to the *Princeton* the following day. Upshur did not attend, instead staying up late in his office to finalize the annexation treaty he had only just hammered out with Texas chargé Isaac Van Zandt. The next morning, however, he joined the president, Secretary Gilmer, and other Washington luminaries, including the seventy-six-year-old Dolley Madison, aboard the *Princeton*. By late afternoon the heaviest of the ship's two twelve-inch guns, the Peacemaker, had already been fired twice, to the delight of the assembled party. While most of the guests, including Tyler, went below to enjoy a "sumptuous collation" of food and drink, Secretary Gilmer persuaded Stockton to fire the massive gun once more. This time the Peacemaker exploded from the inside out, spewing shards of red-hot iron across the deck and killing Upshur, Gilmer, and seven others.[70]

In the aftermath of the disaster, Tyler knew that the delicate state of Texas diplomacy meant he had to act quickly to find Upshur's replacement in the State Department. Within ten days of the tragedy the president nominated John C. Calhoun. It was a natural choice: given the administration's larger foreign policy goals, perhaps no figure in American politics made more sense.[71] Upshur had leaned heavily on Calhoun for advice throughout his tenure at the State Department; on the central questions of British imperial abolitionism and the hemispheric defense of slavery, the two held almost identical views. Yet Upshur had mostly managed to camouflage his aggressive goals with quiet diplomacy, rhetorical restraint, and secretive correspondence. Calhoun took a different approach. Equally committed to the foreign policy of slavery, he saw less reason to disguise his worldview for either domestic or international audiences. In the spring of 1844, at least, this made him much less effective than his predecessor.

Before his death Upshur had expressed confidence that his private lobbying efforts had persuaded more than the necessary two-thirds of the Senate to ratify the treaty. When the finished document was presented to Congress in April, however, Calhoun's correspondence with the British minister in Washington, Richard Pakenham, disturbed this delicate alignment. Responding to the accusations leveled by Duff Green, the *Madisonian*, and other American sources, Pakenham and his foreign secretary, Lord Aberdeen, had publically denied that Great Britain had any plans to interfere in Texas. Although Aberdeen admitted that Britain "shall not desist from those open and honest efforts which we have constantly made for

AWFUL EXPLOSION of the *"PEACE-MAKER"* on board the U.S. STEAM FRIGATE, *PRINCETON*, on WEDNESDAY, 28th FEB: 1844.

The explosion aboard the *Princeton* is dramatically depicted in this 1844
Currier & Ives print. Never before or since has a single incident claimed the lives
of multiple American cabinet officers.

procuring the abolition of slavery throughout the world," he disavowed
any intention to upset the "internal tranquility" of either Texas or "the
American Union."[72] This halfhearted denial failed to satisfy Calhoun. Less
than a week after the Texas annexation treaty was presented to Congress,
the secretary wrote back to Pakenham with more spirit and candor than
Upshur had ever allowed himself as the public mouthpiece of the State
Department.

Britain's cold war on slavery, Calhoun argued, made it "the duty of all
other countries, whose safety or prosperity may be endangered by her
policy, to adopt such measures as they may deem necessary for their protection." By 1844 this notion of a proslavery community of nations came
easily to Calhoun, and he cited it as a fundamental reason for the current
program of annexation. The American absorption of Texas was "the most
effectual, if not the only, means of guarding against the threatened danger"
of British antislavery. In the second half of his letter Calhoun went even
further, plunging into an extended statistical analysis that confirmed slavery

as a positive good. The secretary pronounced black slavery in the American South a "wise and humane" institution while decrying the "vice and pauperism" of free northern blacks. The careful foreign policy of slavery morphed, rather suddenly, into a strident defense of bondage.[73]

Calhoun's inflammatory letter to Pakenham halted the momentum of the annexation treaty in Congress. Although southern newspapers had long denounced Britain's international war on slavery, the administration had not made its public case for Texas on proslavery grounds. President Tyler, although doubtless sympathetic to Calhoun's logic, had scrupulously avoided mentioning the slavery issue when he presented the Texas treaty to the Senate.[74] With most Whigs—even southern Whigs—opposed to annexation, the treaty required near-unanimous support from northern Democrats to gain the necessary two-thirds vote. When Calhoun turned the Texas issue into a debate about slavery, northern expansionists withdrew their support. In June the Senate rejected annexation by the embarrassingly decisive count of 35 to 16.[75]

Yet this would not be the final word on the Texas question: 1844, after all, was an election year. In April both Henry Clay, the leading Whig candidate for president, and Martin Van Buren, the leading Democrat, made public statements opposing the immediate annexation of Texas. The door was open for a pro-Texas candidate to squeeze into the election. At the Democratic convention in Baltimore a determined brigade of southerners successfully blocked Van Buren's nomination. After multiple ballots the eventual nominee, James K. Polk of Tennessee, emerged on a platform of immediate and uncompromising annexation. The political battle between Polk and Clay kept the Texas question very much alive throughout the summer and fall of 1844.[76]

In the meantime, Tyler and Calhoun began to explore other possibilities for annexation. If they could not procure a two-thirds majority in the Senate, perhaps it was possible to manage a joint resolution of Congress, requiring only simple majorities in the House and Senate. Tyler and his cohort did not appear troubled by the idea that the United States had never before added state-sized pieces of territory without ratifying a formal treaty. In 1803 some strict constructionists had felt that Thomas Jefferson had overstepped his bounds in acquiring Louisiana by treaty rather than a constitutional amendment. Now Tyler argued that even a treaty was unnecessary. "The power of Congress" alone was "fully competent" to permit the Union to swallow an entire foreign republic, hundreds of thousands of

square miles in size. By now it was clear that only political reality, not constitutional restraint, could prevent Tyler from annexing Texas.[77]

Within the State Department Calhoun continued to use the Texas debate
as a means to stretch the geographic and ideological boundaries of proslavery politics. His August letter to the new minister to France, William
King, contained yet another impassioned attack on British abolitionism,
joined to yet another stentorian defense of bondage. But what was most
striking about this "King letter," as it came to be known, was the clear intention that it be used as international proslavery propaganda. The triumph of
British abolitionism in Texas, Calhoun declared, would produce a "war of
races all over South America, including Mexico, and extending to the Indian, as well as the African race; and mak[ing] the whole scene one of blood
and devastation." France and "the other great continental Powers," Calhoun
argued, had no interest in such a disaster. "Is it not better for them, that they
should be supplied with tropical products, in exchange for their labor, from
the United States, Brazil, Cuba, and this continent generally?"[78]

At home, southerners cheered Calhoun's magnificent exposé of British
abolition—"[Y]ou have thrown a hand-grenade into their canting camp,"
wrote one ally—while suspicious northerners in Congress demanded to
see the secretary's full correspondence with Paris. But both friends and enemies alike recognized that the King letter's significance lay beyond the traditional borders of the sectional conflict. His South Carolina friend James
Gadsden thought Calhoun deserved "the gratitude of the world, where trade
is stimulated by the production of black & slave labor"; the antislavery press
complained that he had proposed "a grand slaveholding League, of Brazil,
Spain, and France, with the United States at its head."[79]

Calhoun could hardly have put it better himself. Under the secretary's
direction the State Department distributed the King letter to Texas, Brazil,
and "all our Diplomatick agents in Europe." From Rio de Janeiro, where he
had yet to stir up trouble with his hosts, Henry Wise reported that "Mr Calhoun's letter to Mr King had a good effect here" in encouraging the Brazilian government to resist British abolitionism.[80] In Paris King received
the dispatch with enthusiasm, adding only a request for secret-service funds
to place articles "in the Paris papers . . . calculated to disabuse the public
mind here, as to the actual condition of the Slaves of our Country." Calhoun
sent him the money, along with a "confidential" and even more explicit
statement about the white supremacist alliance he had hinted at in his
August letter. "England," he warned, had become "the patron of the coloured

races of all hues, negroes, indians & mixed, ag[ai]nst the white"; France must join the global forces ranged against this abolitionist horde. In the end, it is unclear whether Calhoun and King's proslavery politicking had much impact on French policy, but over the course of 1844–45 France ultimately refused to participate in even tentative British efforts to oppose the American annexation of Texas.[81]

Calhoun also extended Upshur's efforts to provide the strongest possible security guarantee to anxious Texans, who worried that another Mexican invasion loomed in the fall.[82] What could the U.S. military do to help Texas without the consent of Congress? According to one Texas official in Washington, Calhoun was the administration's most "case-hardened" advocate of intervention: "[H]ad he the power, the army would doubtless be ordered right into Texas to repel any attack against her."[83] In September the secretary of state found a rationale that might provide sufficient cover for the administration to deploy American troops. Pierce Butler, U.S. agent to the Cherokee in Indian Territory, had accused the Mexican government of "instigating the Indian Tribes on our south western frontier." By the terms of the U.S.-Mexico treaty of 1831, Calhoun concluded, the United States was authorized to send troops into Texas to "restrain" any possible Indian incursions into the area.[84]

In truth, by 1844 most of the vast plains encompassing western Texas and northern Mexico were under the effective dominion of a powerful Comanche-led empire. The Comanches, Kiowas, and other tribes in the region needed little incitement or assistance from the Mexican government, which could barely sustain its own northern settlements against Indian attacks, let alone manipulate the Indians. No further evidence against Mexico ever surfaced to support the accusations made by Butler, a former South Carolina governor and Calhoun confidant. But it was characteristic of both U.S.-Mexican relations and the foreign policy of slavery that Calhoun drew on the threat of Indian attack to bypass Congress and secure troops for Texas.[85]

In November James K. Polk narrowly defeated Henry Clay to win the presidential election. "[T]he Republic is safe," crowed Andrew Jackson. "Texas is sure under Polks administration to be annexed to the United States." Tyler and Calhoun, however, were determined not to wait until Polk took office. As soon as Congress reconvened in December, the lame-duck administration and its allies pushed forward the joint resolutions on Texas. Congressional critics considered the effort an outrageous and hypocritical abuse of the Constitution. It was "not a little surprising," remarked New York Democrat George Rathbun, "that a gentleman from South Carolina, considered as the standard-bearer of strict construction," should be the author of this annexation policy. Calhoun "could not hear of an appropriation for opening a harbor, improving a railroad, cutting a canal, or chartering a bank, because the power to perform these things is not specifically granted in the constitution," but he was now eager to swallow a sovereign state without ratifying a formal treaty.[86]

Still the advocates of annexation pressed forward in Congress. After a long debate, the House passed a resolution admitting Texas into the Union under conditions very similar to Tyler's original treaty. In the Senate skeptical northern Democrats led by Thomas Hart Benton demanded further discussion on the timing and circumstances of annexation, especially in regard to border disputes between Texas and Mexico. Finally, by a tight vote of 27 to 25, the Senate passed a resolution admitting Texas as a state, but giving the President discretion to conduct additional negotations with Texas authorities. After meeting with President-elect Polk, Benton's faction in the Senate acted under the impression that the incoming administration would proceed with these additional talks to set the terms of annexation. [87]

But at a cabinet meeting two days before their terms of office expired, President Tyler and Secretary of State Calhoun decided that more negotiations would risk further British meddling in Texas. "It was enough," Tyler remembered later, "that Congress had given me the power to act by the terms of the resolutions, and that the urgency of the case was imminent." The outgoing administration determined to flout expectations and move to acquire Texas at once, under the loosest understanding possible. By the time Polk took office, the wheels of annexation were already in motion.[88]

Tyler's aggressive decision, undertaken in the waning hours of his presidency, caught both supporters and opponents of the Senate compromise off guard. In his diary James Henry Hammond confessed to misgivings about acquiring Texas by joint resolution: "The Constitutionality of it I think doubtful." Still, he rejoiced in the larger success of annexation, for it was "an event of great magnitude" and "strengthens the South and the slave interest."[89] For neither the first nor last time in antebellum political history, cold principle dissolved before the demands of hot ambition.

Beyond expediency, however, a deeper logic guided the southern annexationists. Their willingness to use all the muscle and machinery of the federal government to obtain Texas reflected their larger view of U.S. power in foreign affairs. As northern opponents of annexation observed, the new territory would further enhance the military capacity of the nation. The acquisition of Texas, Joshua Giddings told Congress, will "require a large increase of our army," an extensive "circle of fortifications," and an expansion of "our naval armament, in order that slavery might be protected there as well." John Quincy Adams offered an even more vivid picture of how Texas would further the growth of the United States as an imperial behemoth:

> This Texas annexation we deem the turning-point of a revolution which transforms the North American Confederation into a conquering and warlike nation. Aggrandizement will be its passion and its policy. A military government, a large army, a costly navy, distant colonies, and associate islands in every sea, will follow of course in rapid succession.[90]

Giddings and Adams latched onto something real. Tyler and his allies would not have characterized their project in those terms, but as a rule, they proved willing to expand the powers of the central government in order to complete the project of annexation. The British attempt to abolish slavery in Texas, Calhoun stressed in his letter to Pakenham, required an unequivocally national response: "It is felt to be the imperious duty of the Federal Government, the common representative and protector of the States of this Union, to adopt, in self defence, the most effectual measures to defeat it." In the debate over the joint resolutions Virginia congressman Thomas Bayly laid out the constitutional reasoning behind the administration's policy. "There are two classes of powers conferred upon the general government," Bayly explained, "the one relating to our foreign, and other to our domestic relations." Under America's "wise system . . . there is a plenary delegation of power to the general government in all that concerns of external affairs, and a restricted delegation in what relates to our domestic." Thus "liberal construction" should be observed in the former area but "strict construction" in the latter. Given the obvious "importance of Texas to us as a means of military defence," Bayly hoped that Congress would grant the administration all conceivable latitude in managing its annexation.[91]

Southerners may have understood these arguments as useful justifications for a Texas policy that was governed by sectional self-interest, not larger political ideas. But they may also have simply meant what they said. For Tyler, Calhoun, and others, the federal government represented the strongest and most reliable weapon for the defense of hemispheric slavery. It stood to reason that they interpreted its international powers liberally. The founders of the Republic, one pro-Texas essayist argued, took an expansive attitude toward "the duties of the federal government in strengthening our frontiers and fortifying the defenses of freedom. [Their] views [were] broad, capacious, and eminently national." In the 1840s the southerners in charge of American foreign policy were more than content to apply this formulation to contemporary affairs. What, after all, could be more eminently national than the protection of American slavery?[92]

––––––––––

The annexation of Texas was perhaps the quintessential achievement of the foreign policy of slavery. The measure involved all the central aspects of that evolving program: feverish attention to the international balance between slavery and freedom; unquestioning belief in the power of the South to command American foreign policy, and the power of American foreign policy to command the world; and a willingness to bring the full weight of the U.S. government to bear on the question. Its realization brought despair to opponents of bondage on both sides of the Atlantic. "The annexation of Texas looks like one of those events which retard or retrograde the civilization of the ages," wrote Ralph Waldo Emerson in Massachusetts. For the British historian T. B. Macaulay, America's Texas diplomacy defined the essence of its role on the world stage: "The United States' Government has openly declared itself the patron, the champion, and the upholder of slavery. . . . [I]t renders itself illustrious as the evil genius of the African race." American leaders "put themselves at the head of the slave interest, just as Queen Elizabeth put herself at the head of the Protestant interest in Europe." Just as Elizabeth's victories against Spain were triumphs for world Protestantism, so the American victory in Texas was a triumph for world slavery.[93]

Southern slaveholders celebrated their accomplishment in similar international terms. The acquisition of Texas, crowed Henry Wise in Brazil, confirmed America's "monopoly . . . of the cotton trade of the world." The balance of power between Great Britain and the United States would never be the same, declared Major William Chase, commandant of U.S. forces at Pensacola: "A British ministry declaring war against the United States could not remain in power more than forty-eight hours. . . . By the annexation of

Texas the United States have secured the monopoly of growing the great staple of the world."[94]

The South's international triumphalism, however, extended beyond the early stirrings of King Cotton. In a postannexation speech William Lowndes Yancey of Alabama called Congress's attention to "the situation of the two rival industries of the world—the free and the slave labor." The former, though aided by the might of the world's greatest power, Great Britain, was falling behind. But "the other, seeming to derive renewed vigor from the decaying fortunes of its rival, is springing forward with an elasticity and speed that will soon defy rivalry." Texas represented another jewel in the crown of world slavery; under American protection it would doubtless provide yet more evidence of "the immense superiority of a system of associated slave labor over free individual labor in every species of tropical cultivation."[95]

In 1845 the Martinique planter Thomas Jollivet helped translate and publish a Paris edition of Calhoun's now-famous King letter—the lead item in a new collection of American proslavery writing aimed at French readers. Southern commentators cheered and clamored for more. "[A]ll documents calculated to furnish Foreign States with the arguments of the Southern States," urged one South Carolina magazine, "should be sent abroad as widely and rapidly as possible." Perhaps the tide of international antislavery opinion was beginning to retreat, and Europe's "[c]ommon sense" would soon "assert its sway." After the successful annexation of Texas, proslavery propagandists had reason to feel that their cause might receive a fuller hearing both at home and abroad.[96]

Their optimism reflected the great strides the foreign policy of slavery had made in the four years since Tyler had entered the White House. To be sure, slavery's dominoes still arranged themselves precariously on the Atlantic game board; the specter of British abolitionism still loomed across the hemisphere. But thanks in part to American vigilance, none of the dominoes had fallen. The collective forces of antislavery—whether European, American, or African in origin—appeared to have made little headway in their battle against bondage in the Caribbean basin. Above all, the absorption of Texas into the American union immeasurably strengthened the position of hemispheric slaveholders. As Memucan Hunt had observed to Duff Green in early 1844, "The slave interest is too small in N. America to be maintained without molestation if held by two governments. . . . To make it secure one government should protect it all." By 1845 that one government was the United States, and its confidence in the sole possession of cotton and slavery was immense. In the years that followed, the southerners at the helm of national power continued to look for ways to strengthen the slave interest in the Americas, both inside and outside the borders of the United States.[97]

5

The Young Hercules of America

IN MANY WAYS THE PRESIDENCY OF JOHN TYLER represented the high-water mark for the foreign policy of slavery. No White House before or since devoted itself so comprehensively to the international defense of bound labor. As a president without a party and an administration without a national constituency, Tyler and his cabinet answered only to their own ideological predilections. Although they saw their strategic exertions in Cuba, Brazil, and Texas as part of a national effort, their nationalism was the untainted and unbounded product of a distinctively proslavery vision for the United States.

This was not precisely the case in the succeeding administration of James K. Polk. An experienced Tennessee planter and politician, Polk had a record of sturdy opposition to antislavery measures on the national level.[1] But unlike his predecessor, Polk owed his election to both northern and southern voters; once in office, he believed himself responsible not only for the government of the United States but also for the national Democratic Party. Throughout his presidency Polk maintained a balanced cabinet and worked closely with northern allies in Congress. His aggressive diplomacy— above all, his desire to obtain California from Mexico—reflected an expansionistic impulse that derived equally from northern and southern sources. Polk's stalwart Democratic partisanship even sparked a bitter quarrel with John C. Calhoun and his faction of southerners, disrupting the broader proslavery unity that had characterized the Texas annexation struggle.[2]

Nevertheless, the Polk administration proved a worthy legatee of the foreign policy of slavery. From 1845 to 1849 the United States avoided war with Great Britain over Oregon, defended the physical integrity of Texas and the security of its slaves, and extended the southwestern American border all the way to the Pacific. Vigorously embracing the power of the centralized state, in peace and in war Polk sought to assure U.S. hegemony over all North America, from the far western deserts to the near Gulf and the Caribbean basin. In this bare catalog of achievements, Polk accomplished scarcely much more, but certainly no less, than a hypothetical President Calhoun might have done. To be sure, neither the national Democratic Party nor the burgeoning dogma of manifest destiny remained the exclusive property of proslavery southerners. But for the slaveholding elites intimately involved in U.S. foreign policy, the military and diplomatic triumphs of the late 1840s represented an exhilarating sequel to the annexation of Texas. The consolidation of America's continental empire, as they saw it, strengthened the South's position within the United States and strengthened the United States' position in global affairs. Both goals were ideologically congruent with the foreign policy of slavery.

Peace on the Pacific, War on the Rio Grande

The sharpest differences between President Tyler and President Polk were biographical and aesthetic. Where Tyler, the genteel son of tidewater Virginia, was intricate, elliptical, and occasionally grandiose, Polk, who was born in western North Carolina and came of age in middle Tennessee, tended toward a rougher sort of shrewdness in politics, dry rigidity in judgment, and narrow practicality in rhetoric. But from the perspective of U.S. foreign relations, such discrepancies were palpable without being profound. Both presidents saw black servitude as an inarguably national institution and professed shock and dismay when they found their foreign projects interrupted by the domestic politics of slavery. Both packed their state papers with genuflections toward the secular god of limited government, but viewed the overseas power of the state as a weapon best left in the unfettered hands of the chief executive. And neither president, in their labors to defend U.S. national security, proved immune to the charms of U.S. imperial power. The careful accumulation of a hemispheric empire, often through an aggressive foreign policy directed at antislavery enemies, remained the defining characteristic of the Tyler-Polk regime across the 1840s.[3]

One major diplomatic theater on which the new president focused his attention was the Pacific Northwest. The United States and Great Britain had long disputed which nation controlled the thousand miles of coastline between Russian Alaska and Mexican California. Aggressive claimants on both sides demanded the whole region, but moderates hoped for compromise: the Tyler administration had proposed a boundary at the 49th parallel of latitude, while the British suggested the Columbia River, which ran a few hundred miles to the south. By 1844, however, as more Americans migrated westward, expansionists argued that the United States should possess the entire territory.[4] Polk's 1844 Democratic platform called for the occupation of Oregon all the way up to the 54°40' line. In his inaugural address the new president took a tersely uncompromising stance: "[O]ur title to the country of the Oregon is 'clear and unquestionable.'" During his first year in office Polk continued to insist that "the only way to treat John Bull was to look at him straight in the eye." Concessions and compromise proposals, he believed, would only whet Britain's appetite for more territory. A "bold & firm course on our part," by contrast, was in fact "the pacific one."[5]

Polk's Oregon bluster irritated many southerners, especially those in the Atlantic Southeast. For years John C. Calhoun had advocated a course of "masterly inactivity" toward Oregon; the mass movement of Americans to the West, he argued, would soon win the territory for the United States much more effectually than any diplomatic arrangement. Above all, however, Calhoun and other southerners wanted to avoid war with Great Britain. With the dust still settling on Texas annexation, Calhoun argued that a war would be "calamitous in the extreme.... [M]y fear is, that England will despair of settling [the Oregon question] & run it into the Texian question. If so, she will secretly encourage Mexico to take hostile measures."[6] As in the northeastern boundary crisis of 1841–42, slaveholders worried that an Anglo-American conflict would endanger the vital but vulnerable Caribbean basin. Duff Green conjured the old, frightful image of a British-Mexican-Indian-slave alliance. Francis Pickens explained why Britain's stubborn diplomacy in Oregon was a mere "pretext":

> Her real objects will be the region of the Gulph of Mexico, Cuba, Texas & Florida. I have long thought that the two countries must have another appeal to arms sooner or later. Our systems are at issue and the contest will be for the mastery of the world. One or the other must go down or yield. Our policy is to postpone the final appeal as long as possible, as we are growing in strength & she is stationary.[7]

The South's Oregon doves thus maintained the conventional strategic wisdom among slaveholding elites after 1833: full-scale war with Great Britain was simply not worth the risk. An armed conflict, after all, would mean

subjecting the plantation South to an existential threat. A larger clash between the free and slave labor systems of Britain and the United States
might be inevitable, and America should prepare itself accordingly. But war
in the present tense should be avoided. With the exception of a few aggressive southwestern Democrats, this was the bipartisan southern consensus
in the Twenty-Ninth Congress.[8]

Crucially, the Polk administration agreed. The literal-minded president's statement that he sought a "pacific" course on Oregon was not, in
fact, a greedy geographic pun. Although Polk, like many of his southern
colleagues in 1845, believed that King Cotton would stay Britain's hand in a
showdown with the United States, he too worked to prevent hostilities.[9] In
the summer of 1845, a year bookended by his truculent national speeches
on Oregon, the president offered to settle the boundary dispute at the 49th
parallel, the same compromise solution Tyler had proposed. Secretary of
State James Buchanan's letter to the U.S. minister in London noted the president's doubts about "whether the judgment of the civilized world would be
in our favor in a war waged for the comparatively worthless territory north
of 49°."[10]

Although the administration's negotiating line hardened again that autumn, perhaps reflecting Polk's political obligations to Oregon-hungry
northwestern Democrats, there is no indication that the president seriously
envisioned an armed conflict over the northwestern boundary.[11] On the
contrary, the mere hint of British hostility drove Polk toward rapid compromise. The "extensive warlike preparations" under way in London, wrote U.S.
minister Louis McLane, showed that if a conflict over Oregon did break out,
Britain would be "fully and effectually prepared for it at all points." Receiving
this information in February 1846, the administration reported it to Congress, deliberated for a short period, and then proposed, once again, a compromise settlement at the 49th parallel.[12] To squeeze the best terms out of
Great Britain and to keep the peace in his own party, Polk could afford to engage in tactical bombast and cagey negotiations. He could not afford to fight
a war that would threaten the prosperity of the Union and the security of the
slaveholding South. In this regard there was far more continuity among Tyler,
Polk, and Calhoun than any of them was willing to recognize.[13]

Nowhere was the transition more fluid than in American policy toward
Texas. In Tyler's last act as president, he directed the U.S. envoy to Texas,
Andrew Jackson Donelson, to present an immediate offer of annexation to
the Texas government. Assuming office just hours later, Polk had plenty of

time to countermand these orders if he wished to proceed with the more cautious terms of the Senate's Texas resolution. But six days after Polk's inauguration, Secretary of State Buchanan wrote Donelson woodenly that the president believed "it would be inexpedient to reverse the decision of his predecessor."[14] Polk also dispatched two veteran southern politicians to assist Donelson in Texas. Archibald Yell of Arkansas and Charles Wickliffe of Kentucky—Tyler's postmaster general—arrived in the Texas capital in the spring of 1845, bringing with them $1,000 in secret-service money and instructions to do whatever was necessary to cajole the Texas government into accepting the terms of annexation.[15]

Donelson, Yell, and Wickliffe had their work cut out for them. Although most Texans were recent American immigrants who favored annexation, the republic's leadership still nurtured visions of independence. Just before Polk's agents arrived, Texas president Anson Jones had agreed to postpone annexation for ninety days to give British chargé d'affaires Charles Elliot time to arrange a peace treaty between Texas and Mexico—an agreement that could, at least in theory, remove the most urgent argument in favor of U.S. annexation. The Americans sprang into action, drawing from the deep well of their experience in domestic political deal-making. Donelson negotiated with President Jones, while Wickliffe and Yell barnstormed across the country, scattering their funds and making lavish promises about the federal dollars that would pour into Texas after annexation. In July a special Texas convention agreed to accept the terms of the U.S. offer and began work on an American state constitution.[16]

Back in Washington Polk and his cabinet now confronted the real danger of war with Mexico. The Mexican government still regarded Texas as a lost province of its own and had warned U.S. officials repeatedly in 1844 that annexation would mean a formal break in relations. When the Mexican minister left Washington in March 1845, Polk responded with military rather than diplomatic maneuvers. In April Secretary of the Navy George Bancroft ordered Commodore Robert F. Stockton to report with the *Princeton* and several smaller vessels to Commodore David Conner's Home Squadron. The steam-powered sloop whose armaments had killed Abel Upshur would join the already swollen American naval presence off the coast of Mexico. A total of ten ships and nearly 175 guns now gathered in the waters between Galveston and Veracruz. As Polk boasted privately to a Tennessee friend, "Conner commands the largest and most formidable squadron in the Gulf, that we have ever had together since we have been a Nation."[17]

In its disposition of ground troops the administration was equally assertive. Although both Texas and Mexico claimed possession of the land between the Nueces River and the Rio Grande, Polk ordered his agents to regard any Mexican movement into the disputed territory as an act of war against Texas. The United States annexed not only the Lone Star Republic but also its maximal border claims to the Southwest. Wickliffe and Stockton arranged an exhibition of American naval forces near the Rio Grande, purposely designed to prevent a rumored Mexican "incursion" into the disputed area.[18] Meanwhile, the administration ordered General Zachary Taylor and his U.S. army troops, then stationed at Fort Jesup on the Texas-Louisiana border, to prepare to move into Texas. When the Texas government formally agreed to annexation, Taylor's "army of occupation" moved at once to Corpus Christi at the mouth of the Nueces. Polk pledged to Donelson that he would "maintain the Texan title to the extent she claims it to be & not permit an invading army to occupy a foot of the soil East of the Rio Grande."[19]

Clearly, the administration had committed itself to an aggressive course in Texas. In his first six months in office Polk accelerated Tyler's effort to accomplish annexation by joint resolution, authorized federal dollars for a secret propaganda campaign inside the borders of a sovereign nation, assembled the largest fleet in national history in foreign waters, and ordered American troops to prepare for a march into fiercely disputed territory.[20] On the rare occasions when the president expressed doubt about the legality of this program, he found key southern allies ready to defend it. In a summer meeting with Senator Arthur Bagby of Alabama, Polk wondered about the "necessity or propriety of calling Congress, in the event of a Declaration of War or an invasion of Texas by Mexico." With Congress out of session until December, a war might begin months before the legislative branch could react. The senator dismissed these concerns: "Mr. Bagby gave it as his clear opinion that Congress should not be called," Polk wrote in his diary, and declared his "zealous" support for administration policy on the Texas-Mexico border.[21]

Although Polk's agents usually avoided the explicit proslavery rhetoric that filled the correspondence of Tyler's State Department, the administration understood that securing Texas for the Union meant securing slave property throughout the Gulf basin. As Buchanan wrote Wickliffe in March, Texans should be reminded that once they joined the United States, "their peculiar institutions" would be "protected against the attacks of English and French fanatics." The British chargé in Texas, for his part, was grimly specific about annexation's effect on the security of slavery. "Men, Women, and Children," he wrote in July 1845, "have risen in value at least 30 per Cent since this scheme was proposed by Mr. Tyler." Annexation was "no doubt an immense triumph to the great Slave Trade interests of this Country."[22]

The vote of the Texas special convention appeared to settle the annexation question for good. But U.S.-Mexico relations remained in a parlous state: official representatives in both Washington and Mexico City had left their missions in a huff, depriving the two nations of any direct means of communication. In September the new Mexican president, José Joaquín Herrera, indicated that he might be willing to reopen relations, but only if the United States sent a special "commissioner" to Mexico rather than a general envoy. Characteristically, Polk refused to respect such niceties of form: he appointed John Slidell of Louisiana to travel to Mexico City as the official replacement for the absent American minister. Herrera and his government now faced a stark choice. Mexico could either accept Slidell's credentials, thus meekly swallowing two years' of protests about Texas annexation—or it could reject them, and risk providing the United States with a pretext for war.[23]

While Mexico pondered its options, Polk supplemented his pushy diplomacy with bellicose rhetoric and unrelenting military pressure. In the same December 1845 message in which he blasted British intransigence over Oregon, the president issued a lengthy list of grievances against Mexico. But the difference between the two concurrent crises was dramatic. The U.S. Army and Navy were not gathering with unparalleled force on the borders of British Columbia. Nor had the American government delivered "arms and munitions of war ... sufficient for ten thousand men" to the northwestern theater while urging the commanding officer to occupy the full extent of the disputed territory. Yet this was exactly what the administration was doing in Texas.[24] After a series of impatient orders from Washington, General Taylor left Corpus Christi and encamped on the eastern bank of the Rio Grande. In March 1846 the president informed Congress that he had stationed no less than "two-thirds of our Army on our southwestern frontier."[25]

If Polk wanted Slidell's mission to succeed, he had given the Mexicans very little room to operate. In any event, a military coup led by General Mariano Paredes y Arrillaga toppled the Herrera regime in Mexico City, and the new government abandoned negotiations with the United States.[26] The news made an immediate impact in Washington. "[W]e must take redress for the injuries done us into our own hands," Polk told his cabinet in April, and he began to prepare a war message for Congress. Later in the week the president decided to delay the message, but the direction of his policy had shifted: it moved, in a word, from intimidation to provocation. The administration would wait until Mexican troops attacked Taylor on the Rio Grande. Then it would quickly declare war and invade Mexico. "[I]t was only a matter of time," Polk told Slidell, before the fighting began.[27]

In fact, Polk's plan had already worked perfectly. On April 25 the tense situation on the Rio Grande erupted into conflict: Mexican troops surrounded a detachment of Taylor's men, killing eleven and capturing dozens more. When news of this battle reached Washington, on May 9, Polk summoned his cabinet to a special Saturday-night meeting. On Monday the president issued a formal message to Congress, declaring that Mexico has "at last invaded our territory and shed the blood of our fellow-citizens on our own soil. . . . [W]ar exists, and . . . exists by the act of Mexico herself." Polk called for Congress to "place at the discretion of the Executive the means of prosecuting the war with vigor." Only "the immediate appearance in arms of a large and overpowering force," the president declared, could bring "the existing collision with Mexico to a speedy and successful termination."[28]

Why did Polk, who worked hard for a peaceful solution in Oregon, eagerly embrace war on the Texas border? For Thomas Hart Benton, along with many later commentators, the answer was simple: "[B]ecause Great Britain is powerful and Mexico weak." Surely, too, the administration's hope to acquire much of northern Mexico, including valuable Pacific ports in California, whetted its appetite for conflict.[29] But other observers saw something both more sectional and sinister at work. British chargé Elliot, writing in the summer of 1845, predicted that any war started on the Rio Grande would be "undertaken mainly for the purpose of prolonging and extending the System of Slavery." Joshua Giddings, who had succeeded John Quincy Adams as the loudest antislavery voice in Congress, declared that Polk's war message portended "a bloody war for the purposes of conquest and the extension of slavery." Because Texas slaves were escaping bondage by crossing into Mexico, Giddings alleged, Polk and his southern allies sought to "extend our dominions into Mexico in order to render slavery secure in Texas."[30]

The truth was more complicated. Unlike Tyler's push for Texas, Polk's war with Mexico did not spring directly from proslavery politics. Many of its chief architects—including Secretary of State Buchanan (Pennsylvania),

Secretary of War William Marcy (New York) and Secretary of the Navy Bancroft (Massachusetts)—hailed from free states and seldom expressed enthusiasm or concern over slavery. Certainly, compared with Calhoun, Upshur, Green, and the rest of Tyler's Texas clique, they remained quiet about the war's relationship to the domestic and international struggle between free and slave labor. Even Polk gave little indication that he considered the war a proslavery crusade. When Congress began to debate the role of slavery in territory seized from Mexico, the president professed ignorance: "What connection slavery had with making peace with Mexico it is difficult to conceive," he wrote in his diary. Slavery, Polk told Calhoun in December, "would probably never exist" in New Mexico or California. If the Mexican-American War was an executive conspiracy to extend bondage or add new slave states, the conspirator in chief was asleep at the wheel.[31]

But if the struggle with Mexico was not precisely a war for slavery, it was nevertheless a war sanctioned by and acceptable to slaveholders. The presence of Taylor's army on the Rio Grande, as Giddings suggested, did in fact help secure slavery's southernmost frontier.[32] The congregation of American ships in the Gulf strengthened the naval defenses of the southern coast, still a serious concern for slaveholders in 1846.[33] And unlike a war with Great Britain, a clash with Mexico was not likely to expose the South to antislavery invasion. The prospect of a Mexican-American naval struggle, if anything, struck coastal southerners as an opportunity rather than a danger. The U.S. Navy should "invest the entire west coast of Mexico" and plan to seize Veracruz, urged one ardent New Orleans editor. The chance to extend American strategic dominance across the Gulf basin must not be lost.[34]

Some leading southerners, including Calhoun, received Polk's war message with suspicion. In the Senate Calhoun joined a Whig effort to deny that the recent skirmish on the Rio Grande really constituted a full-scale war between Mexico and the United States. When this was blocked by the Democratic majority, he abstained from the Senate vote on the final resolution (which passed by a vote of 40–2) and complained that Polk had maneuvered the nation into a war without Congress's consent.[35] In private, however, Calhoun admitted that he was more worried about Great Britain's response than about the war with Mexico itself. "As a Mexican question," he wrote his son-in-law, "it is to be deplored without looking beyond; but I regard that far less so, than its effects on our European relations. I fear, that it may . . . introduce the interference of both England & France before it is concluded."[36]

In June, after the Oregon dispute was settled and news of Zachary Taylor's early triumphs on the Rio Grande reached Washington, Calhoun's position evolved: "The war has opened with brilliant victories on our side & I trust, may soon be brought to a close. I give it a quiet, but decided support, as much as I regret the occurrence." In the summer of 1846 even the most entrenched southern skeptics went no further than this in their criticism of the war.[37]

The majority of slaveholding elites stood behind the president. This support remained firm even as the Polk administration mobilized the full, clanking force of the federal machine, first to intimidate and then to invade America's southern neighbor.[38] Just before the war broke out, Mexico's foreign minister noted the concentrated weight of U.S. military power on his frontiers, unilaterally directed there the single commander in chief. "[A] powerful & well consolidated State," he observed, was "availing itself of the internal dissensions of a neighbouring nation."[39] In the war that followed, Polk no less than Tyler understood himself to be governing not a loose federation but a "well consolidated State." Throughout the period from 1846 to 1848 this expansive view of executive power in foreign affairs—sustained, crucially, by a dominant group of southerners—continued to define the American war with Mexico.

To Change the Character of the War

The Mexican-American War was an event unprecedented in the history of the United States. It involved the mass deployment of tens of thousands of American soldiers and sailors, the seizure of millions of square miles of enemy territory, and ultimately the capture and occupation of a foreign capital half a continent away from Washington. From a strategic perspective, Polk's war plan anticipated the Union mission in the Civil War: the penetration and subjugation of a large, hostile state. But unlike the Civil War or any other American conflict until the close of the nineteenth century, the decisive actions in the war with Mexico required naval coordination in both the Atlantic and Pacific Oceans, the amphibious landing of American troops on foreign shores, and the subjugation of densely populated foreign territory in which the U.S. Army had few if any native allies.[40] The war furthermore witnessed several extremely determined efforts on the part of the Polk administration to sponsor a coup d'état that would replace the Mexican government with a regime willing to make a favorable peace with the

United States. In these respects and others the conquest of Mexico bears more resemblance to the overseas American military entanglements of the twentieth century than it does to the American Revolution, the War of 1812, or the major Indian conflicts of the antebellum period.[41]

To be sure, it is easy to overstate the magnitude of the war. Although Polk called for up to fifty thousand volunteers, far fewer saw action at any one time. As war veteran Ulysses S. Grant recalled in his memoirs, the "little army of ten or twelve thousand men" with which the United States conquered Mexico paled in comparison to the titanic troop organizations of the Civil War. And in defiance of John Quincy Adams's prediction that southwestern expansion would produce "a military government," by 1848 U.S. armed forces had shrunk to prewar levels.[42] Yet both in principle and in practice many Americans were right to believe that the war with Mexico represented something wholly new for the United States. "The war with Mexico exhibited us in a new aspect," crowed one postwar commentator in the *Southern Quarterly Review*. "It is one thing for a people to show themselves equal to the defense of their homes and firesides; but the greatest test of the powers and resources of a nation will be found to consist in its capacity for foreign warfare."[43]

After the invasion of Mexico, there could be little doubt about the capacity of the United States for imperial conquest. The war was "one of the most unjust ever waged by a stronger against a weaker nation," Grant later wrote. "It was an instance of a republic following the bad example of European monarchies." Many contemporaries, both pro- and antiwar, described the conflict in similar comparative terms. As Ralph Waldo Emerson observed in 1846, "France, England, and America" were all at peace with each other, but that fact had not prevented "poor Algerines, Sikhs, Seminoles, or Mexicans" from being "devoured by these peace-loving States at the same moment."[44] On the other end of the spectrum, Thomas Clemson, Calhoun's son-in-law and the U.S. chargé to Belgium, thought that General Taylor's early success in battle "contrasts well with the doings of the French in Algiers & the English in the Punjaub." Months later Calhoun found the analogy a troubling one: the conflict in Mexico, he feared, was "like to turn out as the war in Algeria has—a war between races & creed, which can only end in the complete subjection of the weaker power—a thing not easily effected in either case."[45]

Part of what drove these far-ranging imperial comparisons, as Calhoun's observations implied, was a general sense that Algerians, Punjabis, and

Mexicans were all racially inferior to their Euro-American conquerors.[46]
The reality of Comanche Indian power over much of northern Mexico encouraged Polk and others to imagine the U.S. invasion as a kind of colonial
civilizing mission—an effort to reclaim the broad plains of Nuevo Mexico
and Alta California from "the occupation of the savage," as Virginia senator
Robert M. T. Hunter put it.[47]

The enormous geographic ambition of the American war plan made
the imperial parallels even more apt. Rather than fighting a limited conflict
over the disputed Nueces strip in Texas, Polk at once organized a war of conquest and expropriation. The day after Congress accepted the president's
war message, the secretary of war directed Colonel Stephen W. Kearney to
march eight hundred miles from Kansas southwest to Santa Fe, which he
was ordered to seize and hold. In the Pacific, Commodore John Sloat and
his squadron had been dispatched months earlier to capture Mexican ports
in California in the event of war; by July, U.S. forces occupied Sonoma, San
Francisco, and Monterey. Just three months after the first skirmish on the
Rio Grande, Polk had effectively seized an entire third of Mexico.[48]

While American troops secured California and the continental interior,
the president hatched a secret attempt to overthrow the Mexican government. Before the war began, Polk had listened with interest to a proposal
made by Colonel A. J. Atocha, a naturalized Spanish American who arrived
in Washington with a message from deposed Mexican president Santa
Anna. The hero and villain of the Texas Revolution was now living in exile
in Havana and, as one historian put it, "intriguing on a scale not to be matched
again, even in Mexico, before the arrival there of Leon Trotsky."[49] In two
February meetings with Polk, Atocha proposed that the president secretly
deposit Santa Anna in Mexico with sufficient funds to seize control of the
government, negotiate a favorable treaty with the United States, and suppress any potential revolts that might follow. "[W]ith half a million in hand,"
Atocha believed, Santa Anna "could make the Treaty and sustain themselves
for a few months, and until the balance was paid."[50] The entire clandestine
project bore more than a passing resemblance to an American-sponsored
coup d'état. Among conceivable Russian revolutionary analogies, a better
parallel might be imperial Germany's decision in April 1917 to send Lenin to
Petrograd in a sealed train. Polk, like Kaiser Wilhelm, provided money and
transport for a charismatic exile to return to his native country and surrender
land for peace.

When the war broke out, Polk's administration began to put the plan in motion. In July 1846 navy commander Alexander Slidell Mackenzie met the exiled leader in Cuba and worked out an agreement to grant him transit to Mexico and ready money in return for Santa Anna's support for peace and territorial concessions. It all went off without a hitch: in August Mexican army officers friendly to Santa Anna removed General Paredes from power; less than a week later the ex-president and his entourage boarded a British mail steamer and sailed unmolested through the American blockade. Arriving in Veracruz, they were in command of the Mexican capital by the middle of September.[51]

The regime change unfolded just as Polk might have hoped, but its aftermath ran less smoothly. Santa Anna reneged on his peace promises and rallied Mexican forces for an even more determined struggle against the United States. Yet Polk's deep involvement in this covert scheme reflected a general truth about the character of his administration. "Never," avowed Thomas Hart Benton years later, "were men at the head of a government less imbued with military spirit, or more addicted to intrigue." But even that formula, which still guides many historical portraits of the Polk administration, remains incomplete.[52] Polk's addiction to covert action went beyond personal temperament and reflected the president's consistently broad understanding of executive power in foreign affairs. None of the correspondence (never mind oral instructions) behind the Santa Anna plot was ever vetted or observed by Congress; the funds for the scheme came from a block appropriation Polk sought for unspecified expenses relating to peace negotiations. An overseas coup, like an overseas conquest of foreign territory, was, for this president, simply not a matter in which Congress had a relevant role to play.

Polk's use of undercover agents also mirrored the policy and the philosophy of his predecessor. Tyler had relied on secret-service monies to pay Duff Green for two trips to Europe; Secretary of State Webster had drawn on executive funds to help propagandize for the Webster-Ashburton Treaty along the Maine border. In April 1846, when the House opened an investigation of Webster's conduct, Polk sprang to the defense of the Tyler administration: "[O]ur foreign relations," he argued in a message to Congress, "are wisely and properly confined to the knowledge of the Executive during their pendency.... [T]he experience of every nation on earth has demonstrated that emergencies may arise in which it becomes absolutely necessary for the public safety or the public good to make expenditures the very object of which would be defeated by publicity."[53]

This expansive interpretation of executive power marked a new development in presidential history. Commanders in chief since George Washington had made use of secret agents and had drawn on secret funds, but no president had explicitly defended, on principle, the idea of absolute executive secrecy in foreign policy. (Polk's comments have helped make him the only nineteenth-century American president quoted on the contemporary CIA's website.) In the president's view, his covert plotting to overthrow the Mexican government required justification only by reference to "the public safety," as defined by Polk himself. No recourse to constitutional interpretation was necessary.[54]

For most of the summer of 1846, while hopes for a Santa Anna–brokered peace remained intact, Polk concentrated his military energy on the vast and distant territories he hoped to take from Mexico. But when it became clear that the new Mexican government would not negotiate, the president altered his course. "[M]y strong impression," he told Marcy and Bancroft in September, "was that the character of the war we were waging in Mexico should be in some respects changed." To begin with, the United States would no longer "pay liberally for the supplies drawn from the country." Instead, he recommended that invading American armies live off the land. The war already entailed expropriation of Mexican territory; why should it not involve expropriation of Mexican property as well? In northern Mexico the Americans' confiscation of weapons and supplies and their occasional atrocities against Mexican citizens earned them the nickname "Comanches of the North."[55]

More dramatically, Polk approved plans for a large-scale invasion of the Mexican heartland. The ambitious scheme called for General Winfield Scott to land an army at Veracruz on the Gulf, march some 250 miles over the Sierra Madre, and end the war with the triumphant seizure of Mexico City. "Nothing like the Mexico City campaign exists in American military history for sheer audacity of concept," one historian has written, "except for Mac-Arthur's Inchon-Seoul campaign of 1950." For the first six months of fighting, Polk had hoped to end the war by consolidating American territorial gains as simply as possible. But since Mexico refused to cooperate, Polk believed, it fell to the U.S. Army to conquer a peace, even if it required a strategic gusto and imperial prerogative that would not be matched for another hundred years.[56]

In Congress the administration fought doggedly for the funds it needed to expand the war effort. Marcy requested money to add ten new regiments to the army, or nearly ten thousand new regular troops; after extended debate in both the House and the Senate, the new forces were authorized in February 1847. That same month Foreign Relations Committee chairman Ambrose Sevier of Arkansas proposed a $3 million appropriation to help the president "bring the existing war with Mexico to a speedy and honorable conclusion."[57] The previous year a similarly vague request for $2 million had run aground when David Wilmot unveiled his famous amendment to bar slavery from any land seized from Mexico. (The Wilmot Proviso, in its first incarnation, did not prevent the spread of slavery in the territories, but it did briefly scramble Polk's plans to fund a puppet government in Mexico City.)[58] In March, however, administration allies in Congress managed to pass the $3 million bill without any slavery-related amendments attached. That same month Scott's army took Veracruz and began the march on Mexico City. Polk had successfully changed the "character of the war."[59]

Winfield Scott's landing at Veracruz, shown in this 1847 *Currier & Ives* print, was the first major amphibious assault in U.S. military history.

Consensus within Conflict

Polk's legislative triumph in early 1847 came at a price: John C. Calhoun and his small band of supporters in Congress, long skeptical about the president's policy in Mexico, appeared to turn against the administration. On February 8 Calhoun held up the ten-regiment bill in the Senate, voting with Whigs to deny the president the power to appoint inferior officers directly. A frequently cited passage in Polk's diary that evening recorded the president's frustration: "I now regard Mr. Calhoun to be . . . the most mischievous man in the Senate."[60] The next day Calhoun spoke against the $3 million bill and unveiled his own strategic plan for the war: rather than invade the Mexican heartland, he proposed that U.S. troops adopt "a defensive position" along "the line we now occupy," from the Rio Grande to California. This "defensive-line" policy, as it came to be known, reflected Calhoun's doubts about an offensive thrust into the "hot regions" of Mexico and also his fears about a northern effort to exclude slavery from even more newly gained territories.[61]

These acts, along with his private murmurings about the "folly & wantoness" of U.S. policy toward Mexico, helped convince both contemporaries and historians that Calhoun had deserted both Polk and the war.[62] But how meaningful was Calhoun's turn against the administration? The delay of the ten-regiment bill may have infuriated the president, but it hardly affected his larger plan to expand the war. In early 1847, Calhoun's faction in Congress passed up a ready-made opportunity to reject the enlargement of the army on states'-rights grounds.

Polk's request for ten thousand new troops sparked opposition not only from antiwar Whigs but also from some northern Democrats, who objected to a general increase of the "standing army." For Hannibal Hamlin of Maine, Polk's bill encouraged a dangerous "tendency to centralization." The "glorious doctrine of State rights," he suggested, would be better served if each state organized its own "independent corps" of volunteers. But despite their doubts about the war, hostility toward Polk, and customary devotion to states' rights, Calhoun and his friends refused to make a stand on the principle of centralization. Andrew Butler, Calhoun's South Carolina colleague in the Senate, even stressed the flexibility of executive authority in military affairs: "The President was the commander-in-chief of the army of the United States, and had the right to make the appointments." Just two days after he had supposedly withdrawn his support from the war effort,

Calhoun voted for a revised bill that still provided appropriations for ten thousand new federal troops. Whatever his distaste for a war of conquest, Calhoun did his part to fund the armies that marched on Mexico City.[63]

Calhoun also resisted the $3 million bill with words rather than deeds. Despite his intermittent worries about the "enormous expense of the government, from its increased military & naval establishments," the South Carolinian did not fight to reduce Polk's unspecified war appropriations. In December 1846, during a "frank & pleasant" conversation with the president, he promised to he would support a budget of $4 million, or even more, to fund negotiations with Mexico. When southern legislators successfully weeded David Wilmot's antislavery language out of the $3 million bill, Calhoun, Butler and their Senate allies voted to give the administration its money.[64]

Historians are fond of quoting Calhoun's biblical admonition about the land Polk and his armies sought to take from America's southern neighbor: "Mexico is to us the forbidden fruit; the penalty of eating it would be to subject our institutions to political death."[65] In the decades to come, the analogy proved prophetic, but in 1847 it hardly reflected Calhoun's actual position on the seizure of Mexican territory. For the South Carolinian, only the apple of central Mexico was truly forbidden; the rest of the Edenic produce of Texas, New Mexico, and California could be consumed without worry. Months before the war began, Calhoun and Polk had agreed privately that the ideal U.S.-Mexico boundary would run along the 32nd parallel of latitude. Later, in another closeted meeting with the president, Calhoun agreed that in any treaty with Mexico, Polk should seek to obtain "the Provinces of New Mexico, Upper and Lower California." The fundamental premise of the defensive-line policy, after all, was that the United States must dig in and hold its conquests of the greater Southwest.[66]

For all his private broodings and public mischief, Calhoun proved an indispensable ally in Polk's war effort. On all the major war measures that passed through Congress, Calhoun expressed a degree of dissent but went forward and supported the administration anyway. Although he and his southern faction held a potential swing vote in war arguments between Senate Democrats and their Whig opponents, Calhoun did not use this power to bargain for material changes to Polk's war policy.[67] The defensive-line policy was articulated with great energy and then simply hung out to dry. Satisfied with the irrelevant grandeur of his oratory, Calhoun congratulated himself on his independence: "By having done my duty fully in reference to the Mexican war," he wrote his son-in-law, "as it relates both to its origin & the mode it ought to have been conducted, I stand free of all responsibility." This was lofty self-delusion. In his votes on the origin and especially the mode of the conflict, Calhoun had helped make the war against Mexico possible.[68]

Polk, for his part, seemed perfectly able to distinguish between the "mischievous" South Carolinian and his real enemies: for all his private complaints, the president continued to consult regularly with Calhoun for the duration of the war. In the legislative struggle against the Wilmot Proviso and against northern antislavery in general, the two slaveholders remained firm friends.[69] Finally, in the long debate about a peace treaty with Mexico, Polk and Calhoun worked to achieve the same tangible goal. In April 1847, after American forces captured Veracruz, the president dispatched State Department clerk Nicholas Trist to accompany the invading U.S. army. Trist was authorized to offer Mexico up to $30 million in exchange for a boundary at or near the 32nd parallel—the same line Polk and Calhoun had agreed on before the war began. When the Mexican government still refused to negotiate on Polk's terms, even after the fall of Mexico City, the president grew more aggressive. That autumn he recalled Trist, instructed Scott to renew his offensive against Mexican resistance, and announced his intention to "fight with increased energy and power in the vital parts of the enemy's country."[70]

With the prospects for peace as dim as ever, a vocal movement for the acquisition of all of Mexico gathered force, especially among northwestern Democrats. "To attempt to prevent the American people from taking possession of Mexico," declared Michigan's Lewis Cass, "would be as futile in effect as to undertake to stop the rushing of the cataract of Niagara." Calhoun and his Senate allies, however, stood against the waterfall. Virginia's Robert M. T. Hunter declared that a close "association with the Mexican people" was a thing "to be dreaded, both in view of its influence on southern institutions, and on account of the impracticability of amalgamating races so distant and irreconcilable." The absorption of Mexico would add millions of square miles of new territory unfit for slavery and millions of new citizens unfit for participation in a white man's republic.[71]

While this debate raged in Washington, Trist disobeyed his orders and remained at work on a peace agreement in Mexico City. In late January he and his Mexican negotiating partners agreed on a treaty that gave Polk all he had sought for the vast majority of the war: Upper California and New

Mexico, with a boundary running from the 32nd parallel to the Rio Grande.[72] Trist's treaty arrived in Washington in February 1848 and sent the politics of the Mexican cession into a confused frenzy. Between Democratic ultraexpansionists and Whig who rejected any major land seizure, it was unclear who would support and who would oppose the compromise agreement. But in the end the balance of forces that favored compromise on peace and territory proved greater than the forces that were willing to tolerate further conflict. On March 10 the Senate officially ratified Trist's agreement.[73]

David Potter's verdict reflects the entrenched historical assessment of the Treaty of Guadalupe Hidalgo: "Thus, by the acts of a dismissed emissary, a disappointed president, and a divided Senate, the United States acquired California and the Southwest."[74] Potter's characterizations are all accurate in a limited sense, but the bitterly ironic flavor of his formulation can be misleading. Trist's treaty allowed the administration and its southern allies to escape the danger of all-Mexico expansion without sacrificing the conquest of western North America. In truth, Polk and Calhoun, despite their personal rivalry, managed to find a kind of modus vivendi in international affairs—a zone of partial but considerable agreement that effectively controlled U.S. foreign policy from 1845 to 1848.

Independently, the two men construed their foreign policy goals and principles in very different ways: Polk emphasized national expansion, assertive diplomacy, and the vigorous prosecution of war, while Calhoun stressed the security of slavery, international commerce, and the avoidance of dangerous conflict. In practice, however, their visions proved much easier to reconcile. The United States successfully defended Texas, escaped a confrontation with Great Britain, made aggressive war on Mexico, and tailored its continental expansion to gain the maximum territory with the minimum threat to slave labor. Polk's swagger did not lead to a military conflict over Oregon; Calhoun's uneasiness about international conflict did not cause him to undermine the war with Mexico. To put it another way, although Polk and Calhoun did not agree about every aspect of foreign affairs, the administration never achieved a result that cut directly against the essentials of Calhoun's position. The same cannot be said about Polk and any of the northern Democrats within his governing coalition.[75]

A kind of southern median—fragments of an international worldview shared by Polk, Calhoun, and the spectrum of southern Democrats between them—governed U.S. actions during the war with Mexico. If this was not an explicit foreign policy of slavery, it was nevertheless a foreign policy that accommodated slaveholders' needs and responded to slaveholders' desires. When the dust settled on the war, many southern elites still doubted whether their domestic institutions could be exported to the arid Southwest. But there was good reason to believe that the acquisition of new territory made bound labor safer where it already existed. "As far as the interests of the slaveholder are concerned," a Texas newspaper observed in 1848, "when the adjacent territory, even though slavery is not established in it, is owned by the United States . . . he has the right, under the constitution and laws, to reclaim persons held to service." The national character of slavery protected American slaveholders even if the newly acquired territories ultimately outlawed the institution. After 1848, the enhanced U.S. military presence in the southwest meant that even fugitive slaves who had escaped to Mexico faced a greater danger of reenslavement. In this sense Polk's war contributed significantly to both the physical and psychological security of anxious borderland slaveholders.[76]

The foreign policy of Polk and Calhoun, above all, embraced the full power of the federal government to advance its international goals. In Congress Calhoun made occasional efforts to distinguish between the militarized southwestern diplomacy of Polk, which he ostensibly opposed, and the militarized southwestern diplomacy of Tyler, which he himself had crafted. His colleagues, including newly seated Mississippi senator Jefferson Davis, were not convinced. Calhoun, Davis noted, "says that the President has not the right to move the army into any disputed territory. . . . But I would ask the Senator, how comes it, that even before the annexation of Texas, the navy of the United States was ordered to the Gulf of Mexico for the protection of Texas?"[77] In the end, such flimsy distinctions collapsed, and Calhoun threw his reluctant but decided support to Polk's audacious war of invasion and conquest. He and the dominant majority of slaveholders did this, neglecting its consequences for the theory and practice of states' rights, in large part because they believed that an American victory in the war would strengthen the United States on the global stage.

For many historians, the war against Mexico sounded the death knell of the early American republic. The invasion and its aftermath have become synonymous with the onset of sectional discord, endless argument about slavery, the collapse of the Jacksonian political system, and finally the outbreak of civil war.[78] It is often the dark omens of the late 1840s that claim pride of place in historical treatments of the war: Calhoun's analogy of Mexico as "forbidden fruit" or Emerson's prediction that "the United States will conquer Mexico, but it will be as the man swallows the arsenic, which brings him down in turn. Mexico will poison us."[79] But between Calhoun at his most morose and Emerson at his most oracular lay a wide expanse of political opinion. For most slaveholding elites, especially, the war was not a gloomy portent but an extraordinary and historic triumph.

On the shores of Bayou Boeuf, Louisiana, the kidnapped African American Solomon Northup remembered that "news of victory" in Mexico produced "only sorrow and disappointment" in his slave cabin, but "filled the great house with rejoicing."[80] Word of American triumphs in Mexico electrified slaveholders far beyond the bayou. Southern envoys in Europe were especially gratified. "I am glad to see that peace is to be conquered by vigorous war," wrote William R. King from Paris. "The blows already inflicted have been felt abroad as well as in Mexico. . . . They have *commanded* respect." From The Hague the Louisianan Auguste Davezac explained that Europeans had long doubted the American capacity to convert "a defensive, into an offensive war." But the "glorious victories obtained by our armies,—the conquests of New-Mexico and California, achieved with such wonderous vigor in execution . . . have refuted that prevision."[81]

The acquisition of a continental empire, as Polk boasted in his 1848 annual message, meant that "the United States are now estimated to be nearly as large as the whole of Europe." Control of Oregon and California put the United States in position to dominate "the rich commerce of China, of Asia, of the islands of the Pacific, of western Mexico, of Central America, the South American States, and the Russian possessions bordering on that ocean." While Europe erupted in revolution in 1848, the economic and strategic position of the United States appeared stronger than ever. "The old thrones of Europe," boasted Louisiana editor James D. B. De Bow, "are being shaken down by the young Hercules of America."[82]

Southern slaveholders stood behind this project of enhancing the power of the United States in world politics. To be sure, a handful of conservative Whigs warned that the war and the new territory it brought would endanger slaveholding interests. But for the Polk administration and its southern allies, American power and American slavery were symbiotically linked. "Our foreign policy," complained the South Carolina novelist and sometime politician William Gilmore Simms in the spring of 1847, "has always been feeble & purposeless." When Scott's army marched into Mexico City, Simms exulted, noting that "our Mexican conquests" would secure "the perpetuation of slavery for the next thousand years."[83] In Mexico, declared ex-President John Tyler in 1850, the United States "have exhibited a prowess which has excited the wonder and admiration of the world." Tyler was writing two years after the conclusion of the war, amid a bitter congressional battle over slavery in the new western territories. Still he considered U.S. victories on the "battlefields of Mexico" a milestone in America's global progress: they confirmed that "all other governments and all other people" were destined to be "but mere dependencies of this mighty Republic." ... [84]

Inside the cramped teleology imposed by the Civil War, it is difficult to find room for Tyler's expansive imperial vision. Even so, it was just as fully a product and legacy of the Mexican-American war as Emerson's dire omen. The war transformed the basic strategic calculus in the Western Hemisphere. It established, in terms humiliating to Mexico and unmistakable to Europe, the cold fact of U.S. dominance over all of North America. It converted the United States, in the words of the *Southern Literary Messenger*, from "a merely continental confederacy" to a "vast empire" with vital interests in both the world's great oceans.[85] And it demonstrated the enormous investment southern slaveholding elites held in the progress of American world power. In the turbulent decade that followed, even as the sectional struggle cast heavy shadows over domestic affairs, southerners like John Tyler continued to place their faith—and often, at times, their near-delirious confidence—in the golden future of American empire.

6

King Cotton, Emperor Slavery

NEVER HAD AMERICAN SLAVEHOLDERS BEEN MORE CONFIDENT in their grasp on international power than in the 1850s. The successful conquest of Mexico, organized and commanded disproportionately by southerners, expanded the limits of America's imperial horizon. In Europe, the breakdown of the Congress of Vienna system after the revolutions of 1848 enhanced slaveholders' belief in the superior fortitude of their own social and political systems. Spiking global demand for cotton, meanwhile, left them flush with wealth and ecstatic about the dependence of the entire industrial world on a commodity that only American slaves could produce with profit. Amid an Atlantic world of bloody social strife and great-power wars, the United States—both stabilized and energized by its slave economy—had emerged as a power to be reckoned with. In an international context, slaveholding power and slaveholding confidence seemed at their zenith.

But for southern elites, that same decade—what we might call the long 1850s, from the storming of Chapultepec to the fall of Fort Sumter—was also a period of great weakness and anxiety. After California's admission to the Union in 1850, free states outnumbered slave states for the first time in American history. Over the course of the decade slavery was prohibited in the Pacific states, came under attack in Kansas, and appeared unable to attach itself to any of the great open spaces of the new Southwest. After 1854 sectional arguments shattered the second party system, which for thirty years had kept the slavery question on the margins of national politics. Out of its ruins grew a new and frighteningly powerful political organization, the antislavery Republican Party, whose essential principle was hostility

toward the South's most fundamental institution. By the end of the decade
the combination of northern population growth and expanding antislavery sentiment made the slave South's grip on national politics more
tenuous than ever. In a domestic context, slaveholding power and slaveholding confidence were approaching their nadir.

It is this element of the 1850s that has most occupied the attention of
modern historians. The narrative of the sectional crisis generally follows
the political seesaw of rising northern might and deepening southern
weakness, culminating with the victory of Abraham Lincoln and the Republicans in 1860. Beyond the battle for supremacy in the federal government, scholars of the antebellum South have fixated on the region's conscious sense of vulnerability from within. Rapid economic modernization,
the unstable loyalties of white nonslaveholders, the restive behavior of
slaves—all these factors heightened slaveholders' uneasiness about the
South's position in the Union and ultimately hastened their desire to leave
it during the secession crisis of 1860–61.[1]

From this perspective, it is easy to be skeptical about slaveholders'
claims of self-assurance. Grand statements about "King Cotton" or a slave
empire in the tropics may strike contemporary readers as large but hollow
overcompensations, bursts of desperate arrogance that sought unsuccessfully to hide the fact of southern weakness. The elite South's global confidence may well seem like a phenomenon that grew out of—and was ultimately defeated by—domestic politics. In this view, would-be southern
expansion had as much to do with the composition of the U.S. Senate as
with anything in the Caribbean basin; the rhetoric of King Cotton was
aimed at sympathetic northern businessmen or wavering southern nonslaveholders, not at an international audience.[2]

Nevertheless, the South's international confidence demands an independent analysis.[3] Over the course of the long 1850s southern self-assurance
bloomed in a multitude of forms, but its roots were essentially economic,
and its vital nourishment was slavery's role in the expanding global marketplace. In the spring of 1850, as Congress debated the future of slavery in
the territories seized from Mexico, Virginia senator Robert M. T. Hunter
proposed a provocative thought experiment: "Suppose that, in 1833, African slavery had been abolished all over the world—in the colonies of
France and Spain, in Brazil, in the United States, wherever, in short, it existed." While his colleagues pondered this alternate history, Hunter encouraged them to consider what global emancipation would have meant for

global commerce. "I ask how such a policy would have operated upon the world at large? No cotton! No sugar! But little coffee, and less tobacco! Why, how many people would thus have been stricken rudely and at once from the census of the world?"[4]

As one journalist argued, cotton, sugar, coffee, and tobacco had become "the four articles most necessary to modern civilization." And these goods, southerners insisted with growing persuasiveness, could be cultivated only by enslaved workers. The staple export crash that followed slave emancipations in the colonial West Indies, they predicted, would persuade elites on both sides of the Atlantic to reconsider slavery's merits as an engine of economic production. "[T]he abolition fever has nearly or quite extinguished itself in Europe," declared James Henry Hammond in 1858. Both Great Britain and France had come to understand that the "great agricultural staples" could "never be produced as articles of wide extended commerce, except by slave labor."[5]

The ripening bravado of King Cotton was the most audible consequence of the South's international confidence in the 1850s. But proslavery economic thought ranged wider and sank deeper than the familiar boasts about cotton's blunt market power. If global commerce really had come to depend on slave-produced goods, many southern leaders believed, then the rest of the nonslaveholding world must, however reluctantly, come to accept the economic logic that upheld African servitude. Under political duress at home, slavery stood stronger and prouder than ever in the markets of the world. Cotton, sugar, coffee, and tobacco might not have any votes in the Senate, but they demonstrated the clear trajectory of international economic development. It was only a matter of time before global economics trumped domestic politics.[6]

Free Trade, Bound Labor

The foreign policy of slavery originally sprang from a theory of political economy. In the early 1840s Duff Green, John C. Calhoun and others argued that Great Britain's antislavery activism across the Western Hemisphere reflected a deeper commitment to colonial mercantilism: by ending black bondage in the Americas, Britain sought to advance the cotton and sugar exports of its East Indian empire.[7] But by the second half of the decade southerners found reason to believe that this formula no longer applied. In early 1845 the British government reduced a wide range of import duties—including the tax on sugar and the tax on raw cotton, which was eliminated altogether. Could Britain be reversing its established policy of imperial protectionism and antislavery advocacy? Calhoun ventured an optimistic prediction: "They have already succeeded in repealing the duty on cotton," he wrote a northern correspondent in 1845, "& will not stop until they repeal them on food.... In repealing, they look to the foreign trade."[8]

His forecast proved spectacularly accurate. In June 1846 Parliament settled years of debate by abolishing the Corn Laws and opening the home market to foreign grains—a major setback for Britain's landed gentry and a major boost to advocates of free trade.[9] When the Whig leader John Russell replaced Robert Peel as prime minister in 1846, he moved almost at once to reduce and eventually repeal the tariff on imported slave-grown sugar.[10] The decade's final trade laws to fall were the British Navigation Acts. Part of the notorious parcel of mercantile regulations that had helped trigger the American Revolution, the acts prohibited the importation of key overseas goods (including sugar and tobacco) into Great Britain in foreign ships. In 1849, after a prolonged debate in Parliament, Russell's government succeeded in abolishing most of the restrictions.[11]

Britain's embrace of free trade delighted but did not astonish the proslavery South. The original foreign policy of slavery, as conceived by Calhoun and others, did not contemplate a ceaseless or irreconcilable conflict between Great Britain and the United States. On the contrary, a determined American defense of slavery, its advocates always maintained, would channel British policy in a more congenial direction. If the United States acted forcefully, Duff Green predicted in 1842, Great Britain "will hesitate, and may be compelled to fall back on the principles of free trade. She will, in that event ... cease to annoy our domestic institutions." By decade's end a few proslavery observers thought that this was exactly what had happened. "As soon as the annexation of Texas became certain," one commentator noted in 1850, "the views of England in respect to slavery underwent a change." The very success of the foreign policy of slavery now fundamentally altered the conditions that had first brought it into being.[12]

The germ of free trade quickly spread far beyond its British host. In July 1846, the same month Parliament repealed the Corn Laws, the U.S. Congress passed its own major package of tariff reductions. Over the next ten years a wide range of European and American states—often prodded by insistent British and U.S. diplomacy—undertook free-trade reforms. In 1853 the annual report of President Franklin Pierce's Treasury secretary exulted in the sheer number of open markets: "[T]he free lists of England, France, Belgium, Portugal, Brazil, Austria, Spain, Russia, Cuba, the Zoll Verein, Chili, Netherlands, Hans Towns, Norway, Mexico, and Sweden . . . mark the progress of free trade among commercial nations."[13]

The decline of transatlantic protectionism coincided with an end to the economic hard times that had gripped the United States since the panic of 1837. Victory in the war with Mexico, along with the discovery of gold in the new territory of California, helped spring the U.S. economy out of the sluggish 1840s and into the general transatlantic boom of the long 1850s. Global tariffs fell while cotton prices rose—from an average of six to eight cents a pound before 1847 to a level at or significantly above ten cents a pound in the decade that followed.[14]

But slaveholders did not cheer the spread of free trade simply because it lined their pockets. It also appeared to confirm a larger theory of global economic development that flattered the South's sense of importance. The "wealth, prosperity, and power of the more civilized Nations of the Temperate Zone," Calhoun had argued in 1844, "depends on the exchange of their commerce with those of the tropical regions." The opening of trade on both sides of the Atlantic implied that even the world's most advanced industrial nations now recognized the economic primacy of southern agricultural staples. Transatlantic urbanization, industrialization, and economic growth hinged more than ever on the production of these goods, especially "those which supply clothing and food—such as cotton, sugar, coffee, and rice." Almost all these products were grown in the southern United States, and all of them, of course, were cultivated with the labor of African slaves.[15]

The propulsive New Orleans editor James Dunwoody Bronson De Bow took the lead in composing and disseminating information on slavery's relation to international trade. The role Duff Green had played for the covert foreign policy of slavery in the 1840s—philosopher, propagandist, indomitable master spirit—De Bow eagerly assumed on behalf of the public economic policy of slavery in the 1850s. His *Review,* the most widely circulated magazine in the antebellum South, trumpeted the global vitality of slave labor in every issue between 1846 and 1861.[16] De Bow maintained a professional interest in statistics—he served as director of the U.S. census from 1853 to 1857—and in his journal a continuous discharge of tables, charts, and figures reinforced the regular volleys of proslavery rhetoric. In this effort he did not hesitate to enlist northern artillerists, especially those whose quantitative enthusiasm matched his own. A favorite piece by New York journalist Thomas Kettell, which De Bow reprinted on at least three occasions, attempted a universal calculation of slavery's contribution to U.S. foreign trade. Cotton, tobacco, rice, sugar, naval stores, and other slave-cultivated exports, Kettell calculated in 1851, added up to nearly $100 million in a total trade of under $135 million. "It is thus apparent," he concluded, "that 75 per cent of the exports of the Union are the product of slave labor."[17]

The arc of such calculations often bent toward sectional resentment. By stressing export figures, clever partisans could make the South appear to be the great producer of national wealth, while the North parasitically siphoned off the profits through tariffs and trading middlemen.[18] In truth, these statistics conveniently skirted the much larger internal economy in which the nonslaveholding states played a dominant part. As northern economists noted, international exports accounted for no more than 10 percent of the total economic product of the United States. The value of inland goods arriving in New York City alone in 1860—grains, meat, dairy, wool, lumber, and other products—equaled the value of the whole of southern cotton output for that year.[19]

But while northern and southern partisans butted heads over the significance of exports, proslavery boosters also articulated a broader, if subtler, argument about international commerce. The power of slavery in the world economy, after all, stretched far beyond U.S. borders. In 1855 De Bow excerpted an essay by the Cincinnati journalist David Christy, which called attention to American *imports* of "coffee, tobacco, sugar and molasses." These goods, harvested by "the hand of the slave, in Brazil and Cuba," were valued at over $34 million, a striking testament to the commercial progress of this *"foreign slavery,"* especially the Brazilian coffee and Cuban sugar industries. In fact, the global market for both was booming.[20]

From 1830 to 1854, yearly Brazilian coffee production grew from 64 million pounds to "the astonishing quality of 400,000,000 lbs." Meanwhile, as De Bow reported, Cuba's annual exports more than doubled in value between 1828 and 1847, and from 1849 to 1857 its sugar crop surged from 220 to nearly 370 tons.[21] "The whole commerce of the world turns upon the product of slave labor," summed up one 1854 *Richmond Daily Dispatch* column that found its way into newspapers from Georgia to Texas. "What could commerce be without cotton, sugar, tobacco, rice, and naval stores?"[22] The annual value of global goods produced by "African slave labor," another journalist calculated in 1858, amounted to $236 million and served a white

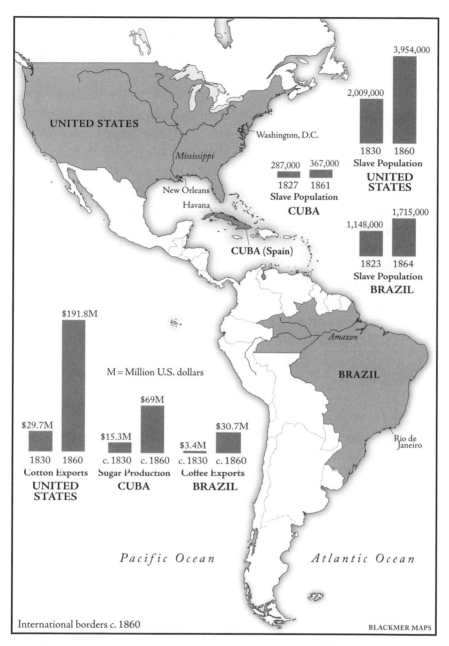

The growth of slavery in Brazil, Cuba, and the United States, c. 1830–1860
Slave population figures from Philip D. Curtin, *The Atlantic Slave Trade: A Census* (Madison: University of Wisconsin Press, 1969), 34; Stanley J. Stein, *Vassouras: A Brazilian Coffee County, 1850–1900* (Princeton: Princeton University Press, 1985 [1958], 295. Cotton, sugar and coffee figures from Douglass North, *The Economic Growth of the United States, 1790–1860* (Englewood Cliffs, N.J.: Prentice-Hall, 1961), 233; David Eltis, *Economic Growth and the Ending of the Transatlantic Slave Trade* (New York: Oxford University Press, 1987), 284, 286.

population of no fewer than 255 million souls—virtually the entire population of Europe and the Americas.[23]

The vitality of trade in slave-produced staples convinced some southerners that they were witnessing a fundamental shift in world opinion, not only regarding agriculture and commerce, but also African slavery itself. In the late 1840s the British debate over the sugar duties served as a particularly fruitful source of evidence for this idea. Parliament's elimination of the tariff on slave-grown sugar, argued one South Carolina newspaper, reflected a dawning awareness that West Indian slave abolition had been "an almost irremediable blunder." Without the ability to coerce the labor of their former slaves, planters in Jamaica and elsewhere were unable to maintain a competitive level of sugar production. Rather than manipulate tariff rates to prop up its failing West Indian colonies, southerners argued, Britain had reluctantly but wisely determined to let the market have its way—even if the market favored the slave-grown sugar of Cuba and the United States. By 1850, when the Alabama judge and future Supreme Court justice John A. Campbell penned a long essay for the *Southern Quarterly Review* on the state of the British West Indies, the subject was all but settled. Campbell had little trouble concluding that the end of the sugar duties represented not only the triumph of free trade but also the international vindication of African slavery as an economic system.[24]

The 1848 emancipation of the French West Indies, on the other hand, represented a significant defeat for southerners freshly optimistic about the position of slavery in the world economy. Five years earlier it might even have inspired a wave of panic. William R. King, after all, had once feared that French colonial emancipation could push Spain and Brazil toward free labor.[25] But in the more confident commercial environment of the late 1840s the older domino theory no longer applied so stringently. It was not long before slaveholders converted the apparent rebuff of French emancipation into another data point showing the failure of worldwide abolitionism. The "emancipated population" of the French islands, wrote one southern essayist in 1848, "are disorderly and inefficient, and the cost of producing their labor is so great, that competition with the organized and contented labor of other countries, is hopeless." Free Martinique's pain would be enslaved Cuba and Louisiana's gain. In just the first year after emancipation, Thomas Kettell demonstrated, French West Indian sugar production dropped by 50 percent. In 1852 Virginia congressman Charles James Faulkner summarized a comfortable consensus when he lumped the French in with the wider fiasco of black freedom in the Caribbean—the "ruinous emancipation policy which has marked the course of Denmark, England, and France over their West Indian possessions."[26]

Proofs of emancipation's apparent failure only strengthened the economic position of slavery. The liberalization of commerce all across the Atlantic world, southerners argued, was more than just a technical adjustment on the part of world markets. It reflected a larger ideological transformation: the American political economy of slavery and free trade had defeated the rival British model of abolition and mercantilism. "The whole scheme of a monopoly of raw products . . . based on a colonial system" had failed decisively, Kettell concluded in an 1850 essay for De Bow. "The great staples which keep in operation the workshops of England are slave products." After the embarrassment of multiple emancipations, Britain's commercial elite at last recognized that they must remain slave products. Both the foreign and the economic policies of imperial abolitionism were now dead; the repeal of the antislavery sugar duties had marked their funeral. Great Britain, Kettell predicted, had begun to "prepare the public mind of England for a toleration of slavery, as the best means of ameliorating the condition of the blacks."[27]

This confidence in the economic power of slave agriculture has occasionally struck modern scholars as absurd. Slaveholders, critics point out, were only peripheral players in a global capitalist system whose true power brokers were merchants and industrialists in London and New York, not producers of raw materials in Virginia or Mississippi. A few frustrated southerners did indeed see things this way. But over the course of the long 1850s, the South's most powerful leaders generally came to share the triumphant view presented by men like De Bow and Kettell. Their convictions cannot be dismissed because they were overtaken by later events or refuted by later investigations into the structure of the world economy.[28]

Slaveholders' optimism, in fact, reflected the particular character of the global economy at mid-century. The "subjection" of global agriculture to "the industrial world economy," as Eric Hobsbawm has written, was certainly a major development of the Age of Capital. Yet this process, however impossible to mistake by 1880, had not definitively emerged in the 1850s. King Cotton, not King Coal, still commanded the world market; the decline of global tariffs and the rise of global prices testified equally to his might.[29]

And it was not just cotton, either. The world's reliance on slave-grown products, southern elites convinced themselves, underpinned the larger

social and political developments of the era. Whatever Europeans or
northerners professed to think about slavery, they could not escape their
dependence on it. The onward march of Western civilization—from the
bustling metropolises of the North Atlantic to the jungles of South America
and from the colonial governors of Asia to the pioneers of California—
proceeded atop a foundation of coercive agriculture. For leading slaveholders, this was one great constant in an age of upheaval.

The Slavery Principle

John C. Calhoun did not enjoy a restful retirement. The fierce congressional
debates over the war with Mexico and slavery in the territories took a severe toll on his health: a vigorous sixty-three-year-old at the time of Texas
annexation, by 1850 Calhoun "stood visibly in the shadow of death and
spoke audibly in a voice from beyond the grave." In his last appearance before the Senate, just weeks before he died, Calhoun could hardly speak at
all. This image of the great South Carolinian still haunts our history of the
sectional crisis: an enfeebled and embittered old man, staring ahead with
hollow eyes, while Virginia senator James Murray Mason read his last implacable sermon against compromise. In the familiar drama of disunion,
Calhoun's sickly gloom personified the South's mortal struggle, inside and
outside of Congress, to preserve its fragile position inside the Union.[30]

It would be a mistake, however, to let Calhoun's tuberculosis stand in
for the overall condition of the slave South. In the two years before his
death, even the dour South Carolinian found reason to hope that on an international plane, at least, the power of slavery remained ascendant. Amid
his broodings on the diminution of southern strength within the Union,
Calhoun took solace in signs that Great Britain, once "the great Apostle of
emancipation," had fundamentally altered its position in regard to American slavery. He was not too modest to take some credit for the change of
course. In 1848, as the Senate debated sending U.S. troops to intervene in a
civil conflict in the Yucatán, James Westcott of Florida warned that Britain
sought to seize both southern Mexico and Cuba in order to "assail" slavery
in the South. When Westcott cited a fragment from Calhoun's magnum
opus of proslavery Anglophobia, his August 1844 letter to William King,
Calhoun himself rose to dispute the point. His letter to King, he noted "with
an honest pride," had helped "produce a change of sentiment in England,

which had now diminished her attachment to abolition." Westcott's fears of an antislavery offensive in the Caribbean were now out of date.[31]

Calhoun and other southerners believed that the triumph of free trade had changed the commercial logic that informed British foreign policy. And there were other signs—less concrete but perhaps even more suggestive—that British opinion on slavery was shifting. Beginning in the late 1840s, observers on both sides of the Atlantic noted the rise of antiabolitionist invective in the British press. "The question, *Slavery,* begins to be much better understood, and more liberally considered than formerly," an English correspondent informed Calhoun in 1848. "The London Times which is our most influential organ has most emphatically espoused the cause of the West India Proprietors. . . . [T]he effect produced by its taunts against the Abolition party have been powerful in their operation upon the public mind."[32]

Across the next decade southern periodicals diligently tracked down and reproduced these taunts for a receptive domestic audience. James D. B. De Bow was especially assiduous in this regard. His *Review* and his multi-volume encyclopedia *The Industrial Resources, etc., of the Southern and Western States* repeatedly excerpted antiabolitionist remarks from the *London Times, Blackwood's Magazine,* the *Economist,* and other leading British publications. The collapse of sugar exports after West Indian emancipation, the African's congenital unsuitability for freedom, and the retreat of the "rose-water philanthropy" of "Clarkson and Wilberforce"—these were the notes sounded in the British press that appealed most reliably to southern publishers.[33] Over the course of the 1850s, as eminent Britons like Thomas Carlyle and Anthony Trollope pronounced West Indian emancipation an economic and social failure, proslavery editors in the South highlighted the evidence that mainstream British opinion now regretted its experiment with black freedom.[34]

To be sure, slaveholding observers could not be certain that Great Britain, or Europe as a whole, had turned against abolitionism. In the early 1850s the runaway success of Harriet Beecher Stowe's *Uncle Tom's Cabin* generated a fresh round of popular antislavery feeling in Europe. Slaveholders abroad witnessed *Uncle Tom*–inspired public speeches, theatrical performances, and paintings at a royal gallery in London.[35] But the same southerners who encountered abolitionist sentiment in the Old World were quick to point out that Europeans nevertheless envied the economic progress of the slaveholding states. "I feel it my duty to say that all Europe is against us," noted

Randal McGavock in his 1854 travelogue *A Tennessean Abroad*. "Ignorant of
our peculiar institution . . . [t]hey . . . say to us that it is a system unworthy
of the age." But Europe's high ground on the slavery question, McGavock
insisted, was undercut by its virtual confession that colonial emancipation
had failed: "Having ruined and rendered bankrupt the citizens of her colonies by the abolition of slavery, they look with jealousy upon the cotton-
growing region of our country." Calhoun's Savannah correspondent Jacob
Levy offered an even more caustic perspective on the structural weakness
of European abolitionism: "You have not failed to notice what a large seg-
ment in the circle of European & American industry, the Slave labor con-
tributes. . . . The very Moralists who denounce slavery almost in the same
breath urge the use of its products." British antislavery, he predicted, could
not long thrive in a larger commercial environment whose health was
linked so intimately to slave-grown staples.[36]

If Europe's cultural attitudes still lagged behind economic reality, many
slaveholding leaders across the 1850s believed that the gap would soon
close. James Gadsden, the U.S. minister to Mexico, shared his optimism
with Jefferson Davis in 1854: "The statesmen of the world . . . are awakening
to the great truths which the Harpers and McDuffies of my little State first
foreshadowed as to African slavery." Great Britain's "antislavery feeling is
running to seed," pronounced James Henry Hammond in 1853. "The grand
politico-religious fervour is nearly evaporated, and *slavery, this day, stands on
a firmer basis than it has ever done!*" The Royal Academy and the West End might
still cherish their sentimental assumptions about the forward progress of
free labor, Gadsden and Hammond implied, but international men of affairs
knew better.[37]

The sturdiest and most familiar foundation of such proslavery confidence, naturally, was the global importance of southern cotton exports.
Slaveholders in the 1850s seldom passed up an opportunity to sketch the
inexorable syllogism of King Cotton: the American South produced nearly
all the world's usable raw cotton; this cotton fueled the industrial development of the North Atlantic; therefore, the advanced economies of France, the
northern United States, and Great Britain were ruled, in effect, by southern
planters.[38]

The conclusions southerners drew from this King Cotton model were
no less grandiose than their premises. De Bow's encyclopedia declared that
cotton was the "most beneficent product that commerce has ever transported for the comfort of the human family."[39] While cotton did its part to

civilize the planet, it also underlined the South's indispensable role in both American and international affairs. For the "*slave-holding* states of the Union," De Bow continued, cotton "is the great source of their power and their wealth, and the main security for their peculiar institutions." The power of King Cotton, in this view, expressed itself on several different levels. It simultaneously gave structure to the world economy, leverage to the United States in foreign relations, and strength to the South in U.S. domestic politics.[40]

This last prong of King Cotton ideology, of course, eventually helped justify southern secession and organize Confederate foreign policy. But King Cotton, in his antebellum rather than Civil War regalia, deserves another examination. In the global marketplace of the 1850s, did cotton command slavery, or did slavery command cotton? The Ohio journalist David Christy, whose 1855 book *Cotton Is King* coined the famous phrase, had no doubt about where the power resided: "KING COTTON cares not whether he employs slaves or freemen. It is the *cotton,* not the *slaves,* upon which his throne is based."[41]

But for many southerners the inverse proposition seemed at least equally true. In early 1854 the South Carolina novelist William Gilmore Simms reviewed a new book by Charles Edwards Lester, a Connecticut-born antislavery activist. Lester's argument was straight forward: Until abolitionists developed a rival source of cotton production, in India or elsewhere, their protests against slavery would remain hopeless. In its emphasis on the South's position of strength within the global marketplace, Lester's book emerged from many of the same premises that upheld King Cotton dogma. Simms, nevertheless, flipped the abolitionist's logic upside down: "'Cotton is the support of negro slavery,' quoth Mr. Lester. It would read more sensibly to say that negro slavery is the soul of cotton. Take away the latter, and you will have but a flemish account of the former, whether in India or America."[42]

Cotton's international importance, Simms argued, could be traced back to essential facts on both its demand *and* its supply side. If it was true that the West's surging desire for cotton imports gave the product its immense value, it was no less true that the only truly successful cotton export model in existence depended on southern slave labor. Lester's hope that Indian railroads would stimulate exports neglected the reality that profitable cotton production required bound labor. "Negro slavery," he concluded, "is established in the equal necessities of the world.... A necessity in social and national affairs, is something stronger than a mere truth. It is a law, with a certain vital principle working restlessly within it, which forbids that it should grow obsolete."[43] Many other southerners agreed: King Cotton's throne was propped up by the industry of African slaves. Without the vital system of "slave labor," extensive cotton production would not be possible.[44]

And slavery's empire, of course, extended far beyond the mere kingdom of cotton. "This instance of cotton," the *Charleston Mercury* noted, "is only one among many that stare every observer in the face, of the superiority of slave labor." The *Mercury*'s global survey of bound-labor regimes found that "the serfs of Russia produce by far the cheapest wheat in Europe"; that the slave economy of Brazil had made "enormous advances in competition with a dozen free labor countries" in coffee production; and that "the same may be said of the sugar culture in Cuba."[45]

This portrait of the world economy struck antislavery critics as grotesquely inhumane. As one Ohio abolitionist wrote, proslavery economics seemed to envision, and indeed to celebrate, "a world toiling and sweating for the benefit of a few capitalists." Everything depended on whether, "by the wear and tear of millions of lives . . . a few hundred thousand masters can succeed in raising a certain amount of cotton, sugar, and coffee, for export, one or two cents cheaper than it could be produced under a system of free labor."[46] But for slavery's boosters, such moral arguments, however passionate, could not dent the steely logic of global commerce. In fact they conceded what they set out to disprove: if slave labor produced cheaper export goods than free labor, even nonslaveholders would eventually have to acknowledge its power. By the 1850s, some southerners contended, that process was already under way. European capitalists were not merely observing the failure of emancipation; they were acknowledging the failure of free labor itself. Beyond mere antiabolitionism, modern political economy had arrived at an active defense of slavery.

The Virginia social theorist George Fitzhugh distinguished himself as an especially conscientious and enthusiastic reporter of proslavery trends in international economic thought. "So far as the slaves are concerned," he remarked in his 1854 treatise *Sociology of the South*, "opinion is fast changing." As Europeans began to "look more closely at what the slaveholders have been doing since our Revolution, they find that they have been exceeded in skill, enterprise and industry, by no people under the sun." As the 1850s progressed, Fitzhugh claimed to have found "a counter current" that had begun to sweep across Europe. Citing Carlyle, the Scottish economist John

Ramsay McCulloch, and others, he affirmed that British political economy had already started to trump British cultural prejudice. The many failures of free society—in the West Indies and in Europe itself—would prepare the way for a transatlantic return to the "slavery principle."[47]

Not all of slavery's defenders were so optimistic about the progress of economic theory. In an 1856 essay for the *Southern Quarterly Review*, George Frederick Holmes acknowledged that the old free-labor critique of slavery's inefficiency was far from dead. It continued to shape mainstream British economics, including John Stuart Mill's influential 1848 textbook *Principles of Political Economy*. Holmes conceded the narrow point that free labor was often cheaper than slave labor; in response, he argued that there were greater matters at stake than the optimal accumulation of wealth. Slavery's value as a stabilizing, patriarchal system—one that allowed the South to avoid mass poverty, mob rule, and other "social leprosies"—far outweighed its economic defects. The efficiency of free labor only proved its superior capacity for exploitation and cruelty.[48]

But for every paternalist like Holmes who surrendered the economic field to free labor, another of slavery's champions appeared to rejoin the battle. Just months after Holmes published his essay, Louisa McCord flooded the pages of *De Bow's Review* with a powerful rebuttal. Born and married into the highest grade of South Carolina's planter aristocracy, McCord distinguished herself as a poet, playwright, and essayist. In the 1850s she emerged as perhaps the most aggressive defender of slavery in the South. Contemporaries were sometimes bemused to see a woman writing about politics, but more often they were simply staggered by her "masculine vigor" and "sinewy strength of thought." When an admiring southern critic called one of McCord's works a "brilliant anamoly of our literature," the reference was to her prose, not her person.[49]

McCord replied to Holmes with characteristic force. Slavery, she argued, could not afford to surrender to its economic critics: "if free labor is cheaper and more productive than slave labor, slavery is a wrong." Yet even a passing glance at recent history was enough to disprove this premise. "[T]he wonderful development of this western continent," she explained, was achieved only "by means of slavery—her immense produce scattered all over our globe, carrying food and clothing to the hungry and the destitute; her cotton and sugar sustaining not only herself but the might of Europe's most powerful nations." McCord did not reject Holmes's domestic portrait of bondage as a paternal sanctuary, but she paired it with an international

diagram of bondage as an economic locomotive. "Slavery, which is the negro's protection, is the world's wealth."[50]

In any case, McCord added, John Stuart Mill's "vulgar prejudice" against
bondage should not stand in for all European economic thought. *"[F]ree
trade, not free labor"* was the guiding principle of contemporary commercial
wisdom: "[T]he true principles of Political Economy" have "carried the day
in favor of slavery." As evidence she brandished excerpts from the sugar duties
debate in Parliament, speeches given at the 1853 Manchester Peace Conference, and recent essays by the liberal Belgian economist Gustave de Molinari. Molinari praised West Indian emancipation as a "noble and generous
enterprise" but admitted that it had been an economic disaster. Despite
their sentimental preference for free labor, McCord concluded, Europe's
leading thinkers and actors could no more resist the economic power of
slavery than a bull could do battle against a railway car.[51]

Beyond the boundaries of the United States, even paternalist conservatives like Holmes often shared the buoyant faith of McCord's "politico-
economic school." One region on the map, in particular, tended to evaporate
the disagreements between proslavery paternalists and economists: the
vast, fertile expanse of Latin America. From Mexico to Brazil, southerners
of different stripes united to insist on the necessity of slavery in the tropical
portions of the Western Hemisphere. Not just the future of slavery but the
future of world civilization itself was at stake. Holmes's glance at South
America showed that he, too, had fallen under the ideological spell of proslavery economics:

> The interior of South America . . . would alone support more inhabitants
> than the population of Europe. . . . The only agency which can be effectu-
> ally applied to the cultivation of the feracious lands of the torrid zone is
> negro slavery. Under its operation . . . the whole of humanity would be re-
> lieved by the diminution of population where it was too dense, and by the
> simultaneous increase of markets and alimentary products.[52]

Holmes's Malthusian worries about population density reflected his
conservative pessimism about economic progress, and in this he remained
distinct from eager market triumphalists like McCord and De Bow. But in
his overarching belief that the system of slave labor must serve as the foundation of global commerce, he was their cousin, and in his specific ideas
about the importance of an enslaved Latin America to the future of that
commerce, Holmes served as the perfect representative of the larger tribe.

It was not merely King Cotton who presided over the markets of the world. The stronger sovereign was Emperor Slavery, and his dominion commanded sugar, tobacco, rice, and coffee—in a phrase, the chief "alimentary products" of the entire Western world.

The World Will Fall Back on African Labor

In June 1853 the *Charleston Southern Standard* printed an editorial titled "The Destiny of the Slave States," which went on to become one of the most widely reproduced and discussed newspaper essays in antebellum southern history. The *Standard*, a moderate, cooperationist paper in the universe of South Carolina politics, had recently fallen under the editorial control of a singularly immoderate and uncooperative fire-eater named Leonidas W. Spratt. The new editor's June column sounded the first "clarion call for the re-opening of the African slave trade." If slavery was indeed a positive social good, Spratt insisted, the slave trade was an equal good. The South's failure to defend the instrument that had made American slavery possible represented a craven surrender to the logic of abolitionism. Spratt's stance represented a major milestone in southern politics. Previous defenders of the Atlantic slave trade, especially in the early republic, had mounted narrow economic arguments for the importation of more laborers from Africa. Never before had a southerner made such a direct moral and ideological case for the beneficence of the overseas slave traffic.[53]

Yet "The Destiny of the Slave States" was more than a landmark argument on behalf of African slave importation. In fact, the slave trade occupied a relatively small share of Spratt's essay. When James D. B. De Bow reprinted the piece in his review, he excised the few paragraphs that discussed the African trade. For De Bow, as for many other contemporary readers, the most significant aspect of the article was, instead, its visionary portrait of the wider Western Hemisphere.[54] Operating from forward bases in Australia, China, and California, Spratt noted, the great powers of the Atlantic world had begun to penetrate the fabled Pacific market. New conduits of commerce were sure to follow. "[A]ll this vast trade and accumulation of gold," Spratt predicted, must "force its way across the Isthmus of Panama into the Gulf of Mexico." This fortunate region was positioned at the center of not one but two major world-economic intersections: it lay between the Atlantic and the Pacific and also between the Amazon and the Mississippi river valleys.

"These are the two greatest valleys upon the face of the earth. . . . [I]f properly developed, they are capable of producing what is produced at present by the whole civilized world."[55]

The key phrase in Spratt's analysis was "properly developed," and it was a phrase with a specific meaning. "These two great valleys of the Amazon and the Mississippi," he continued, "are now possessed by two governments of the earth, most deeply interested in African slavery—Brazil and the United States." Racial slavery was "the perfect system by which the vast tropical regions of the earth are to be developed." The "Caucasian race" lacked the physical stamina to survive "under the miasma of its exuberant and mighty plains and swamps." Now that Britain and France's "miserable experiment" in the West Indies had debunked the fashionable claims for free black labor, the "reflecting parts of mankind" must soon accept the necessity of servitude. To hurry along this gradual enlightenment, Spratt suggested, "our true policy is to look to Brazil as the next great slave power." A firm Brazilian-American partnership could dominate the Caribbean basin while placing "African slavery beyond the reach of fanaticism at home or abroad." In time, Spratt concluded with a flourish, the irresistible gravity of the slave system would pull the entire globe back within its orbit: "The world will fall back upon African labor, governed and owned in some shape or form by the white man, as it has always been." Black slavery was "the only system" that allowed "the industrious but poor laborers of the Northern climates . . . to enjoy the coffee, rice, sugar, and cotton for cheap clothes." Slavery, Spratt declared, "was the true progress of civilization."[56]

"The Destiny of the Slave States" was no ordinary editorial. The extravagant breadth of its imagination was matched, perhaps, only by the wide ambit of its circulation. Over the next year southern newspaper and journal editors reproduced it liberally; Duff Green, ever alert to the latest developments in proslavery internationalism, cut a clipping of the article and saved it with his papers.[57] A wide range of northern papers, too, trembled at what they saw as an unusually explicit statement of the slaveholding worldview. "There is a certain quality of grandeur," remarked the *New York Times* after sampling the article, "in the cool, remorseless, inflexible determination with which the Slave Power thus treads onward to its objects. . . . It belongs to the order of the Infernal Sublime, and challenges a sort of admiration like that sometimes felt for Milton's Satan."[58]

Some of Spratt's arguments were indeed exceptional, even among the untimid minds of the proslavery community. Reviving the African slave trade remained a controversial subject even in the Lower South all the way up to the Civil War, and even the boldest filibuster commandos did not generally advocate a forcible seizure of all the West Indies. But in its larger vision and deeper assumptions "The Destiny of the Slave States" embodied the way southern internationalists understood hemispheric slavery in the 1850s. The core issue was neither the African trade nor the possibility of U.S. expansion to the south. It involved, rather, the fixed laws of geography and political economy—laws that insisted above all on the need for slavery across tropical Latin America.

To be sure, slave-trade advocacy and proslavery internationalism often traveled southward together. The *Charleston Mercury*'s 1854 campaign for African slave-trade revival pointed to "Mexico, Central America, and that world of wonderful resources and untold treasures, Brazil. What hope is there for them under present auspices?" Without a regular supply of freshly enslaved Africans, the *Mercury* and other advocates argued, hemispheric slave societies might cannibalize themselves. Across the long 1850s many of the most articulate and influential slaveholding internationalists, including Spratt, De Bow, and George Fitzhugh, gradually came to embrace the idea of a renewed Atlantic trade.[59] But the cause of hemispheric proslavery, as it might be called, reached much more broadly across the elite South. In fact, the man perhaps most responsible for the quasi-scientific rationale behind Spratt's geographic arguments was a staunch opponent of the slave trade: the Virginia naval reformer Matthew Fontaine Maury.

As a propagandist for southern interests in Latin America, Lieutenant Maury had few equals. His extensive study of global wind and ocean currents, conducted under the auspices of the Navy's Depot of Charts and Instruments, won international acclaim by shortening sailing times between major destinations around the world. And Maury's scientific research, especially in the Western Hemisphere, dovetailed exquisitely with his ideological predilections. Under the lieutenant's examination, the hemispheric laws of wind and sea seemed always to thrust forward American influence, to enhance southern economic opportunity, and to plead for slaveholding engagement with the larger Gulf basin. "Let the *South* not forget to look to the *South*," was Maury's mantra. "Let her study the immensity of the commercial resources which lie dormant in that direction."[60]

Like the author of "The Destiny of the Slave States," Maury regarded the greater Caribbean region as the future epicenter of all global trade. In an 1850 letter to a fellow naval officer he shared his prophetic vision for the hemisphere:

> I have seen the African slave population of America clustered in and around the borders of the [Caribbean] Sea. I have seen this Sea, by Ship Canal and Isthmus highways placed midway between Europe and Asia. It is between two Continents, it receives the drainage of the two greatest river basins in the world, it is natural for the produce of two hemispheres and I have therefore seen in it the Cornu Copia of the world.[61]

Nestled cozily between the Atlantic and the Pacific Oceans and between the Mississippi and Amazon river systems, the Caribbean's "magnificent basin" collected almost the entire agricultural wealth of two continents. Compared with the Mediterranean Sea, its equivalent on the other side of the Atlantic, the wider Caribbean was less encumbered by quirky peninsulas and bays, which lengthened sailing times; the distance from one corner to another was a smooth, straight line across the "broad ocean."[62]

Maury's imperial oceanography further demonstrated the naturally commanding position the United States held within this maritime system. Not only did the mighty Mississippi flow through American soil alone, but because of the nature of Gulf currents, he argued, veteran navigators knew that "the real outlet of the Mississippi river to the ocean, is not at the Balize [at the southern end of the Gulf], but in the straits of Florida." Produce-laden ships heading out of New Orleans did not sail south, into the teeth of the wind, but were pushed east, along U.S. territory. Moreover, even the other great hemispheric river, the Amazon, in distant South America, was for all commercial purposes at the very doorstep of the United States. "To one who has never studied the course of the winds and currents of the sea," declared Maury with the unmistakable authority of one who had, "it appears startling to be told that the shores of the southern states, of Florida and the Carolinas, are on the way-side of vessels bound from the mouth of the Amazon." For a sailing ship, even "Norfolk is not half as far, in point of time, from the mouth of the Amazon as is Rio in Brazil."[63]

Such wind and current analysis drove Maury's tireless efforts to induce Brazil to accept open international navigation of its great river.[64] In 1850 he helped persuade Secretary of the Navy William Graham of North Carolina to send a U.S. naval expedition down the Amazon to report on its commercial potential. The officer chosen to lead the mission, William

Lewis Herndon of Virginia, was Maury's close confidant and relative: it was in his pre-expedition letter to Herndon that Maury vouchsafed his vision of the Caribbean as a "Cornu Copia" of slave agriculture. Although Graham's official instructions remained silent on the subject of slavery, Maury's private correspondence with Herndon made it clear that the two Virginians understood the trip as "the first link in that chain which is to end in the establishment of the Amazonian Republic"—a great slaveholding colony settled by American citizens, with all "their goods and chattels." "That valley," as Maury noted elsewhere, "is a slave country"; the labor needed to civilize it must "be done by the African, with the American axe in his hand."[65]

Maury's vision of the Amazon, however, did not depend on bondsmen imported directly from Africa. Unlike Spratt, he worried that the U.S. South contained too many black slaves, not too few. As he explained in a letter to his cousin, Maury hoped that American slaves would travel with their masters to Brazil, "relieving our own country" of black people and thus avoiding a horrific "war of races" at home. Perhaps, as Gerald Horne has suggested, he hoped that his native Virginia could serve as a profitable breeding ground for the sale of black slaves to South America. Whatever the case, there is no reason for historians to doubt Maury's sincere opposition to the African slave trade.[66]

The necessity of slavery in the Caribbean basin was a subject that both advocates and opponents of the trade could agree on. Henry Wise, like Maury, belonged to the latter group. As U.S. minister to Brazil in the 1840s, he had energetically combated American involvement in the African traffic. In 1854 Wise continued to decry the "foul pollution of such a trade." But none of his strictures on slave trafficking applied to domestic slavery on the South American continent. Brazil, he declared, was "a negro heaven," a "country which is paradise compared to Africa." The *Charleston Mercury* scolded Wise lightly for his "exaggerated picture of the horrors of the slave trade" but applauded the way in which he "vindicates slavery" in Brazil. Wise and the *Mercury* might differ on the slave trade, but they found fellowship in their view of black bondage in South America.[67]

Writing in the *Southern Quarterly Review*, James Henry Hammond rejected Maury's idea that the American South had a problem with "excess slaves." In fact, the region required "about one hundred thousand" more slaves per year: "[T]here is a world of work to do, and labour is *wanting*." Without it, "the great staples would not be yielded sufficiently to satisfy the world." But Hammond, too, saw enormous value in Maury's work on South

America. If Maury's proposed steamship line was established between Charleston and the Amazon, he believed, the South could dominate the commerce of the continent and trigger "a revolution of trade" across the Atlantic world. The essential ingredient, of course, was slavery, since Brazil required black labor "to extract the agricultural wealth of a region, where no others of the human family can toil under a burning sun." For Hammond, Brazil's prosperity depended on some form of the African slave trade, which he optimistically predicted would expand and develop as its economy grew.[68]

But the slave trade was only a means, not an end. A strengthened and expanded hemispheric slavery was the true end, and there were multiple ways to attain it. "The institution of slavery in Brazil," Hammond continued, "on a scale greatly more extended, would entice our southern planters, with their slaves ... to emigrate to the fertile valley of the Amazon." Here Hammond once again converged with Maury. Whether the Caribbean basin was supplied by captured Africans or Virginia bondspeople remained, in a fundamental sense, a question of secondary importance. What mattered most was that the potential wealth of this region was opened to the wide world, and this, of course, required slavery: "systematic culture by African labor, governed by the energy and intelligence of the white man."[69]

Southern commentary on Latin America in the 1850s reflected this virtual consensus. Lieutenant Herndon, who traveled through both Peru and Brazil, declared that the indigenous population in both countries simply "will not work." But in Brazil, at least, black slaves could provide "the compulsory labor necessary to cultivate her lands." In the Senate Jefferson Davis applied this kind of proslavery development economics to the whole hemisphere. "[T]he products of Mexico," he declared in 1850, "once so important and extensive, have dwindled into comparative insignificance since the abolition of slavery. And it is also on that account that the prosperity of Central and Southern America has declined, and that it has been sustained in Brazil, where slavery has continued."[70]

Southern diplomats in South America continued to draw connections between Brazilian and American slavery. In 1857 the arriving U.S. minister, Richard Kidder Meade of Virginia, presented his credentials to Emperor Dom Pedro II with a short speech that referred uncryptically to "an institution common to both countries, fixed and deeply rooted in their soil." Without pronouncing the word "slavery," Meade nonetheless made it clear that he hoped the common bond of bondage would foster a profound unity of action and feeling" between Brazil and the United States." Other proslavery diplomats were even more forthcoming. "No two countries in the world have greater mutual interests than this beautiful Empire and our own Republic," proclaimed Robert G. Scott, the Virginian serving as U.S. consul in Rio de Janeiro. "[T]hey are the two greatest and only powers on the globe with negro slavery recognized and governed by law."[71] This attempt to build a "grand Proslavery alliance with the Brazilian Empire," as an appalled *New York Times* put it, showed that the preservation and enhancement of slavery remained a central priority of U.S.-Brazilian diplomacy in the 1850s, as it had been in the 1840s.[72]

Unofficial southern visitors in Brazil also paid careful attention to the status of the local slave institutions. Charles Fenton Mercer Garnett, a Virginia engineer who worked on Brazilian railroads for three years in the late 1850s, was struck by the "very unsound state of public opinion here on the subject of slavery. In fact there is a strong leaning to abolition. Public sentiment requires educating." Richard Morton, another southern railway engineer, took away the opposite impression: "I believe that ⅞ of the landowners of Brazil are firmly wedded to slavery and would vote *for its extension*," he wrote in his diary. "I venture the assertion that *slavery* lasts as long as the present constitution." Where Garnett and Morton agreed absolutely, however, was on the importance of the Brazilian slave system. Garnett even asked his cousin, the fire-eating Virginia congressman Muscoe Russell Hunter Garnett, for a proslavery "pamphlet" to be distributed in Brazil. "Nothing that has been written in our country suits this latitude," he cautioned. Muscoe's essay "must be perfectly free from *democracy*, and it must say nothing against hereditary monarchy." In his support of the slave-holding regime, Garnett added, "I am quite a Monarchist out here."[73]

For proslavery internationalists in the 1850s, formal political principles faded into irrelevance under the tropical sun. Republican government in itself availed little without the critical ingredient of slave labor—the social cohesion it supported, the political stability it encouraged, and the future wealth it could unleash. Some southerners remained skeptical that Brazil could preserve its domestic slavery without the African slave trade, which had ended under British naval pressure in 1850. Others, including De Bow, foresaw a new and self-sustaining era of Brazilian bondage: "[W]ith 3,000,000 slaves to start with the Brazilians, with ordinary care, can have an annual increase of at least 100,000, which will be consistent with the widest development of agricultural wealth to come." Brazil pessimists called for a revived slave trade, while optimists put their trust in careful slave breeding. But both agreed on a fundamental point. "Certain this is," wrote one southern correspondent from Rio de Janeiro: Brazil's "existence depends upon the development of her slave labor, and the increase of her wealth is to be measured by its welfare and extension."[74]

In the 1850s the proslavery South's leading politicians and intellectuals confronted a new and urgent set of domestic challenges, beginning with the eclipse of southern parity in the Senate, and accelerating into a sectional crisis of unprecedented intensity. Why, then, did so many of them bother to develop an opinion about labor relations in faraway South America? Unlike slavery in Kansas, the Southwest, or even Cuba or Mexico, the fate of Brazilian bondage had little direct bearing on the domestic politics of the United States. Southern thinkers and actors concerned themselves with the condition of labor in Latin America for reasons that went beyond the raging sectional struggle, immediate commercial interest, or even the anxious geopolitics that guided Tyler and Calhoun's foreign policy in the 1840s. South American slavery mattered most of all to southern elites because it gave concrete expression to a larger economic truth that they believed the world had only just begun to understand.

The ascendancy of free trade, the perceived failure of emancipation, and the progress of slaveholding regimes across the hemisphere all offered evidence for this truth. Yet in some ways it reached far past the Americas and went beyond even the specific institution of African servitude. The largest truth, some slaveholders began to argue in the 1850s, involved the two indispensable principles of race and coercion. "If the experience of mankind has solved a single industrial problem," Louisiana's Judah Benjamin informed the Senate, it was this: "[T]ropical products can be maintained, on a scale to meet the requirements of civilized man, by compulsory labor alone." The announcement provoked one antislavery wag to wonder whether it was "not time for the slaveholder of the tropical regions . . . to take his turn at the splendid system of compulsory labor? Off jackets, Messrs. Benjamin & Company, and take to the cotton-field!"[75]

But Benjamin's reference to "compulsory labor" was not merely a bland euphemism, for he meant to include both black slaves and a new category of worker that had arrived in the tropics: "persons bound to service under the name of apprentices, coolies, or colonists." In fact, racialized forms of bound labor seemed to be making an international comeback in the 1850s, as European states scrambled to enlist Chinese, Indian, and African workers to match the demand for tropical products. What did the spread of these new arrangements portend for the future of slavery? For many southerners, they showed that the great powers of Europe had joined their ranks—if not yet in words, then in deeds. The moral principle of free labor was in retreat, while the tangible facts of racial hierarchy and "compulsory" toil grew stronger with every hour. Looking beyond the frustrations of the sectional conflict at home, slaveholders eagerly counted the ways in which the modern world was moving in their direction.

7

Slaveholding Visions of Modernity

"NO WORD IN THE ENGLISH LANGUAGE," remarked the South Carolina planter Frederick Porcher in 1854, "is used so much as the dissyllable progress. In America we use it so much, that we have made a verb of it. This is an age of progress—a country of progress—a people of progress." But what, in the mid-nineteenth century United States, did "progress" entail? "[T]he most satisfactory answer appears to be, that it means cotton manufactories and railways. . . . If this standard is the test for enlightenment," Porcher predicted, "we may expect that some future Yankee geographer will . . . thus prove conclusively against us a case of retrogression."[1]

It was not just Yankees who rendered such a verdict. For nearly 150 years after the Civil War, historians across a wide range of ideological positions and methodological practices often identified the slave South as a case of retrogression. Conservatives and Marxists, statisticians and culturalists, sectional partisans and global theorizers—nearly all tended to conclude that chattel slavery disqualified the South from entering the nineteenth century's mad dash toward modernity.[2] What is more, most scholars agreed, the planter elite knew this and even celebrated it. "The car of progress crushes too many under its wheels," George Fitzhugh declared in 1860. "We are not advocates of change, but, on the contrary, a system that shall prevent change." While the North rushed forward, embracing industrial development, urbanization, and the strong national state, the slave South regarded such modern changes with ambivalence, if not downright hostility.[3]

In the twenty-first century this venerable interpretation—seldom uncontested but never toppled—has faced its most comprehensive challenge yet. A burst of research has reconfigured familiar social and economic data in strikingly unfamiliar ways. In the decade before the Civil War, we now know, the slave South was urbanizing at a faster relative rate than England, France, or the U.S. Midwest. By 1861 it claimed almost ten thousand miles of railroad track, more than any European nation, with a larger number of railroad depots and junctions per white citizen than the northern states. Even by the old Yankee standard of "cotton manufactories," southern industry seems to have grown faster and to have incorporated slave labor more successfully than its critics previously allowed.[4] These statistics do not exactly transform the conventional estimate of the differences between antebellum northern and southern society. In absolute terms the North was far more urban and far more industrial: this brute fact remains. Nevertheless, it now seems clear that slavery did not entirely forbid the kind of economic development customarily associated with modernity; it only assured that this development took a distinctive shape.[5]

Along those lines, we may wonder whether the accepted yardsticks of modernity can accurately measure the size and shape of the late antebellum South. In 1860 the value of southern slaves amounted to $3 billion, far more than all the "railways and cotton manufactories" in America combined. In the Civil War, those slaves proved far less valuable to the South than the war-making power of the North's infrastructure, but it is not clear why the units of military mobilization should be the only way to gauge modern development. As southern commentators frequently pointed out, the 1850s were "times of profound peace and general prosperity" in the United States. For wealthy white Americans, fewer places were more prosperous than the booming precincts of the slave South, in 1860 home to the nation's four richest states and twelve richest counties, at least as measured by wealth per free man.[6]

How did slaveholders view the position of their slave society within a modernizing and industrializing world economy? One clue comes from contemporary language, which points toward a mid-nineteenth-century understanding of the relationship between "industry" and slavery that has sometimes eluded later historians. When Judah Benjamin announced that "mankind has solved a single industrial problem," he was referring not to advances in factory production, but to the discovery that coerced labor was necessary to cultivate tropical goods on a large scale. When James D. B. De Bow titled his 1853 encyclopedia *The Industrial Resources, etc., of the Southern and Western States,* he did not limit his focus to the South's increasingly visible textile mills, tobacco plants, or iron works. Instead, he

meant to consider the total productive resources of the southern states—
including, of course, their slave plantations. In the economic vocabulary of
the 1850s it was perfectly possible for George Fitzhugh to offer praise for
"slavery, as an industrial institution." "Manufacturing" was one thing, but
"industry" had not yet acquired its predominant association with mechanized production.[7] For southern elites, indeed, slavery did not figure as an
obstacle or an antonym to nineteenth-century industrial development, but
as a vital constituent of it. Given the enormous and variegated role that
slavery played in American economic life up to 1861, this was the only definition that made sense.

So much for "industry," but what about the proslavery understanding of
"modernity"? Although historians have largely abandoned the stiff sequences
of modernization theory, the notoriously elusive concept of "the modern"
continues to play a critical role in framing, periodizing, and explaining the
transformations of the nineteenth-century world.[8] If a defining feature of
modern experience is "the breakdown of all traditional legitimations of the
political order," as one leading authority has put it, then the southern defense
of slavery might seem to be ruled out of bounds at once.[9] What else could
the proslavery argument have been other than a powerful, if rather belated,
attempt to legitimize a traditional order that had already begun to crumble
under the onslaught of modernity?

The lamentations of men like Porcher and Fitzhugh appear to confirm
the point: by the middle of the nineteenth century, southern slaveholders
found themselves besieged by social and ideological forces increasingly antagonistic to the basic structure of their society. Great wealth and economic
dynamism notwithstanding, their only option left was a staunch defense of
slavery's citadel against the oncoming "car of progress"—a defense they
made, first with ink and then with blood, until in the Civil War they too
were crushed under modernity's wheels.[10]

Yet this view of slaveholding politics and ideology ignores at least as
much as it explains. Proslavery spokesmen adopted a language of debate as
varied and adaptable as slave labor itself: biblical, paternalistic, and moral-
istic defenses of bondage combined and alternated fluidly with racial, economic, and pragmatic arguments.[11] Within this heterogeneous mixture
there were indeed ample doses of rhetoric that claimed to reject modern
improvements altogether, while celebrating slavery precisely because it preserved a traditional social order. But the antimodern defense of bondage was
not the only strain of proslavery thought. Among the slaveholders at the top

of the South's political pyramid, it was not even the dominant strain. In fact, the most powerful slaveholders generally embraced much more optimistic and forward-looking arguments.[12] Not merely apologists or legitimators of bound labor, they are better seen as its boosters and champions, and their efforts were crowned by a belief that slavery and human development were inextricable. In this respect leading slaveholders sought less to uphold a "traditional" order than to demonstrate the superior fitness of their system for the supremely modern task of "actively constructing society" to suit human needs.[13]

The historian Frederick Cooper has called for scholars to stop "shoehorning political discourse into modern, antimodern, or postmodern discourses" and instead to "listen to what is being said in the world."[14] Over and over again, slavery's champions said the same thing: "modern civilization" depended on "compulsory black labor." Even George Fitzhugh argued that "modern experience" insisted on the subjugation of racial inferiors, and that black slavery "put the South at the lead of modern civilization."[15] The region's prodigious wealth served as one eloquent proof that slavery was compatible with contemporary political economy. But in the 1850s proslavery leaders went even further than this, beginning to sketch a theory of global modernity that named racial coercion as its single indispensable feature.[16]

If theirs was a self-consciously "modern" view of slavery, it was also a self-consciously international one. "Yankee geographers" might well crow about their factories and cities, but on a global rather than a national scale, southerners identified a significant cluster of trends that seemed to affirm slavery's position in the emerging world order. The mid-nineteenth-century rise of free trade corroborated their belief that slave-cultivated agricultural products dominated the commercial markets of the world. European states, too, appeared to have rejected the underlying logic of emancipation. In their Caribbean, West African, and East Indian colonies, even the officially antislavery great powers had embraced a model of production whose fundamental principles were racial hierarchy and bound labor. Only coerced, dark-skinned workers—whether "slaves," "coolies," or "apprentices"—could grow the agricultural staples on which the modern world economy depended. The spread of European imperial power into the far reaches of Asia and Africa affirmed the propriety of the South's paternalistic system at home, while paralleling its vision of an expanded slaveholding power across Latin America. And in the progress of the latest nineteenth-century scientific research, southerners found new evidence to extend their old understandings of racial hierarchy and social organization.

Slavery, according to the American abolitionist slogan, was local; freedom was national.[17] For many of slavery's boosters, the best response to this attack was to widen the parameters of argument. "Freedom," in the destructive way the North understood it, might be increasingly national; but in more than one sense, slavery spanned the breadth of the globe.

A Higher Law than the "Higher Law"

The introduction of migrant workers from India and China into the Western Hemisphere was perhaps the most geographically ambitious labor experiment of the nineteenth century. Under the stewardship of European colonial administrators, these so-called coolie laborers, along with purportedly free "apprentice" workers from West Africa, arrived in the Caribbean basin en masse during the 1850s, especially in the emancipated sugar colonies of Britain and France, but also in enslaved Spanish Cuba and Dutch Surinam. Were these new systems of contracted migrant labor a danger to the political and economic future of black slavery? Some American slaveholders feared they were. Insofar as historians have probed the antebellum South's response to the influx of Asian workers into the Caribbean, they have largely emphasized these doubts and anxieties.[18]

But if southerners often denounced the abuses of coolie labor, and occasionally worried about its threat to slavery's dominance in the production of tropical staples, they also argued that these new systems reflected a deeper ideological victory. After the emancipation of their West Indian colonies, James Henry Hammond announced in 1858, Great Britain and France had "ransacked the universe" for alternative sites and alternative methods of staple production. "They have failed everywhere. . . . [S]ugar, rice, tobacco, coffee, can never be produced as articles of wide extended commerce, except by slave labor. This at length they found out." In desperation, then, Britain and France "renewed the slave trade. Not in name. Oh no!" But the importation of "hundreds of thousands of Chinese and Hindoo Coolies," Hammond argued, was a virtually identical procedure. The two great powers whose "adoption of this abolition crotchet alone made it respectable and influential," he continued, "have thoroughly renounced it, practically, almost in theory." As shocking as all this might seem, Hammond concluded, "there is nothing to surprise us in all this, if we are correct in our views of African slavery." The laws of economics made slavery's global triumph a foregone conclusion: Britain and France's experiments with forced labor showed that they had accepted a version of this inevitability.[19]

From Paris U.S. minister John Y. Mason took a similar view. France had recently announced its plan to bring thousands of free African "apprentices" to the Americas; Napoleon III's foreign minister had frankly admitted that the French West Indies "were languishing for want of labor." Mason, a Virginian, felt more empowered than alarmed by this news: "I feel quite confident," he wrote Secretary of State Lewis Cass in 1858, "that in the future we will see the fanatical denunciations of American slavery greatly moderated, if not silenced, in France, perhaps in England." For Mason, France's African apprentice policy was simply another sign that Europe had turned its back on abolitionism. "[N]ow, to repair the error [of emancipation] in its politico-economic sense," he noted, "measures are resorted to which amount essentially and necessarily to the restoration of slavery, whether . . . that of the coolie or the African emigrant, or the transported Indian sepoy."[20]

Hammond and Mason both exaggerated considerably. In both principle and practice there were enormous differences between chattel slavery and the new imperial labor regimes.[21] Only slavery, after all, awarded masters a property right over the bodies of their workers. Southerners seldom neglected this point when they denounced the abuses inherent in coolie systems: unlike the South's responsible master class, whose workers represented both labor and capital, European imperialists treated their workers wretchedly. The Asian coolie trade, according to Hammond, was organized "under conditions compared with which the Algerine slavery of the last century was merciful."[22]

But while some southern elites decried coolie importation as a moral crime, many also saw its rise as a chance to declare victory in the global argument over labor. For all their abuses, coolie work regimes recognized a fundamental principle in common with domestic bondage in the South: the necessity of compulsory labor performed by nonwhite workers. In 1854 the *Charleston Mercury* cited the arrival of Asian contract laborers in California to make this point with combative aplomb. Four years earlier the antislavery New York senator William Seward had famously invoked "a higher law than the Constitution"—a law established by "the Creator of the universe" that made slavery a moral wrong. But for the *Mercury*'s editors, California's substitution of "Chinese slavery" for "African slavery" had exposed the impotence of Seward's apothegm: "There is a 'higher law' than the 'higher law' itself." The "demand for labor"—for cheap, inferior, and thus compulsory labor—was "a law inherent in the nature of society," and thus a law "which denies all the villainy of abolition." The moral claims of anti-slavery activists, in other words, crumbled under the economic mandate of labor coercion.[23]

Empirical observations of global agriculture confirmed that forced labor rested at the heart of profitable staple production. James Bolton Davis, a South Carolina planter sent by the Polk administration to observe planting operations in the Ottoman Empire, reached that conclusion in 1849. "The experience I have had in the cultivation of Cotton in Turkey," he wrote John C. Calhoun, "satisfies me that Cotton cannot be made without loss, if *controllable* labour is not used." The *Washington Union,* the official organ of the Pierce administration, argued that Britain's attempts to stimulate cotton production in India depended on the ability to coerce the local laborers: "[Y]ou must have a quiet, obedient, and above all, either a people industrious from habit or inclination, or who can be made to work against their inclinations."[24]

Many southerners were skeptical that even the new coercive systems could match the economic efficiency of black bondage. The *Southern Cultivator,* a Georgia agricultural magazine, mocked the "worthlessness of the laborers" in British India: physically weaker and less well fed than American blacks, Indian workers also suffered from a hybrid system of "hireling labor" that did not demand the "watchful guardianship of owners." Only the intensely personal form of surveillance and domination that characterized American slavery, he implied, could produce tropical profits.[25] Other slaveholders wondered whether the new labor arrangements might produce formidable rivals in the global staple market. The latest turns of "European policy," Duff Green argued in 1858, showed that the great powers now sought to promote "African slavery in Africa." Both cotton and sugar, after all, could be grown just as easily by *"sending the white master to the black slave, instead of bringing the black slave to the white master."* Brushing aside the legal fictions that Europeans would use to reconcile this fresh form of coercion with their stated opposition to slavery, Green predicted a coming commercial clash between "[o]ur planters in the South" and "French and British planters in Africa."[26]

But even when the new labor systems presented a material challenge, they offered an ideological reinforcement, confirming both the necessity of compulsion and the fixed hierarchy of race. For Virginia congressman

Thomas Bocock, Europe's imperial programs reflected the modern world's recognition that blacks would not work "continuously and effectively without the coercion of a master." By relying on the dark-skinned labor best suited for the tropics—whether "the swarthy Hindoo, the negro, [or] the coolie"—European administrators implicitly recognized the racial chain of command that must govern any productive social or economic system.[27]

The rise of coolie and apprentice labor also fueled southern belief in the international momentum of slavery. In 1854 the *Southern Literary Messenger* published an extensive rebuttal of Charles Sumner's widely reprinted speech on the Kansas-Nebraska Act. Sumner, the Massachusetts senator, surveyed the globe and found that slave labor was everywhere confined and retreating, from India to Ottoman Turkey. Even in tsarist Russia serfdom had been "carefully restricted by positive prohibition." Trumpeting this "Wilmot Proviso of Russia" and celebrating the global movement toward "the Equality of Men," Sumner noted that "alone in the company of nations" the United States remained tenaciously committed to its slave institutions.[28]

The *Messenger*'s anonymous author rejected the first premise of Sumner's catalog. "The Russian, the Turk, the Moor, and the Algerine! Mild, estimable, tender-hearted people, how can we resist the contagion of their example!" Rather than examining the supposed philanthropy of worn-out empires on the margins of the modern world, the *Messenger* recommended turning to the recent activity of the "civilized and christian nations." Their doings told a rather different story. Great Britain, for instance, "bitterly repented the emancipation of the negroes in Jamaica." Now "she is seeking to repair her own errors by the re-institution of slavery in Jamaica under another designation." France, "in pursuance of the same policy, is directing her energies to tropical Africa, and preparing for extensive colonization, cultivation and commerce with that fruitful region."[29]

Slavery, then, was not in retreat; in fact, it was advancing all across the Atlantic world, from the Straits of Florida to the Cape of Good Hope. According to some observers, it had even tightened its grip on colonial Java.[30] By expanding the definition of global bondage to include coolie and apprentice labor, slaveholders refuted Sumner's claim that the United States stood alone in its "hateful championship" of servitude. "Slavery," intoned the *Messenger*, "is now, and must be for years to come, an inexorable necessity." It was necessary not merely to organize southern society, to protect slaveholders' property, or to provide a conservative bulwark against the dangerous energies of the age. It was also the necessary product of modernity—an irresistible, international force that was both a lead driver and an inevitable passenger in the van of civilization.[31]

The Hot Breath of Civilization

The new migrant-labor systems in the Americas, as both their critics and their supporters understood, depended on the power of European empires far outside the Western Hemisphere. If not for British rule over India, French colonialism in Africa, and the forcible European penetration of China, neither sepoys, apprentices, nor coolies would have been available to work in the staple-crop fields of the Caribbean. "The nations of the world," barked James D. B. De Bow in 1850, "are engaged in the great race for position and for empire."[32] At midcentury the crack of the starter's pistol echoed far around the globe. During the ten years before the American Civil War, Great Britain consolidated its control over India, Australia, and New Zealand, widened the perimeters of empire in South Africa and Burma, and fought new imperial wars against Persia and China. France completed its conquest of Algeria, expanded its possessions along the Senegal River, and claimed its first colony in Southeast Asia. The same decade also saw the Russians conquer Chechnya, the Dutch seize much of Sumatra, and the Spanish extend their enclave in Morocco. "Never," affirms Eric Hobsbawm, "did Europeans dominate the world more completely and unquestionably than in the third quarter of the nineteenth century."[33]

De Bow's message was clear: the United States must follow its triumph in Mexico with an aggressive foreign policy suited to this worldwide scramble for empire. And what was the larger relationship between global imperialism and American slavery?[34] Historians have recognized that the slaveholding South's enthusiasm for aggrandizement in Latin America borrowed some of its language and élan from contemporary European empire builders.[35] But readers of *De Bow's Review* in March 1850 did not have to contemplate Caribbean territorial expansion to perceive a closer link between imperialism and slavery. On the same page where De Bow reached his stirring conclusion on the link between "human progress" and the race for empire, the editor reprinted a section of William Harper's "Memoir on Slavery." By now regarded as a canonical statement of southern thought, Harper's essay emphasized that "the coercion of slavery" formed one of the central "foundations of civilization." In all centuries and on all continents, "the progress of society" required "the command of another's labor," especially when the laborers were drawn from a race "naturally inferior in mind and character." The wheel of global development was turned by forced labor and racial hierarchy—the reciprocal energies of both bondage and empire. In the 1850s American slavery and European imperialism shared an ideological bond that reached far beyond "manifest destiny," territorial expansion, and failed filibuster invasions of Cuba and Nicaragua.[36]

Edmund Ruffin, the influential Virginia agronomist, was just one proslavery writer who cheered the progress of European imperialism across the globe. Like many southerners in the 1850s, Ruffin despised British antislavery, fretted over British intrusion into the Western Hemisphere, and considered British imperialism generally rife with "injustice & cruelty." But also, like many of his compatriots, Ruffin applauded the advance of the British Empire in Asia. When news of the Indian Rebellion reached Virginia in 1857, Ruffin denounced British abuses but noted that a successful native revolution would be disastrous for "the commerce & well-being of the civilized world." "[E]very friend of civilization," he continued, should desire that "the European & superior race shall be dominant" in South Asia. All humanity would benefit if "mongrel and semi-barbarous communities" around the world were improved by civilized conquest. For Ruffin, this category included Japan, Mexico, and Venezuela. "It is strange," he mused perplexedly, "that no foreign power should think them worth being conquered."[37]

Ruffin's untroubled vision of worldwide white supremacy, empire, and commercial exploitation stands out for the simplicity and even the crudeness of its outlines. But he was far from the only proslavery writer who saluted the advance of European imperialism. In 1851 Louisa McCord lamented the plight of "the slaughtered Tasmanian, the starved Australian, the enslaved Coolie, and even the fast-perishing negro of our own free States." Yet their fates were inevitably fixed: "*God's* will," she wrote, "formed the weaker race so that they dwindle and die out by contact with the stronger." In the middle decades of the nineteenth century this view was not the sole possession of slaveholders. A broad spectrum of European and American elites believed that modern world history had disclosed a racial hierarchy that governed human affairs. But unlike their white supremacist peers in London, Paris, or New York, American southerners saw this emergent racial order, above all, as an international vindication of their own slave system. "Slavery, then, or extermination," McCord concluded, "seems to be the fate of the dark races." It was the white man's burden, in her view, not merely to conquer and control the other peoples of the world but to enslave them.[38]

The more immediate imperial history of the Americas gave slave-holders additional evidence that the arc of progress bent toward a familiar kind of racial domination. "The settlement of this western world," noted the *Charleston Mercury,* was accomplished through "the annihilation of myr-iads of human beings." But the total destruction of the "fast-fading Indian" was no crime—"[W]e see in [it] the progress of man's development, and we heartily rejoice at it." So too should Americans celebrate the future con-quest and enslavement of Africa.[39] What gave this historical analogy its power was the idea that black bondage in the Americas took its place on an international spectrum of racial coercion in the name of civilized progress. Viewed as part of a burgeoning imperial order that involved the subjuga-tion of "the chiefs of Australia," the "rajahs of India," and the "barbarians of Africa," American slavery did not appear as a retrograde or isolated phe-nomenon in world politics. By the 1850s it represented something closer to the opposite—the most successful system that civilization had yet devel-oped for managing the relationship between Euro-American conquerors and the inferior peoples they encountered elsewhere. By conscripting the labor of these subordinates and harnessing it to energize the world market, European empire builders only duplicated a technique perfected by slave-holding southerners. If those of "the negro race," as one observer put it, were the quintessential "aboriginals of the soil," then southern masters were the world's exemplary imperialists.[40]

Slaveholders who drew this imperial comparison sometimes stressed the paternalistic function of slavery. The European conquest of the New World, one *De Bow's* contributor calculated, had come at the cost of thirty million lives. Now "aboriginal" populations all over the planet faced a par-allel threat from expanding European empires: "[T]he hot breath of civili-zation withers them away like a sirocco." Southern slavery represented the world's only functioning model of a colonial system that could prevent such "wholesale murder." In truth, the South's "three hundred thousand masters" constituted an imperial army, "standing guard over a nation of four million negroes, and absolutely preserving their lives from destruction."[41]

Other southern writers concentrated on the material benefit of slavery as a globally exportable imperial prototype. Both American slavery and Euro-pean imperialism, declared the Mississippi essayist E. N. Elliott, flowed from the same source: the law of material development. God had commanded man to "replenish the earth, and subdue it," and Elliott took this dictum as "the warrant for the conflict of civilization with barbarism."[42] The divine commandment to generate wealth justified Europe's imperial penetration of closed economies all over the world. It also justified the indefinite expansion of that marvelous engine of wealth production, African slavery. "[B]y legitimate deduction," Elliott argued, "[t]hese principles . . . are as applicable to the rights of labor, as to the rights of commerce." Just as "China and Japan should be required to open their ports," unproductive Africans should be enslaved and compelled to work "for the benefit of the human race."[43]

Elliott's invocation of a divine commandment to justify conquest and enslavement reflected the pervasive Protestantism of antebellum American culture. Southern ministers and other religious authorities, of course, frequently turned to the Bible to defend slavery in the face of northern criticism. Theological vindications of slavery sometimes adopted a pessimistic interpretation of human development, seeing human bondage, like poverty and sickness, as among "the badges of a fallen world," in the words of South Carolina clergyman James Henley Thornwell. Yet for all the intellectual influence of this religious conservatism, it did not prevent secular writers like McCord and Elliott—or their even more boosterish political colleagues—from mobilizing the rhetorical authority of "*God*'s will" to generate a powerfully optimistic vision of slavery's role in global progress.[44]

Along the same lines, southern historians customarily emphasize the ideological tension between paternalistic and materialistic justifications for bondage. But the theorists of American slavery, like the philosophers of global empire, frequently joined the arguments together without the slightest indication of stress. "If civilized man has a right to subdue, tame, teach, and civilize wild men," argued the Georgia agriculturalist Daniel Lee, striking a paternalistic note, then "the plow, the hoe, and the whip are the best known means to accomplish such purposes." In an "age of wonderful industrial activity, of bold and unbounded enterprise," he added, switching effortlessly to a materialistic register, "the great interests of humanity" demanded that the "innumerable tribes in Africa, Asia, and the islands of the sea" be wrangled out of their backwardness and put to work growing staple crops for the benefit of civilization. Both the logic of slavery and the logic of empire, after all, posited that racial hierarchy and coerced labor would improve the barbarian and enrich the white man at the same time.[45]

Europe's recent imperial encounters with formerly unknown African societies afforded an additional range of discoveries about race, labor, and civilization. The famed British explorer Dr. David Livingstone—"a name in every mouth," the *Charleston Courier* reported in 1858—was an opponent of slavery and a friend of "free labor" in Africa. But for southern readers, the objective content of Livingstone's African reportage demolished the "soft-hearted" philanthropy of his political recommendations. By Livingstone's own "honest confession," wrote the Louisiana physician A. R. Kilpatrick, the villagers he encountered in southern Africa lacked "the intellectual powers" and work ethic of the white man. Despite his own questionable politics, Kilpatrick judged, Livingstone had delivered "a fair portraiture of the race. . . . They are servants of servants, and will be to the end of time."[46]

For proslavery readers, these bulletins from the front lines of empire demonstrated not only the settled inferiority of "the negro character" but also the global necessity of black bondage. The Swedish explorer Charles John Andersson, who visited present-day Namibia in the early 1850s, earned praise from the *Courier* for his "unprejudiced" account of African life. Unlike Livingstone, whose "tender consideration for the lower orders of the human species" warped his commentary, Andersson did not waste his time inquiring into the "spiritual capacities and acquirements" of the Africans he met. Instead, "he did what was better. He set them to work." Coerced labor on the southern model, the *Courier* insisted, offered the native African the only hope of improvement: "What a thousand pities that, in this desert country of his, plantations may not be built of sand; and that no one is there to put into his hand a hoe, and let him work out his salvation."[47]

Occasionally the global momentum of such arguments encouraged southern statesmen to advocate for concrete action within the Western Hemisphere. Each of the "privileged races" of the North, declared Matthew Maury, sat adjacent to an inferior continent "which seems more especially commended to its guardianship." While Europe would oversee the social development and economic exploitation of Africa, he argued, the United States must do the same in South America. But the proslavery approach to imperial development did not necessarily depend on such questions of foreign policy. It was the "duty . . . of civilization," William Gilmore Simms urged, to subdue backward peoples, "compel their labor," and bring them forcibly into the modern world.[48] In fact, the United States had already done as much for its own enslaved people of African descent. The concept of "proslavery imperialism," in this sense, did not apply only to southern efforts to expand slavery across the Caribbean or to reopen the slave trade with Africa. Proslavery imperialism also involved an understanding of black bondage in the South as a vital analogue and precedent for global empire building.[49]

In an 1858 essay in the *Southern Literary Messenger*, James Holcombe chided the English historian Thomas Macaulay for offering "fervid denunciations upon Southern slavery" while justifying British imperial rule in India. But Holcombe did not intend simply to scold Macaulay for the traditional English vice of hypocrisy. Since neither "the Hindoo" of India nor "the African" of the South was fitted for liberty, in both cases it was "the duty of the State . . . to establish the relation of personal servitude," or some close equivalent. Virginia senator R. M. T. Hunter drew the same analogy in 1860, suggesting that antislavery activists in the South were like French agents sent to British India "to stir up civil strife [and] produce domestic insurrection." In Calcutta, as in Richmond, white elites had to preserve order and improve civilization by compelling the labor of the racial inferiors that surrounded them.[50]

From this perspective, both the European colonialist and the southern slaveholder understood what abolitionists pretended not to see: that the wide world must be divided by race and driven forward by coerced labor. In this great effort the southern master, thanks to the venerable institution of slavery, was more honest, more humane, and more efficient at his task. The nineteenth century's exemplary imperialists had a duty to share their insights with the rest of the world. "If we are not mistaken," observed Daniel Lee, "it is entirely practicable for the experienced slaveholder of this country to render the great interests of humanity, as teacher of agriculture, a great service." The slave South had the opportunity to act as a global imperial university—the most advanced training ground for a system of racial stratification and economic organization that was beginning to remake the entire planet in its image.[51] "Science," Lee declared, "is making our agriculture a most valuable and instructive School for the benefit of blacks not less than whites." Indeed, it was not just global commerce and global imperialism that vindicated southern slavery, but the progress of knowledge itself.[52]

The World Is Growing Wiser

Slaveholding elites, like their counterparts throughout the Atlantic world, celebrated the mid-nineteenth century as an era of rapid scientific progress. Even the South's most entrenched conservatives generally welcomed the transformations wrought by modern technology: "[T]he merchant-ship,

the railroad, the steam-car . . . and that lightning messenger, the telegraph,"
George Fitzhugh acknowledged, "cannot but become a mighty agency in
diffusing civilization." To be sure, slaveholders also expressed their share of
misgivings about the social consequences of this technological change.[53] But
as southern elites scanned the globe in the 1850s, they saw plenty of reasons
to celebrate the "discoveries and inventions of physical science." Not least
among them was a belief that international scientific inquiry, across a range
of disciplines, was working rapidly to vindicate the social principles that upheld black slavery. In the context of contemporary scientific research—or
what passed for scientific research in the Age of Capital—this belief may
have been optimistic, but it was by no means ludicrous.

Proslavery propagandists' favorite area of knowledge, naturally, was the
emerging science of race. In this field Samuel Cartwright and Josiah Nott
were the two southerners who most notoriously popularized the alliance
between proslavery thought and scientific racism. Cartwright, a Louisiana
physician, gained a wide audience for his pseudomedical musings on "the
diseases and physical peculiarities of the Negro race," many of which found
their way into the pages of *De Bow's Review*. Nott, an Alabama surgeon, constructed an elaborate theory of racial polygenesis that suggested that Africans and Caucasians had evolved from separate species. The researches of
both men ranged from the narrowly anatomical (Cartwright's theory that
black lungs consumed less oxygen) to the grandly anthropological (Nott's
six-thousand-year review of race's role in human history), but all, in the
end, verified the necessity of black slavery.[54]

Not every proslavery southerner swallowed these theories whole. Josiah Nott's view that blacks and whites were two separate species remained
especially controversial since it clashed with the story of singular creation
told in the book of Genesis. But over the course of the 1850s the "ethnological" defense of slavery, in one form or another, claimed an ever-widening
circle of powerful supporters. J. D. B. De Bow, James Henry Hammond, and
Robert Toombs cited modern racial science on behalf of slavery; on the
Senate floor Jefferson Davis expounded on the "natural inferiority" of blacks
in terms that borrowed heavily from Cartwright's fusion of biblical and anthropological arguments. For proslavery statesmen, the intricacies of the debate between racial monogenesis and polygenesis shrank to irrelevance next
to the central finding that Africans, according to modern research, lacked
the basic mental capacity of the white race.[55]

The central figure in the American school of ethnology was neither Cartwright nor Nott but a northern man. The Philadelphia craniologist Samuel George Morton devoted his life to the measurement of human skulls from around the world; his findings formed the evidentiary basis for much of Nott's white supremacist theorizing. Beyond Morton stood a range of naturalists and race thinkers on the other side of the Atlantic—the Egyptologist George Gliddon, who supplied Morton with his skulls; the Scottish anatomist Robert Knox, a vigorous champion of Anglo-Saxonism; and the aristocratic French theorist Arthur Gobineau, whose *Essay on the Inequality of Races* inspired a half century of European racialist thought.[56] Above them all, in reputation and influence, stood the Swiss paleontologist and Harvard professor Louis Agassiz, one of the most respected scientists in the midcentury Atlantic world. Agassiz personally opposed slavery, but he was sufficiently convinced by Morton's skull studies to lend his prestige to the doctrine of fundamental biological differences between the races. When he agreed to place an essay in Nott and Gliddon's 1854 tome *Types of Mankind,* Nott rejoiced: "With Agassiz in the war," he wrote, "the battle is ours."[57]

This flowering of scientific racism in the 1850s—in the North, in Britain, and on the European continent—has encouraged historians to downplay the particular significance of such "ethnological" research to proslavery politics in the South. But for slavery's champions, it was precisely the geographic breadth of the new race science that made it such a welcome development. The grave scholarly conclusions of "Englishmen and Northerners" such as Morton, Gliddon, and Knox, argued Louisa McCord, showed that the concept of racial inequality did not emerge from any provincial "weakness or bias towards our Southern institutions," but from impartial scientific research alone. The world's leading authorities had "universally conceded" that the races were distinct, unequal, and "unalterable," declared Texas representative Lemuel Evans in 1857. Citing a wide range of European researchers—the English philologist R. G. Latham, the French physician Eugène Bodichon, and the Danish-French geographer Conrad Malte-Brun—Evans assured Congress that the international progress of "sober science" stood behind the South's own theory of race.[58]

In 1852 a cautious McCord was not yet ready to declare victory over "maudlin" philanthropists who still hoped to empower, rather than subjugate, biologically inferior peoples. "A full and open discussion on the subject of the races," she believed, was "the likeliest mode of warding off the terrible evil" of emancipation. By the end of the decade some leading slave-holders felt that this discussion had made a considerable advance. One of them was Georgia congressman Alexander Stephens. Frail, bone-thin, and pale almost to the point of translucence, Stephens provoked even friendly observers to compare him to a mummy, ghoul, or some other "refugee from a graveyard." Yet this strange and sickly man was capable of heroic energy in the defense of slave property: throughout the long 1850s Stephens served as perhaps the South's single most effective floor leader in the House of Representatives. And despite a naturally melancholy temperament, Stephens maintained a buoyant optimism about the evolution of scientific opinion toward slavery.[59]

On his retirement from Congress in 1859, Stephens delivered a lecture at Augusta that summarized this confident belief. "New truths are always slow in development," he declared, using language that anticipated the famous "Cornerstone Address" he would give as Confederate vice president two years later. "This is the case in all the physical sciences. It was so with the Copernican system in astronomy; so with the application of steam in mechanics." The same resistance to the irresistible, Stephens argued, explained the the world's hostility toward slavery. But now, Stephens reassured his audience, "[t]he world is growing wiser." Recent investigations in natural science had discovered that "subordination is the normal condition of the negro." As new research uncovered fundamental truths about racial hierarchy, Stephens concluded, the slave South could congratulate itself on building a social system explicitly vindicated by modern science, the most powerful progressive force in the nineteenth-century world.[60]

"In these diabolical statements," Frederick Douglass wrote of Stephens's farewell address, "we have. . . . the cool and thoughtful conclusions of the leading minds of the slaveholding States. They let us into the sources of Southern repose, the tranquillity of tyrants, and are valuable as showing the progress of slavery."[61] And in the 1850s, slaveholders' cool confidence did not depend on racial science alone. The American school of ethnology represented only a singular molecule within the great body of what might be called proslavery scientism. Across the decade slaveholders found ways to cite nearly any field of scientific endeavor for their purpose. The emerging disciplines of demography and geography claimed much southern interest; a variety of authors in *De Bow's Review* used black population statistics as fresh evidence that tropical slavery was favored by the laws of nature. Louisa McCord, proclaiming political economy "the science of wealth," avowed that its most recent discoveries vindicated bondage as a superior engine of prosperity. Slavery was a system that increased human productive capacity, simultaneously improving the laborer and making him a "better *wealth machine*."[62]

Intellectuals like Fitzhugh and Henry Hughes, meanwhile, framed their proslavery writings as contributions to the modern study of "sociology." Edmund Ruffin famously championed black bondage and agricultural reform with the same tireless zeal; a parallel vision of slavery and science animated the chief planter-agronomists of the Lower South, including Daniel Lee, David Dickson, and Noah B. Cloud.[63] The South Carolina naturalist and Lutheran minister John Bachman, meanwhile, publicly clashed with Nott and Gliddon over their heretical theory of racial polygenesis. But Bachman devoted much of his zoological and physiological work to reconciling religion and science in light of the "permanent inferiority" of the African race. And Matthew Maury's oceanographic research, aided by a little climatology, tended to advance rather than undermine the boldest projections of hemispheric slave expansionism.[64]

Beyond the specific findings of any particular discipline, proslavery triumphalists aped the positivistic tone and progressive energy of the sciences in general. Casting their antislavery critics as mushy romantics, out of touch with the direction of the modern world, southerners claimed the hard truths of scientific knowledge as their own. "The North," declared Fitzhugh, "surpasses us in taste and imagination, equals us in learning, but is far behind us in logic." Louisa McCord argued that the judgments of economic science—including the failure of colonial emancipation—could be trusted because they were not derived from "sickly sentimentality" but from the scientific method. "Political Economy," she noted, "asks, doubts, studies, questions, and, seeing what appear hopeless ills, seeks to counteract rather than cure them."[65]

The very language of the proslavery argument, even when it did not explicitly take up the subject of science, reflected the authority that modern technological progress claimed within the minds of the slaveholding elite. "Like the electro-magnet," observed E. N. Elliott, "whose power is lost the moment it is insulated from the vivifying power of electricity, so the servile race loses its power when removed from the control of a superior intellect." The white man's power over the black man sent some slaveholders deep into outer space in search of the appropriate analogy: "[O]ur four millions of negroes are as unalterably bound to obey the white man's will," wrote

Samuel Cartwright, "as the four satellites of Jupiter the superior magnetism of that planet."[66] In an effort to describe the natural harmony of plantation life, even the most paternalistic commentators could not resist the lure of a technological metaphor. The "relation between master and slave," argued the *Charleston Mercury,* "becomes part of the habit . . . of a whole people, and the laborers of a plantation move through their easy tasks, like a well-finished piece of machinery." The "kindly" slave system was far more humane than industrial wage labor, but it was no less efficient. It drew on the same settled laws of science and the same wave of technological discovery that character-ized the triumphs of contemporary engineering.[67]

Some scholars, noting the proslavery argument's zeal for science, have interpreted it in the classic terms of "the slaveholder's dilemma"—an inevi-table tension between the progressive wings of modern development and the reactionary deadweight of slave institutions. Slaveholding elites, writes Drew Faust, grabbed at "the prestige of modern science" in order to "legiti-mate tradition and conservatism." "The positivistic standards of the nineteenth-century intellectual" were grafted onto a fundamentally anti-modern set of ideas about social order and racial subjugation. The scientific bent of proslavery rhetoric, in this view, was at best an ideological self-delusion and at worst a cynical debating tactic.[68]

Yet this interpretation obscures the distinct possibility that many leading slaveholders meant what they said and knew what they meant. The advance of global science, as they saw it, really would promote the cause of racial servitude: if not slavery in name, then modernized forms of hier-archy and coercion that were indistinguishable from slavery. Like other en-ergetic elites across the nineteenth century, these southerners embraced scientific discovery as a means to bring physical and ideological coherence to a world that they knew to be in constant motion—a world in which many venerable solidities, like the theory of human biological equality, or the indigenous cultures of the Americas, did indeed seem to be melting into air. For every George Fitzhugh who warned that these modern trans-formations would endanger the South, there was another southerner eager to show how the nineteenth century's rattling "car of progress"—commerce, empire, science—actually strengthened slavery's position in the global order. Likely as not, that southerner would sharpen the point with a scientific metaphor. "[S]lavery," declared South Carolina senator James Chesnut, "is not a mere fixture, irremovable and inactive as an inert mass. It is not a dead body, but one full of life, vigor, and pliability; capable of self-creating power and preservation."[69]

To Formulate the Modern

For all their wide-ranging confidence, De Bow and other proslavery progressives could not fully banish southern fears about the future of slave labor. Nor could they dispel the "alternating moods of cultural chauvinism and despair" that seized an elite that celebrated change while remaining deeply impressed with the necessity of order.[70] Yet in the 1850s, among the most powerful members of that southern elite, it was international chauvinism as much as domestic despair that governed political belief. Despite the setbacks for slavery within the United States, slaveholders looked abroad with confidence on the slow workings of a larger global order that began to emerge in the middle decades of the nineteenth century.

This was a world of unprecedented commerce and connection, of shrunken distances and expanded empires; a world of multiplying profits and advancing technologies, of cotton plantations and electromagnets. It was a world whose economy depended in significant part on slave labor for raw materials, and just as vitally, a world whose dominant political ideas and social patterns did not always seem incompatible with racial slavery. It was a world where Swedish explorers scoffed at southwestern Africans, British troops repressed a servile revolt in India, and French philosophers proclaimed the fixed order of race. In this world, as one British parliamentarian put it, slave labor might well appear as "a steam-engine" alongside other steam engines—a controversial but marvelous machine whose operation would inevitably outpace the flailing "race horse" of emancipated labor.[71]

Individually, foreign capitalists, colonialists, scientists, and statesmen might sneer at the American South, and the South might sneer back. Nevertheless, in the global order they were fashioning together, slavery and progress had proved impressively congruent. A belief in this essential congruence—in profit, power, and ideology—undergirded the South's international confidence in the 1850s. Through their embrace of free-trade economics, their celebration of Europe's turn against abolitionism, their enthusiasm for the future of bondage, and their glorification of global imperialism and scientific progress, southern elites laid out the rudiments of a proslavery vision of the modern world. Racial hierarchy, coerced labor, and open commerce—these, for the proslavery South, were the lineaments of global modernity in the mid-nineteenth century.[72]

Few elements of slaveholding thought captured the spirit of its international confidence better than proslavery anticipations of the future. De Bow's futurism, quintessentially, grew out of statistical projections. In 1850 he calculated that the American slave population would reach 10.6 million by 1910; three years later he revised the figure upward to 13 million slaves in 1900. In 1859 the former Alabama congressman Henry W. Hilliard ventured an even bolder estimate: in the year 1920, he predicted, 31 million American blacks would be in chains.[73]

The future of bondage, of course, extended well beyond the borders of the United States. Southerners took for granted that the advance of civilization in South America, Africa, and Asia depended on the spread of racial slavery, or something that closely resembled racial slavery—"the same thing under another name," as the *New Orleans Daily Picayune* had it, borrowing from Shakespeare's Juliet. The proslavery futurists of the 1850s did not even shy from predicting that the name itself, as well as the thing, might soon experience a hemispheric rebirth. Thomas Carlyle's 1849 essay on what he termed "the negro question" offered initial momentum for southern assertions that the British West Indies would be reenslaved. But over the course of the following decade the idea of a general Caribbean reenslavement developed an independent hold on the proslavery imagination.[74]

"The wants of white men must triumph over the negro's absurd claim to liberty," declared the *Charleston Mercury,* which foresaw "a revival and extension of African slavery" in the British and French West Indies. Nor were existing colonial possessions in the Caribbean the only targets for future reenslavement. Southerners also looked hopefully to Haiti, home to the hemisphere's original antislavery experiment. For half a century the black republic had loomed as a dangerous symbol of violent insurrection, and many slaveholders, to be sure, continued to regard Haiti with concern throughout the 1850s. But in the emerging midcentury world, with tropical commerce and Euro-American imperialism equally on the march, a nation ruled by free blacks struck many southerners not as a revolutionary beacon but as an obvious anachronism. "Why are the armies and navies of the Emperor of the French," asked an 1859 essay in *Russell's Magazine,* sent "to extend the desert limits of Algeria, or to reassert old claims in Cochin China . . . while the loveliest of islands, the most valuable ancient colony of France, is left unreclaimed . . . ?" "If France continues apathetic," the writer concluded, it would be left to "some other power" to "restore wealth, civilization and refinement to the Antilles."[75]

Slavery's eventual return to Haiti also featured prominently in the poetic magnum opus of the proslavery South, William J. Grayson's "The Hireling and the Slave." At once a conservative critique of wage labor and a woozy ode to plantation harmony. It is tempting to consider Grayson's poem, almost eight hundred rhyming couplets in all, just the kind of antiquated absurdity that only the Old South could have produced: "And from the fleecy field the setting sun / Sends home the slave, his easy harvest done."[76] But "The Hireling and the Slave" also offered one of the boldest and most comprehensive statements of proslavery futurism on record. The poem's final section, which De Bow printed in 1855 under the headline "The Indian and the Slave," began with a familiar analogy: "Like their wild woods, before the Saxon's sway, / The native nations wither and decay.... Such, too, the fate the negro must deplore, / If slavery guard his subject race no more." For all Grayson's fanciful archaism of style and form, the point of this comparison was to link Indians and free blacks together as relics of a departed age. Together they were no more than "helpless wanderers," innate inferiors whose sufferings might elicit compassion but whose destruction was required by modern civilization.[77]

So what part could these "subject race[s]" hope to play in the progress of this civilization? Turning his eye to "Hayti's plains," Grayson sketched out the approaching struggle to redeem "the tropic wild" from its current state of decay:

> But even, in climes like this, a fated power
> In patient ambush waits the coming hour....
>   And Europe's multitudes again demand
> Its boundless riches from the willing land
>   That now, in vain luxuriance, idly lies,
> And yields no harvest to the genial skies....
>
>   Then shall the ape of empire meet its doom,
> Black peer and prince their ancient task resume,
>   Renounce the mimicries of war and state,
>   And useful labor strive to emulate.
>   Why peril, then, the Negro's humble joys,
> Why make him free, if freedom but destroys?[78]

Grayson's vision of a revived slavery stretched from Haiti to South America and eventually to "Congo's suppliant shore," where American blacks, improved and empowered by their enslavement, would spread "civilizing art" across the African continent.

It was the task of the "Brain of the New World," Walt Whitman later wrote, "To formulate the Modern—out of the peerless grandeur of the modern.... To limn with absolute faith the mighty living present."[79] In "The Hireling and the Slave" Grayson attempted nothing less than this: the poetic formulation of a particular vision of modernity, in which slavery's "mighty living present" and irresistible future were the central objects in view. Grayson's portrait of the modern illustrated nearly all the key elements of proslavery's absolute faith: the strict law of racial hierarchy, the simultaneous economic and paternal value of coercion, and the defeat of the black Haitian "ape of empire" by the coming Euro-American Age of Empire. It was above all a vision that looked forward, not backward, as Grayson's description of the mechanized African future made clear: "In iron lines continuous roads proceed, / And steam outstrips the ostrich in its speed."[80]

Black slaves and other coerced inferiors, slaveholders understood, were needed to build those railroads and to generate that steam. Their labor constituted a vital element of midcentury modernity, as indispensable and as inescapable as global capitalism, imperial power, or the technological cunning of "the master-race" itself.[81] The question in the 1850s was not whether the slaveholding United States had a role to play in the building of this modern world. The question was what exactly that role would be.

8

Foreign Policy amid Domestic Crisis

IN LATE FEBRUARY 1854 Virginia senator Robert Mercer Taliaferro Hunter rose from his seat to speak on the Kansas-Nebraska bill. Among the augustly named men who populated the political leadership of the antebellum South, Hunter cut an unexceptional figure. He had fought no duels, killed no Mexicans, and, relative to men like Robert Barnwell Rhett or William Lowndes Yancey, ate very little fire. In college his initials had earned him the nickname "Run Mad Tom," but neither his persona nor his political career owed much to excitement or, indeed, locomotion. With his heavy brows and massive head, thick torso and bedraggled waistcoat, Senator Hunter's appearance suggested unpretentious dignity, to his friends, or vegetable torpor, to his opponents. "It is unfortunate," mused his sympathetic son, "that all of Pa's compliments to his mind are the reverse to his person." Even these compliments, such as they were, tended to have a quality of equivocation. "I think he is the sanest, if not the wisest, man in our new-born Confederacy," Mary Chesnut, who liked him, wrote seven years later.[1]

But across the 1850s Hunter's lumpish sanity earned him a larger share of national influence than many of his more charismatic rivals possessed. As the senior senator from the South's most populous state, chairman of the Finance Committee, and a key member of the formidable F Street Mess—a Washington boardinghouse that served as unofficial headquarters for proslavery politics in the capital—Hunter was one of the most powerful men in the Senate.[2] And during the fierce sectional debate over slavery in the Kansas-Nebraska territory, it was the Virginian's sturdy and conventionally southern convictions, no less than his seniority or chairmanship, that

Robert M. T. Hunter.
"His physique would
attract no inspection
in public from either
sex; and his quietness
of demeanor on the
floor of the Senate
would not designate
to the stranger . . . the
triarch of the slavery
party in Congress."
Quoted in John
Savage, *Our Living and
Representative Men*
(Philadelphia: Childs
and Peterson, 1860),
346. This photograph
from the studio of
Matthew Brady
probably dates from
the 1850s.

made his speech worth hearing. Neither a flame-breathing radical nor an
ambivalent moderate, Hunter was fully aware of his influence. No less an authority than James D. B. De Bow agreed that he stood at "the very head and
front of the States-rights" men in the Senate. When he rose to speak on February 24, 1854, colleagues on both sides of the sectional divide had good
cause to listen.[3]

As befitted his talents and reputation, Hunter began his remarks by dutifully enumerating what were by then already familiar southern arguments
in favor of the Kansas-Nebraska bill. He reviewed the political history of

slavery debates since 1820, adverting briefly to the South's patriotic spirit of self-sacrifice, while politely declining to dwell at great length on the North's monstrous inflexibility. He clambered into a thicket of constitutional law and emerged with the not-entirely-unexpected discovery that Congress, in fact, possessed only limited control over the organization of new territories and lacked the legal power to forbid slavery in any of them. He took notice of the latest demographic trends, as reported by the 1850 census, and ventured the comforting observation that even if slavery were extended to every state in the Union, the rapid increase of the white population in the North meant that black bondage would be very unlikely to overwhelm the free states.[4]

Near the end of his ninety-minute speech, however, Hunter ventured onto less familiar ground. Without retracting any of his earlier declamations about the seriousness of the constitutional crisis, the senator paused to consider the entire Kansas-Nebraska controversy from an international perspective. Suddenly, he found its significance wanting. "We stand on the eve of a general European war," he observed, referring to ongoing tensions in the Crimea between Britain, France, Russia, and Ottoman Turkey. With these great powers poised to collide in battle and the "commerce of the world" wavering in the balance, Hunter asked, would the United States let itself be "distracted and divided here at home upon the miserable, pitiful question as to the mode in which a given number of slaves are to be divided between the country east and that west of the Mississippi river?" Rather than engage in this petty bickering, Hunter declared, the nation should be "consolidating our columns for the great march which is before us"—the larger international struggle that would define the rest of the nineteenth century.[5]

As he talked on, it emerged that even this very earthbound Virginian— "[H]e resembles some quiet unpretending farmer," wrote one journalist, "who might have come up from a rural district, to sit in a State legislature"—was capable of viewing minor American squabbles from the magnificent heights of global politics.[6] The foundation of those politics, Hunter believed, was the necessary expansion of "the Anglo-American population" all across the earth. "It is plain that in the course of this progress, ours must rule all inferior races." The fate of slavery in a specific western province, no matter how it was decided, could not dislodge this great fact. But how should such a racialized global order be managed? While Hunter accepted the inevitability of "Anglo" expansion, he was sharply critical of Great Britain's imperial policy: the British, he proclaimed, too often appeared "amongst nations composed of different races as intermeddlers and architects of ruin." The United States must pursue a different course. "The welfare of neighboring nations which are composed of different races," Hunter argued, "depends upon the possession of power by that which is the superior of them all." American respect for the natural hierarchy of races—that is, white supremacy—offered the best hope for prosperity and peace in Latin America.[7]

Hunter's speech, appearing as it did in the thick of the Kansas-Nebraska debate, demonstrates the continuing importance of international politics, even amid the darkest moments of domestic crisis. Few chronologies in U.S. political history are as familiar as the one that preceded the breakup of the Union. The Compromise of 1850, the Kansas-Nebraska Act, "bleeding Kansas," the caning of Charles Sumner, the *Dred Scott* decision, John Brown's raid on Harper's Ferry, the election of Abraham Lincoln—the narrative of disunion is as colorful and complex as it is closely studied.[8] The theatrical intensity of these events, however, has an unfortunate tendency to obscure the importance of what was happening outside national borders. But as Hunter's remarks suggest, even the most dramatic sectional clashes unfolded in a political atmosphere regularly informed by, and strongly sensitive to, the larger universe of world affairs.

Hunter's approach to the Kansas-Nebraska question was structured not only by the conservative creed of states' rights but also by a keen interest in international commerce, foreign relations, and the global spread of empire. His irritation at the "pitiful" scale of the Nebraska debate as compared with these great questions, emerged out of this larger worldview. Within the boundaries of U.S. national affairs, Hunter well understood, the slaveholding South played a part that was small and likely to grow smaller. Population growth in the North, not to mention the spread of antislavery feeling, was making the South a permanent and embattled minority. In this domestic context proslavery politics were bound to be both conservative and defensive—reliant on the narrowest possible readings of history, law, and the Constitution. Hunter had offered these readings in the first hour of his speech.

But from an international point of view, such narrowness was obnoxious and even embarrassing. For if slavery seemed to be losing strength within the domestic councils of American politics, it was only growing stronger on the world stage. Hunter's vision of a ceaseless and unstoppable Anglo advance was also a vision of rapidly expanding black slavery. As the "great Caucasian hive" made its way across the hemisphere, "we shall have to establish some law that would respect the true relations of the races." Black bondsmen, in other words, must travel in tandem with the great white horde. In this sense it was not just the United States but the slave-holding South that stood on the vanguard of international progress. As the home base of an institution that could remake the tropical world and as a successful laboratory for the inevitable race ordering that must await the expansion of Anglo empire, the South occupied a position of particular significance.[9]

Yet for all his proslavery enthusiasm, Hunter retained a national frame of mind. "When I look to the high mission upon which we are sent—the great destiny which is within our reach," Hunter insisted, almost peevishly, "I can scarcely feel the patience which becomes me in dealing with those who have interposed such obstacles." The entire Kansas-Nebraska crisis was a blip on his imperial radar. Despite the looming danger of sectional discord, Hunter still believed that the United States could summon its "united energies" to play a great part on the world stage. "The empire of the seas," he announced, "the all-mastering influence of a great example, and the foremost place in the march of civilization, are the prizes to which we may justly aspire." These lofty goals could be achieved only through a foreign policy that respected the larger racial truths wrought by Anglo-American global dominance.[10]

In his confidence about the future global roles of both section and nation, Hunter revealed the extent to which late antebellum slaveholding leaders—even the most conventional and conservative—remained committed to an ambitious vision of American international power. The domestic battles of the decade, for all their corrosive intensity, did not destroy slaveholders' faith in the ability of the United States to advance the interests of the South in the wider world. Having enjoyed proximate access to American foreign policy since the Revolution, slaveholders were not quick to abandon it in the 1850s. Historians have come to reckon with the South's imperial interest in Latin America, and especially the frantic desire to obtain new slave territory through negotiated purchase or armed filibuster invasion.[11] But the South's most powerful slaveholders, including Hunter, put a higher priority on preserving slavery than on acquiring territory and, for much of the decade, placed their trust in the U.S. government rather than private filibusters. The march of civilization in the Western Hemisphere, as they understood it, required both slave labor and American state power alike.

The School of American Diplomacy

If 1848 was a tumultuous year for Europe, it was a triumphant one for the United States. Americans especially relished their army's victory in Mexico, consolidated that year by the Treaty of Guadalupe Hidalgo and crowned with half a million square miles of new land in the Southwest. The military triumph in Mexico not only demonstrated to a skeptical world the prowess of America's armed forces but also wonderfully enhanced the nation's strategic position. Any European attempt to meddle in hemispheric affairs would have to reckon with a continental empire that now stretched from the Texas flatlands all the way to San Francisco Bay. America's newfound might, predicted Jefferson Davis, one of the South's freshly minted war heroes, "will probably secure to the United States a long exemption from foreign aggression."[12]

Unfortunately for slaveholding elites, the war could offer no comparable exemption from domestic conflict. In the years immediately following the 1848 treaty, southerners in Congress fought doggedly to assure that they and their slaves would not be kept out of the lands taken from Mexico. The battles grew especially bitter after 1849, when the war hero and Whig President Zachary Taylor attempted to admit the territories of California and New Mexico into the Union as free states. Only a fortuitous combination of events in the summer of 1850, including Taylor's sudden death, allowed Congress to pass successful compromise legislation that fall. Lawmakers admitted California, organized New Mexico and Utah with territorial governments, settled the Texas border question, abolished the slave trade in the District of Columbia, and established a more stringent fugitive slave law. Southern reaction to these agreements was mixed. In some Lower South states radical leaders threatened secession and attempted to repudiate the compromise measures through state elections. Although their efforts failed, and sectional rancor abated for a few years, the bitter fights over slavery in the Nebraska Territory, starting in 1854, showed that tensions between North and South were only very superficially pacified by the "armistice of 1850."[13]

From an international perspective, though, things did not look nearly so bad. Increasingly secure about their economic and ideological relationship with the modern world, proslavery foreign policy elites in the long 1850s also felt a new geopolitical confidence. The triumph of free trade in Parliament, Calhoun declared in 1846, "put an end to the hazard of war" with Great

Britain. And the U.S. conquest of Mexico, as one Florida congressman argued, seemed to show that Britain and other European states had given up trying to enforce a balance of power in the Americas: "They are now disposed to acquiesce in our manifest destiny." The dark hours of the early 1840s had passed; British power in the Western Hemisphere no longer presented such an imminent or existential threat to the security of slavery.[14]

To be sure, southern fears about abolitionist subversions in the Caribbean did not disappear in the 1850s. But the position of proslavery and antislavery forces had shifted decisively. Before 1845 the strongest forces troubling the hemispheric balance of power still carried the momentum of British emancipation in 1833: the real and imagined rebellions, reforms, and diplomatic meddling that disturbed existing slave regimes in Cuba, Brazil, and Texas. After 1848 the strongest destabilizing forces came from slaveholders themselves—filibuster invasions of Cuba and Central America, pugnacious diplomacy across the Caribbean, and aggressive boasts about a reenslavement of all tropical America.[15] Before the war with Mexico, the U.S. foreign policy of slavery had been an essentially defensive action. But that action had succeeded, and by midcentury it seemed to have borne significant fruit, most notably in Great Britain's willingness to accept strategic parity with the slaveholding United States. In 1849 the essayist William Henry Trescot spoke for many southern elites when he envisioned a new era of Anglo-American partnership in the hemisphere: "The abandonment by England of her corn laws; the repeal of her navigation laws ... prove ... that she is willing to share with her offspring of the West, the divided allegiance of the world."[16]

Few southerners thought more extensively about the United States' postwar strategic situation than Trescot. A Charleston-educated lawyer and low-country Carolina planter, he was also, perhaps, the most formidable American foreign policy intellectual of the 1850s. Over the course of the decade Trescot authored two book-length diplomatic histories of the early United States and contributed a stream of influential pamphlets on subjects that ranged from reform of the diplomatic corps to the Crimean War in Europe. His career, like R. M. T. Hunter's speech, offers a valuable window into the way in which proslavery elites managed the dilemma of sectional anxiety and international confidence in the 1850s.[17]

Trescot's 1850 essay *The Position and Course of the South* presented a dryly geopolitical case for southern secession. The admission of California as a free state, he wrote, testified to the South's growing weakness within the

Union: "[B]y recent legislation, the Federal Government has declared itself the ally of the North" and the enemy of "the institutions of the South." But southern power abroad was undiminished. Like other proslavery internationalists, Trescot believed that the economic failure of West Indian emancipation had "taught England never again to sacrifice her profits to her philanthropy." While European antislavery dwindled, trade in raw materials boomed; advances in transportation and manufacturing brought distant nations into a single commercial web. "[L]ike the nervous system of the human body," Trescot argued with a characteristically scientific metaphor, "this subtle and all pervading conductor . . . spreads from one great centre—the cotton trade." Through its command of cotton, the slave South practically held "the fortunes of the world in its hand." Given the South's surplus of international power and deficit of national influence, Trescot concluded, slavery would be safer outside the Union than in it. Slaveholding southerners should seize their destiny and secede at once.[18]

Unlike Hunter, who appealed to America's global greatness as a way of belittling a merely local argument about slavery, Trescot made sectional friction the basis of his entire foreign policy analysis. Yet in some sense Trescot was the secessionist exception who proved the nationalist rule. As the whole of his career reveals, Trescot's desire for southern independence was not incompatible with a desire to enhance and extend the international power of the United States.

A year before he published *The Position and Course of the South,* Trescot composed a less well-known pamphlet on the subject of American foreign relations. Under the misleadingly modest title *A Few Thoughts on the Foreign Policy of the United States,* it argued that the nation must claim its true status as a world power. For Trescot, the age-old commitment to republican isolationism had become, in the era of continental empire and transoceanic commerce, little more than an anachronistic taboo. "[A]re not the interests of the United States sufficiently extended—its power sufficiently strong," he asked, "that it should be part and parcel of any great political transaction which affects the history of the world?" The foreign policy vision of George Washington did not suit the age of James K. Polk.[19]

Like other proslavery thinkers of the 1850s, Trescot understood rising American power in the context of European imperial expansion. Turning a sympathetic eye to Great Britain's empire in Asia, he defended its color-conscious social organization: "The connection between the Anglo-Saxon race and the Asiatic nations, on a footing of perfect equality, has never

existed, and . . . can never exist." The British government in India, unlike in
the postemancipation West Indies, had succeeded in establishing a benevo-
lently rigid racial and economic order. Now that Britain had acknowledged
"her utter West Indian failure," Trescot believed that the spread of Anglo-
Saxon colonialism was good both for the world in general and for Americans
in particular. He called for the United States to join Britain in establishing a
favorable balance of power—imperial, racial, and commercial—all across
the globe, from East Asia to the Mediterranean Sea. If an "intelligent Asiatic"
were to embark on a tour of the international cotton trade, from "the plantations of the South" to "the looms of Manchester," Trescot argued, he would
see clearly that this chain of "immense capital, large experience, and unwea-
ried toil" constituted a single and irresistibly powerful global unit. American
slavery and British imperialism could work hand in hand to remake the
world in their common image.[20]

It was just this prospect of an Anglo-southern alliance that encouraged
Trescot's secessionist prescriptions a year later. In *Position and Course* Trescot
sought to relocate the national greatness of *A Few Thoughts* entirely within
the slaveholding South, and to harness the imperial energies of the United
States from inside a strictly southern confederacy, closely aligned with
Great Britain. But the evolution of Trescot's career made it clear that even
after 1850 he did not abandon all hope in the imperial or proslavery power
of the U.S. government. Despite the candor of his secessionist commitment, he did not spend the rest of the decade agitating for southern independence or fulminating against American national power. Instead, like
Jefferson Davis and other influential southerners who also rejected compromise and threatened disunion, Trescot passed the next ten years working
in behalf of that power. The position and course of the South in 1850 may
have argued for secession, but the position and course of William Henry
Trescot in the 1850s argued for the persistence of proslavery nationalism.

In 1852 Trescot became secretary of the U.S. legation in London, a post
he held until 1854; later, in 1860, he served as assistant secretary of state
under President James Buchanan. From these perches, and as a private citizen in Washington and Charleston, Trescot continued to advocate for a
larger American role in world affairs. His essay on the Crimean War suggested that the United States expand its influence in Europe and urged, in
the meantime, the construction of an American navy that was "commen-
surate" with America's overseas commerce, the second largest in the world.
An 1854 article in the *Southern Quarterly Review* praised the statesmanship of

Massachusetts Whig Edward Everett, whose vigorous rejection of an Anglo-French guarantee for Spanish Cuba rightly identified the United States as "the leading power of this western world." And Trescot's 1853 letter to South Carolina senator Andrew P. Butler, later published as a pamphlet, demanded a thorough reform of the U.S. foreign service, higher diplomatic salaries, and a formal recognition that foreign policy mattered more than ever in an age of "increasing closeness of national relations." The United States, he concluded, stood in need of a diplomatic system "calculated to secure and protect the sort of national reputation" the country deserved.[21]

In this regard Trescot's 1850s attitudes were not so different from his views in 1849. "This much is certain," he had predicted in his earlier essay; "in the future relations of the world, our part is destined to be a great one." The "school of American diplomacy" should be "governed as to its ends, by a strong sense of national power, and a solemn conviction of national responsibility." This was a view Trescot never abandoned, even in the maelstrom of sectional controversy. Although his doubts about the Union surely lingered after 1850, Trescot nevertheless saw the national state as a legitimate vehicle for southern and even proslavery power. Everett's forceful Cuba diplomacy, he declared, showed once and for all that "a question characteristically southern, may yet be essentially national." In the universe of world politics, at least, American slavery and American power remained inseparable.[22]

This basic paradigm held for the bulk of the South's political leadership across the 1850s. Regardless of their attitude toward sectional compromise, the most influential slaveholding elites remained deeply invested in the project of national power building. In debates about foreign policy in Latin America and the Caribbean basin, southern leaders demonstrated again and again the strength of their attachment to the international might of the United States.

———————

The U.S. invasion of Mexico in 1846 set the orientation of American foreign relations for the next fourteen years. The South, following Matthew Maury's dictum, was finally looking to the south, although what slaveholders saw there often depended on the eye of the beholder. For some, including Maury himself, the greater Caribbean basin beckoned with unimaginable economic opportunity. For others, Caribbean commerce meant, above all, a conduit between the Atlantic and Pacific Oceans across the Central American isthmus. The 1849 gold rush in the former Mexican province of California triggered the first serious U.S.-led efforts to build an isthmian transit route, and the most successful of these, the Panama Railroad, opened for business in 1855.[23]

Most sensational, of course, were the Americans who looked to the south not merely for commerce but for conquest. The years after the war with Mexico witnessed a number of American efforts to extend the triumphs of Veracruz and Chapultepec by organizing private invasions of Latin American countries. Several mercenary American armies attempted to "liberate" Spanish Cuba; the Tennessee adventurer William Walker conquered and briefly ruled Nicaragua. In the end, these filibuster missions failed without exception, but their efflorescence from 1848 to 1860—a phenomenon unmatched before or since—is one token of the way in which Latin America and the Caribbean occupied U.S. foreign relations in the long decade between the Treaty of Guadalupe Hidalgo and the attack on Fort Sumter.[24]

Propelled by an imperial belief in America's "manifest destiny," often linked to their own economic interests, southern slaveholders played an outsized part in most of these endeavors. Many southern elites hoped the filibuster missions might produce new slave states, and thus new slaveholding legislators to offset the North in Congress.[25] One explanation for the slaveholding South's interest in Latin America in this period groups these activities under the umbrella of proslavery expansionism—commercial, imperial, and, above all, territorial. Yet ultimately this expansionist impulse produced very little actual expansion. The only new territory acquired was an arid slice of Sonora purchased from Mexico by U.S. minister James Gadsden in 1853—land meant for a southern transcontinental railroad that was not built until long after the slave South disappeared. The most persuasive historical treatments of the era have concluded that proslavery expansionism in the 1850s failed not only because of sectional cleavages between North and South but also because the South itself was deeply divided on the issue. While dauntless Gulf Coast Democrats cried loudly for more territory, Upper South moderates, cautious Whigs and ex-Whigs, and even southeastern conservatives generally opposed the most aggressive schemes of expansion.[26]

Under these fault lines, however, lay a relatively sturdy southern consensus. For all their political differences, both the most excitable southern expansionists and the most cautious southern conservatives approached Caribbean and Latin American diplomacy from the same two fundamental premises. First, their understanding of politics in the region was grounded in a deep concern about the security of slave labor. As in the 1840s, when Tyler, Calhoun, and other southern leaders had organized American foreign policy around a hemispheric defense of slavery, both expansionists and conservatives in the 1850s made the preservation of bound labor their top priority in the Caribbean basin.[27]

No question in all the fraught Anglo-American diplomacy concerning Central America so inflamed southern elites as the rumored British attempt to "exclude slavery from Honduras," as Jefferson Davis put it in 1857. Although the radical filibusterism of William Walker divided southern opinions, Walker's last-ditch attempt to install slavery in Nicaragua in late 1856 made him the darling of many slaveholding leaders for the rest of the decade.[28] Even Virginia senator James Murray Mason, chairman of the Foreign Affairs Committee and a prototypical eastern conservative who opposed Walker's expeditions, kept his eyes peeled for abolitionist activity in the Caribbean. In 1855 Mason accused Great Britain and France of opposing U.S. influence in the Dominican Republic by making common cause with "the African race" and offering to block American slavery. Two years later North Carolina congressman Thomas Clingman issued perhaps the boldest of the decade's many portentous warnings that the entire British West Indies might one day be seized and reenslaved by the United States.[29]

Second, slaveholders of all political stripes agreed that American policy in the region should be guided by an understanding that the United States, not Great Britain or any other nation, must be the dominant strategic power in the hemisphere. Despite their disagreements on how exactly America should secure and preserve this regional hegemony, both expansionists and conservatives agreed that hegemony was the ultimate objective. Only the most radical proslavery expansionists linked aggressive filibustering to purely sectional disunionism; and only the most timid conservatives suggested that the United States accept permanent parity with another nation in Latin America.[30] In this regard, too, slaveholders' approach to the Caribbean basin in the 1850s remained of a piece with the precedent established a decade earlier. Although both the domestic and international balances of power may have shifted in the ten years between the presidencies of John Tyler and Franklin Pierce, southern confidence in the proslavery capacity of U.S. power in Latin America remained remarkably consistent.

"It is but too evident," remarked De Bow, "that the destinies of America are in *our* hands." Across the 1850s the muddy politics of isthmian transit resisted clear sectional or ideological divisions; competing business interests, multiple route plans, and the rival scheme for a transcontinental railroad all jostled for influence in Washington. But one theme that emerged from the debates in Congress was the southern willingness to deploy U.S. power in Latin America. Matthew Maury's strict Virginia constructionism became almost comically loose when he considered the possibility of a railway across Panama. "The principle of the 'greatest good to the greatest number' is one of the pillars of the Constitution," he argued in 1849, sensibly declining to provide a citation for this intrepid piece of textual criticism. Technical details like constitutional precedent simply had no role to play in a question that involved American power and the future of global commerce. The U.S. government, said Maury, should stop fussing and take active control of Central America's "common highway" at once.[31]

No space on "the southern continent," announced James M. Mason in 1853, was so "purely of a domestic character" as the Isthmus of Tehuantepec in Mexico. Emptying right into "our own domestic basin, the Gulf of Mexico," and relatively removed from all other foreign powers, Tehuantepec was virtually American territory. By virtue of its geographic position, Mason argued, the United States had "a right of way across Tehuantepec.... Mexico cannot refuse it unless she becomes disloyal to the general compact of nations." Such a flexible conception of both constitutional theory and international law characterized southern sponsors of Central American transit, whether their cause was in Panama, Mexico, or Nicaragua.[32]

America's strategic reach, as proslavery politicians understood it, extended past the Caribbean and deep into the Southern Hemisphere. Slaveholders pressured Brazil to grant free navigation of the Amazon River, urged the United States to secure control of guano-rich islands off the Peruvian coast, and demanded that the Buchanan administration respond with force to an insult suffered by an American ship in Paraguayan waters.[33] An indulgence for South American abuses, Mason lamented in 1858, had weakened U.S. influence across the continent. "[W]hile other nations immediately redress wrongs that are committed against their Governments," U.S. responses were "always tardy" and thus only "proportionally received and respected." The "semi-barbarians" of Latin America, Mason implied, could understand only a demonstration of force, and there was no reason that the United States should hesitate to make that demonstration.[34]

But for all the South's interest in the wider Latin world, the focus of slaveholding attention in the 1850s remained Cuba. Southern elites certainly envisioned the future reenslavement of the free West Indies, but for the present they were most urgently concerned with protecting slave institutions where they still existed. If African slavery were ever to return to Haiti or Jamaica, one essayist predicted in 1853, then it must first be sustained in the Caribbean's largest island: "Cuba thus becomes the hinge or turning point of the future." In the contest between emancipated "savageism" and slaveholding civilization—"the greatest question of modern times"—Cuba remained the central theater. And the U.S. government remained slaveholders' most powerful and most reliable ally.[35]

A Kindred and Slaveholding Republic

After the various slave insurrection panics of the early 1840s, politics in Cuba settled into a steadier rhythm. Spanish governors in the second half of the decade took some limited steps to curtail the African slave trade, but enough new Africans arrived for the Cuban slave economy to sustain its considerable prosperity. Southern representatives in Europe still worried that foreign influence in Spain might produce "a free negro dependency" in Cuba, but for the most part, the facts on the ground militated against any proslavery panics. After 1850 the slave trade surged back into full form, and by the end of the decade it had reached heights unprecedented in the island's history. More slaves, rising demand in Europe, and fewer tariff restrictions all accelerated Cuba's sugar boom. In the twenty-five years before the American Civil War, total Cuban sugar production more than quadrupled; during the 1850s the island's slaves generated a full quarter of the world's sugar supply.[36]

Economic abundance, however, did not guarantee political stability. Although Cuba's increasingly prosperous Creoles sometimes chafed under the grip of Spanish military rule, the gravest threat to Cuba came from the restive United States. After the war with Mexico, the Polk administration first approached Spain with an offer to buy the island for the sum of $100 million. Despite the substantial price—Mexico had only received $15 million for half of western North America—it was rejected at once. (There is little evidence that Spain ever seriously considered any of the innumerable American purchase proposals between 1848 and 1860.) The more insidious danger for Spanish authorities was a U.S.-sponsored local insurrection, combined with a private invasion of Cuban émigrés and American filibusters. A rebellion against the ruling government, receiving informal aid from the U.S., blossoming into a contested independence, and culminating with formal annexation into the United States—this was, after all, how the acquisition of Texas had been accomplished.[37]

Between 1849 and 1851 the Venezuelan adventurer Narciso López mounted three major filibuster invasions aimed at the "liberation" of Spanish Cuba. All three departed from American shores and were manned primarily by American soldiers. The first attempt was foiled when a U.S. Navy cruiser stopped the filibusters' ship off the coast of Mississippi; the second landed successfully in Cuba but was driven off by Spanish troops; the third and final invasion failed to generate popular support and ended with the execution of López and over fifty of his American mercenaries. None of López's expeditions ever really threatened Spanish rule in Cuba, but they did leave an impact on politics in the United States, especially in the South.

Enthusiasm for the military "liberation" of Cuba extended beyond the slaveholding states; New York, as well as New Orleans, emerged as a hub for filibustering recruitment and organization. But without the support of southern expansionists, it is doubtful whether López's missions would ever have left port. Although both Jefferson Davis and Robert E. Lee declined to take command of a Cuban invasion force, the men who fought in López's army were disproportionately southern in origin. Their chief political backers, too, largely hailed from the South. Decrying the oppression of Spanish monarchical rule in Cuba while noting the political advantages of a possible U.S. annexation, southern expansionists celebrated López's filibusters and mourned his final defeat in 1851.[38]

But the most influential minds of the South were conflicted on the issue. The Gulf South remained consistently enthusiastic about Caribbean expansion, but powerful southeastern senators like Mason, R. M. T. Hunter, and Andrew Butler of South Carolina opposed an aggressive American pursuit of Cuba. Their reluctance did not stem from any fundamental doubts about the capacity of the United States to dominate the Caribbean or possess its most important island. "[T]he fruit," Mason predicted, "will ripen"; Cuba's connection with the United States was "inevitable." What worried the anti-expansionists was the possibility that premature American aggression would trigger a violent slave emancipation, spoiling the fruit for good. Few southern leaders, no matter how devoted to expansionism, believed that the United States could digest a meal so unpalatable as a free black Cuba. Mississippi's

Albert Gallatin Brown, a leading advocate of the filibusters, admitted that "a vast amount of my zeal and enthusiasm [for Cuba] would ooze out very suddenly if I knew it was coming in as a free state."[39]

In other words, the central issue was still the safety of Cuba's slave system. Ohio's Joshua Giddings, no longer such a lonely antislavery voice on Capitol Hill, told Congress as much in 1852. The recent publication of Spanish-American diplomatic correspondence, he alleged, "shows to the country and the civilized world, that for thirty years the Executive has exerted our national influence to maintain slavery in Cuba, in order that the institution be rendered more secure in the United States." No American filibustering army, he predicted correctly, would again invade Cuba, because the Spanish colonial government had vowed to free the island's slaves in that event. And southern elites, Giddings concluded, "have no object in obtaining Cuba, unless they can thereby obtain it with slavery."[40]

This was indeed the dilemma. In the event of an American invasion of Cuba, the U.S. envoy to Spain informed his government in 1852, "secret orders have been issued to emancipate the slaves & place arms in their hands for the conquest and maintenance of their own rule & authority in the island." Cuba, declared the Spanish press, "must always be either *Spanish* or *African*." Such talk made leading southern statesmen wary. A peaceful annexation of Cuba, R. M. T. Hunter wrote a Georgia correspondent, would be a great boon for the South. "Cuba with War and a general emancipation of slaves," on the other hand, "would probably get up a contest both at home and abroad which would be more dangerous to the South than any through which we have yet passed." A "single act" by Spain, noted Virginia's Charles Faulkner in 1852, could convert Cuba from a beautiful blessing into a foul curse. The United States must walk a fine line in the upper Caribbean. An "honorable and peaceful purchase" was desirable, but rash acts that stirred Spanish "resentment to us" brought more danger than opportunity.[41]

Some southerners even argued that Cuba was more valuable as a Spanish colony than as a state in the American union. "It would be bad policy for us to acquire Cuba—slaveholding Cuba as it is . . . so long as it can be peaceably held by Spain," declared North Carolina congressman Abraham Venable. "Spain is now interested, and Brazil is interested in preserving th[e] institution" of African slavery. If a unilateral American seizure of Cuba damaged this coalition of powers, it might actually weaken slavery's global clout. William Trescot agreed, arguing that an independent Cuba—free from Spain but still possessed of its slaves—represented the optimal outcome for the United States. "A kindred and slave-holding republic," he observed, would strengthen slavery abroad without inviting a divisive political debate at home. The certain economic success of this regional ally would exercise a benevolent influence over the "community of islands in the Gulf." Hinting at the possible reestablishment of slavery in the emancipated West Indies, Trescot hoped that a prosperous, independent Cuba might restore "well regulated liberty, and profitable industry" to the region and "retrieve the future, and recompense the past, of these beautiful, but stricken lands."[42]

The failure of López's expeditions temporarily quieted the most militant elements within the South. The election of Franklin Pierce as president in 1852, however, raised the prospect of a new round of proslavery expansionism. Pierce hailed from New Hampshire, but he owed his presidency to southern Democratic votes, and his key administrative personnel reflected this reality. The president-elect initially asked R. M. T. Hunter to serve as secretary of state; when the Virginian decided to remain in the Senate, Pierce gave the job to the veteran New York Democrat William Marcy. But aside from Marcy and James Buchanan, sent as minister to Great Britain, Pierce's foreign policy establishment was dominated by proslavery southerners: Jefferson Davis of Mississippi as secretary of war, James Dobbin of North Carolina as secretary of the navy, John Y. Mason of Virginia as minister to France, Pierre Soulé of Louisiana as minister to Spain, and Ambrose Dudley Mann of Virginia as assistant secretary of state. The rank and file of the diplomatic corps, especially in Latin America, also tilted heavily toward the South: after 1854, among the major countries bordering the Caribbean Sea, only Venezuela was represented by an American envoy from a nonslaveholding state.[43]

While the antislavery press denounced Pierce's "slave-breeding diplomacy," slaveholders were elated. Pierce had formed "an Administration which will defend the institution of slavery with every resource of Executive power," declared one Richmond editorialist. "There was never a time," gushed another, "when the South has had better reason for giving an administration its full and entire confidence than now." Southerners who remembered the Tyler-Upshur-Calhoun axis in the early 1840s might have differed with this assessment, but it was clear that the Pierce administration had great regard for slaveholding interests, both at home and abroad.[44]

In contrast to the Whiggish conservatism of his predecessor, Millard Fillmore, the new president promised a forceful American presence in foreign affairs. "[O]ur attitude as a nation and our position on the globe," Pierce

declared in his inaugural address, "render the acquisition of certain possessions not within our jurisdiction eminently important for our protection."[45] Both American power and American institutions, the president
implied none too delicately, might require the annexation of Cuba. To be
sure, Pierce's turn toward the Caribbean did not grow wholly out of his ties
to the proslavery South. It also reflected the expansionistic ardor of the national Democratic Party—and the sweeping imperial vision of the Young
America movement. Yet even in the exuberant year of 1853, with the sectional controversy perhaps quieter than at any time in the past seven years,
the administration's Democratic nationalism remained extensively concerned with Cuban slavery.[46]

In July Secretary of State Marcy wrote Buchanan in London and Soulé
in Madrid with new instructions to investigate rumors of a possible Cuban
slave emancipation. From the broader perspective of midcentury U.S. anxieties about Cuban slavery, nothing in the medley of emancipationist gossip
that worried Marcy was particularly original or striking. Spanish plans to
"render the island worthless" through slave abolition, "whenever she clearly
perceives that she can no longer retain possession," had troubled potential
annexationists for years. A supposed Anglo-French security guarantee for
Spanish Cuba, offered in return for "a change in the internal condition of
the island," was a long-standing American fear. And no Cuban bugaboo
had a longer tenure in Washington than the British abolitionist design to "fill
that Island with emigrants from Africa," eventually converting it into "an
African Colony." Marcy's racial nightmare scenarios, no less than his euphe-
misms for Cuban slavery, could each have been borrowed intact from the
era of Webster, Upshur, and Calhoun.[47]

Above all, the secretary of state's instructions made it clear that it was
the social rather than the political condition of Cuba that most concerned
the United States. "Cuba, whatever be its colonial condition, whether a dependency or a sovereign state," Marcy wrote Buchanan, "is, of necessity our
neighbor. . . . [I]t is imperative upon us to require from it, whatever may be
its condition, all the observances imposed by good neighborhood." Changes
to the Cuban social system, "particularly in regard to the slaves now there,
or to the present system of labor," Marcy wrote, might cause the island to
become "an instrument of annoyance" to the United States. For the Pierce
administration, no act could be less neighborly than the liberation of several
hundred thousand black bondspeople.[48]

If Marcy's initial instructions already betrayed significant concern
about the security of Cuban slavery, events later in the year deepened that

concern into paranoia. The trouble began in the autumn of 1853 with the arrival of a new Spanish captain general in Cuba. Juan de la Pezuela was a former governor of Puerto Rico who had earned a reputation as an enemy of slavery—an opponent of African trafficking, a persecutor of cruel masters, and a friend to abused slaves.[49] From Madrid Soulé reported that Pezuela had been selected "on account of the violent prejudices he was supposed, and with truth, to entertain against us (the yankees)." The appointment, he feared, reflected the Spanish government's decision to appease Great Britain by liberating "all Africans imported into the Island since 1821. . . . If the admission is acted upon rigidly, Cuba has ceased to have a slave."[50]

In truth, Pezuela's intentions were not so clear. Certainly he did not seek to destroy Cuban slave society. But during the winter of 1853–54 the new captain general issued a flurry of decrees that rattled the nerves of slaveholders on both sides of the Florida Straits. New and more extensive punishments for slave traders were announced; a precedent-breaking order allowing racial intermarriage was signed; and steps were taken to establish a new militia that would include free black troops. In January Pezuela released a proclamation that formally liberated all slaves unlawfully imported to Cuba since 1835. In May, he empowered Spanish authorities to search any Cuban plantation suspected of holding such contraband labor. Soulé had reason to worry. If the new decrees were enforced—and more than at any time in Cuba's recent past, it appeared they might be—the island's entire slave system was in jeopardy.[51]

American slaveholders tracked these events with alarm. Even before the new captain general arrived in Havana, the *Richmond Enquirer* lamented the danger of Cuban emancipation, not because it would block American acquisition of the island, but because of its evil consequences for the cause of world slavery. "The *Africanization* of Cuba will isolate the United States from every other Government—will detach the last ally from the support of slavery—will turn the sympathy of Christendom against it, and will erect a fortress of abolitionism on our very border." Southern confidence in the international power of bondage might have been stronger than ever, but Cuba was one domino that slaveholders could not afford to see fall. The result, as Louisiana governor Paul Hébert proclaimed in January 1854, would "add another state to the black empire which would then extend from the mouths of the Oronoco to the outlets of the Mississippi." Hébert demanded immediate action: "Will the federal government, charged with the international interests of States, anticipate the threatened peril?"[52]

Hébert need not have worried about federal indifference. Throughout the winter of 1853–54 Pierce and his cabinet paid close attention to the developing situation in Cuba. Their man in Havana was acting consul William H. Robertson, lately of Mobile by way of New Orleans, and he flooded the State Department with news and rumors relating to Pezuela's antislavery crackdown. In January Robertson reported that Britain and France were sponsoring a program for general Cuban slave emancipation, to be carried out gradually by Spanish authorities over the next several years. A month later he wrote that plans were under way for "a large French and English fleet" to arrive in Havana and help enforce the new policy. In early March Robertson provided the first official news of Spanish authorities' seizure of the U.S. steamer *Black Warrior,* an event that outraged the Democratic press and ratcheted up national attention to developments in Cuba. And in April and May Robertson filled his correspondence with detailed notes on the progress of "the total abolition of slavery in the island."[53]

The most striking feature of Robertson's dispatches was the extent to which they emphasized social rather than political threats to Cuban stability. According to the best-informed residents of Havana, he reported, "the Captain General is about to grant the colored race the right of intermarrying with the whites and also an equality of civil rights." Meanwhile, the Havana newspapers announced a new regulation that required Cuban plantations to "provide land for the negroes to cultivate on their own account, the produce of which they shall be allowed to sell." Robertson considered this direct intrusion into the slave economy "another link in the Africanization chain."[54]

The acting consul was especially eloquent on the subject of the interracial militia, half of which was composed of "colored people.... [T]he number of armed blacks is *intended to be 12.000*—This I can hardly credit— if so, the scenes will indeed be bloody." The consequence of such policies, Robertson predicted, would be the destruction of white supremacy in Cuba: "[T]he moral influence of superiority which to this time, had served as a guaranty for the peace and safety of the whites will disappear like smoke." Cuba's fragile racial order and productive labor system were both endangered. "I do not relate to you the accounts of the growing insolence of the negroes," the consul informed Marcy with evident anxiety. "They speak of the Marquis de la Pezuela as 'titi Juan', or 'Papa Juan', the Patron of Liberty and Equality." Nothing, in Robertson's view, could be more disturbing to American interests than the prospect of Cuban blacks developing an assertive politics of their own.[55]

In March 1854 Pierce and Marcy secretly dispatched Charles W. Davis to Havana, where he was to compile an official report on the possibility of Cuba's "Africanization." No aspect of Cuban labor politics was off-limits for Davis's investigation. Marcy instructed him to learn everything he could about "negro apprenticeship," Yucatánese immigration, and Chinese coolie labor. Most of all, however, Marcy wanted Davis to determine whether Pezuela really contemplated the enforcement of his winter decrees. The governor's plan to liberate all blacks imported since 1835, the secretary noted, "would manumit at least one third of all the slaves on the Island." To see Cuba overrun with free "native Africans, the most debased species of the human race," was an outcome the United States could not tolerate.[56]

Davis's final report, delivered in late May, did not mince words. "The conclusion is irresistible," he began, "that the emancipation of Slaves and consequent Africanization of the Island in the true object had in view." Pezuela, a true "Captain General of Abolition," had embarked on measures that would ensure "the destruction of the wealth of this Island, a disastrous bloody war of the races, [and] a step backwards in the civilization of America." This confirmed what the Pierce administration already believed and was already working to counteract. In early April Marcy directed Soulé in Madrid to begin negotiating for Cuban annexation. Explicitly worried about a "change of policy in Cuba, particularly in regard to supplying the demand for agricultural labor," the secretary authorized Soulé to offer up to $130 million to Spanish officials for U.S. rights to the island.[57]

As it had been for Tyler in Texas in 1844, so it was again for Pierce in Cuba in 1854. A careful eye on international slavery, not a blind instinct toward expansion, dictated the administration's policy. Southern leaders in Congress viewed the situation in Cuba through the same lens. Senator John Slidell of Louisiana noted that for years he had refused to believe the rumors of Cuban emancipation—why, after all, would Spain willingly destroy its most valuable colony? But Pezuela's recent actions betrayed a "concerted plan to Africanize Cuba." The result, intolerable to the United States, would be the formation of a "Black Empire, under a British protectorate," in the center of the Gulf of Mexico. Slidell's Louisiana colleague Judah Benjamin and Florida's Stephen Mallory concurred, with Mallory adding provocative details of Pezuela's latest display of kindness toward Cuban blacks.[58]

The same emphasis on "this question of Cuban Labor," as the *New York Times* put it, characterized the attitude of the proslavery press. "The Southern States of this confederacy," declared the *Richmond Enquirer* in February, "are sensitively alive to any change in the social condition of Cuba, and would never submit to a revolution which would jeopard the stability of their own institutions." The *Charleston Mercury* was even more explicit: "We regard an attempt to Africanize Cuba—to blast with the plague of emancipation that garden of the West, as a crime against civilization, more than all, as a blow aimed at the legitimate progress of this country." Other southern papers denounced Pezuela as an "emancipationist," offered details on the composition of his new black army, and speculated on the horrors that "eight hundred thousand free negroes" might produce if Cuba entered the Union as a free state.[59]

Some contemporary observers, cutting a path later followed by historians, suggested that the Africanization scare was a "hoax," or at least a false alarm deliberately exaggerated to justify the addition of another slave state.[60] But the hysterical tone of southern rhetoric—along with its continual focus on the racial havoc that emancipation would wreak in Cuba—suggests that a good portion of the anxieties were real. Identifying the island's slave society as an extension of their own, slaveholding leaders believed that the U.S. government had a strategic obligation to prevent "such an obscene violation of social life ... as the Africanization of Cuba." The long history of southern attention to Cuba since 1841, moreover, should banish doubts about whether American slaveholders shared authentic concerns about the future of hemispheric bondage.[61]

But if southern opinion on Cuba revolved around what Robertson called the "all absorbing subject of slavery," it did not follow that all southerners agreed on what to do about it. Former Mississippi governor John Quitman, convinced that "if slave institutions perish [in Cuba] they will perish here," began to raise a private army to save Cuban bondage. In the Senate Slidell and other southerners called for the United States to allow Quitman's expedition to land in Cuba without interference. Immediate military action was necessary to forestall Pezuela's abolitionist program before it was too late. But the same dilemma that had haunted the filibustering debates in 1852 hamstrung Quitman and his entourage in 1854. A military expedition risked doing battle against newly emancipated slaves, fighting for their freedom—a force, as even the ardent expansionist Stephen Mallory admitted, that might prove a match for "an army of a hundred thousand men."[62]

Other southerners, equally aghast at the prospect of emancipation, recommended different approaches, but all agreed on the need to act. The *Richmond Enquirer* remained skeptical about filibustering but called for

an expanded American naval presence in the region and demanded unspecified strong government action to halt Pezuela's plan. The *Charleston Mercury,*
never a forceful advocate for Cuban annexation, came down hard against the
"buccanieering spirit" of the filibusters. Yet in some ways the *Mercury's* pre-
scription for Cuba contemplated an even more belligerent national policy:

> If the Africanization of Cuba be a fact worthy of our notice, let us take such
> notice of it as becomes the first Republic of the world. If our interests are
> imperilled, let the Army and Navy be summoned to their duty. Let the
> Government act as a government, through its own organized constitu-
> tional instruments, and with all the ample powers with which it is clothed.

In its call for direct federal intervention in Cuba, the *Mercury* outflanked
Quitman's private plot and mirrored the battle plan recommended by no
less an aggressive expansionist than Pierre Soulé.[63]

Amid the turmoil, there were two points of consensus in southern approaches to the Cuba crisis of the early 1850s. The first was that the security
of Cuban slavery—and the existing racial order in the Gulf of Mexico—
must be preserved at all costs. The second was that the United States, as the
"first Republic of the world," must be the leading guarantor of that slavery
and that racial order. Even antifilibusters like the *Mercury* and Virginia congressman Charles Faulkner agreed that the "whole power of the Government" should be at hand to resist any attempt "to transfer the island to the
black race, the necessary result of emancipation." Cuba, in William Trescot's
European analogy, was "our Belgium. . . . We will assign [the island] her
place." Whether it would be a Spanish colony, an independent state, or an
American province was not up to anyone else but the U.S. government to
decide. And whether that decision would come in the form of a diplomatic
initiative, a legalized filibuster invasion, or direct federal action was, ultimately, not a question of strategy but of mere tactics.[64]

As it happened, the Pierce administration veered uncertainly among all
these tactical options, settling on little and achieving less. Pierce first tacitly
countenanced Quitman's military preparations and then, in the late spring
of 1854, turned against them. The president's May 31 proclamation against
filibustering, together with the government's subsequent prosecution of
Quitman and two associates in June, has frequently been interpreted as the
product of Pierce's political exhaustion after the Kansas-Nebraska battles.
Having already stretched his northern Democratic allies to the limits of
their political lives to protect slavery in Kansas, the president could not ask
for their help in safeguarding bound labor in Cuba.[65]

Domestic political weakness was surely part of the equation, but there were also plenty of good foreign policy reasons for even the most pro-slavery president to shrink from a filibuster invasion of Cuba. Although the threat of sudden American force might prove useful in negotiations with Spain, the reality of racial warfare was not nearly so appealing or such a beneficial outcome for the security of hemispheric slavery. Nor did opposition to filibustering require an American strategic retreat from the Caribbean. Even as a federal prosecutor issued charges against Quitman in a Louisiana court, Pierce, Slidell, Davis, and Mason determined that Secretary Marcy should inform the New Orleans district attorney that the United States still planned to take "immediate and decisive" measures toward Cuba. Secretary of the Navy James Dobbin, expressing the administration's confidence in a more prudent government solution to the crisis, told a Mississippi friend that "if the Filibusters do not spoil things the Island will be ours in twelve months."[66] In Havana the passing of the filibuster threat in early 1855 prompted a sigh of relief from consul Robertson. Quitman's withdrawal, he noted, "may put a new face on things here, and probably put a stop to the intended augmentation of Black troops. . . . This will . . . lead to a more quiet state of things, which is very desirable."[67]

Pezuela, meanwhile, soon found himself in retreat in Cuba. Spanish merchants and Cuban planters alike had recoiled in horror at the captain-general's winter and spring proclamations, and their joint reaction was too much for him to withstand. By the end of May 1854 Pezuela issued another edict that underlined the government's commitment to slavery and even trumpeted the happiness of the Cuban slave in comparison to free European workers. This reversal—both practical and rhetorical—was widely publicized in southern papers and likely helped dissuade American slaveholders from pursuing desperate measures.[68] In July a revolution in Madrid toppled the Spanish government, leading to Pezuela's recall; by late 1854 some southerners were celebrating Spain's repudiation of the "abolitionizing laws" that had characterized the previous regime. James Gadsden of South Carolina, the administration's minister to Mexico, saw Spain's redoubled commitment to slavery as "the nucleus of its restoration in the other [Caribbean] islands, which, by an opposite and mistaken policy of humanity, are rapidly lapsing into barbarism."[69]

U.S. diplomatic entanglement in Cuba did not end there. Pierce still had to contend with the impetuous Pierre Soulé, whose penchant for improvisation did not prove to be an advantage for American diplomacy in Europe.

When Soulé, Buchanan, and John Y. Mason met in Belgium in the fall of 1854 and composed a document asserting the United States' right to "wrest" Cuba from Spain, the overconfident Louisianan leaked it to the press. This "Ostend Manifesto," as belligerent as it was useless, caused the Democratic Party considerable embarrassment for the remainder of the decade But it did not express anything fundamentally new or controversial about the way proslavery leaders understood U.S. rights and duties in the Caribbean.[70]

That understanding persisted across the decade. In 1859 President Buchanan's administration mounted a final antebellum effort to cajole or manipulate Spain into selling Cuba. By then, with the antislavery Republican Party controlling the House of Representatives, the domestic politics of Cuban annexation were desperate, if not hopeless. Yet the international politics remained as favorable as ever, at least as far as proslavery leaders were concerned. As John Slidell told the Senate, the American acquisition of Cuba would fit into a larger pattern of imperial expansion that embraced England's "march of conquest in India," France's "dominions on the southern shores of the Mediterranean," and Russia's subjugation of "her barbarous neighbors in Asia." U.S. hunger for Cuba simply reflected "the tendency of the age": the inevitable "absorption of weaker Powers" and "inferior races" by the stronger and the superior. For Slidell, as for Trescot, R. M. T. Hunter, and other southern elites, whatever their specific positions on the tactics of Cuba diplomacy, the advance of civilization demanded that the United States both preserve hemispheric slavery and amass hemispheric power. This formula remained the ideological foundation for southern relations with Latin America across the 1850s.[71]

What the Africanization episode also demonstrated was the continuing importance of foreign affairs, even in the thick of the sectional crisis. The Cuban panic in the spring of 1854 exploded almost simultaneously with the Kansas-Nebraska debates in Congress. For many in the South, Cuba was the more important topic. Alexander Stephens's indefatigable floor management had been vital to the passage of the Nebraska bill, but the Georgian felt that "the Cuba question" and the "injurious [abolition] policy of Britain and France" were "much greater issues." The present and future politics of slavery were too wide ranging for the South to regard its chief institution in a merely domestic light.[72]

The Africanization episode also revealed the depth of elite slaveholders' attachment to U.S. national power even as they understood that their grip on it might be slipping. With the partial exception of John Quitman and his fellow commandos, southerners in 1853–54 almost universally looked to the federal government as the natural savior of slavery, both at home and abroad. Antiexpansionist conservatives rejected filibustering but still expressed optimism that the "ample powers" of the "first Republic of the world" could dominate affairs in the Caribbean basin.[73] And rabidly profilibustering state officials, such as Louisiana's state assemblymen, also saw a positive role for U.S. national authority in Cuba. "The time has arrived," that state legislature announced in its spring 1854 resolution, "when the Federal Government should adopt most decisive and energetic measures to thwart and defeat a policy conceived in hatred to this Republic."[74]

Ultimately the Pierce administration found no acceptable venue for such aggressive federal measures in the Caribbean. Cuban slavery, it turned out, could be best preserved without recourse to direct intervention. But that did not mean that Pierce and his allies failed entirely to strengthen American regional power in the mid-1850s. The administration's concurrent efforts to expand the U.S. Navy and U.S. Army reflected a firm belief in the capacity of the central state to manage foreign affairs. And the men who led that ambitious project—James Dobbin, Jefferson Davis, and their allies in Congress—were all committed southern slaveholders.

9

The Military South

FEW FIGURES IN AMERICAN HISTORY are more easily evoked than the militant planter of the antebellum South. Hot blooded, quick tempered, and skilled in the arts of war, this swashbuckling cavalier rode, shot, and issued orders with the habit of command that evolved naturally from a lifetime of mastering his slaves. But despite all the mythology that surrounds the slave-holding South's sectional military spirit, neither popular nor academic histories have paid much attention to the South's national military politics.[1] A political narrative that culminates with secession and Civil War has produced an intense interest in martial activity within the future Confederacy—its share of West Point graduates, its private military academies, its local militias, and its rituals of combat. But among the tallies of Mexican War volunteers and accounts of jousting tournaments, what often goes missing is the relationship between the antebellum South's civilian politicians and the U.S. armed establishment. It is a striking omission, for in the long decade before disunion, southerners claimed almost exclusive control over the military politics of the republic.

Between 1847 and 1861 men from the future Confederate states served as secretary of war for eleven of fourteen years and secretary of the navy for nine. In Congress the proportion of southerners leading the Military and Naval Affairs Committees was equally lopsided (see Table 9.1). During a decade in which the future Confederate states accounted for less than a third of the nation's population, and little more than a fifth of its free population, representatives from those states occupied nearly three-quarters of the key federal positions in the formulation of military policy.[2]

Table 9.1. Military and Naval Affairs Chairmen in Congress, 1847–1861

Congressional Committee, 30th to 36th Congress (1847–1861)	Total Sessions	Southern-Chaired Sessions	Northern- or Border State–Chaired Sessions	Southern Percentage
House Military Affairs	14	11	3	79%
Senate Military Affairs	14	6	8	43%
House Naval Affairs	14	10	4	71%
Senate Naval Affairs	14	14	0	100%
Total	**56**	**41**	**15**	**73%**

Source: *House Journal* and *Senate Journal*, 30th Congress, 1st Session, to 36th Congress, 2nd Session (1847–1861).

Note: "Southern" here refers to representatives from one of the eleven future Confederate states. An exception is made for William Gwin of California, Senate Naval Affairs chairman from 1851 to 1855. Gwin was a leading champion of slavery who maintained plantations in Mississippi across the 1850s and returned to them in 1861. See Leonard L. Richards, *The Slave Power: The Free North and Southern Domination, 1780–1860* (Baton Rouge: Louisiana State University Press, 2000), 98–100.

The slave South's power within the Democratic Party, the dominant political organization across the long 1850s, allowed southern elites to command a large number of leadership assignments in both the executive and the legislative branches.[3] It was no coincidence, as Republican senator William Seward lamented in 1856, that slavery's Democratic friends dominated the critical organs of administration and legislation, while antislavery senators like Charles Sumner and John Hale found themselves confined to the committees on pensions, public buildings, and revolutionary claims.[4] Yet the influence of the so-called slave power was not distributed equally across the government. During the 1850s southerners monopolized the Navy and War Departments, but northern and border-state men predominated in four of the five other cabinet posts. Congressional representatives from the future Confederate states took almost no leadership role in the House and Senate committees on commerce, agriculture, and the territories. Instead, as Seward observed, southerners concentrated their strength inside the congressional bodies devoted to "the two great physical forces of the republic," the army and the navy.[5] Even the rank and file of Senate committee membership reflected the South's disproportionate interest in military matters (see Table 9.2).

Nor was southern participation in late antebellum military politics a matter of quietly filling committee seats. Proslavery leaders sought and achieved major changes in the structure, size, and capacity of the U.S. armed

Table 9.2. Committee Appointments in the Senate, 1847–1861

Senate Committee, 30th to 36th Congress (1847–1861)	Total Committee Appointments	Southern Appointments	Northern or Border-State Appointments	Southern Percentage
Naval Affairs	86	45	41	52%
Military Affairs	86	43	43	50%
Judiciary	82	34	48	42%
Foreign Relations	82	31	51	38%
Territories	82	30	52	37%
Finance	82	28	54	34%
Commerce	82	27	55	33%
Agriculture	48	12	36	25%

Source: *Senate Journal*, 30th Congress, 1st Session, to 36th Congress, 2nd Session (1847–1861).
Note: "Southern" again refers to senators from the eleven future Confederate states, along with William Gwin of California. The Senate Agriculture Committee was discontinued in 1857.

forces. Led by executive and legislative officers like Secretary of War and Military Affairs Chairman Jefferson Davis, the army and navy grew to their largest-ever peacetime levels, occupying a historically unprecedented share of the federal budget. In the 1850s, under leadership that was predominantly southern, the U.S. Navy expanded its squadrons and moved decisively out of the age of sail and into the age of steam. The U.S. Army added new regiments, overhauled its frontier deployment strategy, and adopted the battlefield technologies that would define Civil War combat a decade later, the rifled musket and the minié ball.

All this was done within the frenzied domestic politics of a dissolving union. Even as Congress chafed and Kansas bled, ostensibly sectional southern leaders remained deeply invested in national military power. In truth, the antebellum South's commitment to states' rights seldom went much further than the region's commitment to slavery. Across the 1850s southerners frequently claimed the power of the federal government to enforce the Fugitive Slave Act and, depending on the circumstances, safeguard the rights of slaveholders in the western territories.[6] But the advantages of a proslavery national state, for most southern elites in Washington, transcended the direct protections it could offer to the owners of human property. In the realm of military politics, as in foreign affairs generally, proslavery southerners stood out as the late antebellum republic's most aggressive advocates for centralized state power.

Proslavery military enthusiasm in the 1850s shared many of the features that had characterized the southern-led naval reform movement a decade earlier: a belief in the compatibility of sectional slavery and national power; a competitive instinct to measure U.S. capacities against other great powers; and a special concern for the protection of American "institutions" in the Gulf and the Caribbean.[7] But whereas naval reform in the 1840s had been conceived as a strategic rebuttal to the imperial abolitionism of Great Britain, the expansions of the 1850s drew their energy from a freestanding belief in the imperial destiny of the slaveholding United States. The primary role that slaveholders played in these reforms affirmed the South's ongoing commitment to U.S. international power. At the same time, it offered an emphatic and tangible demonstration of the proslavery elite's excitement about its place in the vanguard of modern development.

"Free trade imperialism," a historian of nineteenth-century France has argued, "ultimately relied on hard power." In promoting European-style military organization, cutting-edge weapons technology, and a significant expansion of forces, the South's most powerful slaveholders did not merely indicate their ongoing faith in the broader American state to serve their narrow sectional interests. They communicated a confident belief in the modernizing state itself.[8] Drawing inspiration from the Prussian general staff, the French conquest of Algeria, and the naval administration of Great Britain, slaveholders recognized that in a midcentury world dominated by open commerce and expanding empires, they could not neglect the hard power of the central state. The U.S. government, enhanced by ambitious military reforms, would play an essential role in managing the global transformations they envisioned and in shaping the new era they welcomed into being.[9]

We Must Have a Strong Navy

Ever since Abel Upshur's ambitious attempts at naval reform in the 1840s, slaveholding elites had retained a close connection to American sea power. "[T]he South," Jefferson Davis told an assembly of Mississippi Democrats in 1844, "has a delicate and daily increasing interest in the navy."[10] The same mix of strategic fears and desires that shaped proslavery foreign policy in the Caribbean basin encouraged southern leaders to pay particular attention to naval affairs. Georgia congressman and House Naval Affairs chairman Thomas Butler King, a key figure in the navalist coalition of the Upshur era, continued to advocate for an enhanced and expanded steam navy.[11] In 1847 King persuaded Congress to pass a naval measure long sought by southerners: a new line of government-subsidized Atlantic mail steamers, on the model of the British Cunard line, that could be converted into naval vessels in the event of war. The British mail packets, he proclaimed, were part of a system "skillfully designed to bring down upon us . . . at any unexpected moment, the whole force of British power. More especially this is true with respect to our *southern* coast." Although King disavowed the need for "one of those large and expensive naval establishments" found in Europe, he argued that the new convertible war steamers were necessary to rebut the British threat and ensure U.S. control over its coastal waters.[12]

In debates over the mail steamer bill King and his southern allies insisted on the importance of federal investment in naval projects. Dismissing the notion that "private enterprise, if left untrammeled by Government schemes," could provide the steamers more efficiently, King pointed to Great Britain's massive state support for its navy. Without government aid, American citizens "would be quite incapable of competing for any considerable time with so powerful an opposition." For veteran naval advocate Matthew Maury, the most attractive feature of King's mail steamer plan was that it gave momentum to the larger cause of U.S. naval expansion. The steamers added to "the sinews of that maritime strength, which, when rightly understood . . . and properly carried out by the government[,] will make us in war the strongest power on the ocean that the world ever saw."[13]

It was no coincidence that Maury outlined this grand vision of U.S. naval power in April 1848, just months after the conclusion of the American war with Mexico. The conquest of western North America fired the imaginations of many southern navalists. With the acquisition of California and over eight hundred miles of Pacific coastline, argued the *Southern Literary Messenger,* the United States must now "become a great naval power as well as a great commercial people." For Virginia congressman Richard Kidder Meade, later minister to Brazil, U.S. westward expansion inspired a grandiose naval metaphor. In 1851 he compared naval policy to "the necessity of defending our frontiers from the depredations of the Indians. . . . . Sir, in some sense the various nations of the world are on our frontier—the sea being our domain, and every vessel with an American flag an American hamlet." Meade's notion of an imperial "maritime frontier" naturally required a powerful naval establishment to patrol its far-flung borders. Scorning the idea that "the Virginia delegation" should reject naval expansion because it violated a strict construction of the Constitution, Meade insisted on the federal government's authority to raise whatever kind of sea power it wished.[14]

Even as sectional tensions over slavery engulfed Congress, southern navalists comfortably combined their proslavery politics with an imperial vision of American naval power. In an 1850 letter to the new House Naval Affairs chairman, Frederick Stanton of Tennessee, Thomas Butler King proposed a line of government steamships to help export the South's free blacks to Africa. "The black race," he wrote, "must remain in subjection to the white, or be exterminated. . . . The increase of these free colored people in our southern towns and cities has already become a most serious evil, and a perfect nuisance." The racist language and proslavery logic behind this scheme were characteristic of the colonization movement in the white South of the 1850s. But what is striking about King's plan is that it hoped to solidify white supremacy at home while simultaneously enhancing U.S. naval power abroad. "[A] steam navy," King declared, "has become necessary to our position and safety . . . and for the protection and security of our extensive coasts," which now ranged from Florida to the Puget Sound. The proposed African mail steamers in 1850, like the convertible ships he had requested in 1847, would add vital strength to the U.S. naval steam marine. In King's worldview, there was no reason that the linked demands of American power and American slavery could not be satisfied at the same time.[15]

Besides King's steamer plans, prominent southerners during the Polk, Taylor, and Fillmore administrations urged various other projects for naval development, ranging from the fantastic (Frederick Stanton's idea for a massively armed, high-tech new battleship that would force "the rebuilding of every other Navy" in the world) to the familiar (the Louisiana assembly's petition for a "permanent fleet" stationed off New Orleans harbor). Matthew Maury's direct influence with North Carolina's William A. Graham, secretary of the navy under Fillmore, helped bring about the U.S. Navy's expedition down the Amazon River in 1851. In terms of tangible naval expansion, however, the late 1840s and early 1850s did not yield great progress.[16]

The major southern naval accomplishments of the late antebellum period came during the Pierce administration, and in large measure, they represented the work of one man, James Cochrane Dobbin. A thirty-nine-year-old North Carolinian who had served one term in Congress during the 1840s, Dobbin's appointment as secretary of the navy in 1853 did not exactly provoke hymns of acclamation, even from political supporters. "A lawyer of Fayetteville, N.C., in the prime of life, and of industrious habits" was all one friendly newspaper could muster. (Dobbin's chief qualification for the cabinet, in fact, seems to have been the speech he gave on behalf of Pierce at the Democratic convention of 1852.) Small in stature, modest in personality, and inconspicuous in national politics, Dobbin must have appeared an unlikely figure to lead a revival of southern navalism. Yet he became the first naval secretary in over twenty years to serve through an entire presidential term, and in those four years he helped achieve a transformation of the U.S. Navy.[17]

Dobbin's first annual report, in December 1853, included the most forthright demand for naval expansion in over a decade. The secretary renounced any desire for war but posed a hawkish rhetorical question to members of Congress: "[C]an peace best be maintained by the exhibition of comparative weakness, or by a display of strength and preparation which, while it invites not a conflict, at least defies assaults?" In his emphasis on naval policy as a vital element in America's standing among "the great Powers of the world," Dobbin followed the lead of foreign policy commentators like William Trescot. And in his strategic conception of American sea power, which assumed that "our Navy should *at least be large enough to command our own seas and coast*," the Fayetteville lawyer resuscitated the language of bygone southern navalists from Abel Upshur to John C. Calhoun.[18]

Like his predecessors, Dobbin believed that the best naval defense was a powerful offense; shore fortifications without a navy were merely "a shield without a sword." The new secretary therefore pivoted rapidly from coastal protection to the need for a revamped and technologically advanced American fleet. His most urgent demand was for six new "first-class" steam frigates. These would be heavy, oceangoing warships, equipped with the latest screw-propeller technology and capable of carrying up to fifty guns. To contend with "the overwhelming strength of the navies of the many great nations with which we claim equal rank," the United States needed not mere gunboats, but powerful, state-of-the art steamships.[19]

In Congress Dobbin's key navalist allies hailed almost exclusively from slaveholding states. House Naval Affairs chairman Thomas Bocock explicitly modeled his approach to the navy on the career of his fellow Virginian, "Judge Upshur." In the Senate the most influential figure was Stephen Mallory of Florida. Later the chief of the Confederate navy, in the 1850s Mallory was the Senate's leading supporter of American naval expansion.[20] Dobbin's report reached these men on Capitol Hill in the early months of 1854, just as the Cuban emancipation scare was rattling through Washington. The naval spokesmen of the South did not hesitate to connect the two questions. Spain's ongoing oppression of Cuba, Bocock observed as he brought the steamer bill to the House, might well provoke a "general and determined revolt" on that island. A stronger U.S. naval force in the Caribbean might help "annex that independent island to our Confederacy" and "quiet forever one of the most dangerous questions that claims a solution over our future." Southern newspapers were more explicit about exactly what kind of danger lurked on the nation's southern doorstep. Great Britain and France, declared the *Memphis Daily Appeal*, "may resolve upon the chaotic creation of a negro confederation in the Antilles. . . . To avert so dire a calamity from the race of man, we must have a strong navy. If powerful at sea, we shall keep back the tide of vandalism from our own shores—we will also reflect light to the people of all other lands."[21]

The link between slavery and southern naval policy was obvious. Whether as a useful means to advance Cuban annexation or as a necessary buffer for Gulf and Caribbean slave institutions, the U.S. Navy retained value as a tool of proslavery policy. Yet the vision of southern navalists seldom retreated into a narrow or purely defensive sectionalism. Although the Kansas-Nebraska debates swirled around them, and the future of the Union looked more uncertain than ever, slaveholders inside and outside Washington remained committed to a bold, nationalistic understanding of naval policy. A Virginia conservative in foreign affairs, Bocock had long opposed the doctrine of American "intervention" overseas. But like Robert M. T. Hunter, he saw U.S. foreign policy in the imperial shades of skin color: "It is *manifest destiny* which is bearing the red man of the country westward upon a receding wave into the great ocean of annihilation. It is *manifest destiny* which will ever make a strong, vigorous, and healthful race overrun and crush out a weak and effete one." Predicting that the unstoppable American goliath would eventually incorporate Latin America into its domain, Bocock fastened his grand racial vision to the debate over naval appropriations. "All these considerations urge on us the necessity of preparation. . . . And there is no mode so appropriate as a proper increase of our Navy."[22]

Even if we set aside a portion of this grandiloquence as a virtual requirement in midcentury congressional debate, it is clear that Bocock and other naval advocates were committed to the navy not only as a protection for the South but also as an instrument of national power. Underneath the windy rhetoric of racial manifest destiny, southerners accumulated hard numerical arguments for naval increase. "Naval strength (or weakness)," Stephen Mallory avowed in 1854, "is altogether relative, and must ever be measured by that of its probable adversaries; and in determining what the condition and strength of our service should be, we have first to ascertain those of the only naval Powers whose ability to contend with us on the open sea is unquestioned." After acquiring those facts, southern navalists were doubly convinced that American sea power must grow. "Our Navy is much less than one fifth that of several of the greater Powers of Europe," Secretary Dobbin observed, and "not larger than that of certain other Powers of Europe which are not of the first rank."[23]

In Congress, Bocock and Mallory offered an even more pessimistic portrait of American sea power. The United States, concluded Bocock, "with a commerce and tonnage equal to Great Britain, has only about one eighth of her naval force. This is too great a disparity." Although no southern navalist in the 1850s suggested anything quite like Abel Upshur's heroic ratio of 1841, which foresaw the U.S. Navy growing to half the size of British forces, it was the principle, not the proportion, that counted. American naval forces, like American foreign policy, should be organized to compete with Britain and other European powers on the "open sea." Over half a decade of bitter debate over slavery had not yet persuaded southerners to abandon their belief in U.S. international power. Urged onward by Bocock and Mallory, Congress passed the six-frigate bill in April 1854.[24]

Dobbin's annual reports during the mid-1850s continued to stress the familiar southern navalist talking points. The need to preserve "our rank as a nation" through "steady and gradual enlargement of our Navy" was one of them; the special value and vulnerability of the Gulf of Mexico was another. Like Calhoun, Dobbin drew a critical distinction between domestic federal spending, which enriched foreign investors, and naval appropriations, which employed American workers and augmented "the mechanical skill of the country."[25] Dobbin's practical projects as naval secretary further reflected both the local and global ambitions of proslavery navalists. Commodore Matthew Perry's famous voyage to Japan had been conceived under Secretary Graham during the Fillmore administration, but Dobbin actively supported the mission and trumpeted its result in 1854 as the dawn of a "new era" in "the commerce of the world." Influenced by Matthew Maury's theory that a Central American canal could make the Caribbean the center of transpacific trade, Dobbin organized an ill-fated expedition to the

Darien Gap in Panama. In his final report to Congress the secretary argued that the "peculiar position" of Central America's isthmus had attracted "the attention of the world," and that U.S. interests on the west coast of Central and South America demanded that the navy equip not one but two Pacific squadrons.[26]

Although many of Dobbin's requests remained unmet, and a number of internecine controversies disrupted the efforts of naval reformers in Congress, the secretary's achievement was secure. Dobbin even left the Navy Department on a high note: just hours before Pierce's term expired in March 1857, a combined effort of southern legislators produced funding for five new steam sloops and one thousand additional navy seamen.[27] On the whole, some contemporary observers thought that the southern-led expansion of the mid-1850s represented a major milestone in U.S. naval development. "It is scarcely extravagant to say," the *Charleston Mercury* wrote of Dobbin, "that his administration has been the best which the Navy has ever enjoyed, and will leave fruits behind it that will make it memorable in the history of our military marine."[28]

No less a naval strategist than Alfred Thayer Mahan agreed. In 1856 the future admiral was a teenage midshipman at the Naval Academy, with an appointment secured through family connections to Jefferson Davis. Looking back on the longer-term development of the U.S. Navy, Mahan's memoirs put special stress on the shipbuilding program organized by Secretary Dobbin. The construction of a steam marine during the 1850s was "revolutionary in character," Mahan declared; it ushered the navy into a new epoch. The statesmen who had made it possible were nearly all slaveholding southerners.[29]

Armies and Empires

For the South's leading politicians, and especially those who fancied themselves states'-rights republicans of the old school, it was not always easy to reconcile official principles with actual foreign and military policy preferences. In no case, perhaps, did they face a taller struggle than in their effort to expand the peacetime size of the U.S. Army. Large land forces, unlike a vigorous sea power, violated one of the holy taboos of old republican politics, a distinction often seized upon by naval advocates to justify their own less obvious heresy. "A large standing army," insisted the *Richmond Enquirer* in 1853, "is incompatible with the theory of our Government, and dangerous to civil liberty; but an effective Navy is essential to the protection of American rights, while it is capable only of harming the enemy."[30] Nevertheless, in the 1850s southern military spokesmen rose to the challenge. Their leader, in the key appropriations battles of the decade, was Jefferson Davis.

Davis's personal background revealed a deep immersion in both sectional politics and national military culture. A West Point graduate, he served briefly in the Black Hawk War of 1832 before leaving the army to run a large cotton plantation in Mississippi. Entering Democratic Party politics in the 1840s, Davis became a vocal advocate of Texas annexation and quickly acquired a reputation as a rising star. Like many younger southern Democrats, Davis warmly embraced the ideological legacies of both Andrew Jackson and John C. Calhoun—the pro-southern nationalism of the former, in his eyes, was perfectly compatible with the nationalistic southernism of the latter.[31] When the war with Mexico broke out, Davis supported the Polk administration in both word and deed, accepting an appointment as colonel of the First Regiment of Mississippi. Wounded in heroic fashion at the battle of Buena Vista, he hobbled back to his home state and won a place in the Senate. There he established himself as a leading spokesman for slavery and southern rights, opposing the Compromise of 1850 and waging an anti-Compromise campaign for the Mississippi governorship in 1851. Despite his sectional intransigence, Davis remained deeply committed to national military power: as chairman of the Senate Military Affairs Committee from 1849 to 1851, he led legislative efforts for higher army budgets, new troop regiments, and technological innovation.[32]

Named President Franklin Pierce's secretary of war in 1853, the forty-four-year-old Davis was the highest-ranking southerner within an administration devoted to southern interests. Unlike the diminutive James Dobbin, Davis had an imposing physical presence and an active public career that made him an inviting target for both praise and criticism. Friendly contemporaries, including James D. B. De Bow, thought him "the very soul of President Pierce's cabinet"; the antislavery press imagined that he "sustains the border ruffians [in Kansas], countenances the Cuban filibusters, wields President Pierce, rides Dobbin, commands the army and navy, and, *a la plantation*, whips [Secretary of State William] Marcy and [Attorney General Caleb] Cushing up to their dirty work." In truth, Davis did not quite rule

Jefferson Davis. "His manner is easy, and there is a precision in his phraseology which gives a vigor and force to his speeches that accord well with the military character of the speaker." John Savage, *Our Living and Representative Men* (Philadelphia: Childs and Peterson, 1860), 180. This photograph from the studio of Matthew Brady probably dates from the late 1850s.

over the Pierce administration like a plantation overseer, but his influence in the cabinet was real.[33]

As secretary of war, Davis made it clear that his most fundamental goal was to expand the size of the national army. In the past four decades, his first annual report observed, the United States "has increased in population more than eighteen millions, and in territory a million of square miles," but "the military peace establishment of this country has been augmented by less than four thousand men." The current troop count—formally fourteen thousand men but practically many fewer—was "manifestly inadequate." Although Davis included all the standard disclaimers about America's historic aversion to large standing armies, he argued that even "in peace" a powerful country like the United States should maintain, "a military establishment that is capable of the greatest expansion in war."[34]

In the spring session of 1854 Congress passed some of Davis's smaller proposals, including an increase in the number of cadets at West Point and a general raise of army pay. But it was not until later that year that Davis had any luck in his major effort at army expansion. Half a continent away from Washington, near Fort Laramie in the Nebraska Territory, a dispute between white migrants and Lakota Sioux Indians had exploded into violence. On

August 19, 1854, U.S. Army second lieutenant John Lawrence Grattan led a small detachment of soldiers into the Sioux camp to apprehend an Indian charged with killing a migrant's cow. Young, inexperienced in Indian affairs, and possibly drunk, Grattan showed little concern that the military lacked the formal authority to adjudicate such local quarrels. He arrived in a belligerent mood and demanded that the accused culprit be produced at once; when Sioux leaders refused his request, tensions mounted. With groups of Indian warriors maneuvering around the army band, a nervous American soldier fired into a crowd of Sioux. The ensuing skirmish quickly became a rout. Heavily outnumbered from the start, Grattan and his twenty-nine volunteers were all killed.[35]

News of the "Fort Laramie Massacre" set off a storm of protest across the country, with newspapers decrying a "preconcerted plot" to "murder" Grattan and his men. In Washington the Pierce administration began to organize a punitive army expedition to western Nebraska. The following summer soldiers under Gen. William S. Harney attacked a Lakota camp at Blue Water Creek, killing eighty-six Sioux, at least half of them women and children. But long before Harney's troops marched out of Fort Leavenworth, Secretary of War Davis seized on the frontier bloodshed as evidence for his larger argument that the army needed more men. Davis's public campaign began in the press. As early as October 1854 an essay composed by "Friends of the Administration" appeared in the *Charleston Mercury*, lamenting the "annihilation of Grattan and his followers" and demanding that the army grow in size to prevent future conflicts.[36]

Davis worked hard to keep the administration's military talking points consistent. When Pierce's official organ, the *Washington Union*, attempted to excuse the War Department's responsibility for the Grattan affair by discounting the possibility that there were not enough troops in the West, the secretary reacted at once. Writing directly to the *Union*'s editor, Davis upbraided him for seeming to credit the idea that "there was no lack of troops for the protection of the frontier." This mistaken notion, he declared, "may be an embarrassment to the Administration in its efforts to obtain the necessary increase of the Army." If the paper wanted to cover Indian affairs in the future, Davis promised that the War Department would be happy to provide information underlining "the propriety of increasing the number of mounted troops as well as those of other arms." The correction came swiftly: the very next day the *Union* ran another column, "Indian Massacres," this time making it clear that the puny size of the army was a danger to

American settlers in the West. The secretary of war "must have more troops at his disposal, or the sad intelligence must continue to reach us of the butcheries and violations of women and children by the savages." Thereafter the administration's military propaganda machine functioned in rather better order.[37]

When Davis delivered his second annual report to Congress in December, he knew just what to say. The United States, he wrote, possessed just 11,000 men to cover 10,000 square miles, in land inhabited by 40,000 Indian warriors. "That this force is entirely inadequate to purposes for which we maintain any standing army, needs no demonstration; and I again take occasion to urge the necessity of such immediate increase as will at least give some degree of security to our Indian frontier." Davis described the Grattan affair as "the result of a deliberately formed plan, prompted by a knowledge of the weakness of the garrison at Fort Laramie."[38]

It was vital to the administration's military expansion program that the Laramie incident be viewed in this light. Within the War Department the secretary could rely on the assistance of Adjutant General Samuel Cooper, a New Yorker who had married into a prominent Virginia family, and who, six years later, would become the highest-ranking offer in Davis's Confederate military. Davis and Cooper acted aggressively to suppress or discredit alternative accounts of Grattan's encounter with the Sioux. The Indian agent at Fort Laramie, whose testimony blamed Grattan for the massacre, soon found himself transferred to another department. Later, when the army's own investigation also found Grattan responsible, Cooper accused its author of reproaching "a brother officer" and doing injury to "the gallant dead" at Fort Laramie.[39]

The War Department was moving ahead with full steam, but on Capitol Hill Davis's army proposals ran into political controversy. The same Thirty-Third Congress that had just witnessed the furious sectional clashes over slavery in Kansas and Nebraska now took sides in a passionate and wide-ranging debate about Indian relations, racial identity, and the military responsibilities of empire. What was striking about this second Nebraska debate, however, was that most leading southerners now argued on behalf of federal authority in the territories. R. M. T. Hunter, who only months before had denied the government's right to regulate slavery in Kansas, now insisted that its military power be brought to bear in Nebraska. Only an larger national army, southerners argued, could subdue the Great Plans and reflect the growing international clout of the United States.

This much less well-known Nebraska controversy erupted after an inflammatory speech from former Texas president and current senator Sam Houston. An ambivalent southerner who had opposed the Kansas-Nebraska Act and a conflicted westerner who had spent several years living as a member of the Cherokee Nation, Houston held heterodox views on both slavery and Indian relations. His January 1855 speech indicted U.S. Indian policy across the decades, alleging that almost every instance of Indian aggression "has been induced or provoked by the white man, either by acts of direct aggression upon the Indians, or by his own incaution." The Fort Laramie incident was certainly no exception. Houston rejected the administration's call for four new regiments, avowing that he preferred to "civilize" the Indians rather than simply exterminate them.[40]

The response to Houston's provocation was swift and furious. Florida navalist Stephen Mallory professed shock at the Texan's portrait of Native American innocence: "Why, sir, the Senator must know that the taste of blood is just as natural to the Indian as it is to the tiger." Iowa Democrat Augustus Dodge declared that Houston's speech smacked of "the carping spirit of Abolition." Like Africans, Indians were decreed by God "to give way to the Anglo-Saxon," and "that philosophy which blubbers over it is sickly indeed." No wonder that Houston had "opposed every increase of our military force." For administration allies in Congress, it was vital that Davis receive his troop requests, not only to safeguard the frontier but also to repudiate the radical abolitionist logic that looked unkindly on the U.S. Army.[41]

Southern legislators played a critical role in guiding the military expansion plan through Congress. In the House acting Military Affairs chairman Charles Faulkner of Virginia worked closely with Davis to shepherd the four-regiment bill through committee and onto the floor.[42] In the Senate, where antislavery northerners like Seward and Sumner universally joined the opposition, proslavery champions like Hunter, Mallory, and Albert Gallatin Brown of Mississippi, all spoke in favor of military increase, even if they disagreed on the particulars of troop organization or legislative tactics. No southern dissenter, aside from the idiosyncratic Houston and the Whig moderate John Bell, rejected Davis's plan entirely or introduced principled objections to dangerous "standing armies." In February 1855 the four-regiment bill passed the Senate with ease. Even after the ordeal of Kansas-Nebraska and the dark portent of the previous fall elections, in which pro-southern candidates had been walloped at the northern polls, slaveholding elites largely retained their confidence in the imperial muscle of the U.S. Army. "If we will stretch from ocean to ocean," declared George Badger of North Carolina, "we must necessarily multiply our military means."[43]

There was no question that southern leaders saw the process of American expansion in essentially imperial terms. Houston had begun the debate by comparing U.S. westward settlement to European colonialism in Asia. All across the world, he observed, powerful nations were "seeking to civilize and christianize men on the banks of the Ganges, or the Jordan, or in Burrampootah." Why should the United States not do the same with its own indigenous population? Other southerners accepted this transnational analogy—Nebraska's Indians, said one senator, were "the Arabs of the plain"—but drew rather different conclusions.[44]

Secretary of War Davis, for one, looked to European empires as models for U.S. Army frontier deployment strategy. The wide-open West, Davis declared in his first annual report, was simply too vast to protect in its entirety. Instead, he proposed to concentrate troops in large numbers at "commanding positions" where they might intimidate the native population through striking exhibitions of power. This vision of military deployment, which implicitly acknowledged the U.S. military as an occupying force in fundamentally hostile territory, had much in common with European experiences in Europe and Asia.[45]

In his 1856 report Davis made the link explicit: "The occupation of Algeria by the French presents a case having much parallelism to that of our western frontier, and affords us the opportunity of profitting by their experience." French policy "leaves the desert in the possession of the nomadic tribes"; outposts were established on the limit of settled areas and fortified with "strong garrisons" capable of dispatching large "marching columns" into native territory. For Davis, French colonialism in Algeria was not a moral blot but an instructive example of imperial military organization. In the absence of the much larger army he would have liked to build, this French plan, dependent on vigorous displays of force to subdue a racially inferior population, made practical sense. The secretary of war refused to "blubber" over the fate of either Africans or Indians held in the grip of a superior power. Betraying no qualms about the parallel between the U.S.'s democratic manifest destiny in North America and France's imperial subjugation of North Africa, Davis was satisfied to league his nation, and his army, on the side of empire.[46]

A vision of the United States as a great international power, indeed, shaped the whole of Davis's activities in the War Department. Beyond his plans for troop increases and imperial frontier deployment, the secretary sought to reorganize U.S. Army administration on the model of the Prussian general staff, with a stronger and more centralized military bureaucracy. In 1854 he sent a delegation of officers, including future Union general George McClellan, to Europe to study munitions, tactics, and staff organization in the Crimean War.[47] Davis worked to internationalize army education, adding an additional year of language instruction to the curriculum at West Point. Cadets already learned French, the language of military tactics in Europe, but Davis believed that they must also learn Spanish, the language of military occupation in the Americas. (Army detachments already maintained U.S. power over tens of thousands of Spanish speakers in New Mexico and California; that number would increase exponentially in the event of future southerly acquisitions.) Davis even waged a lonely battle to bring camels into army service for use in the Southwest; the animals, after all, had been used with great success by the French and British Empires in the desert regions of North Africa and the Middle East. It was no coincidence that an expert witness on behalf of the camel scheme was the English Egyptologist and prominent scientific racist George Gliddon.[48]

Like James Dobbin in the Navy Department, Davis saw the United States as a great nation among other great nations. With a massive and growing population, a newly won continental empire to manage, and commercial interests in every corner of the world, the United States in the mid-1850s was well on its way to a triumphant role in global affairs. Whatever the damage that sectional strife had done to American domestic politics, Dobbin and Davis evidently believed that the country's international destiny remained as grand as ever. By 1857 they had succeeded in overhauling the U.S. armed forces. To a steam navy of 14 small vessels, bearing just 71 guns, Dobbin provided for 11 powerful new steamships that carried a total of 308 guns and 1,000 new sailors to man them. Davis, meanwhile, oversaw an army that grew from under 11,000 to nearly 16,000 active troops, a relative increase of almost 50 percent.[49] To be sure, the military establishment remained small compared with the powers of Europe. But the enhanced U.S. Army now boasted a troop number that was comparable to, if not larger than, total British army strength in the Western Hemisphere.[50] And by the historical standards of the American republic, the increases were considerable, if not unprecedented. Altogether the U.S. Army, Navy, and Marines gained about 6,000 new personnel during Pierce's term in office, by far the largest peacetime expansion achieved by any administration since the War of 1812.[51]

Of course, the Dobbin-Davis reform program went beyond a simple expansion of forces. It also involved a large measure of technological modernization. Dobbin and his congressional allies had virtually created a steam navy from scratch, and in 1856 Davis pushed for and won a large appropriation to upgrade the army's arsenal of large and small guns. Under his direction U.S. armories halted production of smoothbore muskets and began to build rifles fitted to fire the grooved minié ball; wrought-iron artillery carriages and improved Colt revolvers entered the service in large numbers. Together, Dobbin and Davis—these "two energetic and far-sighted ministers, brought from the slave states, and identified with their policy," in the words of William Seward—had led the U.S. armed forces out of the age of wood and sail and into the age of metal and steam.[52]

States' Rights, National Security

The sectional partisanship that disfigured the domestic politics of the 1850s did not fatally undermine army and navy expansion. If anything, the fiercest bouts in the ring of military politics were fought between strong-willed southerners themselves. During the Pierce administration Matthew Maury waged a bitter personal battle with Dobbin and Mallory over the salary and standing of nonseafaring naval officers; Jefferson Davis, meanwhile, became embroiled in a vituperative correspondence with the army's top general, Winfield Scott. All these men agreed on the necessity of expanding the army and navy, but this agreement did not prevent them from cordially hating each other or uncordially bombarding their rivals with vicious personal insults. (Scott, said Davis, displayed "petulance, characteristic egoism . . . greed of lucre and want of truth"; Davis, said Scott, was "an enraged imbecile.") Nevertheless, all this individual animosity did not prevent the remarkable collective accomplishment of southern military advocates in the middle 1850s.[53]

Nor did philosophical objections to a powerful central state get in the way of military expansion. To be sure, defensive southerners often brandished small-government and strict-constructionalist arguments to block protective tariffs, western homesteads, and, of course, attempts to limit slavery in the territories. As the sectional crisis mounted, slaveholders viewed such domestic politics of nation building with increasing skepticism. Their doubts about centralized domestic power and its implications for the security of slave property were only heightened by the antislavery turn in northern politics after the Kansas-Nebraska Act. Even federal initiatives that might tangibly benefit the agrarian South met staunch resistance in Congress: over the course of the 1850s, southern legislators repeatedly stymied northern-led efforts to create a department of agriculture and a system of agricultural colleges. In both an ideological and a practical sense the South's leadership was becoming less and less attached to the project of building a national community at home.[54]

But in foreign and military policy, more often than not, southerners could be found in the vanguard of federal expansion, activity, and enterprise. This program extended to the central government's symbolic, as well as strategic, functions. Between 1850 and 1860 Congress appropriated millions of dollars for the construction of a new U.S. Capitol, whose stately new wings, cast-iron dome, and fresco-splashed interior suggested the vaulting ambition of an imperial republic. The most ardent and effective political sponsor of the Capitol extension plan, managed by the War Department, was Jefferson Davis; perhaps its most enduring congressional ally was Robert M. T. Hunter.[55]

In the same years another group of southerners in government led a successful campaign for the reform and enlargement of the U.S. diplomatic corps. Congressman John Perkins of Louisiana and Assistant Secretary of State A. Dudley Mann of Virginia collaborated to produce an 1855 bill that increased the number of ministers abroad, added a secretary of legation to each mission, and raised diplomatic and consular salaries around the world. Only six years later Perkins would chair Louisiana's state secession convention, but for now, he argued, America's "great advances in wealth and power" demanded large-scale State Department reforms. Perkins and James D. B. De Bow, who gave the consular reforms much attention in his *Review*, agreed that a powerful, modern nation like the United States required an army, navy, and foreign service to match.[56]

This concurrent interest in diplomatic reform is revealing because for all their zeal about military expansion, few southerners sought to involve the country in war. Davis might demand unprecedented army appropriations and deliver aggressive speeches about American dominance of the Caribbean, but in the key moment of 1854 he refused to stand up for a Cuban filibuster mission that might have involved the United States in a serious international conflict. In the various diplomatic imbroglios of the 1850s, principally over Cuba and British interference in Central America, some hot-blooded spirits like Pierre Soulé urged military action, but in every case they were overruled by a more cautious and more powerful southern mainstream. Even precious military appropriations could be sacrificed if they portended dangerous conflict. When Stephen Douglas demanded as many as fifty new warships to contest British power in the Americas, Mallory, Davis, and the majority of southern senators opposed him on the grounds that such a precipitate increase might result in an unnecessary and hazardous war.[57]

The proslavery drive for military expansion during the 1850s did not emerge from the blind belligerence of a southern martial culture. It sprang, rather, from a careful and crucial distinction between domestic and international balances of power. As a Mississippian in the American union, Davis genuinely feared the consequences of a vigorous central government hostile to slavery. But as an American in the wider world, Davis understood U.S. national power as the strongest possible mechanism to advance the international interests of his slaveholding class. In making these calculations, leading southerners understood that military power was desirable, even if military action was not. A strong armed establishment, declared R. M. T. Hunter in 1856, added to the American "sense of security; it adds to the respect which foreign nations may feel for us; and I confess that I desire to see this country placed in such a condition that no foreign Power shall ever direct a gun in menace upon our coast without feeling that they do it under the responsibility of aiming at those who have guns enough pointed in return." For like-minded southern leaders, peace, strength, and slavery were mutually reinforcing. A powerful, well-armed American state, at ease with Europe and dominant in its own hemisphere—this was the surest possible guarantee for both the South and its slave institutions.[58]

Antislavery members of Congress had little trouble discerning the relationship between slavery and military expansion. The chief aim of President Pierce's administration, Joshua Giddings announced, was the protection of slave property in both Cuba and the southern states. To this end "the whole power of the nation" was mobilized: "[O]ur Army must be increased; our Navy enlarged; all the paraphernalia of war must be provided." Giddings exaggerated the administration's eagerness to provoke an actual armed conflict: neither Davis nor Dobbin actively sought "a war to maintain Cuban slavery." But his interpretation of the military buildup was not far from the mark. The worldview that produced it, and the policy that gave it shape during the Pierce administration, understood American state power as the bedrock of southern and Caribbean slavery alike.[59]

In March 1854 Giddings spoke as a member of a perpetually aggrieved minority, but the midterm elections later that year transformed the balance of power in Congress. Outraged by the Kansas-Nebraska Act, northern voters turned against the Pierce administration and the Democratic Party. The beneficiaries, however, were not the old Whigs but two new political organizations that had risen from their ashes: the antislavery Republican Party and the anti-immigrant American (or Know-Nothing) Party, whose members together occupied a majority of seats in the new House of Representatives.[60]

The arrival of a mass antislavery party in the House left a major imprint on the politics of military expansion. Led by Giddings and Ohio's John Sherman, Republicans added a proviso to the 1856 army appropriations bill that would prevent any part of the U.S. Army from enforcing the laws enacted by the fraudulent proslavery legislature in Kansas Territory. When the House passed the amended bill on the strength of Republican and Know-Nothing votes, the military's southern sponsors were apoplectic. According to R. M. T. Hunter, Republicans knew full well that the Democratic Senate would never pass such a measure. Instead, they aimed simply to "stop the wheels of Government." If the attempt succeeded, Hunter declared, "then, sir, revolution is accomplished." Republican Benjamin Wade replied that proslavery crimes in Kansas justified a revolution, prompting South Carolina's Andrew Butler to issue an evocative challenge: "Sir, the man who invented the guillotine was the first to have his head cut off by it. Try your guillotine here, as you have proposed, on this bill, and a change of circumstances may subject you to the wheel."[61]

Butler's grasp of French revolutionary history was shaky, but by August 1856, this was something more than a metaphor. In Kansas that summer, the conflict between Missouri border ruffians and free-state militias had erupted into a shooting war. Months earlier, on the Senate floor, Butler's nephew Preston Brooks had battered his colleague Charles Sumner to a pulp for insulting the South Carolinian in a speech. On the army bill, Butler pronounced himself willing to take the Republican dare. Even if Congress withheld funds for "the diplomatic corps, the Army, the Navy, or any one of the branches of the Government," this would not "shake the entire American system." Antislavery fanatics might break down the "miserable bond" of Union, but Butler placed his political faith elsewhere: "We have State governments at home—state governments of autonomous growth and existence . . . that can defy reckless factions."[62]

Butler assumed the characteristic pose of states'rights absolutism. But what made this debate notable was the extent to which leading southerners implicitly rejected this view and claimed "the wheels of Government"—the federal government—as their own. In the House Charles Faulkner described the anarchy that would ensue if Republicans had their way: "Your Army, being wholly unprovided for, must of course be disbanded, and your frontier settlements left to the savage barbarities of Indian warfare; your national armies, arsenals, and military work-shops, will be closed." When Congress adjourned without any agreement on military appropriations, southern newspapers denounced the Republicans' revolutionary attempt to destroy "the existence of our Government."[63]

For their part, Republicans insisted that they were not trying to disband the army but merely to prevent its misuse in Kansas. Yet when antislavery senators were pushed, they offered a view of the armed forces utterly alien to the geopolitical imagination of southerners like Davis or Hunter. "How is the Government to be arrested, even if this Army bill should fail?" asked William Seward. "Is the Army of the United States . . . a necessary and indispensable institution, in our republican system? On the contrary, it is an exception, an anomaly, an antagonistic institution, tolerated, but wisely and justly maintained with jealousy and apprehension." Even if the army disappeared for a few months, said Maine's William Fessenden, the people and government of the United States would be just fine. Southerners and Democrats, however, would not take the dare. Eventually, in a special late summer session of Congress called by President Pierce, House Democrats prevailed on enough Know-Nothings to pass the Senate's army appropriations bill over Republican opposition.[64]

This established the pattern of military politics across the contentious late 1850s. The chiefly southern Democrats at the helm of army and navy policy called for more and better troops, guns, and ships; the growing antislavery bloc in Congress rejected all three. Even after the tightly contested presidential election of 1856, in which James Buchanan held off Republican John C. Frémont by a margin of just two states, southern elites continued to beat the drum for military expansion. Buchanan did not share Pierce's enthusiasm for foreign policy adventures, and his cabinet lacked administrative master spirits on a par with Dobbin or Davis. But the Democratic governing coalition in Washington remained both highly sympathetic to slavery and favorably disposed to military growth.[65]

In December 1857 Buchanan's secretary of war, John Floyd of Virginia, asked for five new army regiments. More troops were needed both to patrol the Indian frontier and to regain federal control over Utah Territory, whose Mormon leadership had committed "flagrant acts of rebellion" against the United States. The Republican Party had expressed its distaste for Mormon practices in its 1856 campaign platform, which labeled slavery and polygamy the "twin relics of barbarism," and called for Congress to bar both from the federal territories. But congressional Republicans overwhelmingly opposed any attempt to exploit the Utah crisis to increase the regular army. Maine senator Hannibal Hamlin remembered the last time a Democratic administration had made this pitch—Jefferson Davis's successful call for four new regiments after the so-called Grattan massacre in Nebraska. What had these troop units achieved? "Not a single thing have they done since they were created, except, on one occasion, to murder a few poor squaws and little children." Hamlin and others denounced the 1855 slaughter of Sioux at Blue Water Creek, rejecting the idea that either Mormon or Indian difficulties could be resolved through military increase.[66]

The legislative captains of the army expansion effort, meanwhile, were the familiar southern suspects. Back in his old post as Senate chairman of the Committee on Military Affairs, Davis hoped to modify Floyd's request by adding companies rather than regiments to the army. (As a Georgia committee member helpfully explained, this mirrored the French method and allowed for more flexibility in troop organization.) Republican opposition to military funding, southerners argued, amounted to a perverse and deranged abandonment of government authority. "Let Kansas bleed; let Utah bleed; let the torch be lighted up all along the line of the frontier," cried Mississippi's Albert Gallatin Brown, "they will stand by, coldly look on, and vote no increase of the Army."[67]

The navy debates of the Buchanan years played out in similar fashion. When House Naval Affairs chairman Thomas Bocock introduced a bill for ten new steam sloops in May 1858, even a sectionalist as notorious as South Carolina's Lawrence Keitt lined up in support of the warships. An outspoken defender of the South's right to secede, months earlier Keitt had called one of his congressional colleagues a "Black Republican puppy" and had touched off a sectional brawl on the floor of the House.[68] On the navy bill, however, he spoke glowingly about the present and future of the American union. "We are every day increasing our resources . . . and enlarging the volume of our power"; the navy should reflect the perpetually expanding sphere of U.S. interests. It would not be long, Keitt continued, before "we have carried our institutions to the furthest South, [and] given form and vitality to the wealth and power which for ages have been sleeping there." For Bocock, Keitt, and the South's leadership at Washington, an enhanced navy was the necessary adjunct of both U.S. global clout and the hemispheric destiny of slavery.[69]

All this legislative activity yielded another substantial increase in the U.S. armed forces. In 1858 Davis failed to get his permanent army companies, but he did gain funding for three new volunteer regiments; Bocock and his allies managed to win money for eight new steamships.[70] Organized by these "sectional" southern legislators and enacted amid the drama of a divided union, national army and navy spending under Buchanan surpassed even the swollen outlays of the Pierce years. By 1859 total military expenditures had more than doubled since 1852 and had grown to occupy nearly 55 percent of the entire federal budget (see Table 9.3).

To be sure, this spending boom was not restricted to the army and navy. Total federal expenditures grew during the flush 1850s, as rising customs revenue freed up more money for post offices, public buildings, lighthouses, and other projects.[71] But it was the engorged military budgets that accounted for the largest increases in federal spending. New Hampshire Republican John Hale pointed out that by some reckonings expenditures in the mid-1850s topped the levels reached during the war with Mexico. "I am sorry to have to state these facts," he joked, "because I am afraid they will encourage the President to go into another war, thinking that war is more economical than peace." More fundamentally, Republicans attacked the aggressive foreign policy premises that justified the surge in military spending. "The most preposterous of all preposterous things," said Illinois antislavery radical Owen Lovejoy, "is that in order to preserve peace you must go armed to the teeth."[72]

Yet by and large, Republicans lacked the votes to obstruct the southern and Democratic military expansion program. Only the panic of 1857 and the consequently depressed state of the Treasury after 1858 finally brought the party to a halt. A Senate retrenchment committee led by Tennessee's Andrew Johnson—like Sam Houston, something of a southern apostate— managed to slash army and navy funding for the year 1859–60.[73] But even

Table 9.3. U.S. Army and Navy Expenditures, 1849–1861

Year	War Department Expenditures	Navy Department Expenditures	Combined Total Expenditures	Share of Federal Budget
1849–50	$9,400,000	$7,905,000	$17,305,000	44%
1850–51	$11,812,000	$9,006,000	$20,818,000	44%
1851–52	$8,225,000	$8,953,000	$17,178,000	39%
1852–53	$9,947,000	$10,919,000	$20,866,000	43%
1853–54	$11,734,000	$10,799,000	$22,533,000	39%
1854–55	$14,774,000	$13,312,000	$28,086,000	47%
1855–56	$16,948,000	$14,092,000	$31,040,000	45%
1856–57	$19,262,000	$12,748,000	$32,010,000	47%
1857–58	$25,485,000	$13,985,000	$39,470,000	53%
1858–59	$23,244,000	$14,643,000	$37,887,000	55%
1859–60	$16,410,000	$11,515,000	$27,925,000	44%

Source: Susan B. Carter et al., eds., *Historical Statistics of the United States, Earliest Times to the Present: Millennial Edition* (New York: Cambridge University Press, 2006), Table Ea 636–643. © Cambridge University Press 2006.

Note: Expenditures are for each year ending on June 30.

in this rearguard action, fought against Republican opponents demanding that the army be cut in half, southern legislators successfully prevented any permanent reductions in the size of the armed forces. Once again some of the South's most celebrated sectionalists did not hesitate to identify their labors with the power of the national government. "It will not do for Congress, because there has been a panic among the financial men of the country, to have a panic here," avowed a grave James Henry Hammond in 1859. "Statesmen must be above such things as that. We are not to abdicate the functions of Government and revolutionize all our affairs according to the prices-current." In the same session Davis and Mallory even sought, with partial success, to win funds for new and heavier artillery weapons "in order that we should keep pace with the rest of the world."[74]

To some degree the southern military enthusiasms of the late 1850s complement rather than challenge the familiar narrative of the sectional crisis. Slaveholding leaders had long viewed the demographic growth of the North with alarm: California's admission to the Union, John C. Calhoun warned, gave the free states "a decided ascendancy" in the House, the Senate, and the electoral college. By 1850 the nonslaveholding states accounted for nearly 60 percent of the U.S. population. But despite Calhoun's fears, the North's simple majorities did not lead at once to "control of the Government and the powers of the system." In fact, the government remained very much in southern hands. As one historian has argued, the year 1857 "marked the high tide of the South's national political power": through their control of the Democratic Party, slaveholders dominated the Buchanan administration, the Supreme Court, and both chambers of Congress.[75]

Nevertheless, the slave South's formal power in government washed over terrain whose political geography fundamentally favored the North—and after the election of 1856 southern leaders knew it. For many analysts of the sectional crisis, the South's political offensives during the Buchanan years—the sweeping *Dred Scott* decision, the proslavery Lecompton Constitution in Kansas, and the demand for a federal slave code in the territories—all flowed from the hydraulic pressure exerted by this mix of power and vulnerability. Driven by the desperate need to protect slavery while they still controlled the government, southern leaders pushed their northern Democratic allies too far, splitting the party and setting the stage for Republican victory in 1860.[76]

In one sense the ongoing southern effort to strengthen the army and navy conforms to this larger series of events. As their 1856 platform proclaimed, Republicans believed that southerners wanted to augment the national "military power of the government" in order to boost the sectional power of slavery.[77] But in another sense southern military endeavors, even during the grimmest hours of the domestic crisis, suggest an entirely different sort of proslavery trust in the federal government. Unlike the fugitive slave law or the prospective territorial slave code, Jefferson Davis's new regiments and Stephen Mallory's new steamships did not extend the power of the U.S. government solely to protect the property rights of slaveholders. They extended the power of the U.S. government to project influence across the Western Hemisphere however it saw fit. In other words, proslavery militarism in 1859, as in 1841, was not simply a matter of rerouting national policy to serve sectional interests. Rather, it involved a remarkable faith in slaveholders' ability to control and define the meaning of national policy itself. In the 1850s that faith emerged not only from the domestic circumstances that had given southerners a lopsided share of federal offices, but also from the international circumstances that seemed to smile on the future of American power and American slavery alike.

The persistence of that faith ultimately exposed southern militarists to no shortage of ironies after the fracture of the Union. Davis's push for the adoption of new regiments and better rifle technology left the U.S. Army in stronger shape to rally its forces against the South in 1861. The shallow-draft steamers that Dobbin, Bocock, and Mallory pushed through Congress were used to great effect in the North's blockade of Confederate ports during the Civil War. The strength of southern confidence in American firepower abroad recoiled backward to help destroy slaveholding society at home. For practically the whole of the 1850s, however, that confidence survived intact. The domestic cords of Union might be slowly snapping, one by one, but the South's belief in American international power was still, perhaps, the sturdiest remaining bond.[78]

10

American Slavery, Global Power

THE ELECTION OF 1860 CONSTITUTED A REVOLUTION in American politics. For the first time in the nation's history, a president was elected on the basis of a purely sectional vote. Abraham Lincoln carried virtually every state in the Union where slavery had been outlawed; he lost every state where slavery endured. The national triumph of the Republican Party, a political organization that existed almost entirely in the nonslaveholding North, had no precedent in the history of the United States. This electoral arithmetic alone made the Republicans unique, but their vocal antislavery political platform made them revolutionary. Never in eighty years of American existence had the country been governed by a chief executive who openly opposed black servitude.[1]

This revolution of 1860, among its many reversals and disruptions, contained dire implications for the foreign policy of slavery. For decades, the share of slave-state representatives in Congress had grown smaller with each election. But in the executive branch southern power and southern influence were never overthrown. The antebellum president least sympathetic to slavery was probably Zachary Taylor, and even he owned three hundred slaves.[2] Throughout the 1840s and 1850s, slaveholding fingerprints remained especially prominent on the levers of executive power that dealt with international relations. In foreign and military affairs southerners could still look forward to a central role in shaping national policy.

The incoming presidential administration offered none of these inducements. In fact the organizing principle of Abraham Lincoln's entire party was resolute opposition to the fundamental beliefs, interests, and aims of the proslavery South. Certainly, there could be no such thing as a foreign policy of slavery in a Republican administration. Southern elites, understanding themselves as the leading architects and principal stakeholders in U.S. international power for the past three decades, now found themselves cut off from their own creation. Their sense of dispossession was profound. "So is the nation gone—forever over to Black Republicanism," brooded Henry Wise. "That breaks the charm of my life." *Richmond Examiner* editor John Moncure Daniel, Franklin Pierce's envoy to Turin, lamented that the rise of northern antislavery would destroy the American empire. "We have built up a great, prosperous, free, glorious country, which would soon over-shadow all the earth"—and now it would all be wrecked by such "feeble canters" as Horace Greeley and William Lloyd Garrison.[3]

Worse yet, the mighty organism that southerners had built now threatened to turn its formidable energies against the institution they held most dear. "The crisis of the 1850s," Steven Hahn has written, "was no longer a battle between expansive and restricted conceptions of federal power. It instead unleashed a full-scale struggle over who would control the state itself." By 1860 it was clear that both sides in this struggle saw the U.S. federal government, for all its supposed weakness, as the weapon that would decide the contest between free and slave labor. A decade of combat against the slave power, James Oakes argues, had convinced Republicans that American slavery could not long survive without "the steadying hand, the stabilizing force, of the national government." Surrounded by a cordon of free states and deprived of the prop of executive power, the slave system would slowly wither and die. For their part, slaveholders generally accepted this formula, and the bitter debates of the 1850s only brought southern leaders closer to the view that slavery required the firm protection of the national state.[4]

The Republican campaign platform promised only to forbid slavery in the federal territories, without immediately threatening it in the South. Nevertheless, Lincoln's victory raised the prospect of new and deadly dangers to the security of the slave system. The rise of a patronage-driven Republican Party in the South; a yeoman revolt against the slaveholding class; direct insurrectionary violence led by newly empowered slaves; the collapse of white supremacy and the patriarchal social order—after November 1860, all these internal calamities seemed terrifyingly possible.[5]

But among the many disturbing consequences of Lincoln's victory, perhaps the most immediate was the Republican Party's capture of the outward-looking American state. Under President Lincoln, the United States suddenly assumed the shape of an antislavery world power. Slaveholders from

Matthew Maury to Jefferson Davis had made heroic efforts to enhance American power in a global context, but now those efforts appeared to have been wasted or, worse, actively misspent. Davis's new infantry regiments and James Dobbin's steam frigates were just a fraction of the trouble. The prospective U.S. secretary of state, William Seward, had only recently declared that freedom and slavery stood in "irrepressible conflict" not just at home but around the world, from South America to Ottoman Turkey. With men like Lincoln and Seward in power, slavery's greatest champion in that conflict, the United States, had abruptly switched sides. The whole of the American national state—its armed forces, its diplomatic corps, its entire institutional capacity for overseas action—might now use its strength to undermine slavery across the Western Hemisphere.[6]

It was a situation liable to produce confusion or even paralysis. And in the fall of 1860 many of the South's most powerful politicians wavered. The foremost practitioners of the foreign policy of slavery did not generally distinguish themselves as aggressive secessionists. Some influential opinion makers, like James D. B. De Bow in New Orleans, quickly joined the ranks of those who demanded immediate separation, but most men in the South's national leadership were less confident and less public about their positions. Jefferson Davis had threatened secession during the 1860 campaign, but after Lincoln was elected, he dutifully returned to Washington for the start of the Thirty-Sixth Congress, leaving the door open for a possible compromise settlement. Stephen Mallory refused to support Florida's separate state secession in December 1860. Even James Henry Hammond, a longtime believer in the theoretical goal of southern independence, found himself struggling quietly, if unsuccessfully. against South Carolina's separatist tide.[7]

In Virginia Robert M. T. Hunter defended the right of secession but wanted national negotiations, not state action. James Mason privately endorsed separation but opposed any movement until the Lower South left the Union first. Longtime veterans in the field of proslavery foreign policy like Duff Green, Matthew Maury, and ex-president John Tyler each spent much of the secession winter attempting to drum up an alternative solution that would keep the United States intact.[8]

Even those who openly advocated southern resistance, like Henry Wise, were often reluctant to relinquish the framework of national power. Wise declared himself in favor of "fighting in the Union" rather than out of it. According to his plan, Virginia and the southern states would not secede but would battle, militarily if necessary, to maintain their rights against Republican oppression. The proposal reflected Wise's eccentric and demagogic politics, but it also indicated the depth of his commitment to the national government. "The Union," he argued, "is not an abstraction: it is a real, substantial thing. . . . [I]t has nationality, lands, treasury, organization of army, navy, ships, dock-yards, arsenals, etc. Should we renounce these rights and possessions because wrong-doers attempt to deprive us of other rights?" Even after Lincoln's election, the physical substance of American power—especially American international power—proved difficult for southerners to surrender.[9]

A Question of Empire

When Congress gathered in Washington nearly a month after Lincoln's election, no southern state had yet left the Union. Movements for secession were gathering steam, especially in South Carolina, but compromise-minded legislators still hoped to hammer out a settlement that would avert disunion. Inside congressional committee chambers and Washington hotel rooms, frantic negotiators put everything on the bargaining table. It was no coincidence, and no surprise, that the conversation ran frequently to the future of slavery across the hemisphere.

The most active and most prominent of the negotiators was Kentucky senator John J. Crittenden. In December 1860 Crittenden proposed to solve the territorial question forever by extending the Missouri Compromise line between freedom and slavery all the way to the Pacific. Lands "hereafter acquired," so long as they were south of the 36°30' boundary, would not be subject to any restrictions; Cuba, Mexico, and all Latin America thus remained theoretically open to slaveholding acquisition. The Lower South's leading statesmen in Washington were cautiously receptive to the plan. Although secession movements were already under way in their home states, Jefferson Davis of Mississippi and Robert Toombs of Georgia, serving on Crittenden's Senate Committee of Thirteen, agreed to support the compromise. The critical provision, in their view, was the clause that guaranteed the possibility of future slave expansion. Toombs, otherwise a staunch secessionist, proclaimed himself willing to accept the bargain so long as slavery would be protected all the way to "the south pole."[10]

Hesitating representatives from Virginia, North Carolina, and Tennessee were even more eager to support Crittenden's compromise. But many of these Upper South men, including John Tyler and James Mason, also made it clear that the deal would become valueless if "territory south" of current U.S. borders were not included in its provisions. On this point virtually the whole of the South's slaveholding leadership was in agreement. In the select compromise committee called by the House of Representatives, an overwhelming majority of southerners even opposed a bargain that would add New Mexico as a slave state if the "hereafter" clause were not also included.[11]

Why were both Lower and Upper South leaders so intent on provisions for future expansion into Latin America? The "hereafter" clause allowed the possibility for new slave states to enter the Union, thus offering hope that the legislative balance of power might someday be restored. But any southern leader with a fragment of practical sense must have understood that this was highly unlikely. After all, Caribbean annexation efforts had failed repeatedly during the 1850s, and a Republican-dominated Congress in the 1860s would be even less receptive to proslavery expansion.[12]

More than a delusive hope for new slave states or a fastidious regard for sectional honor, southerners' insistence on the "hereafter" clause reflected the importance of their vision of the United States' role in world affairs. If the two quarrelling sections could resolve their differences, declared R. M. T. Hunter in January 1861, the restored United States might "play for mastery in that game of nations where the prizes are power and empire." Hunter, remember, was no wild-eyed expansionist. He had not mustered much enthusiasm for James Buchanan's Cuba annexation plan two years earlier. But he was a man with a decided vision of the global future, and words like "mastery" and "empire" did not fall from his lips as hollow ornaments of rhetoric. They reflected a lifelong belief that the international destiny of slavery and the international destiny of the United States were inextricable. If a Crittenden-style compromise on "territory south" was not likely to produce any new slave states in the near future, it nevertheless affirmed the possibility that the foreign policy of slavery, in one form or another, might still have a future in U.S. national politics. It offered hope that American power and American slavery could one day be reconciled.[13]

Republican opposition, however, doomed all such negotiations. Accepting a major constitutional extension of slavery violated the basic raison d'être of the entire Republican Party; it was not compromise but capitulation.[14] And in some ways the implications of the "hereafter" clause seemed the most frightful of all. Republicans sought to contain slavery within the

South in order to kill it, not to watch it metastasize across the hemisphere. "Let there be no compromise on the question of extending slavery," president-elect Lincoln advised congressional Republicans in December 1860. "A year will not pass," he declared in January, "till we shall have to take Cuba as a condition upon which they will stay in the Union." The Republican rejection of the Crittenden compromise was also a decisive rejection of the foreign policy of slavery. As one congressman put it, a constitutional pledge to protect bound labor south of the 36°30' line "would make the Government the armed missionary of slavery" across the Americas. In fact, as John Quincy Adams knew all too well, the U.S. government had often served in that capacity over the past two decades. But with Lincoln in the White House, it would do so no longer.[15]

Only after this rebuff became certain in the waning days of 1860 did Jefferson Davis abandon all hope for a national settlement. Davis and his colleagues in Washington did not originate the secession movement; while they negotiated fruitlessly with the Republicans, a more aggressive substratum of southern elites, operating at the state level, had already begun to act.[16] But when the Lower South's national leaders did embrace secession, they embraced it decisively. In January and February Davis, Toombs, Stephen Mallory, John Slidell, and others backed successful efforts to remove the remaining Lower South from the Union. Nationally powerful elites in the Upper South also began to harden their line. In the Virginia secession debates between February and April, Hunter, Mason, Tyler, and Wise all devoted themselves, in one way or another, to the cause of disunion.

With the significant but almost solitary exception of Alexander Stephens, after January 1861 the antebellum South's most experienced proslavery statesmen accepted the dissolution of the republic they had worked so hard to build. Why did these powerful leaders support this leap into the unknown? They had many reasons, but as the debate over the "hereafter" clause suggests, the future international career of the United States counted among them. These exponents and engineers of the foreign policy of slavery could not think about the crisis of the Union in strictly domestic terms. "The root of the thing," wrote Matthew Maury to a northern relative, "is not in cotton or slavery, nor in the election of Lincoln. . . . The real question is a question of empire." Maury dissembled, of course, when he tried to separate "slavery" from his notion of "empire," but his emphasis on imperial responsibility rings true. The secession crisis involved not only the fate of the existing slave states but also the "vast domain" from the California coast to the

Amazon valley—and, given the rising power of the United States, the wider world beyond.[17]

By 1861 the usual polarities in the American argument over empire had been reversed. In what must have seemed a surreal parody of the military debates of the previous decade, southerners in the Thirty-Sixth Congress now took a vigorous stand against any military or naval expansion whatsoever. When Republican John Hale, the new chairman of the Naval Affairs Committee, brought out a bill to construct seven new steam sloops, the Senate's remaining Upper South slaveholders opposed it unanimously. This was in the second week of February; three days earlier, in Montgomery, Alabama, the seven Lower South states had adopted a constitution and had proclaimed themselves the Confederate States of America. Under these circumstances Republicans could hardly be surprised that southerners like James Mason would view a proposal to "increase the naval armament" as a direct military threat to the "Sovereign States" of the Lower South.[18]

But given the longer history of naval debate in Congress, William Fessenden could not resist feigning shock at Mason's opposition to the bill: "Why sir, look back into your own records of your own party, coming from your own President and your own Senate committee, year after year, and you have precisely this proposition to build these steamers." Indeed, Hale's bill was a virtual carbon copy of the proposals authored and advocated by his predecessor as chairman, Stephen Mallory. But in February 1861 Mallory was no longer in Washington. He was back home in Pensacola, helping negotiate a truce between the Florida militia and the U.S. troops stationed at Fort Pickens. Later that month Jefferson Davis asked him to serve as the secretary of the navy for the new southern Confederacy.[19]

The triumph of the Republican Party in 1860 meant that the overarching question of empire could no longer be resolved through a struggle for control of the American state. Slaveholders had lost that battle; they now resumed the contest within the hastily constructed apparatus of a proslavery state of their own. Very quickly, men like Davis and Mallory—neither flamboyant fire-eaters nor stubborn moderates but mainstream southern elites with extensive experience in Washington—assumed command of the new Confederate government. Southern secession may have emerged out of state-level politics, but the Confederacy rapidly coalesced around the South's foremost national leaders. At Montgomery in February 1861, state representatives selected former U.S. Treasury secretary Howell Cobb to preside over the new Confederacy's constitutional convention.

With little hesitation that same body chose former U.S. secretary of war Davis as president and Alexander Stephens, who had spent nearly two decades in the U.S. Congress, as vice president. Eventually, antebellum statesmen with long federal careers filled out the rest of the Confederate government: Robert Toombs as secretary of state (1861); R. M. T. Hunter as his replacement in the State Department (1861–1862) and then president pro tempore of the Confederate Senate (1862–1865); Judah Benjamin as secretary of war (1861–1862) and secretary of state (1862–1865); Stephen Mallory as secretary of the navy (1861–1865); Thomas Bocock as Speaker of the House (1862–1865); James Mason as minister to England (1862–1865); and John Slidell as minister to France (1862–1865).[20]

Historians have documented the revolutionary effect the election of 1860 produced in such leaders, who feared that with a Republican in the White House, they could no longer control their states, their societies, and even their households. But another reason they were willing to leave the Union by 1861 was that they feared that they could no longer manage their empire.

The Greatest Material Interest of the World

Southern secession, of course, was not a pure product of anxiety and weakness. Slaveholders may have been pushed out of the Union by political defeat, but they were also pulled into the Confederacy by their ravenous ambition. If southern elites had been concerned only about the physical security of slavery as a regional institution or the maintenance of their political standing in a local context, then a risky and potentially violent separation from the Union could never have received their support. And if those same elites had been genuinely convinced of their global isolation or their lack of fitness for international politics, they would never have chosen a course that demanded immediate entrance into world affairs.

The secession movement conformed to the larger shape of proslavery politics in the previous decaded. In domestic terms, it was a defensive maneuver; in international terms, a high-stakes gamble. In the Confederate spring of 1861 southern leaders were confident that their enterprise could thrive on the global stage. The South's institution of African slavery, they believed, had helped establish the safest, strongest, and most successful republican government in history. Fortified by decades of experience at the helm of the world's preeminent slave power—the United States—these new Confederates approached international politics with immense self-assurance.[21]

At the state secession conventions of 1860–61, of course, disunionists had placed slavery at the heart of their case for southern independence. The Republican threat to black servitude—and therefore to white supremacy— required the South to form its own government.[22] But if slavery found itself besieged within the old Union, Confederates argued, its power was only growing in world affairs. Vice President Alexander Stephens, who had converted himself from a dour opponent of secession to a jubilant tribune of the Confederacy, sounded the new note in a famous March 1861 speech at Savannah. The founders of the American republic had believed that slavery was "wrong in principle," he recalled. "Our new Government is founded upon exactly the opposite ideas; its foundations are laid, its cornerstone rests, upon the great truth that the negro is not equal to the white man; that slavery, subordination to the superior race, is his natural and moral condition." Stephens's claim that black slavery was the cornerstone of the Confederacy has rightly become one of the best-known utterances of the Civil War era. Somewhat less well known are his subsequent remarks, which traced the career of this "great truth" over the course of "world history."[23]

Stephens's boast at Savannah was neither a clichéd assertion of racial prejudice nor a reactionary appeal to tradition. As he had done in his 1859 retirement speech at Augusta, the vice president rejected traditional wisdom in favor of a very specific confidence in mid-nineteenth-century scientific progress. Knowledge about the laws of race, he continued, "has been slow in the process of its development, like all other truths in the various departments of science." Stephens likened the progress of scientific racism to Galileo's astronomy, Adam Smith's political economy, and William Harvey's theory of blood circulation. At first, these great discoveries were rejected and scorned by men of science; now, "they are universally acknowledged. May we not, therefore, look with confidence to the ultimate universal acknowledgment of the truths upon which our system rests?"[24]

Stephens and other Confederates knew that this ultimate acknowledgment might be a long way off. By 1861 Europe's most powerful states had abolished slavery; the current governments of Britain, France, Russia, and the northern United States all professed a formal commitment to antislavery principles. Most Confederate leaders recognized that their new republic's chief selling point, in economics and diplomacy alike, would not be slavery but cotton. Europe's need for this crucial raw material, innumerable southerners argued, ensured that its great powers would recognize the Confederacy and guarantee the security of its cotton-producing institutions, whatever their humanitarian scruples about slavery. This confidence in King Cotton formed the basis of the Confederate diplomatic strategy and flavored the rhetoric of Confederate leaders from the start.[25] In his inaugural address as Confederate president, Jefferson Davis refrained from the proslavery bravado that characterized Stephens's cornerstone speech a month later. Instead, the new president stressed the Confederacy's "production of staples . . . in which the commercial world has an interest scarcely less than our own."[26]

Historians have sometimes made much of the distinction between Davis's shrewd restraint and Stephens's impolitic glorification of slavery, occasionally even suggesting that Davis saw Stephens's speech as a tactical blunder.[27] It would go too far, however, to conclude that in the triumphant flush of secession and statehood, southern elites celebrated cotton while downplaying slavery. Davis's second major public address, his April 1861 message to the Confederate Congress, did not skirt the question of racial bondage. The president crowed that the South's slave system had transformed "brutal savages into docile, intelligent, and civilized agricultural laborers," working productively under "the supervision of a superior race."[28]

Alexander Stephens was just the most prominent among many outspoken elites who viewed the worldwide position of bound labor with confidence, not trepidation. In general, secessionists and Confederates did not attempt to obfuscate the economic links between cotton and slavery. More often, they advertised them. Consider this first full paragraph from Mississippi's declaration of secession:

> Our position is thoroughly identified with the institution of slavery—the greatest material interest of the world. Its labor supplies the product, which constitutes by far the largest and most important portions of commerce of the earth. These products are peculiar to the climate verging on the tropical regions, and by an imperious law of nature, none but the black race can bear exposure to the tropical sun. These products have become necessities of the world, and a blow at slavery is a blow at commerce and civilization.

Like Stephens's cornerstone speech, these lines are frequently cited as evidence that slavery, rather than an abstract commitment to states' rights, stood at the heart of the Confederate enterprise. But this emphasis skims past the most striking feature of the declaration. Mississippi's secessionists listed the *global* necessity of slavery as their first and most fundamental reason for dissolving the Union. State leaders also feared that an antislavery government in Washington would threaten "property worth four billions of money" while sowing "insurrection and incendiarism in our midst." But in the declaration even these stark fears came in second place to the international importance of slave labor.[29]

Nor was this secessionist confidence in slavery simply a projection of the familiar southern confidence in cotton. Mississippi's slaves produced nearly 500 million pounds of cotton in 1860, more than any other American state, but its secessionist elite understood that slavery's claim on the world economy reached beyond their own booming plantations. It was no coincidence that the man who wrote the declaration, Alexander M. Clayton, had served as a U.S. consul in Cuba in 1853. A close friend of Jefferson Davis, Clayton had no trouble persuading the rest of the convention to depict slavery in hemispheric rather than domestic terms. Everybody present knew that an "imperious law of nature" made certain that coerced, dark-skinned labor was equally necessary in Mississippi, Matanzas, and São Paulo, and that the products of that labor would be consumed with equal delight in London, Paris, and Hamburg. King Cotton might be at the center of the South's diplomatic strategy, but Emperor Slavery was the center of global commerce and civilization.[30]

In the crisis months of 1860 and 1861 southern leaders affirmed again and again that their slave institutions were not nearly as sectional or as peculiar as antislavery propaganda suggested. All the most ebullient proslavery internationalism of the 1850s bubbled forth in secessionist speeches and broadsides. Perhaps the single most widely read pamphlet, John Townsend's *The South Alone, Should Govern the South,* devoted considerable attention to the international status of slavery. "It is a mistake," Townsend declared, "to suppose that England, France, Germany, Russia, and the other commercial and manufacturing nations of Europe, are hostile to African slavery." In fact, Britain's "disastrous experiment" in the West Indies only confirmed "the romantic absurdity" of emancipation and the absolute necessity of "compulsory labor." Following George Fitzhugh and J. D. B. De Bow, Townsend cited the *London Cotton Supply Reporter,* the *London Times,* and the Caribbean travel diary of Anthony Trollope as evidence that the "intelligent Englishman" now scorned abolitionism and was willing to deal on friendly terms with a southern republic whose cornerstone was slavery.[31]

If the supposed disaster of Caribbean emancipation had shaken Europe's commitment to free labor, subsequent events seemed to show that the world might again embrace the principle of coercion. "[T]he course of France and Great Britain in regard to the coolie and African apprenticeship systems, as introduced into their colonies," R. M. T. Hunter argued in 1860, "afford[s] evidence of a growing change in their opinions upon slavery in general." On this crucial subject, Hunter and other leading slaveholders believed, the "public sentiment of the world" remained in a state of flux. At any rate, the state of international opinion on slavery looked more promising than a generation before, when even southern men had feared to defend slavery as a positive good.[32]

"The proslavery sentiment," agreed the Louisiana secessionist William H. Holcombe, "is of recent development. It is more recent than any of the great inventions which have created the distinctive forms of our modern civilization." The democratic enthusiasms of the Age of Revolution, Holcombe argued in an influential pamphlet, appeared out of date in the wiser and more orderly world of the middle nineteenth century. Certainly, in the decades since abolitionism first made its appearance, the "question of slavery has been thoroughly sifted." Fresh evidence from the scientific laboratories of Europe, the sugar estates of the Caribbean, and the field notes of African explorers all served to confirm the essential truths of proslavery theory. The slaveholding South, Holcombe concluded, could justly claim the mandate of global civilization: "[I]ts principles are based upon large and safe inductions, made from an immense accumulation of facts in natural science, political economy and social ethics."[33]

Not all secessionists shared this confidence in equal measure. An alternative strain of discourse openly acknowledged the general unpopularity of slavery, sometimes even depicting the South's global isolation in romantic terms. By and large, however, leading slaveholders much preferred to see themselves as hardheaded men of the world. Many were willing to admit that slavery still faced considerable obstacles abroad. Great Britain, admitted North Carolina senator Thomas Clingman in February 1861, is "not at all friendly toward our institutions." But in the global order that Britain had fashioned, Clingman asked, was African bondage really so far out of place? Casting his eye over British foreign policy during the past decade, Clingman found a powerful empire guided not by "humanity" but by a stern calculation of material interests. Neither the rise of an "inhuman" coolie trade in the West Indies, nor the bloody Second Opium War with China, nor the use of "torture" to collect land rent in India suggested a tender-hearted British government that would blanch at recognizing the independent "slaveholding community" of the South. To the contrary, recent history seemed to reveal a field of global action whose major players, whatever their official pronouncements, recognized the necessary rule of power, co-ercion, and hierarchy.[34]

A willfully unsentimental mode of analysis suffused the international worldview of the seceding South. "Nations," wrote Townsend, "are not gov-erned by sentiment, much less by sentimentality, but by their interest." The ruling classes of Great Britain, declared Fitzhugh, were not idle dreamers or voluptuous aristocrats but "brave, earnest, well-informed, practical working men." In the cold universe of geopolitics—a world regulated not by emotion but by power and profit—the South could not fail to command respect, if not assistance. "These tall, thin, fine-faced Carolinians are great material-ists," observed British journalist William Howard Russell after spending an April evening in a Charleston drawing room. "Slavery," he thought, had "aggravated the tendency to look at all the world through parapets of cotton bales and rice bags." This style of thought joined the slave South's intellec-tual preference for calm rationality—"cool brains," as Mary Chesnut put it—to the boosterish confidence of antebellum politics.[35] It did not prove a successful hybrid. The belief in a practical, self-interested Britain led southern elites to underrate British antislavery and overrate their own leverage, through cotton exports, over British policy. What made this miscalculation possible was not merely the arrogant arithmetic of King Cotton but a larger set of beliefs about slavery's place in the world.[36]

A belief in slavery, to be sure, did not necessarily amount to an argu-ment for secession. For nearly the whole of the antebellum period, southern confidence in slavery was more often synonymous with confidence in the United States, whose government had done so much to nurture slave insti-tutions throughout the hemisphere. R. M. T. Hunter had applauded the world's evolving opinion on slavery in an 1860 campaign speech that urged the election of John C. Breckinridge and the continued dominance of slave-holding interests within the Union. The Republican victory in that election, however, altered the geography of power in the Atlantic world. Slavery's most dangerous and most determined opponents were now centered not in London or Boston but in the seat of U.S. government. After November 1860 it became an open question whether slavery would fare better within a Union controlled by Republicans, or in a wider world whose dependence on slave goods was a given, and whose objections to slave labor seemed to wane with every hour.

The southern elites who broke up the Union were driven, above all, by the need to protect a society organized around the ownership of slaves. Under a Republican government, slaveholders feared, their society would be vulnerable to a thousand dangers, from outside assault to internal disintegration. This explains the panicked political diagnosis of 1860–61, but it only halfway explains the proposed remedy of secession and Confederate nationhood. A full explanation must confront not just the Union that slaveholders fled but also the world that slaveholders sought to join. Here, too, slave ownership remained at the center of their vision. For men like Davis, Stephens, and Hunter, slavery was never merely the South's social glue—a local institution that allowed masters to carve out a small nook of order in a larger world given to chaos. Slavery was also the political and economic fulcrum of that larger world. In that sense the Confederate project was not designed to escape "modern civilization" but to command it.[37]

Building a Proslavery World Power

The secession of the American South took place in an age of secessions. Across the mid-nineteenth-century Atlantic world, from Texas to Belgium to Hungary, minority groups withdrew—or attempted to withdraw—from larger political units, often claiming that their right to self-government could be achieved only through separation from an oppressive central authority. Southern elites themselves enjoyed drawing parallels between their predicament and that of the beleaguered minorities of Europe. The inauguration of a Republican government in Washington, declared James Mason in 1860, would be "to us the government of a foreign power. We shall stand to such power as Italy to Austria and Poland to Russia." Comparisons of this kind, southern leaders hoped, might induce European powers to recognize and assist the Confederacy,as they had assisted Greece, Belgium, and other young nations.[38] In truth, the Confederate case was strikingly different. Among the secessionists of the mid-nineteenth century, American slaveholders were the only group who had, for eighty years previous, served as the dominant political elite within the government they now abandoned. If the decision to secede from the Union was indeed a revolution, it was a revolution led by the ruling class of the ancien régime.[39]

Slaveholders' long experience atop the U.S. government inevitably shaped the character of the nation-state they created in 1861. The cultural and political vocabulary of the southern Confederacy everywhere bore the

same imprint, from its constitution to its currency to one Mississippi congressman's proposal that the new republic claim the "the name and style of
the United States of America."[40] But the Confederacy did not just inherit
slaveholders' emotional attachment to the old Union. The leaders of the
new regime also brought with them many of the ideological and strategic
assumptions that had defined their years within the U.S. government. In its
confident geopolitical ambitions, capacious view of state power, and close
attention to the international politics of slavery, the new Confederate States
of America strongly resembled its antebellum American progenitor.

Secessionists liked comparing themselves to the oppressed nations of
Europe, but they expected their own independent government to occupy
an altogether different position on the world stage. Visiting South Carolina
to urge secession in November 1860, Georgia orator Francis Bartow insisted on the urgency of collective southern action, in contrast to the willy-
nilly independence seeking of European principalities. "Are we to play the
game now playing in Italy today?" he asked rhetorically. Should South Carolina "be a Tuscany" and Georgia "a Piedmont, with "one little province . . .
under the protection of England, and another tied to France"?[41] Such a frag-
mented form of nationhood would be as absurd as it was degrading. The
South's true course, as nearly every influential secessionist understood, involved not only separation but also consolidation—the melding of several
purportedly "sovereign" states into a united slaveholding republic strong
enough to hold its own in world affairs. Slavery without political mastery
was a dead end. Whether in Abraham Lincoln's Union or in the fierce realm
of international relations, true independence was synonymous with world
power.

Slaveholding elites believed that their southern republic possessed all
the necessary materials for a mighty international career. "The South," declared the report of one Mississippi secession meeting, claimed "over one
million of square miles in territory, capable of sustaining a population of
one hundred fifty millions of inhabitants." Certainly, secessionists tended
to agree, size mattered. In their eyes, the sheer territorial extent of a potential
slaveholding republic was an argument for southern independence. Mea-
suring the South's physical dimensions against other world powers became
a favorite secessionist pastime; the South, said Alabama's Jabez Curry, was
larger than the United States before the Louisiana Purchase; it was "more
than *six* times as large as Prussia," boasted John Townsend.[42]

Some early Confederate writers gloried in the South's noble struggle against the stronger North, anticipating later wartime and postwar propaganda that depicted the Confederacy as a heroic underdog. But in the exuberant spring of 1861 the rhetoric of statehood generally pushed in the opposite direction—toward the power and scope of the new Confederate nation. "Ours," boasted Stephens, "is an area of country more than double the territory of France or the Austrian empire. . . . It is greater than all France, Spain, Portugal, and Great Britain, including England, Ireland, and Scotland, together." The Confederacy's true peers were not weak nations like Poland or Hungary but the great empires that dominated them. After the Upper South joined the Confederacy in the spring of 1861, southern horizons expanded even further: the completed republic, declared the Richmond *Examiner*, now ruled a larger landmass than "that of any country in Christendom, except Russia, Brazil, and the Northern Union."[43]

There are reasons to be skeptical about this kind of braggadocio. Newly minted Confederates confronted critical audiences, both at home and abroad, who doubted that a rump southern state could hold its own on the world stage. They had every incentive to make the grandest possible case for the new nation's future career, both to convince the skeptics and, perhaps, to convince themselves. But popular speeches and newspaper columns were not the only expressions of the South's strategic confidence. The founding of the Confederacy itself was an act of geopolitical ambition. As Francis Bartow suggested in November 1860, most secessionist leaders understood that withdrawal from the Union meant the creation of a new and powerful southern nation-state.

William Henry Trescot, who had just resigned as assistant U.S. secretary of state, advised Howell Cobb in early 1861 to "organize a Southern government immediately. We must meet Lincoln with a President of our own." Most critical, for Trescot, was for the new Confederate regime to find its footing on the world stage: "[A]bove all, our foreign relations ought to be assured as quickly as possible." Feeble as separate international actors, together the southern states could dominate global politics. Through its strategic control over the Gulf of Mexico and its command of the isthmus connection to the Pacific, Trescot had written years earlier, an independent South would eventually become "the guardian of the world's commerce—the grave and impartial centre of [a] new balance of power."[44] The foundation of this towering international confidence was the Confederacy's control of the global cotton supply, which could be manipulated to secure strategic assistance from Europe. But if the means to southern world power was cotton diplomacy, the mechanism was a strong national state. Only through "unity of national feeling and centralization of national government," Trescot wrote in February, could southern independence thrive.[45]

The South's leadership had already begun working toward this vital end. In early February 1861, just days after the last of the Lower South states left the Union, a formidable collection of southern politicians gathered in Montgomery, Alabama, with instructions from their state secession conventions to frame a provisional southern government. What political authority did this improvised assembly possess? A few delegates doubted their ability to do much more than draw up a preliminary constitution and submit it to the states for ratification. But the Montgomery convention, like the Confederacy it spawned, was dominated by worldly state builders, not doctrinaire idealists.[46] Led by a trio of nationally experienced Georgians—Stephens, Howell Cobb, and Robert Toombs—the men at Montgomery acted quickly to lay the groundwork for a strong and united southern state. After just two days of committee deliberation and a mere nine hours of floor debate, delegates agreed on a provisional constitution that gave them instant authority to draft a permanent founding document, pass laws as a Congress, and elect a president. This was no longer a convention; it was a national government. The new regime "sprang forth as if by magic," one Alabama representative later wrote. Amid the thrill of creation, few delegates complained that the theoretically sovereign state legislatures had received no chance to ratify these proceedings.[47]

With Lincoln's inauguration just weeks away, the seceding Lower South states had to work "promptly" to confront the new Republican administration with "a strong government," as one Florida senator put it. Just days after the government was formed, the Confederate States of America had a functioning executive branch, with Davis and Stephens at its head. Speed was of the essence, both to resist any northern efforts to foil secession and to encourage wavering Upper South states to join the new republic. But the astonishingly fast and almost painless birth of the Confederate state also said something about the confidence with which slaveholding leaders viewed the power of government.[48]

Listing his reasons for why the South should quit Lincoln's Union, R. M. T. Hunter placed paramount importance on the relationship between slavery and the central state. In a southern republic, he argued, "[o]ur social system,

THE STARTING POINT OF THE GREAT WAR BETWEEN THE STATES.
INAUGURATION OF JEFFERSON DAVIS

At his inauguration on February 18, 1861, Confederate President Jefferson Davis was introduced to the public by Montgomery Convention President Howell Cobb. This print, produced by a Baltimore company years after the Civil War, was based closely on a photograph taken at the exact hour of Davis's inauguration, 1 o'clock p.m.

instead of being dwarfed and warred upon by the action of the government, would receive all the assistance and means of development which it is proper for a government to render the society which it represents." Hunter did not attend the initial convention at Montgomery—he arrived only after Virginia seceded in April—but his words captured the essential outlook of the men who forged the Confederate state. Secession did not produce a flight away from central authority but the eager embrace of a new and explicitly proslavery central authority.[49]

One month after the Montgomery convention drew up its provisional constitution, the Confederate Congress adopted a permanent founding document. The inspiration and model for the Confederate founders was not Calhoun's *Disquisition on Government* or any other theoretical work; instead, it was the existing Constitution of the United States.[50] Far from installing a regime devoted to the protection of minority rights, the Confederacy's small innovations to the U.S. Constitution tended to enhance rather than restrain the power of the national government, and particularly the power of the executive branch. The Confederate president and vice president would each serve six years rather than four; Confederate cabinet officers, unlike their counterparts in the United States, could sit simultaneously in the House or Senate, allowing the administration to manage legislation directly from the floor of Congress. The president received the power of a line-item veto on budget questions, while Congress was constrained to propose appropriations according to the estimates of department heads. Theoretically a deterrent to legislative logrolling and pork-barrel spending, these measures streamlined the executive's ability to control policy in Congress. Certainly, they would have been welcomed by the southern military reformers of the 1850s, who seldom feared excessive expenditures but often lamented unproductive congressional meddling with War and Navy Department requests.[51]

To be sure, the Confederate Constitution contained a few large and dramatic gestures in the direction of states' rights. Its preamble added a clause acknowledging that each state was "acting in its sovereign and independent character" while omitting the U.S. constitutional clause about promoting "the general welfare." Yet even in this framing paragraph the alterations were ambiguous: whereas the American founders of 1787 had pledged themselves merely to "form a more perfect union," the Confederate state builders of 1861 avowed their intention to create "a permanent federal government." The other major victories won by states'-rights advocates at Montgomery—bans on protective tariffs and national infrastructure spending—functioned much better as rhetorical flourishes than as actual restrictions on federal power, as the course of Confederate history would show.[52]

At the center of the Confederate state-building project stood the institution of slavery. Here, as R. M. T. Hunter had hoped, the Montgomery founders made certain that their new state would not merely let slavery alone but would provide all the positive "assistance and means of development" that a national government could offer. Unlike the U.S. Constitution, which famously avoided all mention of the word "slave," the Confederate Constitution used the word ten times. It affirmed the immutable "right of property in negro slaves," clarified the fugitive slave clause, and declared that in all new territories acquired, "the institution of negro slavery . . . shall be recognized and protected by Congress." Each of these emendations reinforced the power of slaveholders over their slaves; equally important, each of them invested the Confederate government as the ultimate guardian of this power. The Montgomery convention also agreed overwhelmingly to ban the African slave trade, an act that further underlined Confederate willingness to empower a proslavery central government—not individual states or masters—to regulate the boundaries of slave labor within the new nation.[53]

In their years of service and supremacy within the old American Union, slaveholders had often worked to enhance the capacity of the federal government. The executive branch, as the chief conductor of U.S. power overseas—through the army, the navy, and the diplomatic corps—had long been the special property of ambitious southern reformers. It was largely the fear of an internal political threat to slavery that kept slaveholders wary about the encroachments of centralized authority. Now that they sat at the controls of their own "great government," as Howell Cobb called the new regime, it was no surprise that they acted to strengthen the hand of the proslavery state.[54]

The foreign policy posture of the Confederate States, too, reflected the legacy of the antebellum decades. The Confederate Constitution's new clause about the acquisition of territory signaled slaveholders' long-standing appetite for empire. In the early months of 1861 some Confederates called for a bold plan of hemispheric expansion, embracing, in various iterations,

Cuba, Mexico, Central America, Colombia, Brazil, or even the whole of both American continents. The antislavery North, declared greedy imperialists like Edmund Ruffin, had long stood in the way of the South's glorious international career; now that it was unfettered, nothing could prevent the Confederate conquest of the Latin world.[55]

Yet as in the 1850s, the foreign policy of slavery both encouraged and undercut impulses toward territorial expansion. With the world's strongest slaveholding state now reduced to less than half its former capacity and threatened by an antislavery behemoth to the north, the hemispheric balance of power between bondage and freedom became more precarious than ever. "Spain, Brazil, and the South," observed a writer in *De Bow's Review*, "are the only slaveholding countries. If Cuba were detached from Spain, the cause of slavery would be weakened," both in the Americas and in Europe. The Confederate government under Jefferson Davis was acutely aware of its hemispheric peers. "For the future," Davis told an Atlanta audience shortly before his inauguration, "we are to be embraced in the same moral category as Brazil and Cuba." Although Davis alluded to the possibility of expanding into "the West India Isles," he did not want to alienate potential partners in the Caribbean basin. The guiding principle of the Confederacy's hemispheric foreign policy was not expansion but proslavery coalition building.[56]

"It is the policy of the Government of the Confederate States," Secretary of State Toombs informed the Confederacy's Havana envoy in July, "that Cuba shall continue to be a colonial possession of Spain." Shelving any plans for Cuban annexation, the Confederacy instead approached Spain with a plea for "a close and intimate alliance" in the Americas. Hunter, who soon replaced Toombs in the State Department, made the proslavery logic of this proposal explicit in his instructions to the Confederacy's commissioners in London: "Of all the great powers of Europe, Spain alone is interested, through her colonies, in the same social system which pervades the Confederate States." The growth of Spanish "power and influence" across the Americas, Hunter continued, would bring both slaveholding nations together, "armed with the means to protect their common social system."[57]

In Mexico, too, the Confederacy's first moves were cautious and conciliatory, giving precedence to slavery rather than territorial expansion. When the Mexican governor of Coahuila and Nuevo León, just across the Rio Grande from Texas, proposed to join his two provinces to the Confederate republic, Davis firmly declined the offer.[58] Such an annexation might prove more costly than it was worth, and in any case the basis of Confederate-Mexican friendship lay elsewhere. "The institution of domestic slavery in one country and that of peonage in the other," Toombs told the Confederacy's agent in Mexico City, "establish between them such a similarity in the system of labor as to prevent any tendency on either side to disregard the feelings and interests of the other."[59]

As an interpretation of Mexican society and politics, this was myopic, but as a window into the Confederate strategic worldview, it is revealing. Why did Davis's Confederacy so quickly abandon long-standing southern dreams of expansion? The traditional explanation centers on the exigency of the Civil War: after the clash at Fort Sumter in April, the South had to muster all its resources for the military conflict with the North. Under these circumstances it was simple logic to postpone any grand imperial designs in Latin America in favor of a quieter, cheaper policy of alliance and collaboration. But in its emphasis on slavery over expansion, the Confederacy's hemispheric program represented a continuity, not a rupture, with the antebellum era. When Hunter made "social systems" rather than political allegiances the priority in Spanish Cuba, he only followed a long strategic tradition in U.S. foreign policy. When in August 1861 George Fitzhugh proposed that the Confederate States of America discard the Monroe Doctrine and support a French effort to reenslave Haiti, he only borrowed the arguments of New Orleans editors in the 1840s and the visions of South Carolina poets in the 1850s.[60]

None of this is to suggest that an active, engaged foreign policy was the Confederacy's first priority in the early months of 1861. Confident in the political power generated by their slave economy—"the greatest material interest in the world"—the Confederate leadership, if anything, scorned the delicate labors of diplomacy. The strategic cornerstone of southern world power lay in the hands of King Cotton, guided by Emperor Slavery—not the second-rate squad of commissioners Jefferson Davis initially dispatched to Europe and Latin America.[61] The point, rather, is that in its foreign policy, as in its state making, the Confederate States of America inherited the worldview of the proslavery United States. From Madrid to Rio de Janeiro—a sympathetic Brazilian envoy was spotted in Montgomery in May—Confederate leaders approached Atlantic world geopolitics the same way as southern Americans had done for decades: with an ideological and strategic calculus whose fundamental postulate was the protection of slave property.[62]

———————

For American slaveholders, the most decisive rupture was not secession but the Civil War. "Peace," John C. Calhoun had always insisted, "is indeed our policy." At his inaugural address in February 1861 Jefferson Davis repeated Calhoun's claim: "[A]s an agricultural people," he declared, "our true policy is peace." For all the vainglorious Confederates who boasted that slavery would prove an asset in wartime, the South's shrewdest leaders from 1840 to 1860 consistently sought to strengthen slavery while avoiding a major armed conflict.[63]

In April 1861, however, Davis proved unable to secure his sovereign slave republic without bombarding U.S. troops in Charleston harbor. Amid the intoxications of independence, statehood, and nation making, Confederates lost their grip on strategic reality. In just four months they had successfully pulled the Lower South out of the Union and had erected a strong national state on its rich domains—a republic with "all the elements of a high national career," as Alexander Stephens boasted at Savannah. With the Upper South teetering in the balance and the prospect of a united slaveholding empire within reach, the Confederacy was not about to begin that career by remaining idle while the U.S. Navy resupplied the garrison at Fort Sumter. If they had truly created "a Government which would command obedience at home . . . and respect abroad," how could Confederates allow a hostile foreign power to command the gateway to their second-largest city and most important Atlantic port?[64]

This was one of the many ironies of southern nationhood. The same vast confidence that helped slaveholders dominate the Union while they were in it, and assemble a new state so quickly once they were out of it, propelled them to their own destruction. *"Forward,"* wrote Lawrence Keitt at the Montgomery convention, "is the inexorable word in this world."[65] Believing in the progressive force of civilization and the progressive power of their own institutions, slaveholders charged headlong into disaster. War exposed all the frail premises and self-serving perambulations of Confederate strategic thought. Great Britain purchased the South's cotton but did not depend on it. Slave labor may have been one motor driving global capitalism in 1860, but other and even more dynamic engines could be found. The size, strength, and unity of the Confederate States could not prevent the North from waging war to restore the Union nor compel the European powers to recognize the independent South.[66]

As help from abroad failed to materialize, the Confederacy increasingly turned its considerable energies inward. Under the pressures of civil war the strong national government that men like Hunter and Trescot had desired, and the Montgomery Constitution had framed, quickly acquired substance. In its efforts to mobilize men and materiel—through conscription, railroad construction, mass production, labor impressment, and outright property confiscation—Davis's government gradually assumed near-absolute control over vast swathes of the southern economy. By 1863 the rebel leviathan had grown far beyond the scope of any antebellum imagination. Before the war was over, it had enlisted and equipped perhaps a million soldiers, forged a mighty industrial plant out of almost nothing, and transformed the social landscape of the South.[67]

Many observers, then and since, have called attention to this incongruity of the Confederate experience: a revolution commenced in the name of states' rights ended by creating the most invasively organized national government in all nineteenth-century American history. It would be too much to claim that these dramatic wartime transformations flowed naturally out of prewar foreign policy precedents. But two decades of antebellum experience in the United States made it clear that when slavery and international relations crossed paths, slaveholders eagerly grasped for the power of the federal government. And the position of the Confederacy itself was, in some ways, undeniably and irreducibly international—the southern republic was never anything but a state fighting for its survival against an outside invader. Whether the threat to slavery came from British abolitionists or the Union army, southern leaders proved willing to exercise all the power they could muster to achieve their aims.[68]

They did so to no avail. In the war they began at Charleston harbor, slaveholders' oldest and darkest fears were realized. Fearing a British move against Texas in 1843, Andrew Jackson's nightmare had been that an invading "army of 40,000 men" might "take possession of Memphis & Baton Rouge," seize New Orleans, "excite the negroes to insurrection," and arm rebellious slaves across the South.[69] By the summer of 1863 this was no longer a paranoid prophecy but a simple chronicle of events, the only difference being that the revolutionary army in question belonged to the United States of America. When the war came, bondage crumbled.[70] The Confederacy's physical infrastructure, for all its wartime innovations, lacked the resources to compete with the North. Its foreign policy, for all its swollen self-regard, lacked the punching power to compel European intervention. And its social system, for all its boasted resilience, lacked the capacity to cope with the violent disruptions of war. Seeking to confirm their power over the hemisphere, and claim their place in the vanguard of modern progress, slaveholders only hastened their own ruin and obsolescence.[71]

Epilogue

The Rod of Empire

ON A BRIGHT JUNE MORNING IN 1890, twenty-five years after the defeat of the slaveholders' rebellion, Harvard College gathered to celebrate its 239th commencement. The streets of Cambridge swelled with the customary magnificence of a Harvard graduation, as the governor of Massachusetts made his way to Sanders Theatre "in royal state," escorted by a company of cavalry lancers. The roster of eminent Victorians assembled at Harvard reached back deep into the nineteenth century even as it gave hints of the approaching twentieth: Abraham Lincoln's son Robert Todd, class of '64, rubbed elbows with Virginia Woolf's father, the English critic Leslie Stephen. Other dignitaries included former first lady Frances Cleveland, Oliver Wendell Holmes Jr., and no fewer than two distinct John Quincy Adamses—Governor John Quincy Adams Brackett and Harvard alumni association president John Quincy Adams II, the sixth president's grandson.[1]

But even in this company of local Brahmins and illustrious visitors, the most anticipated orator was a lowly undergraduate. A faculty committee had selected the first African American student ever to deliver a graduation-day lecture at Harvard—a twenty-two-year-old philosophy major named William Edward Burghardt Du Bois. This "slender, intellectual-looking mulatto," as the *Nation* haughtily described him, had given his address a title as striking as it was provocative: "Jefferson Davis as a Representative of Civilization."[2]

Davis had died only recently, succumbing to bronchitis in New Orleans the previous December. His death washed away one of the last surviving pillars of the antebellum master class: of the original twelve Lower South

senators who had left Washington after Lincoln's election, none now remained alive. But the old slaveholding elite had hardly been buried before it
began to rise again, cast in bronze and hauled atop pedestals of marble. Just
weeks before Harvard's commencement, on Memorial Day, the city of
Richmond had unveiled a sixty-foot equestrian statue of Robert E. Lee on
Monument Avenue. A fresh aspect of the white South's lost-cause narrative
had begun to emerge, less mournful and embittered by Confederate military defeat, and more optimistic, if not triumphant, about the moral value
of the Confederacy's example to a reunited United States. In different ways
the feeling spread even beyond the South. The late 1880s and early 1890s,
David Blight has argued, were the critical years when the spirit of national
white reconciliation gradually overtook the memory of the war against
slavery. Another guest at Sanders Theatre in June was the poet Richard W.
Gilder, Gettysburg veteran and now editor of *Century* magazine, whose hugely
popular Civil War soldier stories helped Americans remember the late conflict not as a revolutionary clash of nations but as a somber battle between
brothers.[3]

The young Du Bois must have noted all this. Jefferson Davis and his
breakaway Confederate republic had been crushed on the battlefield, but
neither disloyalty toward the United States nor decisive military defeat had
been enough to extinguish his legacy—even in Cambridge, Massachusetts.
(Davis's funeral and the unveiling of Lee's statue had both received sympathetic coverage in regional newspapers.)[4] Indeed the title of Du Bois's lecture
could be interpreted as a taunt aimed at all New England. Even in this cradle
of American abolitionism, Du Bois seemed to imply, the chief "representative of civilization" in 1890 was neither of the two John Quincy Adamses in
attendance, but the ghost of a treasonous Confederate commander.

Yet when Harvard president Charles W. Eliot called the student speakers
to the rostrum, announcing the commencement program in "sonorous
Latin," Du Bois did not rise intending to lament that the South, rather than
the North, was winning the cultural contest for the memory of the Civil
War. His vision ranged much more broadly.[5] "I wish not to consider the
man" Jefferson Davis, he insisted, "but the type of civilization which his life
represented: its foundation is the idea of the Strong Man—individualism
coupled with the rule of might—and it is this idea that has made the logic of
even modern history, the cool logic of the Club." It was an idea that underpinned not only the rise of the Lost Cause in the South, or the triumph of
racist reconciliation in the North, but also the larger pattern of global politics in 1890.[6]

"To the most casual observer," Du Bois continued, "it must have occurred that the Rod of Empire has in these days turned toward the South," toward "Southern North America, South America, Australia, and Africa." Du Bois did not need to elaborate on this point; his Harvard audience surely knew that the past decade had witnessed a feverish scramble for imperial possessions all around the globe. At the Berlin Conference of 1884–85, hosted by German chancellor Otto von Bismarck, the major European powers agreed to carve up nearly the whole of the African continent. Before the nineteenth century was complete, British, French, Russian, German, Dutch, Japanese, American, and other empires would violently extend their dominion over most of the world's indigenous peoples, from central Asia to the South Pacific.[7] Nor did Du Bois need to remind his listeners that these vast conquests were nearly always justified by the code of racial supremacy. It was a Harvard man—Theodore Roosevelt, class of '80—who expressed this imperial dogma most vividly: "It is of incalculable importance," he wrote in *The Winning of the West,* "that America, Australia, and Siberia should pass out of the hands of their red, black, and yellow aboriginal owners, and become the heritage of the dominant world races."[8]

But if the basic outlines of this new imperialism sounded familiar, Du Bois's interpretation of its genealogy was strikingly original. Neither Bismarck nor Roosevelt but Jefferson Davis, Du Bois argued, best personified the contemporary world's obsession with race and thirst for empire. Davis's antebellum career as a U.S. Army officer and secretary of war had been defined by these same brutal pursuits—first "advancing civilization by murdering Indians," then winning heroism in the "national disgrace" of the war with Mexico. As Confederate president, Davis finally became "the peculiar champion of a people fighting to be free in order that another people should not be free." A vision of progress through racial domination had been at the heart of the Confederate enterprise, and although the Confederacy was defeated, Du Bois argued that its fundamental ideas now inspired "the policy and philosophy of the State" in the present day. In fact, the entire political order of the late nineteenth-century world—the rise of "the Strong Nation with its armies"; the conquest of "effete civilization[s]" by these same imperial nation-states; the idea of white supremacy as the basis of international relations—had been anticipated and vividly embodied in the slaveholding American South. The "Rod of Empire," in this telling, grew out of the master's whip.[9]

To reach these conceptual heights, Du Bois certainly simplified the complex history of slavery, race, and empire across the nineteenth century.

It was not quite accurate to suggest that the slave South alone had inspired the ruthless global order he described. From Alaska to Bengal, midcentury opponents of slavery like William Seward and Lord Palmerston laid the groundwork for the late nineteenth century's world of empires. The same overwhelming wealth and weaponry that the industrial North used to conquer the South in 1865 also permitted, and sometimes encouraged, Euro-American imperialists to overrun the planet in the decades that followed. (Very often, in bloody U.S. conflicts from Montana to Korea, it was not just the weapons but the commanding officers that were the same.)[10]

Big steel, not King Cotton, had already begun to dominate the new era; in the world's most powerful countries heavy industry overshadowed staple agriculture, while tariff protections supplanted free trade. Even on an ideological level, where Du Bois grounded his alternate genealogy, the lines of descent seemed equally difficult to trace. The vision of racial civilization that animated men like Theodore Roosevelt did not depend on a strict defense of chattel slavery. On the contrary, white imperialists in Africa, from David Livingstone onward, generally understood themselves as inheritors of the abolitionist crusade. The Age of Empire, in both moral and material terms, was a world that nonslaveholders had made.[11]

Few of these qualifications, however, diminished the power of Du Bois's central insight. American slaveholders were not the only nineteenth-century elites whose vision of progress matched Du Bois's cutting definition: "the advance of a part of the world at the expense of the whole" and "the rise of one race on the ruins of another." But in the strength of their commitment to African bondage at home and across the Americas, slaveholders can be seen as a vanguard for the coercive, state-powered racism that characterized the international relations of the late nineteenth century.[12] Proslavery intellectuals from Matthew Maury to James D. B. De Bow had surveyed "every Southern country" in the Western Hemisphere and had concluded that its future development depended on compulsory nonwhite labor. And proslavery foreign policymakers from Abel Upshur to Jefferson Davis had understood that the "mighty Right arm" of this racialized economic order was the "Strong Nation": the military and diplomatic capacity of the American state. In this ironic sense the very institution that for so long marked the American South as a relic of the seventeenth century—racial slavery—also propelled it to anticipate some of the darkest features of the twentieth.[13]

If by 1890 the commanding heights of the world economy no longer belonged to staple agriculture, the imperial hunger for raw tropical materials—and the deployment of dark-skinned labor to produce them—remained a major feature of global trade.[14] The ferocity of this process would not have surprised American slaveholders. "If civilization, like an ogre, asked for its daily breakfast the heads of one thousand African negroes," the world would provide them, declared a *De Bow's* contributor in 1859, before the Congo Free State was a glimmer in King Leopold's eye. "Conquest, extension, appropriation, assimilation, and even the extermination of inferior races has been and must be the course pursued in the development of civilization," observed George Frederick Holmes in 1856, two years before the birth of Theodore Roosevelt.[15]

Of course, these southerners assumed that chattel slavery would serve as a critical tool in this spread of civilization, and some imagined that the leading civilizers would be American slaveholders. Eric Hobsbawm once speculated that if it had survived into the late nineteenth century, the "slave South, being used to the difference between a free and mass unfree population ... might well have become more like a European empire." The Civil War ensured that none of these dreams were realized. But even a superficial glance at the wider world of 1890—carved into colonies, ranked by race, and fueled by extractive labor—made it clear that not every element of the pro-slavery vision disappeared from view after the defeat of the Confederacy.[16]

This was precisely Du Bois's point. Above all, he insisted, the ideas and the activities of the slave South remained relevant in the late nineteenth century. Here he parted company with most of his white contemporaries, who by 1890 much preferred to isolate the old world of the plantation from the new universe of global politics. Just a generation after American emancipation, transatlantic elites had already begun to decorate slavery's tomb with garlands of myth, romance, and false antiquity. The "splendid virtues" of the southern planter, lamented British prime minister William Gladstone in 1889, had been unjustly blotted out in the present day. Although they were tragically bound to the moral error of slavery, Gladstone wrote, southern masters nevertheless represented true heirs to "the age of chivalry ... worthy to sit with Sir Percival at the 'table round' of King Arthur."[17]

Du Bois, however, refused to condescend to Jefferson Davis and his class. Instead he evaluated them, as the *Nation* noted, "with almost contemptuous fairness." Granting slaveholders the justice of their merits—"stalwart manhood and heroic character"—he also acknowledged the ambition of their political project and the significance of its legacy. This project may have been characterized by "moral obtuseness and refined brutality," but it was a powerful venture of transnational scope, not a faux-medieval daydream.[18]

And here Du Bois still has something to teach us today. Famously, the myth of the lost cause, advanced by the memoirs of men like Davis and Alexander Stephens, divorced slavery from the causes of disunion, distorting Civil War history for generations. Equally important, those same generations constructed their narratives of southern history in the shadows of Confederate defeat. If one read all antebellum history backward from the perspective of Appomattox, it became easy to see the South as weak, defensive, and archaic. Only these illusions could permit later observers, from Westminster to Hollywood, to view the proud slaveholding civilization of Jefferson Davis with such demeaning nostalgia.

But to deal properly with American slaveholders, a dose of contemptuous fairness is required. With Du Bois, we must recognize the full magnitude of the proslavery enterprise—not only its cruelty and blindness but also its power and sophistication. In the decades before the Civil War, slaveholders organized U.S. foreign policy around the effort to defend slavery throughout the Western Hemisphere. They did this not simply to guard their property rights or to solidify their social order, but because they understood slavery as a vital element of global progress. It was the appointed destiny of the United States, slaveholders believed, to uphold the institutions that nourished modern civilization. Only a political revolution that was unprecedented and unrivaled in American experience drove them from power. Even their ultimate defeat unfolded on the grandest of scales: no other slaveholding class in human history led a rebellion that claimed three-quarters of a million lives. Its triumphs, its downfall, and its legacy attest to the vast breadth and fierce confidence of the proslavery political vision. We can be grateful that slaveholders never gained the world they craved, but we achieve nothing by failing to take the true measure of its dimensions.

NOTES

ACKNOWLEDGMENTS

CREDITS

INDEX

Notes

Abbreviations

AHR	*American Historical Review*
CG	*Congressional Globe*
CG Appendix	*Appendix to the Congressional Globe*
CW&M	College of William and Mary
DBR	*De Bow's Review*
DCUS	William R. Manning, ed., *Diplomatic Correspondence of the United States: Inter-American Affairs, 1831–1860*, 12 vols. (Washington, D.C.: Carnegie Endowment for International Peace, 1936–1939)
H.R. Doc.	*House of Representatives Document*
H. Ex. Doc	*House of Representatives Executive Document*
H.R. Rep.	*House of Representatives Report*
JAH	*Journal of American History*
JCWE	*Journal of the Civil War Era*
JDC	Dunbar Rowland, ed., *Jefferson Davis, Constitutionalist: His Letters, Papers, and Speeches*, 10 vols. (Jackson: Mississippi Department of Archives and History, 1923)
JER	*Journal of the Early Republic*
JSH	*Journal of Southern History*
LC	Library of Congress
NA	National Archives
PJCC	Clyde N. Wilson et al., eds., *The Papers of John C. Calhoun*, 28 vols. (Columbia: University of South Carolina Press, 1959–2003)
PJD	Lynda L. Crist et al., eds., *The Papers of Jefferson Davis*, 14 vols. (Baton Rouge: University of Louisiana Press, 1971–2015)
SHC-UNC	Southern Historical Collection, Wilson Library, University of North Carolina at Chapel Hill

S. Doc.	Senate Document
S. Ex. Doc.	Senate Executive Document
S. Misc. Doc.	Senate Miscellaneous Document
S. Rep.	Senate Report
SLM	Southern Literary Messenger
SQR	Southern Quarterly Review
VHS	Virginia Historical Society

THE EPIGRAPH preceding the Introduction is from Karl Marx, "The North American Civil War," *Die Presse* (Vienna), November 7, 1861, in Marx and Friedrich Engels, *The Civil War in the United States*, ed. Richard Enmale (New York: International Publishers, 1937), 64.

Introduction

1. For surveys of this vast history, see David Brion Davis, *The Problem of Slavery in the Age of Revolution, 1770–1823* (Ithaca, N.Y.: Cornell University Press, 1975); Robin Blackburn, *The Overthrow of Colonial Slavery, 1776–1848* (London: Verso, 1988); and Seymour Drescher, *Abolition: A History of Slavery and Antislavery* (New York: Cambridge University Press, 2009), 1–266.
2. For population and trade estimates, see Robin Blackburn, *The American Crucible: Slavery, Emancipation and Human Rights* (London: Verso, 2011), 296–97. On the extraordinary growth of American, Brazilian, and Cuban slavery between 1820 and 1860, see Dale W. Tomich, *Through the Prism of Slavery: Labor, Capital, and World Economy* (Lanham, Md.: Rowman and Littlefield, 2004), esp. 56–71; and Anthony E. Kaye, "The Second Slavery: Modernity in the Nineteenth-Century South and the Atlantic World," *JSH* 75, no. 3 (August 2009): 631–42.
3. Theodore Parker, *The Great Battle between Slavery and Freedom, Considered in Two Speeches.* (Boston: Benjamin H. Greene, 1856), 7–8. On the international dimensions of antislavery struggle, see Blackburn, *American Crucible*, 329–89; and W. Caleb McDaniel, *The Problem of Democracy in the Age of Slavery: Garrisonian Abolitionists and Transatlantic Reform* (Baton Rouge: Louisiana State University Press, 2013).
4. For two distinct but overlapping views of the nineteenth-century United States as the epicenter of a transnational conflict over empire and slavery, see Sven Beckert, *Empire of Cotton: A Global History* (New York: Knopf, 2014), 83–273; and John Craig Hammond, "Slavery, Sovereignty, and Empires: North American Borderlands and the American Civil War, 1660–1860," *JCWE* 4, no. 2 (June 2014), 264–98.
5. Eric Hobsbawm, *The Age of Capital: 1848–1875* (New York: Charles Scribner's Sons, 1975), 141–43, 182–86. For similar arguments from a global history perspective, see Barrington Moore, *Social Origins of Dictatorship and Democracy: Lord*

and Peasant in the Making of the Modern World (Boston: Beacon Press, 1966), 111–56; and Christopher A. Bayly, *The Birth of the Modern World: 1798–1914* (Malden, Mass.: Blackwell, 2003), 161–65, 402–10.

6. See L. Diane Barnes, Brian Schoen, and Frank Towers, eds., *The Old South's Modern Worlds: Slavery, Region, and Nation in the Age of Progress* (New York: Oxford University Press, 2011); Beckert, *Empire of Cotton*; Seth Rockman, "Slavery and Capitalism," in "Forum on the Future of Civil War Era Studies," *JCWE* 2, no. 1 (March 2012): online supplement; Walter Johnson, *River of Dark Dreams: Slavery and Empire in the Cotton Kingdom* (Cambridge, Mass.: Harvard University Press, 2013); Edward E. Baptist, *The Half Has Never Been Told: Slavery and the Making of American Capitalism* (New York: Basic Books, 2014); and Gabriel Winant, "Slave Capitalism," *n+1*, August 2013, https://nplusonemag.com/issue-17/reviews/slave-capitalism.

7. Michael O'Brien, *Conjectures of Order: Intellectual Life in the Old South, 1810–1860* (Chapel Hill: University of North Carolina Press, 2004); Elizabeth Fox-Genovese and Eugene D. Genovese, *The Mind of the Master Class: History and Faith in the Southern Slaveholders' Worldview* (New York: Cambridge University Press, 2005).

8. On the international orientation of the antebellum southern economy, see Douglass North, *The Economic Growth of the United States, 1790–1860* (Englewood Cliffs, N.J.: Prentice-Hall, 1961), esp. 66–134; and Gavin Wright, *The Political Economy of the Cotton South: Households, Markets, and Wealth in the Nineteenth Century* (New York: W. W. Norton, 1978).

9. Important work on American slaveholders and the wider world includes Gerald Horne, *The Deepest South: The United States, Brazil, and the African Slave Trade* (New York: New York University Press, 2007); Matthew Pratt Guterl, *American Mediterranean: Southern Slaveholders in the Age of Emancipation* (Cambridge, Mass.: Harvard University Press, 2008); Edward B. Rugemer, *The Problem of Emancipation: The Caribbean Roots of the American Civil War* (Baton Rouge: Louisiana State University Press, 2008); Brian Schoen, *The Fragile Fabric of Union: Cotton, Federal Politics, and the Global Origins of the Civil War* (Baltimore: Johns Hopkins University Press, 2009); and Peter Kolchin, "The South and the World," *JSH* 75, no. 3 (August 2009): 565–80.

10. Hobsbawm, *Age of Capital*, 57. For varying perspectives on the place of slavery inside the global capitalist economy, see Eric Williams, *Capitalism and Slavery* (Chapel Hill: University of North Carolina Press, 1944); Immanuel Wallerstein, "American Slavery and the Capitalist World-Economy," in *The Capitalist World-Economy* (Cambridge: Cambridge University Press, 1979), 202–21; Elizabeth Fox-Genovese and Eugene D. Genovese, *Fruits of Merchant Capital: Slavery and Bourgeois Property in the Rise and Expansion of Capitalism* (New York: Oxford University Press, 1983), esp. vii–60; Tomich, *Through the Prism of Slavery*, 3–55; and Walter Johnson, "The Pedestal and the Veil: Rethinking the Capitalism/Slavery Question," *JER*, 24, no. 2 (Summer 2004): 299–308.

11. Leonidas W. Spratt, "The Destiny of the Slave States," *Charleston Southern Standard,* June 25, 1853; Eugene D. Genovese, *The World the Slaveholders Made: Two Essays in Interpretation* (New York: Random House, 1969).

12. Johnson, *River of Dark Dreams,* 413. On proslavery's "alternative narrative of progress," see Christa Dierksheide and Peter S. Onuf, "Slaveholding Nation, Slaveholding Civilization," in William J. Cooper Jr. and John M. McCardell, eds., *In the Cause of Liberty: How the Civil War Redefined American Ideals* (Baton Rouge: Louisiana State University Press, 2009), 9–25.

13. L. Q. C. Lamar, speech in House, *CG Appendix,* 36th Cong., 1st Sess., 115 (February 21, 1860); Lemuel Evans, speech in House, *CG Appendix,* 34th Cong., 3rd Sess., 235 (February 4, 1857). See also O'Brien, *Conjectures of Order,* 1044–45; and Fox-Genovese and Genovese, *Mind of the Master Class,* 156, 532.

14. On institutional and ideological approaches to the history of slavery, see Robin Einhorn, "Slavery," *Enterprise and Society* 9, no. 3 (September 2008): 491–508.

15. See Don E. Fehrenbacher, *The Slaveholding Republic: An Account of the United States Government's Relations to Slavery* (New York: Oxford University Press, 2001); David F. Ericson, *Slavery in the American Republic: Developing the Federal Government, 1791–1861* (Lawrence: University Press of Kansas, 2011); and Adam Rothman, "The 'Slave Power' in the United States, 1783–1865," in Steve Fraser and Gary Gerstle, eds., *Ruling America: A History of Wealth and Power in a Democracy* (Cambridge, Mass.: Harvard University Press, 2005), 64–91.

16. Josiah Grinnell, speech in House, *CG,* 38th Cong., 2nd Sess., 199 (January 10, 1865); W. E. B. Du Bois, *Black Reconstruction in America* (New York: Russell and Russell, 1935), 47.

17. On the notion of an "outward state," and its relative strength in a later nineteenth-century period, see Andrew W. Cohen, "Smuggling, Globalization, and America's Outward State, 1870–1909," *JAH* 97, no. 2 (September 2010), 371–98. See also Ericson, *Slavery in the American Republic,* 107–34; and Robert E. Bonner, *Mastering America: Southern Slaveholders and the Crisis of American Nationhood* (New York: Cambridge University Press, 2009), 3–40.

18. Arthur M. Schlesinger, *New Viewpoints in American History* (New York: Macmillan, 1922), 243. See also Richard E. Ellis, *The Union at Risk: Jacksonian Democracy, States' Rights, and the Nullification Crisis* (Oxford: Oxford University Press, 1987); James L. Huston, "Property Rights in Slavery and the Coming of the Civil War," *JSH* 65, no. 2 (May 1999): 249–86; and Manisha Sinha, *The Counterrevolution of Slavery: Politics and Ideology in Antebellum South Carolina* (Chapel Hill: University of North Carolina Press, 2000)

19. For important revisions of the notion of a weak or nonexistent antebellum federal government, especially regarding military affairs, see William J. Novak, "The Myth of the 'Weak' American State," *AHR* 113, no. 3 (June 2008): 752–72; Brian Balogh, *A Government out of Sight: The Mystery of National Authority in Nineteenth-Century America* (New York: Cambridge University Press, 2009); and

Max Edling, *Hercules in the Cradle: War, Money, and the American State, 1783–1867* (Chicago: University of Chicago Press, 2014).

20. Henry Adams, *John Randolph* (Boston: Houghton Mifflin, 1882), 270–71. On antebellum slaveholders' embrace of different forms of state power, both in theory and in practice, see Douglas Ambrose, "Statism in the Old South," in Robert L. Paquette and Louis A. Ferleger, eds., *Slavery, Secession, and Southern History* (Charlottesville: University Press of Virginia, 2000), 101–25; Arthur Bestor, "State Sovereignty and Slavery: A Reinterpretation of Proslavery Constitutional Doctrine, 1846–1860," *Journal of the Illinois State Historical Society* 54, no. 2 (Summer 1961): 117–80; Steven Lubet, *Fugitive Justice: Runaways, Rescuers, and Slavery on Trial* (Cambridge, Mass.: The Belknap Press of Harvard University Press, 2010); and John Majewski, *Modernizing a Slave Economy: The Economic Vision of the Confederate Nation* (Chapel Hill: University of North Carolina Press, 2009), 1–107.

21. *Richmond Enquirer*, May 16, 1854.

22. For four generations of influential scholarship on this question, each primarily concerned with slavery and territorial expansion, see Charles W. Ramsdell, "The Natural Limits of Slavery Expansionism," *Mississippi Valley Historical Review* 16, no. 2 (September 1929): 151–71; Eugene D. Genovese, *The Political Economy of Slavery: Studies in the Economy and Society of the Slave South* (New York: Pantheon, 1965), 243–74; James M. McPherson, *Battle Cry of Freedom: The Civil War Era* (New York: Oxford University Press, 1988), 91–116; and Johnson, *River of Dark Dreams*, 330–93.

23. Marx, "North American Civil War," 65. Diplomatic historians have tended to stress the importance of race rather than slavery in the longer history U.S. foreign relations. But the slaveholders at the helm of antebellum foreign policy were not driven by white supremacy alone; as a class, they sought to advance the interests of a particular system of labor and property. See Michael Hunt, *Ideology and U.S. Foreign Policy* (New Haven, Conn.: Yale University Press, 1988), 46–92; Thomas R. Hietala, *Manifest Design: American Exceptionalism and Empire*, rev. ed. (Ithaca, N.Y.: Cornell University Press, 2003); Reginald Horsman, *Race and Manifest Destiny: Origins of American Racial Anglo-Saxonism* (Cambridge, Mass.: Harvard University Press, 1981), 187–297; and Joseph Fry, *Dixie Looks Abroad: The South and U.S. Foreign Relations, 1789–1973* (Baton Rouge: Louisiana State University Press, 2002).

24. Robert E. May, *The Southern Dream of a Caribbean Empire, 1854–1861* (Gainesville: University Press of Florida, 2002 [1973]); Robert E. May, *Manifest Destiny's Underworld: Filibustering in Antebellum America* (Chapel Hill: University of North Carolina Press, 2002); Amy S. Greenberg, *Manifest Manhood and the Antebellum American Empire* (New York: Cambridge University Press, 2005).

25. On the idea of a "foreign policy of slavery," see St. George L. Sioussant, "Duff Green's 'England and the United States': With an Introductory Study of American

Opposition to the Quintuple Treaty of 1841," *Proceedings of the American Antiquarian Society,* n.s., 40 (Worcester, Mass.: American Antiquarian Society, 1931): 214; and Robert Kagan, *Dangerous Nation: America's Foreign Policy from Its Earliest Days to the Dawn of the Twentieth Century* (New York: Vintage, 2006), 181–223, 445–46.

26. *Richmond Enquirer,* April 20, 1844. On the significance of antebellum invocations of disunion, see Elizabeth R. Varon, *Disunion! The Coming of the American Civil War, 1789–1859* (Chapel Hill: University of North Carolina Press, 2010).

27. On "proslavery Americanism" as a defining feature of the late antebellum southern worldview, see Bonner, *Mastering America,* xi–213.

1. Confronting the Great Apostle of Emancipation

1. [Edgar Allan Poe], "George Balcombe," *SLM,* January 1837, 49–58. On Tucker, see Robert J. Brugger, *Beverley Tucker: Heart over Head in the Old South* (Baltimore: Johns Hopkins University Press, 1978); Beverley D. Tucker, *Nathaniel Beverley Tucker: Prophet of the Confederacy, 1784–1851* (Tokyo: Nan'un-do, 1979); Drew Gilpin Faust, *A Sacred Circle: The Dilemma of the Intellectual in the Old South, 1840–1860* (Philadelphia: University of Pennsylvania Press, 1977); and Eric H. Walther, *The Fire Eaters* (Baton Rouge: Louisiana State University Press, 1992), 8–47.

2. Edward William Sidney [Nathaniel Beverley Tucker], *The Partisan Leader: A Tale of the Future,* 2 vols. (New York: Rudd and Carleton, 1861 [Washington, D.C.: Duff Green, 1836]), quotations 173, 40.

3. On Green, see W. Stephen Belko, *The Invincible Duff Green: Whig of the West* (Columbia: University of Missouri Press, 2006); and Richard R. John, "Affairs of Office: The Executive Departments, the Election of 1828, and the Making of the Democratic Party," in Meg Jacobs, William J. Novak, and Julian E. Zelizer, eds., *The Democratic Experiment: New Directions in American Political History* (Princeton, N.J.: Princeton University Press, 2003), 51–84.

4. Green to Nathaniel Beverley Tucker, September 13, 1836, Tucker-Coleman Collection, CW&M.

5. Richard Hofstadter recorded this as a "traditional gibe" against the intensely serious Calhoun. Richard Hofstadter, *The American Political Tradition and the Men Who Made It* (New York: Vintage, 1948), 73.

6. On British emancipation, see Robin Blackburn, *The Overthrow of Colonial Slavery, 1776–1848* (London: Verso, 1988), 419–72; David Brion Davis, *Inhuman Bondage: The Rise and Fall of Slavery in the New World* (New York: Oxford University Press, 2006), 231–50; and Christopher L. Brown, *Moral Capital: Foundations of British Abolitionism* (Chapel Hill: University of North Carolina Press, 2006).

7. On British abolition as a major event in the history of the American South, see Joe B. Wilkins, "Window on Freedom: The South's Response to the Emancipation of the Slaves in the British West Indies, 1833–1861" (PhD diss., University of

South Carolina, 1977); Edward B. Rugemer, *The Problem of Emancipation: The Caribbean Roots of the American Civil War* (Baton Rouge: Louisiana State University Press, 2008); and Steven Heath Mitton, "The Free World Confronted: The Problem of Slavery and Progress in American Foreign Relations, 1833–1844" (PhD diss., Louisiana State University, 2005).

8. Don E. Fehrenbacher, *The Slaveholding Republic: An Account of the United States Government's Relations to Slavery* (New York: Oxford University Press, 2001), 89–134; Eliga H. Gould, *Among the Powers of the Earth: The American Revolution and the Making of a New World Empire* (Cambridge, Mass.: Harvard University Press, 2012), 145–77.

9. Charles C. Tansill, *The United States and Santo Domingo, 1798–1873* (Baltimore: The Johns Hopkins Press, 1938); Rayford Logan, *The Diplomatic Relations of the United States with Haiti, 1776–1891* (Chapel Hill: University of North Carolina Press, 1941); Tim Matthewson, "Jefferson and Haiti," *JSH* 61, no. 2 (May 1995): 209–48; Ashli White, *Encountering Revolution: Haiti and the Making of the Early Republic* (Baltimore: Johns Hopkins University Press, 2010).

10. On antimaroon activities in Florida, see William Earl Weeks, *John Quincy Adams and American Global Empire* (Lexington: University of Kentucky Press, 1992), 62–65, 106–7. On state power and the spread of continental slavery in this period, see Adam Rothman, *Slave Country: American Expansion and the Origins of the Deep South* (Cambridge, Mass.: Harvard University Press, 2005); Matthew Mason, *Slavery and Politics in the Early Republic* (Chapel Hill: University of North Carolina Press, 2006); and John Craig Hammond, "Slavery, Settlement, and Empire: The Expansion and Growth of Slavery in the Interior of the North American Continent, 1770–1820," *JER* 32, no. 2 (Summer 2012): 175–206.

11. George Washington and Thomas Jefferson may well have employed a "proslavery foreign policy" in Haitian-American relations, but I would distinguish between a concrete opposition to one nation and the much broader, more aggressive proslavery worldview that developed after 1840. See Tim Matthewson, *A Proslavery Foreign Policy: Haitian-American Relations during the Early Republic* (Westport, Conn.: Prager, 2003); and Alfred N. Hunt, *Haiti's Influence on Antebellum America: Slumbering Volcano in the Caribbean* (Baton Rouge: Louisiana State University Press, 1988).

12. Caitlin Fitz, "Our Sister Republics: The United States in an Age of American Revolutions" (PhD diss., Yale University, 2010), esp. 102–46. On the absence of the slavery issue in the 1823 Monroe Doctrine discussions, see Jay Sexton, *The Monroe Doctrine: Empire and Nation in Nineteenth-Century America* (New York: Hill and Wang, 2012), 76.

13. John Randolph, speech, *Register of Debates*, 19th Cong., 1st Sess., 112–13 (March 1, 1826); John Berrien, speech, *Register of Debates*, 19th Cong., 1st Sess., 291 (March 14, 1826). See N. Andrew N. Cleven, "The First Panama Mission and the Congress of the United States," *Journal of Negro History* 13, no. 3 (July 1928):

225–54; Fitz, "Our Sister Republics," 236–62; and Nicholas Wood, "John Randolph of Roanoke and the Politics of Slavery in the Early Republic," *Virginia Magazine of History and Biography* 120, no. 2 (Summer 2012): 106–43.

14. Sexton, *Monroe Doctrine*, 74–84; Fitz, "Our Sister Republics," 263–90; Andrew R. L. Cayton, "The Debate over the Panama Congress and the Origins of the Second American Party System," *Historian*, 47, no. 2 (February 1985): 219–38.

15. John Floyd, speech, *Register of Debates*, 19th Cong., 1st Sess., 2449 (April 20, 1826).

16. Thomas Jefferson, quoted in Robert W. Tucker and David C. Hendrickson, *Empire of Liberty: The Statecraft of Thomas Jefferson* (New York: Oxford University Press, 1990), 45. On the Jeffersonian "reconciliation with Great Britain" after 1815, see William Earl Weeks, *The New Cambridge History of American Foreign Relations*, vol. 1, *Dimensions of the Early American Empire, 1754–1865* (New York: Cambridge University Press, 2013), 95–96.

17. Henry Clay, *In Defence of the American System: Against the British Colonial System* (Washington, D.C.: Gales and Seaton, 1832), 11. On America's "dependent development" within a British-led Atlantic world, see A. G. Hopkins, "The United States, 1783–1861: Britain's Honorary Dominion?," *Britain and the World* 4, no. 2 (September 2011): 232–46; and Sam W. Haynes, *Unfinished Revolution: The Early American Republic in a British World* (Charlottesville: University of Virginia Press, 2010). On the Anglo-American cotton trade in the early nineteenth century, see Sven Beckert, *Empire of Cotton: A Global History* (New York: Knopf, 2014), 98–174; and Brian Schoen, *The Fragile Fabric of Union: Cotton, Federal Politics, and the Global Origins of the Civil War* (Baltimore: Johns Hopkins University Press, 2009), 100–145.

18. Jefferson to Monroe, October 24, 1823, in Andrew A. Lipscomb and Albert E. Bergh, eds., *The Writings of Thomas Jefferson*, 20 vols. (Washington, D.C.: Thomas Jefferson Memorial Association, 1907), 15:477; James Madison, quoted in Hopkins, "United States, 1783–1861," 238. On Canning's proposal and the geopolitical considerations that shaped the Monroe Doctrine, see Sexton, *Monroe Doctrine*, 47–61; and Weeks, *Dimensions of the Early American Empire*, 114–20.

19. James Hamilton, speech, *Register of Debates*, 19th Cong., 1st Sess., 2154 (April 10, 1826); John Floyd, speech, *Register of Debates*, 19th Cong., 1st Sess., 2449 (April 20, 1826).

20. John Randolph, speech, *Register of Debates*, 19th Cong., 1st Sess., 119 (March 2, 1826); emphasis in the original.

21. The Royal Navy's budget in 1833 was roughly £4.9 million; see B. R. Mitchell, *British Historical Statistics* (Cambridge: Cambridge University Press, 1988), 580. On apprenticeship and compensation, see Thomas C. Holt, *The Problem of Freedom: Race, Labor, and Politics in Jamaica and Britain, 1832–1938* (Baltimore: Johns Hopkins University Press, 1992), 13–112; and Nick Draper, *The Price of Emancipation:*

Slave-Ownership, Compensation and British Society at the End of Slavery (Cambridge: Cambridge University Press, 2009).

22. For southern responses along these lines, see *Richmond Enquirer,* June 18, 1833; *Georgia Telegraph* (Macon, Ga.), July 3, 1833; and *United States Telegraph,* June 18, 1833.

23. Richard H. Brown, "The Missouri Crisis, Slavery, and the Politics of Jacksonianism," *South Atlantic Quarterly* 65 (Winter 1966): 55–72; Sean Wilentz, *The Rise of American Democracy: Jefferson to Lincoln* (New York: W. W. Norton, 2005), 218–53; Robert Pierce Forbes, *The Missouri Compromise and Its Aftermath: Slavery and the Meaning of America* (Chapel Hill: University of North Carolina Press, 2007); Donald J. Ratcliffe, "The Decline of Antislavery Politics, 1815–1840," in John Craig Hammond and Matthew Mason, eds., *Contesting Slavery: The Politics of Bondage and Freedom in the New Nation* (Charlottesville: University of Virginia Press, 2011), 175–206.

24. Rugemer, *Problem of Emancipation,* 145–290; Edward B. Rugemer, "The Southern Response to British Abolitionism: The Maturation of Proslavery Apologetics," *JSH* 70, no. 2 (May 2004): 221–48.

25. Legaré to Isaac Holmes, April 8, 1833, in Mary S. Legaré, ed., *Writings of Hugh Swinton Legaré,* 2 vols. (New York: Da Capo Press, 1970 [Charleston, 1846]), 1:215; emphasis in the original. On the very real opportunities that Caribbean and Atlantic proximity provided for the circulation of antislavery ideas and actors in the early nineteenth century, see Julius Scott, "The Common Wind: Currents of Afro-American Communication in the Era of the Haitian Revolution" (PhD diss., Duke University, 1986); Jane G. Landers, *Atlantic Creoles in the Age of Revolutions* (Cambridge, Mass.: Harvard University Press, 2011); and Ada Ferrer, *Freedom's Mirror: Cuba and Haiti in the Age of Revolution* (New York: Cambridge University Press, 2015).

26. *Southern Patriot* (Charleston, S.C.), May 4, 1833. See also Wilkins, "Window on Freedom," 45–60; and Rugemer, *Problem of Emancipation,* 114–24, 156–60.

27. Gelien Matthews, *Caribbean Slave Revolts and the British Abolitionist Movement* (Baton Rouge: Louisiana State University Press, 2006); Robin Blackburn, *The American Crucible: Slavery, Emancipation and Human Rights* (London: Verso, 2011), 329–89.

28. On postemancipation Great Britain as an "antislavery state" at the helm of an economic and geopolitical "world system," see Richard Huzzey, *Freedom Burning: Antislavery and Empire in Victorian Britain* (Ithaca. N.Y.: Cornell University Press, 2012), 40–74. See also David Brion Davis, *Challenging the Boundaries of Slavery* (Cambridge, Mass.: Harvard University Press, 2006), 61–94; and Seymour Drescher, *The Mighty Experiment: Free Labor versus Slavery in British Emancipation* (New York: Oxford University Press, 2003), 144–78. To be sure, American slaves had received ad hoc assistance (rather than systematic state support) from Great Britain before 1833; see Gerald Horne, *Negro Comrades of the Crown:*

African Americans and the British Empire Fight the U.S. before Emancipation (New York: New York University Press, 2012), 17–104.

29. On the diplomacy of the shipwrecked slave cases, see Fehrenbacher, *Slave-holding Republic*, 104–7; and Rugemer, *Problem of Emancipation*, 197–204.

30. Francis Fry Wayland, *Andrew Stevenson: Democrat and Diplomat, 1785–1857* (Philadelphia: University of Pennsylvania Press, 1949); Howard Temperley, "The O'Connell-Stevenson Contretemps," *Journal of Negro History* 47, no. 4 (October 1962): 217–33.

31. Stevenson to Lord Palmerston, July 1836, included in Stevenson to Forsyth, August 6, 1836, *S. Doc. No. 174*, 24th Cong., 2nd Sess. (1837); Forsyth to Stevenson, March 27, 1837, in *S. Doc. No. 216*, 25th Cong., 3rd Sess. (1839). On Forsyth, see A. L. Duckett, *John Forsyth, Political Tactician* (Athens: University of Georgia Press, 1962).]

32. Forsyth to Stevenson, March 27, 1837, and Stevenson to Lord Palmerston, December 23, 1837, *S. Doc No. 216*, 25th Cong., 3rd Sess. (1839).

33. Stevenson to Lord Palmerston, January 14, 1837, and Forsyth to Stevenson, March 27, 1837, *S. Doc No. 216*, 25th Cong., 3rd Sess. (1839).

34. Stevenson to Lord Palmerston, May 12, 1837, *S. Doc No. 216*, 25th Cong., 3rd Sess. (1839).

35. Stevenson to Lord Palmerston, June 16, 1837, Stevenson Family Papers, LC.

36. Howard Jones and Donald A. Rakestraw, *Prologue to Manifest Destiny: Anglo-American Relations in the 1840s* (Wilmington, Del: Scholarly Resources, 1997), 1–70; Howard Jones, *To the Webster-Ashburton Treaty: A Study in Anglo-American Relations, 1783–1843* (Chapel Hill: University of North Carolina Press, 1977); Horne, *Negro Comrades of the Crown*, 114–19.

37. *Richmond Enquirer*, April 14, 1840; Francis Pickens, speech in House, *CG Appendix*, 25th Cong., 3rd Sess., 299–300 (March 1, 1839). See also *Southern Patriot*, January 27, 1840.

38. Calhoun, "Remarks on the *Caroline Affair*," in Senate, January 9, 1838, *PJCC*, 14:79–80; Henry Wise, speech, *CG*, 26th Cong., 1st Sess., 311 (April 9, 1840).

39. Muriel Chamberlain, *Pax Britannica? British Foreign Policy, 1789–1914* (London: Longman, 1988), 75; John Darwin, *The Empire Project: The Rise and Fall of the British World-System, 1830–1870* (New York: Cambridge University Press, 2009), 26–41. For anonymous assessments in southern periodicals, see "A Succinct Account of the Sandwich Islands," *SLM*, July 1837, 423–24; "China and the Chinese," *SLM*, February 1841, 152–55; and "The British in Affghanistan," *Magnolia; or, Southern Appalachian*, August 1842, 122–24.

40. Hammond to Calhoun, April 29, 1840, *PJCC*, 15:193; Stevenson to Forsyth, November 23, 1840, Stevenson Family Papers, LC. See also Kinley J. Brauer, "The United States and British Imperial Expansion, 1815–1860," *Diplomatic History* 12 (Winter 1988): 19–38; and Elizabeth Kelly Gray, "American Attitudes toward British Imperialism, 1815–1860" (PhD diss., College of William and Mary, 2002).

41. *Georgia Telegraph*, March 12, 1839 (emphasis in the original); *Louisville Courier-Journal*, quoted in the *Richmond Enquirer*, October 16, 1838.

42. John C. Calhoun, speech in Senate, March 30, 1840, *PJCC*, 15:149–50. See Bruno Gujer, "Free Trade and Slavery: Calhoun's Defense of Southern Interests against British Interference, 1811–1848" (PhD diss., University of Zurich, 1971), 112–13.

43. *PJCC*, 15:154.

44. Ibid., 15:152, 156.

45. Robert Monroe Harrison to Webster, March 22, 1841, quoted in Rugemer, *Problem of Emancipation*, 205.

46. Forsyth, "Address to the People of Georgia," August 29, 1840, in the *Georgia Telegraph*, September 22, 1840. On the domestic "politics of slavery," see William J. Cooper Jr., *The South and the Politics of Slavery, 1828–1856* (Baton Rouge: Louisiana State University Press, 1978).

47. *Richmond Enquirer*, April 14, 1840. On the relationship between southern fear of domestic abolitionism and fear of British power, see Haynes, *Unfinished Revolution*, 177–203.

48. *CG*, 26th Cong., 2nd Sess., 170–71 (February 13, 1841). On Pickens, see John B. Edmunds Jr., *Francis W. Pickens and the Politics of Destruction* (Chapel Hill: University of North Carolina Press, 1986).

49. Edward D. Jervey and C. Harold Huber, "The *Creole* Affair," *Journal of Negro History* 65, no. 3 (Summer 1980): 196–211; Howard Jones, "The Peculiar Institution and National Honor: The Case of the *Creole* Slave Revolt," *Civil War History* 21, no. 1 (March 1975): 28–50.

50. "Resolutions of the Legislature of Mississippi" in *H.R. Doc 215, 27th Congress, 2nd Sess.* (1842).. On this question, see Phillip Troutman, "Grapevine in the Slave Market: African American Geopolitical Literacy and the 1841 *Creole* Revolt," in *The Chattel Principle: Internal Slave Trades in the Americas*, ed. Walter Johnson (New Haven, Conn.: Yale University Press, 2004), 203–33.

51. *CG*, 27th Cong., 2nd Sess., 47 (December 22, 1841).

52. Tyler speech at the Virginia Colonization Society, January 10, 1838, in Lyon Gardiner Tyler, ed., *Letters and Times of the Tylers*, 3 vols. (New York: Da Capo Press, 1970 [1884–1896]), 1:567–70.

53. Abel P. Upshur to Nathaniel Beverley Tucker, June 14, 1837, Tucker-Coleman Collection, CW&M

54. Ben E. Green, undated reminiscences, Duff Green Papers, SHC-UNC; Duff Green, *Facts and Suggestions, Biographical, Historical, Financial, and Political, Addressed to the People of the United States* (New York: Richardson and Co., 1866); Belko, *Invincible Duff Green*, 316–31. On Green's influence within the Tyler administration, see Edward P. Crapol, *John Tyler: The Accidental President* (Chapel Hill: University of North Carolina Press, 2006), 71–74.

55. Green to Abel P. Upshur, April 28, 1842, Green Papers, SHC-UNC; St. George L. Sioussant, "Duff Green's 'England and the United States': With an Introductory

Study of American Opposition to the Quintuple Treaty of 1841," *Proceedings of the American Antiquarian Society*, n.s., 40 (Worcester, Mass.: American Antiquarian Society, 1931): 176–82.

56. Upshur to Nathaniel Beverley Tucker, August 7, 1841, August 28, 1841, Tucker-Coleman Collection, CW&M; John Quincy Adams, speech at Dedham, Massachusetts, quoted in *Niles' Register*, November 4, 1843; Frederick Merk, *Slavery and the Annexation of Texas* (New York: Knopf, 1972), 14.

57. On the Anglo-American fracas over the slave trade and the right of search, see Fehrenbacher, *Slaveholding Republic*, 161–72; and Hugh G. Soulsby, *The Right of Search and the Slave Trade in Anglo-American Relations, 1814–1862* (Baltimore: Johns Hopkins Press, 1933). For a detailed analysis of British domestic politics and the logic behind the Quintuple Treaty, see Mitton, "Free World Confronted," 55–86.

58. Green's article in *Le Commerce*, March 4, 1842, quoted in Sioussant, "Duff Green's 'England and the United States,'" 209. See also Lawrence Jennings, "France, Great Britain, and the Repression of the Slave Trade, 1841–1845," *French Historical Studies* 10, no. 1 (Spring 1977): 101–25.

59. Green to Edward Everett, January 18, 1842, Green Papers, SHC-UNC.

60. Green to Tyler, January 24, 1842, Green Papers, SHC-UNC.

61. Green to Everett, January 18, 1842, Green Papers, SHC-UNC; Green to Calhoun, January 24, 1842, reprinted in Green, *Facts and Suggestions*, 153–55; Green to Tyler, January 24, 1842, Green Papers, SHC-UNC. Several of Green's most important letters in this period are also reprinted as an appendix in Merk, *Slavery and the Annexation of Texas*, 183–290.

62. Green to Everett, January 18, 1842, Green Papers, SHC-UNC. See *United States Telegraph*, August 21, 1833; *Georgia Telegraph*, August 29, 1835, August 13, 1839, October 13, 1840; and *Natchez Free Trader*, n.d., reprinted in *African Repository and Colonial Journal*, December 15, 1840.

63. Calhoun to Green, April 2, 1842, *PJCC*, 16:209.

64. *Madisonian* (Washington, D.C.), April 1, 1842. For additional examples, see *Charleston Mercury*, March 18, 1842; *New Orleans Commercial Bulletin*, April 23, 1842; Robert Carter Nicholas to Calhoun, May 16, 1842, *PJCC*, 16:249–52; Calhoun to Nichols, [June?] 1842, *PJCC*, 16:273–74; and Gro. Wright of Virginia to Congressman Robert M. T. Hunter, April 16, 1842, Robert M. T. Hunter Papers, Library of Virginia.

65. "East India Cotton," *SQR*, April 1842, 446–92. On the influence of this essay, see Rugemer, *Problem of Emancipation*, 204–8; and Schoen, *Fragile Fabric of Union*, 168–72.

66. Alisdair Roberts, *America's First Great Depression: Economic Crisis and Political Disorder after the Panic of 1837* (Ithaca, N.Y.: Cornell University Press, 2012); Edward E. Baptist, *The Half Has Never Been Told: Slavery and the Making of American Capitalism* (New York: Basic Books, 2014), 261–307.

67. Beckert, *Empire of Cotton*, 120–35; Drescher, *Mighty Experiment*, 144–78; Andrea Major, *Slavery, Abolitionism, and Empire in India, 1772–1843* (Liverpool: Liverpool University Press, 2012), esp. 321–39.

68. Huzzey, *Freedom Burning*, 40–74; Mitton, "Free World Confronted," 22–86. See also Keith Hamilton and Patrick Salmon, eds., *Slavery, Diplomacy, and Empire: Britain and the Suppression of the Slave Trade* (Brighton: Sussex Academic Press, 2009); and Howard Temperley, *British Anti-slavery, 1833–1870* (London: Longmans, 1972).

69. *Southern Patriot*, February 29, 1840.

70. Hammond to Calhoun, April 29, 1840, *PJCC*, 15:193; "East India Cotton," 492.

71. Duff Green, "The United States and England, by an American," *Great Western Magazine*, September, 1842, 78. On the widespread enthusiasm about America's future greatness, see Robert Kagan, *Dangerous Nation: America's Foreign Policy from Its Earliest Days to the Dawn of the Twentieth Century* (New York: Vintage, 2006), 7–70.

72. Green, "United States and England," 13; John C. Calhoun, speech in Senate, March 16, 1842, *PJCC*, 16:193–94. For similar expressions of confidence in the efficiency of American slave labor, see Francis P. Blair to Andrew Jackson, September 10, 1840, in John Spencer Bassett, ed., *The Correspondence of Andrew Jackson*, 6 vols. (Washington, D.C.: Carnegie Institute, 1926–1935), 6:75–76; *New Orleans Commercial Bulletin*, August 11, 1841; *Madisonian*, April 6, 1842; and "Indian and American Cotton," *Magnolia; or, Southern Appalachian*, August 1842, 122–30.

73. Upshur to Duff Green, May 20, 1843, Duff Green Papers, SHC-UNC.

2. The Strongest Naval Power on Earth

1. *Daily Picayune*, October 6, 1841. On Upshur, see Claude H. Hall, *Abel Parker Upshur: Conservative Virginian, 1790–1844* (Madison: State Historical Society of Wisconsin, 1964); and Michael O'Brien, *Conjectures of Order: Intellectual Life in the Old South, 1810–1860* (Chapel Hill: University of North Carolina Press, 2004), 803–6, 833–36. Upshur's major proslavery essay was "Domestic Slavery, as It Exists in Our Southern States . . . ," *SLM*, October 1839, 677–87.

2. *Schenectady Cabinet: or, Freedom's Sentinel*, October 5, 1841 ("Calhoun"); *New Orleans Commercial Bulletin*, September 22, 1841 ("ultra-Jeffersonian"); *Georgetown [D.C.] Advocate*, September 21, 1841 ("metaphysician").

3. According to Upshur, the existing U.S. Navy in 1841 was roughly one-eighth the size of British forces. *S. Doc. No. 1/6, 27th Cong., 2nd Sess.: Report of the Secretary of the Navy* (1841), 379; hereinafter cited as *Report of the Secretary of the Navy* (1841).

4. *Report of the Secretary of the Navy* (1841), 375. Upshur to Nathaniel Beverley Tucker, October 21, 1841, Tucker-Coleman Collection, CW&M. See also Hall, *Abel Parker Upshur*, 120–30; and John H. Schroeder, *Shaping a Maritime Empire: The Commercial*

and Diplomatic Role of the American Navy, 1829–1861 (Westport, Conn.: Green-wood Press, 1985), 57–78.

5. *Report of the Secretary of the Navy* (1841), 379–80.

6. Ibid., 380; emphasis in the original.

7. Ibid.

8. Ibid., 381.

9. John Quincy Adams, *Memoirs of John Quincy Adams,* ed. Charles Francis Adams, 12 vols. (New York: AMS Press, 1970 [1874–1877]), 11:95, 139–40. See also John Quincy Adams, speech at Braintree, Massachusetts, September 17, 1842, reprinted in *Niles' National Register* 13 (November 12, 1842): 173; and Steven Heath Mitton, "The Free World Confronted: The Problem of Slavery and Progress in American Foreign Relations, 1833–1844" (PhD diss., Louisiana State University, 2005), 146.

10. Neither political nor diplomatic historians have sufficiently explored this movement. For partial but notable exceptions, see Schroeder, *Shaping a Maritime Empire;* Edward P. Crapol, *John Tyler: The Accidental President* (Chapel Hill: University of North Carolina Press, 2006), 74–80; Thomas R. Hietala, *Manifest Design: American Exceptionalism and Empire,* rev. ed. (Ithaca, N.Y.: Cornell University Press, 2003), 13–14, 57–58; and Walter A. McDougall, *Throes of Democracy: The American Civil War Era, 1829–1877* (New York: Harper Perennial, 2008), 247–53.

11. Even as they have rejected traditional understandings of "manifest destiny," many valuable treatments of foreign policy aggressiveness in antebellum America concentrate primarily on territorial expansion. See Hietala, *Manifest Design;* Sam W. Haynes and Christopher M. Morris, eds., *Manifest Destiny and Empire: American Antebellum Expansion* (College Station: Texas A&M University Press, 1997), 115–45; and Michael A. Morrison, *Slavery and the American West: The Eclipse of Manifest Destiny and the Coming of the Civil War* (Chapel Hill: University of North Carolina Press, 1997). For a fuller discussion of the origins and historiography of southern naval advocacy, see Matthew Karp, "Slavery and American Sea Power: The Navalist Impulse in the Antebellum South," *JSH* 77, no. 2 (May 2011): 283–324.

12. The most complete scholarly treatment of Maury's life verges on hagiography: Frances Leigh Williams, *Matthew Fontaine Maury: Scientist of the Sea* (New Brunswick, N.J.: Rutgers University Press, 1963). See also Chester G. Hearn, *Tracks in the Sea: Matthew Fontaine Maury and the Mapping of the Oceans* (New York: McGraw-Hill, 2002); and John Grady, *Matthew Fontaine Maury, Father of Oceanography* (Jefferson, N.C.: McFarland, 2015).

13. On Maury's proslavery activities in the later antebellum years, see Chapters 6–9; on his work for the Confederacy and Maximilian, see Williams, *Matthew Fontaine Maury,* 348–441; and John Majewski and Todd Wahlstrom, "Geography as Power: The Political Economy of Matthew Fontaine Maury," *Virginia Magazine of History and Biography* 120, no. 4 (2012): 340–71.

14. Harry Bluff [Maury] to Secretary Paulding, *Richmond Whig,* August 18, 1838 (quotation); "Will Watch [Maury] to His Old Messmate Harry Bluff," *Richmond Whig,* December 20, 22, 24, 1838; Charles Lee Lewis, *Matthew Fontaine Maury: The Pathfinder of the Seas* (Annapolis, Md.: United States Naval Institute, 1927), 33–35.
15. Williams, *Matthew Fontaine Maury,* 120–29.
16. Harry Bluff [Maury], "Scraps from the Lucky Bag, No. 1," *SLM,* April 1840, 237. Maury also lobbied privately for naval expansion; he told his cousin that he "went to Washington to urge ... the expediency of increasing the effective force afloat." Maury to Mat Maury, March 3, 1840, Matthew Fontaine Maury Papers, LC.
17. Harry Bluff [Maury], "Scraps from the Lucky Bag, No. 1," 233–40.
18. On Perry, Stockton, and other northern naval reformers, see Schroeder, *Shaping a Maritime Empire,* 42–44.
19. Harry Bluff [Maury], "Scraps from the Lucky Bag, No. 2," *SLM,* May 1840, 309, 310.
20. William Henry Chase, "Memoir and Estimate on the Improvement of the Bar of Pensacola," November 29, 1829, and "Memoir on Fortifications of Pensacola," September 30, 1829, both in "Letters Sent by Captain William H. Chase, Corps of Engineers, 1829–1836," Record Group 77, Entry 145, NA. On U.S. coastal fortification policy, especially in Florida, see Mark A. Smith, *Engineering Security: The Corps of Engineers and Third System Defense Policy, 1815–1861* (Tuscaloosa: University of Alabama Press, 2009).
21. *Southern Patriot* (Charleston, S.C.), May 4, 1833; *New Orleans Bee,* May 8, 1833; Captain Charles Stewart, "The Navy Yard at Pensacola," *Army and Navy Chronicle,* February 9, 1837, 83; Hugh Legaré, speech, January 11, 1839, in Mary S. Legaré, ed., *Writings of Hugh Swinton Legaré,* 2 vols. (New York: Da Capo Press, 1970 [Charleston, 1846]), 1:334 (quotation). See also Gerald Horne, *Negro Comrades of the Crown: African Americans and the British Empire Fight the U.S. before Emancipation* (New York: New York University Press, 2012), 105–63.
22. Ernest F. Dibble, *Antebellum Pensacola and the Military Presence* (Pensacola, Fla.: Bicentennial Series, 1974), 31–60; George F. Pearce, *The U.S. Navy in Pensacola: From Sailing Ships to Naval Aviation, 1825–1930* (Gainesville: University Press of Florida, 1980), 36–42, 67–71.
23. Chase to General Charles Gratiot, February 22, 1836 (first and second quotations), August 27, 1836 (third and fourth quotations), Chase Letters, NA.
24. William Henry Chase, "Harbor of Pensacola," *Pensacola Gazette,* March 21, 1839, reprinted in the *Army and Navy Chronicle* (April 18, 1839): 244; see also Chase, "Communication with the Pacific," *Army and Navy Chronicle* (January 31, 1839): 68.
25. John C. Calhoun, "Remarks on the Cumberland Road Bill," speech in Senate, April 1, 1840, *PJCC,* 15:169, 171–72.
26. John C. Calhoun, "Remarks on Public Expenditures," speech in Senate, May 7, 1840, *PJCC,* 15:202; Calhoun, "Remarks on Naval Appropriations Bill," speech

in Senate, July 11, 1840, ibid., 15:304–5; Calhoun, "Remarks on the Cumberland Road Bill," speech in Senate, April 1, 1840, ibid., 15:171–72.

27. John C. Calhoun, "Speech on the Bill to Distribute the Proceeds of the Sales of Public Lands to the States," speech in Senate, August 24, 1841, *PJCC*, 15:727–31; emphasis in the original.

28. John C. Calhoun, speech in Senate, *CG*, 26th Cong., 2nd Sess., 522 (July 11, 1840).

29. In his earlier career Tyler spoke against the Missouri Compromise, recorded the only Senate vote against Andrew Jackson's "force bill" in the nullification crisis, and demanded that northern states act vigorously to suppress the abolitionists. See Lyon Gardiner Tyler, ed., *Letters and Times of the Tylers*, 3 vols. (New York: Da Capo Press, 1970 [1884–1896]), 1:316–22, 446–58, 574–79; and Crapol, *John Tyler*, 57–88.

30. On Tyler's break with the Whigs and the domestic political confusions of the early 1840s, see Sean Wilentz, *The Rise of American Democracy: Jefferson to Lincoln* (New York: W. W. Norton, 2005), 521–546

31. *H.R. Rep. No. 3*, 27th Cong., 2nd Sess. (1841). A manuscript draft of this report can be found in Folder 467, Thomas Butler King Papers, Southern Historical Collection, Wilson Library, University of North Carolina at Chapel Hill. On Thomas Butler King, see Edward M. Steel, *T. Butler King of Georgia* (Athens: University of Georgia Press, 1964).

32. The ongoing diplomatic tension with Great Britain helped the Home Squadron bill zip through the House by a vote of 184 to 8. For the brief debate, including King's remarks, see *CG*, 27th Cong., 1st Sess., 238–40 (July 21, 1841).

33. *Report of the Secretary of the Navy* (1841), 380.

34. For southern navalist support for Upshur's program, see the *Fredericksburg (Va.) Argus*, December 20, 1841; *New Orleans Commercial Bulletin*, December 27, 1841; and *Columbus (Ga.) Inquirer*, reprinted in the *Madisonian* (Washington, D.C.), January 5, 1842.

35. *CG*, 27th Cong., 2nd Sess., 47, 48 (December 21, 1841); John C. Calhoun to James Henry Hammond, December 31, 1841, *PJCC*, 16:29; *Georgia Telegraph*, March 29, 1842.

36. Harry Bluff [Maury], "Harry Bluff, On the Right of Search," *SLM*, April 1842, 297; *Madisonian*, March 29, 1842.

37. Harry Bluff [Maury], "Harry Bluff, On the Right of Search," 298, 300; emphasis in the original.

38. With their constant references to a "black-a-moor" invasion, the navalists were perhaps just as afraid of the black enemy within as the British or abolitionist enemy without. See Kenneth Greenberg, *Masters and Statesmen: The Political Culture of Antebellum Slavery* (Baltimore: Johns Hopkins University Press, 1985), 107–23.

39. *Natchez Free Trader*, reprinted in *New Orleans Commercial Bulletin*, December 7, 1841; Harry Bluff [Maury], "Harry Bluff, On the Right of Search," 296.

40. *S. Doc. No. 216*, 27th Cong., 2nd Sess. (1842), 2; *S. Doc. No. 98*, 27th Cong., 2nd Sess. (1842), 1–2; *H.R. Doc. No. 220*, 27th Cong., 2nd Sess., (1842), 22–25, 33–34.

41. Upshur to Commander Andrew Fitzhugh, December 21, 1841; Upshur to Lieutenant Oscar Bullins, March 2, 1842; Upshur to Captain William D. Salter, July 21, 1842; Upshur to Captain William M. Armstrong, October 19, 1842; Upshur to Commodore Charles Stewart, December 5, 1842, "Letters Sent by the Secretary of the Navy to Officers, 1798–1868," Record Group 45, microfilm record M149, reels 33–35, NA; Upshur to Tucker, March 28, 1842, Tucker-Coleman Collection, CW&M.

42. *S. Doc. No. 1/8*, 27th Cong., 3rd Sess., No. 1/8: *Report of the Secretary of the Navy* (1842), 535..

43. Jones to Upshur, September 13, 1842; Jones to Captains James Armstrong, C. K. Stribling, and Thomas A. Dorwin, September 8, 1842, "Pacific Squadron Letters, 1841–1886," Record Group 45, microfilm record M89, reel 31, NA (second and third quotations. The official correspondence relating to the Monterey affair was reprinted for Congress: *H.R. Doc. No. 166*, 27th Cong., 3rd Sess., No. 166 (1843). On Jones, see Gene A. Smith, *Thomas ap Catesby Jones: Commodore of Manifest Destiny* (Annapolis, Md.: Naval Institute Press, 2000).

44. Smith, *Thomas ap Catesby Jones*, 93–122; George M. Brooke Jr., "The Vest Pocket War of Commodore Jones," *Pacific Historical Review* 31, no. 3 (August 1962): 217–33.

45. Upshur's biographer notes that the secretary and the captain "held several informal conferences" in Washington in 1841; it is certainly possible that Jones received an oral briefing not preserved in his official instructions. Upshur to Jones, December 10, 1841, Letters Sent to Officers, NA; Hall, *Abel Parker Upshur*, 177.

46. Jones to Upshur, September 13, 1842, Pacific Squadron Letters, RG 45.

47. Jones to Captains James Armstrong, C. K. Stribling, and Thomas A. Dorwin, September 8, 1842, Pacific Squadron Letters, RG 45. In fact, the British fleet was making a routine stop off the Nicaraguan coast. "Cession of the Californias," *Army and Navy Chronicle*, March 5, 1840, 150; the article was originally published in the *New Orleans Courier*, February 18, 1840.

48. Upshur to Dallas, March 6, 1843, Letters Sent to Officers, NA.

49. Jones repeatedly complained about the small size and technological backwardness of his forces, especially in comparison to British and French squadrons: Jones to Upshur, March 22, 1842, and Jones to Upshur, August 31, 1842, Pacific Squadron Letters, RG 45.

50. Wilbur D. Jones, *Aberdeen and the Americas* (Athens: University of Georgia Press, 1958); Kenneth Bourne, *Britain and the Balance of Power in North America, 1815–1908* (London: Longmans, Green, 1967).

51. For these southern fears, see H.R. Rep. No. 3, 27th Cong., 2nd Sess. (1841), 3–6; Madisonian, March 9, 1842; Southern Patriot, April 7, 1842.

52. *New Orleans Commercial Bulletin,* April 2, 1842.

53. Southerners were continually on the lookout for a technological silver bullet that might give the U.S. Navy an immediate advantage over all other world powers. In 1841 and 1842 Upshur, T. B. King, and Henry Wise each urged Congress to build a ship made "altogether of iron"; *Report of the Secretary of the Navy* (1841), 382; King, *CG,* 27th Cong., 2nd Sess., 777 (July 22, 1842); Wise, *CG,* 27th Cong., 2nd Sess., 399–400 (April 8, 1842); *New Orleans Commercial Bulletin,* April 24, 1842.

54. *Report of the Secretary of the Navy* (1841), 378; Hall, *Upshur,* 136–38. See also David F. Long, "The Navy under the Board of Commissioners, 1815–1842," and Geoffrey S. Smith, "An Uncertain Passage: The Bureaus Run the Navy, 1842–1861," in *In Peace and War: Interpretations of American Naval History, 1775–1984,* 2nd ed., ed. Kenneth J. Hagan (Westport, Conn.: Prager International, 1984), 63–106.

55. *CG,* 27th Cong., 2nd Sess., 970–73 (August 30, 1842).

56. For the full debates on naval appropriations, see *CG,* 27th Cong., 2nd Sess., 497–522, 633, 638–41, 672–73. Despite the failure to increase funding, naval expenditures in 1842 were higher than they had ever been since the War of 1812; see *S. Ex. Doc. No.* 345th Cong., 1st Sess., (1877), 156; Charles Oscar Paullin, *Paullin's History of Naval Administration, 1775–1911* (Annapolis, Md.: Naval Institute Press, 1968), 176; and Harold and Margaret Sprout, *The Rise of American Naval Power, 1776–1918* (Annapolis, Md: Naval Institute Press, 1980), 145–48.

57. Maury to William M. Blackford, November 19, 1843, Matthew Fontaine Maury Papers, LC; Schroeder, *Shaping a Maritime Empire,* 65–68.

58. Williams, *Matthew Fontaine Maury,* 144–50; Crapol, *John Tyler,* 79–80.

59. Sprout and Sprout, *American Naval Power,* 140–51; McDougall, *Throes of Democracy,* 251–52. On southern navalism after the Tyler administration, see Chapter 9.

60. Upshur to Tucker, September 10, 1841, Tucker-Coleman Collection, CW&M; Upshur to Tucker, January 12, 1842, Tucker-Coleman Collection, CW&M.

61. Abel P. Upshur, *A Brief Enquiry into the True Nature and Character of Our Federal Government: Being a Review of Judge Story's "Commentaries on the Constitution of the United States"* (Philadelphia: John Campbell, 1863 [1840]), 106.

62. *S. Doc. No.* 1/8, 27th Cong., 3rd Sess., No. 1/8: *Report of the Secretary of the Navy* (1842), 550–51; see also Upshur to Tucker, October 25, 1842, Tucker-Coleman Collection, CW&M.

63. "Our British Relations," *Magnolia; or, Southern Monthly* 4 (June 1842): 333. On slavery and the distinction between domestic and international federal power, see Robert E. Bonner, *Mastering America: Southern Slaveholders and the Crisis of American Nationhood* (New York: Cambridge University Press, 2009), 41–78.

3. A Hemispheric Defense of Slavery

1. John Quincy Adams, *Memoirs of John Quincy Adams*, ed. Charles Francis Adams, 12 vols. (New York: AMS Press, 1970 [1874–1877]), 11:117; "Letter from John Quincy Adams," July 29, 1844, *Liberator*, August 9, 1844, 127.
2. "Letter from John Quincy Adams," 127.
3. *S. Doc. No. 1/6*, 27th Cong., 2nd Sess.: *Report of the Secretary of the Navy* (1841), 380.
4. [Washington] *Daily Madisonian*, January 28, 1842.
5. On the diplomacy leading up to the treaty, see Howard Jones and Donald A. Rakestraw, *Prologue to Manifest Destiny: Anglo-American Relations in the 1840s* (Wilmington, Del: Scholarly Resources, 1997), 121–50; on the financial interests that mitigated against war, see Jay Sexton, *Debtor Diplomacy: Finance and American Foreign Relations in the Civil War Era, 1837–1873* (Oxford: Oxford University Press, 2005), 33–40.
6. John C. Calhoun, "Speech on the Treaty of Washington," in Senate, August 19, 1842, *PJCC*, 16:393–410; John Tyler, Second Annual Message, December 6, 1842, in James D. Richardson, ed., *A Compilation of the Messages and Papers of the Presidents*, 10 vols. (new York: Bureau of National Literature,1897), 5:2047–49; Upshur to Nathaniel Beverley Tucker, August 21, 1842, Tucker-Coleman Collection, CW&M.
7. William C. Rives, speech in Senate, *CG Appendix*, 27th Cong., 3rd Sess., 62 (August 17 and 19, 1842).
8. Duff Green, article in *Le Commerce*, March 4, 1842, quoted in St. George L. Sioussant, "Duff Green's 'England and the United States': With an Introductory Study of American Opposition to the Quintuple Treaty of 1841," *Proceedings of the American Antiquarian Society*, n.s., 40 (Worcester, Mass.: American Antiquarian Society, 1931): 209; Harry Bluff [Matthew Maury], "Harry Bluff, On the Right of Search," *SLM*, April 1842, 297–98.
9. Harry Bluff [Maury], "Scraps from the Lucky Bag, No. 1," *SLM*, April 1840, 233–40; [Maury], "Our Relations with England," *SLM*, June 1842, 381–95.
10. John C. Calhoun, "Speech on the Treaty of Washington," August 19, 1842, *PJCC*, 16:402; *New Orleans Commercial Bulletin*, August 31, 1842.
11. Tyler, Second Annual Message, 4:194–96; Tyler, message to the House of Representatives, February 27, 1843, *Compilation of the Messages and Papers of the Presidents*, 4:2082–84. As late as 1858 Tyler continued to insist that the treaty had "distinctly repudiat[ed] the claim of Great Britain" to the right of search: "The idea of my conceding to Great Britain any thing! Fudge!" John Tyler to Robert Tyler, August 29, 1858, in Lyon Gardiner Tyler, ed., *Letters and Times of the Tylers*, 3 vols. (New York: Da Capo Press, 1970 [1884–1896]), 2:239–42.
12. Calhoun, "Speech on the Treaty of Washington," August 19, 1842, *PJCC*, 16:393–410; Bruno Gujer, "Free Trade and Slavery: Calhoun's Defense of Southern Interests against British Interference, 1811–1848" (PhD diss., University of Zurich, 1971), 100–121.

13. William Harper, *Memoir on Slavery, Read before the Society for the Advancement of Learning of South Carolina* (Charleston: James S. Burges, 1838), 50.]

14. [Maury], "Our Relations with England," *SLM*, June 1842, 395; "Thornton on Slavery," *SLM*, March 1842, 234–36.

15. Upshur to Tucker, April 10, 1841, Tucker-Coleman Collection, CW&M; *Report of the Secretary of the Navy* (1841), 380. For Pickens's report, see *CG*, 26th Cong., 2nd Sess., 170–71 (February 13, 1841).

16. Upshur to Tucker, January 12, 1842, and January 28, 1842, Tucker-Coleman Collection, CW&M.

17. Upshur to Duff Green, April 6, 1842, Green Papers, SHC-UNC; Upshur to Tucker, April 20, 1842, and August 21, 1842, Tucker-Coleman Collection, CW&M.

18. John C. Calhoun, speech in Senate, March 30, 1840, *PJCC*, 15:156; Upshur to Tucker, April 20, 1842, Tucker-Coleman Collection, CW&M. Tyler agreed with Upshur's analysis of the Quintuple Treaty: Tyler to Webster, n.d. [1842?], *Letters and Times of the Tylers*, 2:233.

19. Thomas Hart Benton, speech in Senate, *CG Appendix*, 27th Cong., 3rd Sess., 1–27 (August 18, 1842). But see also Calhoun's proslavery rebuttal, "Speech on the Treaty of Washington," August 19, 1842, *PJCC*, 16:405.

20. *CG*, 27th Cong., 3rd Sess., 2 (August 20, 1842).

21. *Daily Madisonian*, September 9, 1842, November 14, 1842, December 13, 1842, December 16, 1842.

22. On Dew and Harper as foundational proslavery thinkers, see Michael O'Brien, *Conjectures of Order: Intellectual Life in the Old South, 1810–1860* (Chapel Hill: University of North Carolina Press, 2004), 942–53. On southern intellectual interest in other slave societies throughout history, see Elizabeth Fox-Genovese and Eugene D. Genovese, *The Mind of the Master Class: History and Faith in the Southern Slaveholders' Worldview* (New York: Cambridge University Press, 2005), 201–24.

23. Thomas Roderick Dew, "Professor Dew on Slavery," in *The Proslavery Argument; as Maintained by the Most Distinguished Writers of the Southern States* (Charleston: Walker, Richards, and Co., 1852), 485–88.

24. William Harper, *Memoir on Slavery*, 42–44. On Harper as the exponent of "a proslavery argument firmly rooted in modernity," see Brian Schoen, *The Fragile Fabric of Union: Cotton, Federal Politics, and the Global Origins of the Civil War* (Baltimore: Johns Hopkins University Press, 2009), 163–68. On southern identification with other Caribbean slave societies, see Matthew Pratt Guterl, *American Mediterranean: Southern Slaveholders in the Age of Emancipation* (Cambridge, Mass.: Harvard University Press, 2008), esp. 1–78.

25. Joel Roberts Poinsett, *Notes on Mexico, Made in the Autumn of 1822* (Philadelphia: H. C. Carey and I. Lea, 1824), 219–21. As the first U.S. minister to Mexico, Poinsett opposed both Mexican emancipation and a rumored antislavery invasion of Cuba in 1829. See "Texas and its Revolution," *SLM*, May/June 1841,

407–9; and J. Fred Rippy, *Joel Poinsett, Versatile American* (Durham, N.C.: Duke University Press, 1935), 104–17.

26. Thomas Jefferson, quoted in Louis A. Perez Jr., *Cuba and the United States: Ties of Singular Intimacy* (Athens: University of Georgia Press, 2003), 39; James M. Callahan, *Cuba and International Relations: A Historical Study in American Diplomacy* (Baltimore: The Johns Hopkins Press, 1899), 127–30.

27. See, for instance, Don E. Fehrenbacher, *The Slaveholding Republic: An Account of the United States Government's Relations to Slavery* (New York: Oxford University Press, 2001), 126–31, 180; Frederick Merk, *The Monroe Doctrine and American Expansionism, 1843–1849* (New York: Knopf, 1966), 233–77, 280–85; and Arthur F. Corwin, *Spain and the Abolition of Slavery in Cuba, 1817–1886* (Austin: University of Texas Press, 1967), 77–78, 98–104, 116–27.

28. Callahan, *Cuba and International Relations*, 63–328; Perez, *Cuba and the United States*, 34–47; Lester D. Langley, *The Struggle for the American Mediterranean: United States–European Rivalry in the Gulf-Caribbean, 1776–1904* (Athens: University of Georgia Press, 1976).

29. *Richmond Enquirer*, June 20, 1837.

30. See the speeches of James Hamilton and John Floyd discussed in Chapter 1: *Register of Debates*, 19th Cong., 1st Sess., 2154 (April 10, 1826), 2449 (April 20, 1826).

31. *New Orleans Commercial Bulletin*, October 5, 1841, November 3, 1841, November 16, 1841.

32. *New Orleans Commercial Bulletin*, October 26, 1842.

33. On the "sugar revolution" in Cuba, which took off in the 1830s, see Franklin W. Knight, *Slave Society in Cuba during the Nineteenth Century* (Madison: University of Wisconsin Press, 1970), 25–46; Dale Tomich, "World Slavery and Caribbean Capitalism: The Cuban Sugar Industry, 1790–1868," *Theory and Society* 20, no. 3 (June 1991): 297–319; David R. Murray, "Statistics of the Slave Trade to Cuba," *Journal of Latin American Studies* 3, no. 2 (November 1971): 131–49; and Christopher Schmidt-Nowara, *Empire and Antislavery: Spain, Cuba, and Puerto Rico, 1833–1874* (Pittsburgh: University of Pittsburgh Press, 1999), 3–6.

34. John C. Calhoun, Speech at Montgomery, Alabama, on May 8, 1841, *PJCC*, 15:538; Thomas Butler King to Henry Lloyd Page King, December 14, 1856, Thomas Butler King Papers, SHC-UNC.

35. A Physician [J. G. F. Wurdemann], *Notes on Cuba, Containing an Account of Its Discovery and Early History* (Boston: James Munroe and Company, 1844), 12, 158–59, 263, 263–67.

36. For a paradigmatic statement of this policy, see Secretary of State John Forsyth to Aaron Vail, July 15, 1840, *DCUS*, 11:22–24.

37. Waddy Thompson to William Butler, November 24, 1841; John Tyler to Daniel Webster, December 16, 1841, in Kenneth E. Shewmaker, ed., *The Papers of Daniel Webster: Diplomatic Papers*, vol. 1, *1841–1843*, (Hanover, N.H.: Dartmouth University Press, 1983), 367–69. See also Robert L. Paquette, *Sugar Is Made with Blood:*

The Conspiracy of La Escalera and the Conflict between Empires over Slavery in Cuba (Middletown, Conn.: Wesleyan University Press, 1988), 183–205.

38. Robert L. Paquette, "The Everett–Del Monte Connection: A Study in the International Politics of Slavery," *Diplomatic History* 11, no. 1 (Winter 1987): 1–21.

39. Daniel Webster to Robert B. Campbell, January 14, 1843; Webster to Washington Irving, January 17, 1843, *DCUS*, 11:26–30; emphasis in the original.

40. Irving to Webster, March 10, 1843, *DCUS* 11:331–32; Webster to Irving, March 14, 1843, *DCUS*, 11:30–31.

41. Calhoun to Upshur, August 27, 1843, *PJCC*, 16:381–83.

42. *New Orleans Commercial Bulletin*, September 9, 10, 1843.

43. The Upshur-Argaiz agreement was informal and likely oral, but it is discussed in considerable detail in Upshur's correspondence with Washington Irving in Madrid: Upshur to Irving, January 9, 1844, *DCUS*, 11:31–32; Irving to Upshur, March 2, 1844, *DCUS*, 11:335–36.

44. Aaron Vail to Webster, December 28, 1841, *DCUS*, 11:329–30; Robert Blair Campbell to Upshur, October 5, 1843, Despatches from U.S. Consuls to Havana, 1783–1906, Record Group 59, vol. 19, NA; hereinafter cited as Despatches from Havana. See also David Turnbull, *Travels in the West: Cuba, with Notices of Puerto Rico, and the Slave Trade* (London: Longman, 1840); and David R. Murray, *Odious Commerce: Britain, Spain and the Abolition of the Cuban Slave Trade* (New York: Cambridge University Press, 1980), 133–58.

45. On Harrison, see Edward B. Rugemer, *The Problem of Emancipation: The Caribbean Roots of the American Civil War* (Baton Rouge: Louisiana State University Press, 2008), 185–97, 208–16.

46. Robert Monroe Harrison, quoted in Rugemer, *Problem of Emancipation*, 209–10; Campbell to Upshur, October 5, 1843, Despatches from Havana, vol. 19; *DCUS*, 11:332–34.

47. Campbell to Upshur, October 24, 1843, November 9, 1843, Despatches from Havana, vol. 19; Paquette, *Sugar Is Made with Blood*, 203–5.

48. O'Donnell's fall 1843 report is summarized and quoted extensively in Thomas Caute Reynolds to James Buchanan, August 12, 1847, *DCUS*, 11:418.

49. Turnbull, *Travels in the West*, 188–89.

50. Paquette, *Sugar Is Made with Blood*, 209–66; Murray, *Odious Commerce*, 159–207.

51. Campbell to O'Donnell, June 28, 1844, Despatches from Havana, vol. 19. The consul also protested against the treatment of American citizens detained in O'Donnell's crackdown, but his chief objection was that "negro testimony" had caused innocent civilians to be wrongfully arrested, including one American "from the slave holding states."

52. Upshur to Irving, January 9, 1844, *DCUS*, 11:31–32.

53. Irving to Upshur, March 2, 1844, *DCUS*, 11:335–36. On Irving as a diplomat, see Stanley T. Williams, *The Life of Washington Irving*, vol. 2 (New York: Oxford University Press, 1935), 181–86.

54. Calhoun to Campbell, June 26, 1844, *DCUS*, 11:33–34; see William R. Manning's commentary, *DCUS*, 11:33–34.

55. On Webster as a willing diplomatic servant of slavery, at least until 1843, see Fehrenbacher, *Slaveholding Republic*, 108–10.

56. Campbell to O'Donnell, June 28, 1844, Despatches from Havana, vol. 19; Irving to Ramón María Narváez, March 10, 1845, *DCUS*, 11:344; Benjamin G. Wright to Calhoun, October 5, 1844, *PJCC*, 20:34; James J. Wright to Calhoun, November 6, 1844, *PJCC*, 20:219–20.

57. Webster to Campbell, January 14, 1843, *DCUS*, 11:26–29 (emphasis in the original); James J. Wright to Calhoun, November 6, 1844, *PJCC*, 20:220.

58. John Forsyth to Aaron Vail, July 15, 1840, *DCUS*, 11:22–24.

59. Memorandum of Charles Jared Ingersoll, March 15, 1844, quoted in William M. Meigs, *The Life of Charles Jared Ingersoll* (Philadelphia: J. P. Lippincott, 1897), 263.

60. Expansionist northerners often expressed a similar position; see Alexander Hill Everett, "Cuba," *SQR*, April 1842, 377–97; Paquette, "Everett–Del Monte Connection," 19–21.

61. *New Orleans Commercial Bulletin*, April 25, 1842.

62. *New Orleans Commercial Bulletin*, April 23, 1842, April 29, 1842.

63. On Monroe's 1823 message interpreted as "a proslavery declaration" in the 1840s, see Jay Sexton, *The Monroe Doctrine: Empire and Nation in Nineteenth-Century America* (New York: Hill and Wang, 2012), 86–97.

64. Wurdemann, *Notes on Cuba*, 252; Count de Ofalia to John H. Eaton, February 22, 1838, *DCUS*, 11:307–9; Campbell to Upshur, October 5, 1843, Despatches from Havana, vol. 19. On Cuban Creole admiration for the southern United States, see Schmidt-Nowara, *Empire and Antislavery*, 15–16.

65. For early Spanish-American conversations about naval cooperation, see Vail to Forsyth, January 15, 1841, *DCUS*, 11:314.

66. Thomas C. Reynolds to James Buchanan, July 27, 1847, *DCUS*, 11:418; Reynolds to Calhoun, October 16, 1844, *DCUS*, 11:342–43. On Jollivet, see Lawrence C. Jennings, *French Antislavery: The Movement for Abolition of Slavery in France, 1802–1848* (Cambridge: Cambridge University Press, 2000), 223–25.

67. Calhoun to Green, September 8, 1843, *PJCC*, 17:424–25.

4. Slavery's Dominoes

1. "The Valley of the Amazon," *SQR*, July 1847, 135; *CG*, 27th Cong., 1st Sess., Appx., 74 (June 8–9, 1841); *CG Appendix*, 27th Cong., 2nd Sess., 334 (April 15, 1842); "United States Exploring Expedition," *SLM*, May 1845, 305–8. See also Gerald Horne, *The Deepest South: The United States, Brazil, and the African Slave Trade* (New York: New York University Press, 2007).

2. Green to Tyler, January 24, 1842, and Green to Tyler, April 28, 1842, Duff Green Papers, SHC-UNC; Duff Green, "The United States and England, by an American,"

Great Western Magazine, September 1842, 56–58 ("first induced Cuba and Brazil"); Green to Calhoun, October 18, 1843, *PJCC,* 17:511–12 ("Let England succeed"); Horne, *Deepest South,* 55–57. On British antislavery pressure in Brazil, see Alan K. Manchester, *British Preeminence in Brazil* (Chapel Hill: University of North Carolina Press, 1933), 254–56.

3. Green to Upshur, October 17, 1843, Duff Green Papers, SHC-UNC. See also Green to Calhoun, September 29, 1843, *PJCC,* 17:470–72.

4. Upshur to George Proffit, August 1, 1843, *DCUS,* 2:122–26.

5. Calhoun to Wise, May 25, 1844, *DCUS,* 2:126–28.

6. See William Lloyd Cumiford, "Political Ideology in United States–Brazilian Relations" (PhD diss., Texas Tech University, 1977).

7. Calhoun to Wise, May 25, 1844, *DCUS,* 2:126–28.

8. "Glances at Congress," *United States Magazine and Democratic Review* (October 1837): 72–74, quoted in Barton H. Wise, *The Life of Henry Wise of Virginia, 1806–1876* (New York: Macmillan, 1899), 67–68.

9. John Quincy Adams, *Memoirs of John Quincy Adams,* ed. Charles Francis Adams, 12 vols. (New York: AMS Press, 1970 [1874–1877]), 10:409. On Wise's role in 1830s debates over slavery, see William Lee Miller, *Arguing about Slavery: The Great Battle in the United States Congress* (New York: Knopf, 1996), 338–40, 360–72, 388–92.

10. On Wise's suspicious attitude toward Great Britain, see his speeches, *CG,* 26th Cong., 1st Sess., 311 (April 9, 1840); and 27th Cong., 2nd Sess., 497 (May 13, 1842); on his loyalty to Tyler, see Craig M. Simpson, *A Good Southerner: The Life of Henry A. Wise of Virginia* (Chapel Hill: University of North Carolina Press, 1985), 45–59. The appointment to Brazil made Wise an envoy extraordinary and minister plenipotentiary, the highest rank in the U.S. diplomatic service, equaled only by the envoys to Britain, France, Spain, Prussia, and Russia.

11. Wise to Calhoun, November 1, 1844, and December 14, 1844, in Despatches from U.S. Ministers to Brazil, 1806–1906, Record Group 59, M121, Reel 15, NA; hereinafter cited as Despatches from Brazil. Reprinted in *H.R. Doc. No. 248,* 28th Cong., 2nd Sess. (1845), 39–40, 54–55. On American participation in the African slave trade in Brazil, see W. E. B. Du Bois, *The Suppression of the African Slave Trade to the United States of America, 1638–1870* (York: Russell and Russell, 1965 [1898]), 162–67; Lawrence Hill, *Diplomatic Relations between the United States and Brazil* (New York: AMS Press, 1971), 110–45; and Horne, *Deepest South,* 1–84.

12. Hamilton Hamilton to Wise, March 4, 1845, in Wise Family Papers, VHS; Calhoun to Thomas G. Clemson, June 23, 1845, *PJCC,* 21:598; Wise to James Buchanan, December 9, 1846, in Despatches from Brazil, Reel 18; also in *DCUS,* 2:369–71.

13. Simpson, *Good Southerner,* 61–69; Horne, *Deepest South,* 67–69.

14. Wise to França, September 24, 1844, and Wise to Calhoun, October 11, 1844, in Despatches from Brazil, Reel 15, NA; *DCUS,* 2:256–67. Wise's rhetoric matched

the language of leading Brazilian conservatives in the 1840s, who deeply admired American proslavery politics; see Rafael de Bivar Marquese and Tâmis Peixoto Parron, "Internacional escravista: A política da Segunda Escravidão," *Topoi* 12, no. 23 (July–December 2011): 97–111; and Marquese and Parron, "The Proslavery International and the Politics of the Second Slavery," paper presented at "The Politics of the Second Slavery" conference, Binghamton, N.Y., 2010.

15. Wise to Calhoun, September 1, 1844, and November 1, 1844, Despatches from Brazil, Reel 15, NA. On U.S.-Brazilian naval cooperation, see Richard Carl Froehlich, "The United States Navy and Diplomatic Relations with Brazil, 1822–1871" (PhD diss., Kent State University, 1971), 201–330.

16. Wise to Calhoun, January 12, 1845, Despatches from Brazil, Reel 15, NA; *PJCC*, 21:98–103. In the case of the Brazilian Empire, which lacked even the form of a republican government, the meaning of "institutions" is especially difficult to hide.

17. Wise to Caleb Cushing, December 6, 1845, Wise Family Papers, VHS; Wise to "Dear Bob" [probably Robert I. Paulson], March 15, 1846, quoted in Horne, *Deepest South*, 74–75. Wise to Buchanan, March 6, 1846, in Despatches from Brazil, Reel 17, NA. This letter, along with much of Wise's other correspondence, is printed in *H.R. Ex. Doc. No. 61*, 30th Cong., 2nd Sess., 61 (1849).

18. Wise to Calhoun, October 11, 1844 ("colonies at Demerara"), Wise to Hamilton, December 1, 1844 ("offenders at home"), and Wise to Maxwell, Wright & Co., December 9, 1844 ("Old and New World"), Despatches from Brazil, Reel 15, NA. See also Barton Wise, *Life of Henry Wise*, 110–15; and Horne, *Deepest South*, 70–72.

19. Tyler, Message to Congress, February 20, 1845, in James D. Richardson, ed., *A Compilation of the Messages and Papers of the Presidents*, 10 vols. (New York: Bureau of National Literature, 1897), 5:2215–18; Bruno Gujer, "Free Trade and Slavery: Calhoun's Defense of Southern Interests against British Interference, 1811–1848" (PhD diss., University of Zurich, 1971), 208–13.

20. John C. Calhoun, "Speech on the Treaty of Washington," August 19, 1842, *PJCC*, 16:402; Domingo Del Monte, quoted in Alexander H. Everett to Calhoun, April 13, 1844, *PJCC*, 18:224–29.

21. Wise to Calhoun, February 18, 1845, Despatches from Brazil, Reel 15, NA; Froehlich, "United States Navy and Diplomatic Relations with Brazil," 383.

22. See especially Wise to Hamilton Hamilton, July 31, 1846, in *British and Foreign State Papers, 1846–47* (London: Harrison and Sons, 1860), 35:479–537.

23. Wise to James Buchanan, May 1, 1845, Despatches from Brazil, Reel 15, NA; A Physician [J. G. F. Wurdemann], *Notes on Cuba, Containing an Account of Its Discovery and Early History* (Boston: James Munroe and Company, 1844), 267.

24. "Glances at Congress," 74.

25. Wise to Buchanan, November 24, 1845, Despatches from Brazil, Reel 15, NA; Buchanan to Wise, September 27, 1845, in John Bassett Moore, ed., *The*

Works of James Buchanan, 12 vols. (Philadelphia: J. B. Lippincott Company, 1909), 6:267–71.

26. Buchanan to Wise, March 29, 1847, *Works of James Buchanan*, 7:260–65. Wise loftily attributed his quarrels with the Brazilian government to his "Republican heart" and hatred for court ceremony. Wise to Buchanan, February 27, 1847, Henry A. Wise Papers, VHS; Wise to Cmdr. Lawrence Rousseau, April 6, 1847, Wise Family Papers, VHS; Cumiford, "Political Ideology in United States–Brazilian Relations," 96–101.

27. Wise to Edward Hopkins, April 12, 1846, *DCUS*, 2:337; Marquese and Parron, "Internacional escravista."

28. Wise to França, February 4, 1845, Despatches from Brazil, Reel 15, NA; see also Buchanan to John F. Crampton, September 2, 1847, *Works of James Buchanan*, 7:407–9.

29. See especially Jeffrey Needell, *The Party of Order: Conservatives, the State, and Slavery in the Brazilian Monarchy, 1831–1871* (Stanford, Calif.: Stanford University Press, 2006), 138–55, 272–74; Leslie Bethell, *The Abolition of the Brazilian Slave Trade* (New York: Cambridge University Press, 1970), 296–387; Marquese and Parron, "Internacional escravista"; and Robert Slenes, "The Brazilian Internal Slave Trade, 1850–1888: Regional Economies, Slave Experience, and the Politics of a Peculiar Market," in Walter Johnson, ed., *The Chattel Principle: Internal Slave Trades in the Americas* (New Haven, Conn.: Yale University Press, 2004), 325–70.

30. Adams, *Memoirs*, 12:195–97.

31. Wise later aggressively repudiated all suggestions that he worked against slavery in Brazil; see Wise to P. H. Aylett, 23, 1854, Aylett Family Papers, VHS; and John Coles Rutherfoord diary, July 16, 1857, VHS.

32. Anthony M. Brescia, "The Naval and Military Strength of the British West India Islands in 1842: A Report by Secret Agent Albert Fitz with a Foreword by Anthony M. Brescia," *Bermuda Journal of Archaeology and Maritime History* 6 (1994): 194–206; Edward P. Crapol, *John Tyler: The Accidental President* (Chapel Hill: University of North Carolina Press, 2006), 96–97. On Guiana, see Green to Upshur, November 14, 1843, Duff Green Papers, SHC-UNC.

33. Calhoun to John Hogan, February 22, 1845, *PJCC*, 21:342–43; Calhoun to Nicholas Trist, September 18, 1845, *PJCC*, 22:150; Hogan to Calhoun, September 22, 1845, *PJCC*, 22:160–61; Gujer, "Free Trade and Slavery," 202–4. For evidence that Calhoun drew on the secret-service fund to provide arms to the white Dominicans in their ongoing struggle with Haiti, see Crapol, *John Tyler*, 84–85.

34. The two envoys were Allen A. Hall of Tennessee and Vespasian Ellis of Missouri. Hall to Calhoun, May 25, 1844, *PJCC*, 19:611–13; Hall to Calhoun, October 28, 1844, *PJCC*, 20:137–40; Ellis to Calhoun, December 10, 1844, *PJCC*, 20:514–17; emphases in the original. See also Judith Ewell, *Venezuela and the United States: From Monroe's Hemisphere to Petroleum's Empire* (Athens: University of Georgia Press, 1996), 39–49.

35. Jefferson to James Monroe, May 14, 1820, in Andrew A. Lipscomb and Albert E. Bergh, eds., *The Writings of Thomas Jefferson*, 20 vols. (Washington, D.C.: Thomas Jefferson Memorial Association, 1907), 15:251; David M. Pletcher, *The Diplomacy of Annexation: Texas, Oregon, and the Mexican War* (Columbia: University of Missouri Press, 1973), 66–69.

36. *CG*, 24th Cong., 1st Sess., 460–61 (May 16, 1836). On slavery and the politics of Texas independence, see Randolph B. Campbell, *An Empire for Slavery: The Peculiar Institution in Texas, 1821–1865* (Baton Rouge: Louisiana State University Press, 1989), 10–49;,, see Andrew J. Torget, *Seeds of Empire: Cotton, Slavery, and the Transformation of the Texas Borderlands, 1800–1850* (Chapel Hill: University of North Carolina Press, 2015), 98–176; and Sarah K. M. Rodriguez, "'Children of the Great Mexican Family': Anglo-American immigration to Texas and the making of the American Empire, 1820–1861," PhD. diss., University of Pennsylvania, 2015.

37. For official diplomatic fears that Britain might assist Mexico in threatening Texan or American slavery, see Powhatan Ellis to John Forsyth, May 19, 1835, June 25, 1835, and August 3, 1836, all in *DCUS*, 8:326–38; and Andrew Stevenson to John Forsyth, October 29, 1836, Stevenson Family Papers, LC.

38. *Southern Patriot* (Charleston, S.C.), April 18, 1842; *New Orleans Commercial Bulletin*, March 18, 1842.

39. Wise's speech was transcribed by the *National Intelligencer* (Washington, D.C.), April 15, 1842. See Frederick Merk, *Slavery and the Annexation of Texas* (New York: Knopf, 1972), 192–200. Merk's account of annexation grants slavery its central importance but suffers from an unfortunate tendency to dismiss slaveholding fears as the product of cynical propaganda rather than genuine ideology.

40. The *National Intelligencer* recorded "[a] laugh in certain portions of the House" when Wise argued that true abolitionists should support Texas annexation. Quoted in Merk, *Slavery and the Annexation of Texas*, 197.

41. John Quincy Adams, speech in House, *CG*, 27th Cong., 2nd Sess., 422–24 (April 15, 1842).

42. A year later Adams seemed to have realized the prescience of Wise's bombastic oration. All of Tyler's foreign policy, he wrote in his diary, was originally laid out in "Wise's speech of 14th April last." Adams, *Memoirs*, 11:344–46.

43. The literature on the politics of Texas annexation is large. See Merk, *Slavery and the Annexation of Texas*, 3–32; Thomas R. Hietala, *Manifest Design: American Exceptionalism and Empire*, rev. ed. (Ithaca, N.Y.: Cornell University Press, 2003); William W. Freehling, *The Road to Disunion*, vol. 1, *Secessionists at Bay, 1789–1854* (New York: Oxford University Press, 1990); William J. Cooper Jr., *The South and the Politics of Slavery, 1828–1856* (Baton Rouge: Louisiana State University Press, 1978); Michael A. Morrison, *Slavery and the American West: The Eclipse of Manifest Destiny and the Coming of the Civil War* (Chapel Hill: University of North Carolina Press, 1997), 13–38; and Sam W. Haynes, "Anglophobia and the Annexation of Texas:

The Quest for National Security," in Sam W. Haynes and Christopher M. Morris, eds. *Manifest Destiny and Empire: American Antebellum Expansion* (College Station: Texas A&M University Press, 1997), 115–45.

44. Robert Walker's "Letter . . . Relative to the Annexation of Texas," the most influential example of this safety-valve thesis, was intended for distribution in the North alone. Walker's primary pamphlet intended for southern audiences, titled "The South in Danger," stressed the importance of Texas for the security of slavery. See Frederick Merk, *Fruits of Propaganda in the Tyler Administration* (Cambridge, Mass.: Harvard University Press, 1971), 95–130, 221–52; and Stephen J. Hartnett, *Democratic Dissent and the Cultural Fictions of Antebellum America* (Urbana: University of Illinois Press, 2002), 124–31.

45. Gilmer's letter, dated January 10, 1843, was published in the *Baltimore Republican and Argus*, January 19, 1843, and the *Madisonian* (Washington, D.C.), January 23, 1843; it is reprinted in Merk, *Slavery and the Annexation of Texas*, 200–204. See also Pletcher, *Diplomacy of Annexation*, 113–16; and Freehling, *Secessionists at Bay*, 368–71.

46. Hunt to Gilmer, March 21, 1843, Tyler Family Papers, CW&M; emphasis in the original. For more on Hunt's geopolitical imagination, see Robert E. Bonner, *Mastering America: Southern Slaveholders and the Crisis of American Nationhood* (New York: Cambridge University Press, 2009), 24–29.

47. Jackson to Aaron V. Brown, February 9, 1843, in John Spencer Bassett, ed., *The Correspondence of Andrew Jackson*, 6 vols. (Washington, D.C.: Carnegie Institute, 1926–1935), 6:201–2. By uniting Jackson, Tyler, and Calhoun behind the same banner, Texas annexation proved to be a foreign policy bond that transcended many domestic political divisions; see Robert V. Remini, *Andrew Jackson and the Course of American Democracy, 1833–1845* (New York: Harper and Row, 1984), 487–511.

48. On Tyler's political aspirations in 1843, see Crapol, *John Tyler*, 176–94; and Norma Lois Peterson, *The Presidencies of William Henry Harrison and John Tyler* (Lawrence: University Press of Kansas, 1989), 176–201.

49. Green's informant was Ashbel Smith, the Texas envoy in London; the evidence was a letter from a Galveston abolitionist who boasted of British support for his antislavery efforts in Texas. Andrew Yates to W. J. Converse, March 19, 1843, and Green to Tyler, May 31, 1843, Duff Green Papers, SHC-UNC; see also Freehling, *Secessionists at Bay*, 372–85.

50. Green to Tyler, May 31, 1843, July 3, 1843, and August 29, 1843, Duff Green Papers, SHC-UNC; Ashbel Smith to John C. Calhoun, June 19, 1843, *PJCC*, 17:252–53.

51. Ephraim D. Adams, *British Interests and Activities in Texas, 1838–1846* (Baltimore: Johns Hopkins Press, 1910); Lelia M. Roeckell, "Bonds over Bondage: British Opposition to the Annexation of Texas," *JER* 19, no. 2 (Summer 1999): 257–78; Pletcher, *Diplomacy of Annexation*, 113–207.

52. See Upshur to Tucker, March 13, 1843, Tucker-Coleman Collection, CW&M. For a somewhat different interpretation of Upshur's motives, with a greater

emphasis on conscious southern sectionalism and domestic party politics, see William W. Freehling, "Unlimited Paternalism's Problems: The Transforming Moment on My Road toward Understanding Disunion," in *The Reintegration of American History* (New York: Oxford University Press, 1994), 105–37.

53. Steven Heath Mitton, "The Upshur Inquiry: Lost Lessons of the Great Experiment," *Slavery & Abolition* 27 (April 2006): 89–124. On Robert Monroe Harrison, see Edward B. Rugemer, *The Problem of Emancipation: The Caribbean Roots of the American Civil War* (Baton Rouge: Louisiana State University Press, 2008), 185–97, 208–12.

54. Calhoun to Upshur, August 27, 1843, *PJCC*, 17:381–83.

55. Upshur to Murphy, August 8, 1843, September 22, 1843, *DCUS*, 12:44–49, 51–52; Pletcher, *Diplomacy of Annexation*, 125–38.

56. *Madisonian*, September 27, 1843; see also September 23–28, November 14, and November 23–25. Upshur may well have authored these pieces; see Claude H. Hall, *Abel Parker Upshur: Conservative Virginian, 1790–1844* (Madison: State Historical Society of Wisconsin, 1964), 198–99.

57. *Charleston Mercury*, November 11, 1843; Upshur to Tucker, October 26, 1843, Tucker-Coleman Collection, CW&M.

58. Calhoun to Upshur, August 27, 1843, *PJCC*, 17:381–83; Upshur to Murphy, August 8, 1843, *DCUS*, 12:44–49. Duff Green's letters to Upshur and Calhoun continued to connect Brazil, Cuba, Texas, and Atlantic commercial politics: Green to Upshur, October 17, 1843, Duff Green Papers, SHC-UNC; Green to Calhoun, October 18, 1843, *PJCC*, 17:511–12.

59. William R. King to Calhoun, October 10, 1844, *PJCC*, 20:61–64. For similar statements, see J. B. Plauche to Jackson, June 2, 1844, *Correspondence of Andrew Jackson*, 6:297; and Upshur to Everett, September 28, 1843, *DCUS*, 7:6–17.

60. Thompson to Upshur, March 25, 1844, *DCUS*, 8:581. A former Virginia congressman wrote Calhoun with the same opinion: "[I] think it best for her and the U. States, if [Texas] can be independent of Foreign powers with her southern institutions, to remain as she is. She will be a protection to us, and we to her against northern fanatics." Mark Alexander to Calhoun, July 20, 1844, *PJCC*, 19:404.

61. Upshur to Murphy, August 8, 1843, *DCUS*, 12:44–49.

62. Upshur to Tucker, August 7, 1841, Tucker-Coleman Collection, CW&M ("Southern man"); Upshur to Calhoun, November 8, 1843, *PJCC*, 17:535 ("Mason & Dixon"); Upshur to Tucker, October 26, 1843, Tucker-Coleman Collection, CW&M. In actuality, Everett was far from an abolitionist; see Paul A. Varg, *Edward Everett: The Intellectual in the Turmoil of Politics* (Selinsgrove, Pa.: Susquehanna University Press, 1992), 87–126.

63. Green to Upshur, January 10, 1844, Duff Green Papers, SHC-UNC; Robert Walsh to Calhoun, April 26, 1844, *PJCC*, 18:340–41. Tyler first proposed Henry Wise for the French ministry, but the Senate rejected the nomination.

64. Upshur to Calhoun, August 14, 1843, *PJCC*, 17:356; emphasis in the original. For interpretations of Texas annexation that stress the role of a consciously sectionalist ideology, see Freehling, *Secessionists at Bay,* 353–452; and John McCardell, *The Idea of a Southern Nation: Southern Nationalists and Southern Nationalism, 1830–1860* (New York: W. W. Norton, 1979), 230–36.

65. Upshur to Murphy, August 8, 1843, *DCUS*, 12:44–49.

66. Calhoun to Wilson Lumpkin, December 1841, *PJCC*, 16:20; Jackson to William B. Lewis, October 31, 1843, in *Correspondence of Andrew Jackson*, 6:238–39; Edward P. Crapol, "John Tyler and the Pursuit of National Destiny," *JER* 17, no. 3 (Autumn 1997): 467–91. On Jackson's lifelong fusion of slaveholding southernness and militant American nationalism, see Mark R. Cheatham, *Andrew Jackson, Southerner* (Baton Rouge: Louisiana State University Press, 2013).

67. Upshur to Tucker, December 4, 1843, Tucker-Coleman Collection, CW&M; emphases in the original. That same December a former law student of Tucker's wrote his professor to mock a classmate who had transformed himself into a "Calhoun crusader and Texas champion.... My dear Judge, our bulwark is the Constitution, not Texas, is it not?" Upshur, Calhoun, and even Tucker were not so sure. Robert Ould to Tucker, December 31, 1843, Tucker-Coleman Collection, CW&M. On Upshur and Tucker's exchange, see Crapol, *John Tyler,* 199–200; and Robert J. Brugger, *Beverley Tucker: Heart over Head in the Old South* (Baltimore: Johns Hopkins University Press, 1978), 150–51.

68. Murphy to Anson Jones, February 14, 1844, *DCUS*, 12:326–27. See Pletcher, *Diplomacy of Annexation,* 130–33; Lyon Gardiner Tyler, ed., *Letters and Times of the Tylers,* 3 vols. (New York: Da Capo Press, 1970 [1884–1896]), 2:282–90; and Robert Seager, *And Tyler Too: A Biography of John and Julia Gardiner Tyler* (New York: McGraw-Hill, 1963), 213–14.

69. *CG,* 27th Cong., 2nd Sess. (April 24, 1842); Adams, *Memoirs,* 11:515–16. On the USS *Princeton,* see Hall, *Abel Parker Upshur,* 209–13.

70. On the *Princeton* disaster, see Seager, *And Tyler Too,* 203–6; and Crapol, *John Tyler,* 207–10.

71. Some confusion still surrounds the process that led to Calhoun's selection; for conflicting accounts, see Henry Wise, *Seven Decades of the Union* (Philadelphia: Lippincott, 1881), 221–25; Charles M. Wiltse, *John C. Calhoun: Sectionalist, 1840–1850* (Indianapolis: Bobbs-Merrill, 1951), 161–63; and St. George L. Sioussat, "John Caldwell Calhoun," in Samuel Flagg Bemis, ed., *The American Secretaries of State and Their Diplomacy* (New York: Knopf, 1928), 5:127–233.

72. Aberdeen to Pakenham, December 26, 1843, quoted in Gujer, "Free Trade and Slavery," 151–52.

73. Calhoun to Pakenham, April 18, 1844, *PJCC*, 18:273–78. Historians have unearthed a remarkable variety of motivations for Calhoun's letter, including genuine Anglophobia, sectionalist provocation, the imperatives of South Carolina

politics, and shrewd electoral calculation—by associating Texas with slavery, he could dissuade Martin Van Buren from supporting annexation and cripple the New Yorker's chances of receiving the Democratic presidential nomination. See Sean Wilentz, "The Bombshell of 1844," in Gareth Davies and Julian E. Zelizer, eds., *America at the Ballot Box: Elections and Political History* (Philadelphia: University of Pennsylvania Press, 2015), 36–58; Gujer, "Free Trade and Slavery," 152–57; Freehling, *Secessionists at Bay*, 408–10; Cooper, *Politics of Slavery*, 375–76; Sam W. Haynes, *Unfinished Revolution: The Early American Republic in a British World* (Charlottesville: University of Virginia Press, 2010), 243–45; and Charles G. Sellers, *The Market Revolution: Jacksonian America, 1815–1846* (New York: Oxford University Press, 1991), 413. Perhaps the most convincing explanation, however, is simply that Calhoun felt no need to separate his personal proslavery views from official American policy; as he saw it, they were one and the same.

74. Tyler, Message to the Senate, April 22, 1844, *Compilation of the Messages and Papers of the Presidents*, 5: 2160–66.

75. In 1844 congressional divisions on Texas followed party rather than sectional lines. Southern Whigs generally opposed annexation, arguing that Texas would dilute American economic strength and embroil the country in a profitless war with Mexico. In this sense the leaders of the Texas junto did not represent the whole of the South, only its most powerful and controlling faction. See Sean Wilentz, *The Rise of American Democracy: Jefferson to Lincoln* (New York: W. W. Norton, 2005), 547–76; Joel Silbey, *The Storm over Texas: The Annexation Controversy and the Road to Civil War* (New York: Oxford University Press, 2005), 28–90; and Michael F. Holt, *The Rise and Fall of the American Whig Party: Jacksonian Politics and the Onset of the Civil War* (New York: Oxford University Press, 1999), 168–88.

76. The best account of the raucous Democratic convention of 1844 is still found in Charles G. Sellers, *James K. Polk: Continentalist* (Princeton, N.J.: Princeton University Press, 1966), 85–107.

77. Tyler, Message to the House of Representatives, June 10, 1844, *Compilation of the Messages and Papers of the Presidents*, 5:2176–77; Merk, *Slavery and the Annexation of Texas*, 83–84. No less an authority on executive power than John Yoo has observed that Tyler's effort to acquire Texas by "statute, rather than a treaty . . . set a precedent for future Presidents, who used what would become known as congressional-executive agreements to adopt the Bretton Woods agreement and GATT in the wake of World War II." John Yoo, *Crisis and Command: A History of Executive Power* (New York: Kaplan, 2011), 191. For more critical commentary, see Hermann E. von Holst, *John C. Calhoun* (Boston: Houghton, Mifflin, 1899), 245–55; and Peter Zavodnyik, *The Age of Strict Construction: A History of the Growth of Federal Power, 1789–1861* (Washington, D.C.: Catholic University of America Press, 2007), 225–30.

78. Calhoun to King, August 12, 1844, *PJCC*, 19:568–78; Wiltse, *John C. Calhoun*, 201.

79. George Gliddon to Calhoun, December 26, 1844, *PJCC*, 20:630; Gadsden to Calhoun, December 14, 1844, *PJCC*, 20:547; *Cincinnati Weekly Herald and Philanthropist*, May 7, 1845; *CG*, 28th Cong., 2nd Sess., 24 (December 12, 1844).

80. Calhoun to Clemson, September 14, 1844, *PJCC*, 19:781; Wise to Buchanan, May 19, 1845, *DCUS*, 2:280 (quoted). Calhoun further dispatched his letter to Great Britain, Prussia, Spain, Russia, Austria, the Netherlands, and Belgium; in Cape Verde the U.S. consul had the letter translated into Portuguese. See *PJCC*, 19:671; and Seymour Drescher, *The Mighty Experiment: Free Labor versus Slavery in British Emancipation* (New York: Oxford University Press, 2003), 273.

81. King to Calhoun, October 6, 1844, *DCUS*, 6:540–41; King to Calhoun, October 10, 1844, *PJCC*, 20:63–64; Calhoun to King, December 13, 1844, *PJCC*, 20:543–45. On French diplomacy regarding Texas, see Pletcher, *Diplomacy of Annexation*, 156–62, 185–90.

82. Anson Jones to Tilghman Howard, August 6, 1844, Howard to Jones, August 6, 1844, and Howard to Calhoun, August 7, 1844, *DCUS*, 12:360–65.

83. Charles H. Raymond to Anson Jones, September 12 and 13, 1844, quoted in Sioussat, "John Caldwell Calhoun," 230; Gujer, "Free Trade and Slavery," 159.

84. Calhoun to Andrew Jackson Donelson, September 17, 1844, *PJCC*, 19:800–803; Gujer, "Free Trade and Slavery," 159–64.

85. On Indian power in the southwestern plains and its function in justifying U.S. aggrandizements across the 1840s, see Brian Delay, "Independent Indians and the U.S.-Mexico War," *AHR* 112, no. 1 (February 2007): 35–68; and Pekka Hamalainen, *The Comanche Empire* (New Haven, Conn.: Yale University Press, 2008).

86. Jackson to Andrew Jackson Donelson, November 18, 1844, *Correspondence of Andrew Jackson*, 6:329–30; *CG Appendix*, 28th Cong., 2nd Sess., 132 (January 22, 1845); Merk, *Slavery and the Annexation of Texas*, 139–47.

87. *Joint Resolution for annexing Texas to the United States*, U.S. *Statutes at Large* 5 (1845), 797–98; Merk, *Slavery and the Annexation of Texas*, 152–56; Sellers, *James K. Polk: Continentalist*, 171–73, 186–89, 205–8.

88. Tyler to Charles A. Wickliffe, November 20, 1848, in John Tyler Letters, VHS; Calhoun to Donelson, March 3, 1845, *DCUS*, 12:83–85. See also *Letters and Times of the Tylers*, 2:362–65; Pletcher, *Diplomacy of Annexation*, 179–83; and Crapol, *John Tyler*, 215–22.

89. Hammond, diary entry March 9, 1845, in Carol Bleser, ed., *Secret and Sacred: The Diaries of James Henry Hammond, a Southern Slaveholder* (New York: Oxford University Press, 1988), 144. For similar sentiments from another South Carolinian, see Robert Barnwell Rhett's speech in the House, *CG Appendix*, 28th Cong., 2nd Sess., 55 (January 4, 1845).

90. Giddings, speech in House, *CG Appendix*, 28th Cong., 2nd Sess., 342–46 (January 22, 1845); Adams, *Memoirs*, 12:49.

91. Calhoun to Pakenham, April 18, 1844, *PJCC*, 18:273–78; Thomas Bayly, speech in House, *CG Appendix*, 28th Cong., 2nd Sess., 122–28 (January 7, 1845); see also

Richmond Enquirer, January 10, 1845. Robert Brugger speculates that Upshur and Tyler's friend Nathaniel Beverley Tucker may have coached Bayly in his constitutional exegesis; see Brugger, *Beverley Tucker,* 150–51, 248; and Bonner, *Mastering America,* 41–78.

92. "Annexation of Texas," *SQR,* October 1844, 494–96. The *Southern Literary Messenger,* in pursuit of the same argument, even quoted the Federalist John Jay on the flexibility of executive power in foreign affairs: "The Editor" [B. B. Minor], "The Annexation of Texas," *SLM,* May 1844, 315–20. For similar views among Calhoun's correspondents, see Wilson Lumpkin to Calhoun, September 24, 1844, *PJCC,* 19:833–34; Francis Pickens to Calhoun, October 31, 1844, *PJCC,* 20:102; and John Mathewes to Calhoun, December 1, 1844, *PJCC,* 20:435–38.

93. Ralph Waldo Emerson, journal entry, March 1845, in Bliss Perry, ed., *The Heart of Emerson's Journals* (Boston: Houghton Mifflin, 1926), 212; Macaulay in *Hansard,* HC Deb 26 February 1845, vol. 77, c1298; also quoted in "European Correspondence," *SLM,* May 1845, 323.

94. Henry Wise to Caleb Cushing, December 6, 1845, in Henry A. Wise Papers, VHS; William Henry Chase, *Memoir on the Defence of the Gulf of Mexico* (New Orleans: Jeffersonian Office, 1846), 18–19.

95. *CG,* 28th Cong., 2nd Sess., 85–89 (January 7, 1845).

96. "American Politics in France," *Southern and Western Monthly Magazine and Review,* May 1845, 360–61. On Texas and the state of European attitudes toward slavery in the 1840s, see Drescher, *Mighty Experiment,* 166–72.

97. Memucan Hunt to Duff Green, March 11, 1844, Duff Green Papers, SHC-UNC.

5. The Young Hercules of America

1. Charles G. Sellers, *James K. Polk: Jacksonian, 1795–1843* (Princeton, N.J.: Princeton University Press, 1957); William Dusinberre, *Slavemaster President: The Double Career of James Polk* (New York: Oxford University Press, 2003).

2. On Polk's struggle to lead an increasingly divided Democratic Party, see Sean Wilentz, *The Rise of American Democracy: Jefferson to Lincoln* (New York: W. W. Norton, 2005), 577–86; and Charles G. Sellers, *James K. Polk: Continentalist* (Princeton, N.J.: Princeton University Press, 1966), 162–212.

3. On Polk's personality and leadership style, see Sellers, *James K. Polk: Continentalist,* v–vi, 213–14, 324–26; Sam W. Haynes, *James K. Polk and the Expansionist Impulse,* 2nd ed. (New York: Longman, 2002), 75–93; David M. Pletcher, *The Diplomacy of Annexation: Texas, Oregon, and the Mexican War* (Columbia: University of Missouri Press, 1973), 229–33; Robert F. Merry, *A Country of Vast Designs: James K. Polk, the Mexican War, and the Conquest of the American Continent* (New York: Simon and Schuster, 2009), 2–11; and Amy S. Greenberg, *A Wicked War: Polk, Clay, Lincoln, and the 1846 U.S. Invasion of Mexico* (New York: Knopf, 2012), 25–33, 65–72. For an older work that treats Polk and Tyler's foreign policy as a

single entity, see Jesse S. Reeves, *American Diplomacy under Tyler and Polk* (Baltimore: The Johns Hopkins Press, 1907).

4. On the Oregon question, see Pletcher, *Diplomacy of Annexation*, 89–110; Norman A. Graebner, *Empire on the Pacific: A Study in American Continental Expansion* (New York: Ronald Press, 1955), 1–102; and Shomer S. Zwelling, *Expansion and Imperialism* (Chicago: Loyola University Press, 1970), 16–45.

5. James K. Polk, Inaugural Address, March 3, 1845 in James D. Richardson, ed., *A Compilation of the Messages and Papers of the Presidents*, 10 vols. (New York: Bureau of National Literature, 1897)5:2231; Polk, diary entry, January 4, 1846, in *The Diary of James K. Polk during His Presidency, 1845 to 1849*, ed. Milo Milton Quaife, 4 vols. (Chicago: A. C. McClurg and Co., 1910), 1:155.

6. Calhoun to James Henry Hammond, August 30, 1845, *PJCC*, 22:100–101. See also Charles M. Wiltse, *John C. Calhoun: Sectionalist, 1840–1850* (Indianapolis: Bobbs-Merrill, 1951), 247–62; and Bruno Gujer, "Free Trade and Slavery: Calhoun's Defense of Southern Interests against British Interference, 1811–1848" (PhD diss., University of Zurich, 1971), 271–82.

7. Green to J. McGregor, January 26, 1846, cited in Pletcher, *Diplomacy of Annexation*, 337; Pickens to Calhoun, September 21, 1845, *PJCC*, 22:158.

8. On the handful of southern Oregon hawks in Congress, see John Hope Franklin, "The Southern Expansionists of 1846," *JSH* 25, no. 3 (August 1959): 323–38.

9. For Polk's confidence in the power of cotton, see *Washington Daily Union*, September 24, 1845; Polk, *Diary*, 1:191–92 (January 24, 1846); and Thomas R. Hietala, *Manifest Design: American Exceptionalism and Empire*, rev. ed. (Ithaca, N.Y.: Cornell University Press, 2003), 74–78.

10. James Buchanan to Richard Pakenham, July 12, 1845, in *The Works of James Buchanan*, ed. John Bassett Moore (Philadelphia: J. B. Lippincott Company, 1909), 6:194–204; Haynes, *James K. Polk and the Expansionist Impulse*, 126–32, 143–48; Graebner, *Empire on the Pacific*, 105.

11. Thomas Hietala and Shomer Zwelling argue that Polk was prepared to go to war in Oregon, but neither presents any direct evidence; Hietala, *Manifest Design*, 80–82; Zwelling, *Expansion and Imperialism*, 46–76. On the thinness of Polk's military preparations in the Northwest—a marked contrast to his activity before the war with Mexico—see Howard Jones and Donald A. Rakestraw, *Prologue to Manifest Destiny: Anglo-American Relations in the 1840s* (Wilmington, Del: Scholarly Resources, 1997), 235–36; and Julius M. Pratt, "James K. Polk and John Bull," *Canadian Historical Review* 24 (1943): 341–49.

12. McLane to Buchanan, February 3, 1846, S. Doc. No. 117, 29th Cong., 1st Sess., 117 (1846), 3; Polk, *Diary*, 1:209–11, 242–49 (February 4–5, 23–24, 1846); Haynes, *James K. Polk and the Expansionist Impulse*, 138–39.

13. Tyler, Calhoun, and their allies denounced Polk's Oregon diplomacy in 1845, but their hostility stemmed from a conflict over partisanship and patronage,

not ideology or foreign policy strategy. See Robert Tyler to John C. Calhoun, April 19, 1845, in Lyon Gardiner Tyler, ed., *Letters and Times of the Tylers*, 3 vols. (New York: Da Capo Press, 1970 [1884–1896]), 3:160–61; and Calhoun to R. M. T. Hunter, March 26, 1845, *PJCC*, 21:447–50.

14. Buchanan to Donelson, March 10, 1845, *DCUS*, 12:85–88; see also Sellers, *James K. Polk: Continentalist*, 215–20; and Thomas Hart Benton, *Thirty Years View; or, A History of the Working of the American Government for Thirty Years, from 1820 to 1850*, 2 vols. (New York: D. Appleton, 1854–1865), 2:637–39. On Donelson, see Mark R. Cheatham, *Old Hickory's Nephew: The Political and Private Struggles of Andrew Jackson Donelson* (Baton Rouge: Louisiana State University Press, 2007), esp. 170–86.

15. Buchanan to Wickliffe, March 27, 1845, *DCUS*, 12:88–90. See also A. Brooke Caruso, *The Mexican Spy Company: United States Covert Operations in Mexico, 1845–1848* (Jefferson, N.C.: McFarland, 1991), 18–21.

16. Wickliffe to Buchanan, May 21, 1845, reprinted in C. T. Neu, "The Annexation of Texas," in George P. Hammond, ed. *New Spain and the Anglo-American West: Historical Contributions Presented to Herbert Eugene Bolton*, 2 vols. (Los Angeles: Lancaster Press, 1932), 2:82–83; Pletcher, *Diplomacy of Annexation*, 190–97.

17. Polk to Robert Armstrong, September 13, 1845, in Wayne Cutler, ed., *Correspondence of James K. Polk*, 12 vols. (Knoxville: University of Tennessee Press, 1958–2013), 10:221. See also Bancroft to Conner, July 11, 1845, in Neu, "Annexation of Texas," 2:95; the *Richmond Enquirer*, August 22, 1845; and K. Jack Bauer, *Surfboats and Horse Marines: U.S. Naval Operations in the Mexican War, 1846–48* (Annapolis, Md.: United States Naval Institute, 1969), 7–9.

18. Wickliffe to Buchanan, May 21, 1845, in Neu, "Annexation of Texas," 2:84–85.

19. Polk to Donelson, June 15, 1845, quoted in Pletcher, *Diplomacy of Annexation*, 254. Most historians agree that the Texas (and U.S.) claim to the Rio Grande was legally dubious; Frederick Merk, *The Monroe Doctrine and American Expansionism, 1843–1849* (New York: Knopf, 1966), 133–60; Dean B. Mahin, *Olive Branch and Sword: The United States and Mexico, 1845–1848* (Jefferson, N.C.: McFarland, 1997), 36–38.

20. For allegations that Polk sought to provoke war with Mexico in the summer of 1845, see Richard R. Stenberg, "The Failure of Polk's War Intrigue of 1845," *Pacific Historical Review* 4, no. 1 (March 1935): 36–58; Glenn Price, *Origins of the War with Mexico: The Polk-Stockton Intrigue* (Austin: University of Texas Press, 1967); and Caruso, *Mexican Spy Company*, 23–36. For more skeptical readings of the evidence, see Pletcher, *Diplomacy of Annexation*, 197–99; and Sellers, *James K. Polk: Continentalist*, 222–30.

21. Polk, *Diary*, 1:13 (September 1, 1845). On the same day Polk also sought and received the support of Virginia Whig William Archer.

22. Buchanan to Wickliffe, March 27, 1845, *DCUS*, 12:88–90; Elliot to Aberdeen, July 3, 1845, in Ephraim D. Adams, ed., *British Diplomatic Correspondence Concerning*

the Republic of Texas—1838–1846 (Austin: Texas State Historical Association, n.d.), 511.

23. Mahin, *Olive Branch and Sword*, 47–49; Pletcher, *Diplomacy of Annexation*, 275–79.

24. Polk, First Annual Message, December 2, 1845, *Compilation of the Messages and Papers of the Presidents*, 5:2235–66; Ebenezer Allen to E. A. Rhodes, August 30, 1845 ("arms and munitions"), in George P. Garrison, ed., *Diplomatic Correspondence of the Republic of Texas* 2 vols. (Washington, D.C.: Government Printing Office, 1911), 2:397.

25. Polk further asked Congress for a general expansion of the army and the navy: Message to the Senate, March 24, 1846, *Compilation of the Messages and Papers of the Presidents*, 5:2276–78; K. Jack Bauer, *The Mexican War, 1846–1848* (New York: Macmillan, 1974), 33.

26. Pletcher, *Diplomacy of Annexation*, 276–78; Greenberg, *Wicked War*, 76–79.

27. Polk, *Diary*, 2:354, 382 (April 25, 1846; May 8, 1846).

28. Polk, Message to Congress, May 11, 1846, *Compilation of the Messages and Papers of the Presidents*, 5:2287–93; Greenberg, *A Wicked War*, 102–104

29. Benton, quoted in Haynes, *James K. Polk and the Expansionist Impulse*, 147. See also Buchanan to Thomas O. Larkin, October 17, 1845; and Buchanan to Slidell, November 10, 1845, *DCUS*, 8:169–82; Sellers, *James K. Polk: Continentalist*, 230–35, 398–409; Pletcher, *Diplomacy of Annexation*, 368–92, 576–611; and Norman Graebner, "The Mexican War: A Study in Causation," *Pacific Historical Review*, 49, no. 3 (August 1980): 405–26.

30. Elliot to Lord Aberdeen, August 31, 1845, in Adams, *British Diplomatic Correspondence*, 546; Giddings speech, *CG Appendix*, 29th Cong., 1st Sess., 641–45 (May 12, 1845).

31. Polk, *Diary*, 2:75, 283 (August 10, 1846; December 19, 1846).

32. On slavery's southern frontier, see Sarah E. Cornell, "Citizens of Nowhere: Fugitive Slaves and Free African Americans in Mexico, 1833–1857," *JAH* 100, no. 2 (September 2013): 351–74; William Carrigan, "Slavery on the Frontier: The Peculiar Institution in Central Texas," *Slavery & Abolition* 20, no. 2 (August 1999): 63–86; Sean Kelley, "'Mexico in His Head': Slavery and the Texas-Mexico Border, 1810–1860," *Journal of Social History* 37, no. 3 (Spring 2004): 709–23; and Ronnie C. Tyler, "Fugitive Slaves in Mexico," *Journal of Negro History* 57, no. 1 (January 1972): 1–12.

33. See L. Troost, "Military and Naval Resources and Necessities of the South and West," *DBR*, March 1846, 251–64; and James Gadsden to Calhoun, May 18, 1846, *PJCC*, 23:119.

34. *New Orleans Commercial Bulletin*, reprinted in the *Richmond Enquirer*, May 12, 1846.

35. Calhoun, "Remarks on the President's War Message," May 11, 1846, *PJCC*, 23:92–95. See also Ernest McPherson Lander, *Reluctant Imperialists: Calhoun, the South Carolinians, and the Mexican War* (Baton Rouge: Louisiana State University Press, 1980), 1–24.

36. Calhoun to Thomas Clemson, May 12, 1846, *PJCC*, 23:96; Merk, *Monroe Doctrine and American Expansionism*, 161–93.

37. Calhoun to Clemson, June 11, 1846, *PJCC*, 23:96, 171–72; John H. Schroeder, *Mr. Polk's War: American Opposition and Dissent, 1846–1848* (Madison: University of Wisconsin Press, 1973), 25–32.

38. On southern enthusiasm for the war in Congress, see Joel Silbey, *The Shrine of Party: Congressional Voting Behavior, 1841–1852* (Pittsburgh: University of Pittsburgh Press, 1967), 76–78.

39. Joaquín M. de Castillo y Lanzas to Slidell, March 12, 1846, *DCUS*, 8:821.

40. In its occupation of the Confederacy, of course, the Union army could count on the cooperation of enslaved people and sometimes southern unionists. See Daniel Walker Howe, *What Hath God Wrought: The Transformation of America, 1815–1848* (New York: Oxford University Press, 2007), 747; and Robert W. Johannsen, *To the Halls of the Montezumas: The Mexican War in the American Imagination* (New York: Oxford University Press, 1985).

41. For further parallels between the Mexican-American conflict and later U.S. wars, see Schroeder, *Mr. Polk's War*, ix–xv; and Walter Nugent, "The American Habit of Empire, and the Cases of Polk and Bush," *Western Historical Quarterly* 38 (Spring 2007): 5–24.

42. Ulysses S. Grant, *Memoirs and Selected Letters*, ed. Mary Drake McFeeley and William S. McFeeley (New York: Library of America, 1990), 87; John Quincy Adams, *Memoirs of John Quincy Adams*, ed. Charles Francis Adams, 12 vols. (New York: AMS Press, 1970 [1874–1877]), 12:49. The total number of American soldiers who fought in the war was not inconsiderable: roughly 73,000 volunteers and 27,000 regulars. But the size of the actual U.S. armies on the ground seldom ran above 10,000 to 15,000 men. See John C. Pinheiro, *Manifest Ambition: James K. Polk and Civil-Military Relations during the Mexican War* (Westport, Conn.: Prager, 2007); and Bauer, *Mexican War*, 392–99.

43. "The Conquest of California, and the Case of Lieutenant Colonel Fremont," *SQR*, July 1849, 412–14; John Hope Franklin, *The Militant South* (Boston: Beacon Press, 1956), 7–10.

44. Grant, *Memoirs and Selected Letters*, 41. Emerson's speech of July 4, 1846, is reprinted in Louis Ruchames, "Two Forgotten Addresses by Ralph Waldo Emerson," *American Literature* 28, no. 4 (January 1957): 425–33.

45. Clemson to Calhoun, June 27, 1846, *PJCC*, 23:234; Calhoun to Anna Clemson Calhoun, December 27, 1846, *PJCC*, 24:44.

46. On the widespread belief in Mexican racial inferiority, see Reginald Horsman, *Race and Manifest Destiny: Origins of American Racial Anglo-Saxonism* (Cambridge, Mass.: Harvard University Press, 1981), 228–48; on how that racism shaped the conflict on the ground, see Paul Foos, *A Short, Offhand, Killing Affair: Soldiers and Social Conflict during the Mexican-American War* (Chapel Hill: University of North Carolina Press, 2002), esp. 113–54.

47. Robert M. T. Hunter, quoted in Brian DeLay, "Independent Indians and the U.S.-Mexico War," *AHR* 112, no. 1 (February 2007): 63. See also Brian DeLay,

War of a Thousand Deserts: Indian Raids and the U.S-Mexican War (New Haven, Conn.: Yale University Press, 2009), 253–96; and Pekka Hamalainen, *The Comanche Empire* (New Haven, Conn.: Yale University Press, 2008), 141–43, 233–38.

48. Within days of the declaration of war, Polk told his cabinet that he intended to "obtain California"; see Polk, *Diary*, 1:396–99 (May 14, 1846); and Greenberg, *Wicked War*, 108–10.

49. Bernard DeVoto, *1846: The Year of Decision* (New York: Little, Brown, 1942), 71.

50. Polk, *Diary*, 1:222–25, 227–30 (February 13 and 16, 1846).

51. Caruso, *Mexican Spy Company*, 62–79; Pletcher, *Diplomacy of Annexation*, 445–47.

52. Benton, *Thirty Years View*, 2:680. On secrecy and intrigue as elements of Polk's political personality, see Sellers, *James K. Polk: Continentalist*, 216–20; Merry, *Country of Vast Designs*, 128–30; Pletcher, *Diplomacy of Annexation*, 454–55; and Greenberg, *Wicked War*, 70–71.

53. Polk, Message to the House of Representatives, April 20, 1846, *Compilation of the Messages and Papers of the Presidents*, 4:431–35; Polk, *Diary*, 1:431 (May 27, 1846). On Tyler's use of confidential agents, see Edward P. Crapol, *John Tyler: The Accidental President* (Chapel Hill: University of North Carolina Press, 2006), 71–74, 108–11, 126–27; and Robert V. Remini, *Daniel Webster: The Man and His Time* (New York: W. W. Norton, 1997), 610–18.

54. Caruso, *Mexican Spy Company*, 65–67; Stephen F. Knott, *Secret and Sanctioned: Covert Operations and the American Presidency* (New York: Oxford University Press, 1996), 127; Central Intelligence Agency, Center for the Study of Intelligence, "Our First Line of Defense: Presidential Reflections on U.S. Intelligence," https://www.cia .gov/library/center-for-the-study-of-intelligence/csi-publications/books-and -monographs/our-first-line-of-defense-presidential-reflections-on-us-intelli gence/polk.html.

55. Polk, *Diary*, 2:144–45 (September 19, 1846); DeLay, *War of a Thousand Deserts*, 279–88.

56. Bauer, *Mexican War*, 323. On the strategic planning behind the Veracruz attack, see Pletcher, *Diplomacy of Annexation*, 465–83.

57. *CG*, 29th Cong., 2nd Sess., 300 (February 2, 1847).

58. *CG*, 29th Cong., 1st Sess., 1214–21 (August 8–10, 1846); Polk, *Diary*, 1:76–77 (August 10, 1846).

59. *CG*, 29th Cong., 2nd Sess., 556, 573 (March 1, March 3, 1846). On the Veracruz landing and Scott's Mexico City campaign, see Bauer, *Mexican War*, 232–325; and Greenberg, *Wicked War*, 200–213.

60. Polk, *Diary*, 2:371 (February 8, 1847); see Lander, *Reluctant Imperialists*, 58–79; Howe, *What Hath God Wrought*, 764–65; and Schroeder, *Mr. Polk's War*, 63–88.

61. Calhoun, speech in Senate, February 9, 1847, *PJCC*, 24:115–36; Gujer, "Free Trade and Slavery," 309–12.

62. Calhoun to Clemson, June 15, 1847, *PJCC*, 24:399.

63. *CG*, 29th Cong., 2nd Sess., 110–11, 276 (January 4 and 28, 1847). The *Charleston Mercury*, declared that the regular army should "make this obstinate and infatuated

people feel the full force of our arms." *Charleston Mercury,* May 30, 1846; January 7, 15, 16, and 27, 1847. For the final Senate vote on the ten-regiment bill, see *CG,* 29th Cong., 2nd Sess., 375–77 (February 10, 1847); Lander, *Reluctant Imperialists,* 65–66; Schroeder, *Mr. Polk's War,* 72–73; and Pinheiro, *Manifest Ambition,* 51–58.

64. Calhoun to Wilson Lumpkin, April 6, 1847, *PJCC,* 24:299–300. For the $4 million offer, see Polk, *Diary,* 2:282–84 (December 19, 1846); for the final Senate vote on the $3 million bill, see *CG,* 29th Cong., 2nd Sess., 555–56 (March 1, 1847).

65. John C. Calhoun, speech in Senate, February 9, 1847, *PJCC,* 24:118. For scholarly quotation, see Richard Hofstadter, *The American Political Tradition and the Men Who Made It* (New York: Vintage, 1948), 110; Remini, *Daniel Webster,* 619; and Jay Sexton, *The Monroe Doctrine: Empire and Nation in Nineteenth-Century America* (New York: Hill and Wang, 2012), 79.

66. Polk, *Diary,* 1:312 (March 30, 1846); 2:282–84 (December 19, 1846).

67. On the decisive voting power of Calhoun's band, which included Andrew Butler of South Carolina, David Yulee and James Westcott of Florida, and later Robert M. T. Hunter and James M. Mason of Virginia, see Schroeder, *Mr. Polk's War,* 73.

68. Calhoun to Clemson, June 15, 1847, *PJCC,* 24:399. The only military appropriation Calhoun actually joined with the Whigs to defeat came well after the war had ended: *CG,* 30th Cong., 1st Sess., 477–80, 496–503 (March 16–17, 1848); Lander, *Reluctant Imperialists,* 170.

69. William J. Cooper Jr. has observed that after the Proviso the Calhounites and the regular southern Democrats "stood much closer together than historians have usually admitted"; Cooper, *The South and the Politics of Slavery, 1828–1856* (Baton Rouge: Louisiana State University Press, 1978), 236–38. See also Polk, *Diary,* 4:19–21 (July 16, 1848); and Dusinberre, *Slavemaster President,* 143. Polk's diary also shows his close cooperation with Calhoun allies like David Yulee of Florida and Robert Barnwell Rhett of South Carolina, even long after the Calhounites had supposedly split with the administration: Polk, *Diary,* 2:463 (April 7, 1847); 3:236 (December 2, 1847).

70. Buchanan to Trist, October 6 and 25, 1847, *DCUS,* 8, 214–18. Polk, Third Annual Message, December 7, 1847, *Compilation of the Messages and Papers of the Presidents,* 5:544–46.

71. *CG,* 30th Cong., 1st Sess., 79 (December 30, 1847); *CG,* 30th Cong., 1st Sess., 26 (December 15, 1847), 310 (February 7, 1848). See also Lander, *Reluctant Imperialists,* 150–70; and John D. P. Fuller, "The Slavery Question and the Movement to Acquire Mexico, 1846–1848," *Mississippi Valley Historical Review* 21, no. 1 (June 1934): 31–48.

72. On Trist and his negotiations, see Wallace Ohrt, *Defiant Peacemaker: Nicholas Trist in the Mexican War* (College Station: Texas A&M University Press, 1997), 135–46; and Greenberg, *Wicked War,* 214–24, 238–40.

73. Pletcher, *Diplomacy of Annexation,* 551–63; Frederick Merk, *Manifest Destiny and Mission in American History* (New York: Knopf, 1963), 180–201.

74. David M. Potter, *The Impending Crisis: America before the Civil War, 1848–1861* (New York: Harper and Row, 1976), 6.

75. Expansionist Democrats in the Northwest were stymied by the administration's caution in the Oregon negotiations; Free Soil Democrats in the Northeast were forced to swallow the defeat of the Wilmot Proviso.
76. *Galveston Civilian,* April 28, 1848. On fugitive slaves in Mexico after 1848, see Cornell, "Citizens of Nowhere," 365–66.
77. For the full Davis-Calhoun exchange, see *JDC,* 1:191–201.
78. See Potter, *Impending Crisis,* 1–18; and Michael A. Morrison, *Slavery and the American West: The Eclipse of Manifest Destiny and the Coming of the Civil War* (Chapel Hill: University of North Carolina Press, 1997), 66–95.
79. Emerson's prophecy, in particular, appears with metronomic regularity in major treatments of the war: see James M. McPherson, *Battle Cry of Freedom: The Civil War Era* (New York: Oxford University Press, 1988), 51; Howe, *What Hath God Wrought,* 821; Pletcher, *Diplomacy of Annexation,* 581; Schroeder, *Mr. Polk's War,* 117; Haynes, *James K. Polk and the Expansionist Impulse,* 205; Greenberg, *Wicked War,* 269; and George C. Herring, *From Colony to Superpower* (New York: Oxford University Press, 2005), 176. On Polk's rejection of both Emerson's and Calhoun's visions of the war, see Walter A. McDougall, *Throes of Democracy: The American Civil War Era, 1829–1877* (New York: Harper Perennial, 2008), 306–7.
80. Solomon Northup, *Twelve Years a Slave* (New York: Penguin, 2012 [1853]), 164.
81. King to James Buchanan, July 20, 1846, *DCUS,* 6:570; emphasis in the original. Auguste Davezac to James Buchanan, February 9, 1847, *DCUS,* 10:17. For similarly triumphant reports from southerners abroad, see (from Spain) Thomas C. Reynolds to James Buchanan, July 27, 1847, *DCUS,* 11:410–12; and (from Prussia) Andrew Jackson Donelson to John C. Calhoun, September 27, 1848, *PJCC,* 26:67; see also Johannsen, *To the Halls of the Montezumas,* 303–8.
82. Polk, Fourth Annual Message, December 5, 1848, *Compilation of the Messages and Papers of the Presidents,* 4:637–38; James D. B. De Bow, "The South American States," *DBR,* July 1848, 8. See also *Richmond Enquirer,* May 2, 1848; "Conquest of California," 414.
83. Simms to James Henry Hammond, May 1, 1847, July 15, 1847, in Mary C. Simms Oliphant, et al, eds., *Letters of William Gilmore Simms,* 6 vols. (Columbia: University of South Carolina Press, 1952–1982), 2:311, 332–33.
84. Tyler to Samuel Gardiner, November 26, 1850, Tyler Family Papers, CW&M.
85. "Our Foreign Policy," *SLM,* January 1850, 1. On Britain's rueful recognition of this altered reality, see Kenneth Bourne, *Britain and the Balance of Power in North America, 1815–1908* (London: Longmans, Green, and Co., 1967), 170–205.

6. King Cotton, Emperor Slavery

1. On the numerous internal fault lines in antebellum southern society, see Stephanie McCurry, *Masters of Small Worlds: Yeoman Households, Gender Relations, and the Political Culture of the Antebellum South Carolina Low Country* (New York:

Oxford University Press, 1995); J. Mills Thornton III, *Politics and Power in a Slave Society: Alabama, 1800–1860* (Baton Rouge: Louisiana State University Press, 1978); Michael P. Johnson, *Toward a Patriarchal Republic: The Secession of Georgia* (Baton Rouge: Louisiana State University Press, 1977); Steven Hahn, *The Roots of Southern Populism: Yeomen Farmers and the Transformation of the Georgia Upcountry* (New York: Oxford University Press, 1983); Lacy K. Ford, *Origins of Southern Radicalism: The South Carolina Upcountry, 1800–1860* (New York: Oxford University Press, 1988); and William A. Link, *Roots of Secession: Slavery and Politics in Antebellum Virginia* (Chapel Hill: University of North Carolina Press, 2003).

2. See, for instance, Eugene D. Genovese, *The Political Economy of Slavery: Studies in the Economy and Society of the Slave South* (New York: Random House, 1966), 243–70; David M. Potter, *The Impending Crisis: America before the Civil War, 1848–1861* (New York: Harper and Row, 1976), 177–98; James M. McPherson, *Battle Cry of Freedom: The Civil War Era* (New York: Oxford University Press, 1988), 91–116; James Oakes, *The Ruling Race: A History of American Slaveholders* (New York: Random House, 1983), 225–35; and John McCardell, *The Idea of a Southern Nation: Southern Nationalists and Southern Nationalism, 1830–1860* (New York: W. W. Norton, 1979), 71–90, 227–76. For more focused work on southern imperialism that largely grants interpretive priority to domestic considerations, see Robert E. May, *The Southern Dream of a Caribbean Empire, 1854–1861* (Gainesville: University Press of Florida, 2002 [1973]); William W. Freehling, *The Reintegration of American History* (New York: Oxford University Press, 1994), 158–75; and Walter Johnson, *River of Dark Dreams: Slavery and Empire in the Cotton Kingdom* (Cambridge, Mass.: Harvard University Press, 2013), 280–420.

3. For recent scholarly investigations see Edward B. Rugemer, *The Problem of Emancipation: The Caribbean Roots of the American Civil War* (Baton Rouge: Louisiana State University Press, 2008); Robert E. Bonner, *Mastering America: Southern Slaveholders and the Crisis of American Nationhood* (New York: Cambridge University Press, 2009); Brian Schoen, *The Fragile Fabric of Union: Cotton, Federal Politics, and the Global Origins of the Civil War* (Baltimore: Johns Hopkins University Press, 2009).

4. Robert M. T. Hunter, speech in Senate, *CG Appendix*, 31th Cong., 1st Sess., 381 (March 25, 1850).

5. [Thomas P. Kettell], "The Future of the South," *DBR*, February 1851, 137; James Henry Hammond, speech at Barnwell Court House, October 29, 1858, in Clyde N. Wilson, ed., *Selections from the Letters and Speeches of the Hon. James H. Hammond, of South Carolina* (Spartansburg, S.C.: Reprint Company, 1978), 347–48.

6. Slaveholders' late antebellum confidence that European policy would ultimately be driven by interest, not principle, aligns with James Oakes's argument that the South experienced a major ideological shift after 1850: Oakes, "From Republicanism to Liberalism: Ideological Change and the Crisis of the Old South," *American Quarterly* 37, no. 4 (Autumn 1985), 551–71.

7. See, for instance, John C. Calhoun to Duff Green, April 2, 1842, *PJCC*, 16:209; "East India Cotton," *SQR*, April 1842, 446–92.

8. Calhoun to Robert M. T. Hunter, March 26, 1845, and Calhoun to Abbott Lawrence, May 15, 1845, *PJCC*, 21:447–50, 550; Bruno Gujer, "Free Trade and Slavery: Calhoun's Defense of Southern Interests against British Interference, 1811–1848" (PhD diss., University of Zurich, 1971), 91–121.

9. On the Corn Laws and the 1840s as a turning point in British commercial policy, see Paul Bairoch, "European Trade Policy, 1815–1914," in Peter Mathias and Sidney Pollard, eds., *Cambridge Economic History of Europe*, 8 vols. (New York: Cambridge University Press, 1989), 8:1–160; and Anthony Howe, "Free Trade and Global Order: The Rise and Fall of a Victorian Vision," in Duncan Bell, ed., *Victorian Visions of Global Order: Empire and International Relations in Nineteenth-Century British Political Thought* (New York: Cambridge University Press, 2007), 26–46.

10. On the sugar duties, see Eric Williams, *Capitalism and Slavery* (Chapel Hill: University of North Carolina Press, 1944), 136–42; Seymour Drescher, *The Mighty Experiment: Free Labor versus Slavery in British Emancipation* (New York: Oxford University Press, 2003), 176–88; C. Duncan Rice, "'Humanity Sold for Sugar!' The British Abolitionist Response to Free Trade in Slave-Grown Sugar," *Historical Journal* 13, no. 3 (September 1970): 402–18; and Richard Huzzey, "Free Trade, Free Labour and Slave Sugar in Victorian Britain," *Historical Journal* 53 (2010): 359–79.

11. On the Navigation Acts, see J. H. Clapham, "The Last Years of the Navigation Acts," pts. 1 and 2, *English Historical Review* 25, no. 99 (July 1910): 480–501; 25, no. 100 (October 1910): 687–707. For an enthusiastic southern response to their repeal, see D. J. M. [David James McCord], review of "The Anatomy of the Navigation Acts," *SQR*, January 1850, 417.

12. Green to Webster, January 24, 1842, in Duff Green, *Facts and Suggestions, Biographical, Historical, Financial, and Political, Addressed to the People of the United States* (New York: Richardson and Co., 1866), 150–52; Green to Tyler, July 3, 1843, Green Papers, SHC-UNC; [Thomas P. Kettell], "Stability of the Union," *Commercial Review of the South and West*, April 1850, 354–56.

13. "Report of the Secretary of the Treasury," December 6, 1853, *CG Appendix*, 33rd Cong., 1st Sess., 2. On the broader spread of free trade, see Bairoch, "European Trade Policy," 23–36; C. P. Kindleberger, "The Rise of Free Trade in Western Europe, 1820–1875," *Journal of Economic History* 35, no. 1 (March 1975): 20–55; David Todd, "John Bowring and the Global Dissemination of Free Trade," *Historical Journal* 51, no. 2 (2008): 373–97; and Schoen, *Fragile Fabric of Union*, 190–95. On the complexities of commercial opinion within the planter class, see John Majewski, *Modernizing a Slave Economy: The Economic Vision of the Confederate Nation* (Chapel Hill: University of North Carolina Press, 2009), 108–39; and Brian Schoen, "The Burdens and Opportunities of Independence: The Political Economies of the Planter Class," in L. Diane Barnes, Brian Schoen, and Frank Towers,

eds., *The Old South's Modern Worlds: Slavery, Region, and Nation in the Age of Progress* (New York: Oxford University Press, 2011), 66–84.

14. See Alisdair Roberts, *America's First Great Depression: Economic Crisis and Political Disorder after the Panic of 1837* (Ithaca, N.Y.: Cornell University Press, 2012), 175–202; and Susan B. Carter et al., eds., *Historical Statistics of the United States, Earliest Times to the Present: Millennial Edition* (New York: Cambridge University Press, 2006), Table Cc 205–266.

15. Calhoun to King, August 12, 1844, *PJCC*, 19:573; "Consumption and Production of Cotton, Sugar, Tobacco, and Rice," *New York Weekly Herald*, April 11, 1857, reprinted in the *Charleston Mercury*, April 23, 1857; "Slavery in the Tropics," *Charleston Mercury*, May 15, 1857. Industrial development in the temperate North Atlantic did powerfully stimulate the demand for tropical and subtropical staples between 1840 and 1860; see Eric Hobsbawm, *The Age of Revolution, 1789–1848* (New York: New American Library, 1962), 351; Dale W. Tomich, *Through the Prism of Slavery: Labor, Capital, and World Economy* (Lanham, Md.: Rowman and Littlefield, 2004), 56–71; and Robin Blackburn, *The American Crucible: Slavery, Emancipation and Human Rights* (London: Verso, 2011), 280–327.

16. John F. Kvachs, *De Bow's Review: The Antebellum Vision of a New South* (Lexington: University Press of Kentucky, 2014); Robert F. Durden, "J. D. B. De Bow: Convolutions of a Slavery Expansionist," *JSH* 17, no. 4 (November 1951): 441–61; Ottis Clark Skipper, *J. D. B. De Bow, Magazinist of the Old South* (Athens: University of Georgia Press, 1958).

17. [Kettell], "Future of the South," 137; James D. B. De Bow, *The Industrial Resources, etc., of the Southern and Western States . . .* , 3 vols. (New Orleans: Pudney and Russell, 1853), 3:37–45; *DBR*, September 1856, 308–23. On slaveholders' embrace of the gospel of prosperity, see Oakes, *The Ruling Race*, 123–38.

18. Thomas Kettell, *Southern Wealth and Northern Profits*, ed. Fletcher Green (Tuscaloosa: University of Alabama Press, 1965 [1860]). On cotton exports and the politics of sectional grievance, see Schoen, *Fragile Fabric of Union*, 242–50, Majewski, *Modernizing a Slave Economy*, 111–16; and Johnson, *River of Dark Dreams*, 280–301.

19. Stephen Colwell, *The Five Cotton States and New York: Remarks upon the Social and Economical Aspects of the Southern Political Crisis* ([Philadelphia], 1861), 36–37; Daniel Lord, *The Effect of Secession upon the Commercial Relations between the North and South* (New York: Office of the New York Times, 1861), 37–38. On the rise of the internal economy and its consequences, see Louis Bernard Schmidt, "Internal Commerce and the Development of a National Economy before 1860," *Journal of Political Economy* 47, no. 6 (December 1939): 798–822; Marc Egnal, *Clash of Extremes: The Economic Origins of the Civil War* (New York: Hill and Wang, 2009), 101–22; and Ariel Ron, "Developing the Country: 'Scientific Agriculture' and the Roots of the Republican Party" (PhD diss., University of California–Berkeley, 2011), 57–96.

20. David Christy, "'Cotton' Is King," *DBR*, September 1855, 263–68, 308–16; emphasis in the original.

21. "The Coffee Trade—Its Production and Consumption over the World," *New York Herald*, August 20, 1856; reprinted in the *Charleston Courier*, January 16, 1857; *Georgia Telegraph* (Macon, Ga.), January 27, 1857; *DBR*, September 1857, 285–89. On Cuban sugar, see *DBR*, May 1852, 572; *DBR*, May 1859, 589; "A Trip to Cuba," *Russell's Magazine*, April 1858, 65–66.

22. Under the heading "Slavery and Commerce," this brief comment first appeared in the *Richmond Daily Dispatch* of December 30, 1854, and spread widely thereafter; see the *Georgia Telegraph* (Macon, Ga.), January 16, 1855; *Texas State Gazette* (Austin, Tex.), January 27, 1855; *Memphis Daily Appeal*, January 28, 1855; *Kansas Weekly Herald* (Leavenworth, Kans.), May 4, 1855; *Arkansas State Gazette* (Little Rock, Ark.), June 1, 1855; and *DBR*, June 1856, 739.

23. "Our Relations with Africa," *New York Herald*, February 17, 1858; reprinted in the *Charleston Courier*, March 10, 1858.

24. *Charleston Evening News* article reprinted in the *Milledgeville Federal Union*, September 8, 1846; J. A. C. [John A. Campbell], "The British West Indies Islands," *SQR*, January 1850, 342–77. On Campbell's essay, see Rugemer, *Problem of Emancipation*, 265–66; on the sugar duties and the West Indies, see Thomas C. Holt, *The Problem of Freedom: Race, Labor, and Politics in Jamaica and Britain, 1832–1938* (Baltimore: Johns Hopkins University Press, 1992), 117–25.

25. William R. King to Calhoun, October 10, 1844, *PJCC*, 20:61–64. For an overview of French emancipation, see Robin Blackburn, *The Overthrow of Colonial Slavery, 1776–1848* (London: Verso, 1988), 494–506.

26. "C," "The French Republic," *SQR*, July 1848, 234–35; [Kettell], "Future of the South," 132–36; Charles James Faulkner, speech at public dinner, December 16, 1852, Faulkner Family Papers, Box 70, VHS.

27. [Kettell], "Stability of the Union," 354–56. The actual relationship between slavery, antislavery, and British free trade imperialism was somewhat more ambiguous; see Ronald Robinson and John Gallagher, "The Imperialism of Free Trade," *Economic History Review* 6, no. 1 (1953): 1–15; Todd, "John Bowring and the Global Dissemination of Free Trade," 391–92; Richard Huzzey, *Freedom Burning: Antislavery and Empire in Victorian Britain* (Ithaca, N.Y.: Cornell University Press, 2012), 98–176; and Marc-William Palen, "Free Trade and Transatlantic Abolitionism: A Historiography," *Journal of the History of Economic Thought* 37, no. 2 (June 2015): 291–304. But in the 1850s it was easy for southerners to believe that the new open-market imperialism could coexist quite comfortably with enslaved labor in the South, Brazil, Cuba, and elsewhere.

28. Arguments about slavery and the capitalist economy that fall along these lines include Immanuel Wallerstein, "American Slavery and the Capitalist World-Economy," in *The Capitalist World-Economy* (Cambridge: Cambridge University Press, 1979), 202–21; and Scott Reynolds Nelson, "Who Put Their Capitalism in

My Slavery?" *JCWE* 5, no. 2 (June 2015), 289–310. To understand the course of nineteenth century political struggle—rather than simply to produce an accurate map of nineteenth century economic development—historians must treat mistaken southern ideas as seriously as prescient northern ones.

29. Eric Hobsbawm, *The Age of Capital: 1848–1875* (New York: Charles Scribner's Sons, 1975), 141–43, 182–86. Whether the South's vision of global economic development—extensive and mercantile, rather than intensive and industrial— definitively set it apart from the burgeoning capitalist order of the late nineteenth century is a question for theorists and world historians: persuasive answers in the affirmative include Giovanni Arrighi, *The Long Twentieth Century: Money, Power, and the Origins of Our Times* (London: Verso, 1994), esp. 1–37, 223–25, 289–301; and Sven Beckert, *Empire of Cotton: A Global History* (New York: Knopf, 2014), esp. xv–xxii, 165–98. But what seems clear is that in the specific moment of the 1850s, it was perfectly possible for southern elites to comprehend a pattern of development that put them in the vanguard, not the rearguard, of economic progress.

30. John C. Calhoun, speech in Senate, March 4, 1850, *PJCC*, 27:187–210. On Calhoun's deathlike appearance as a symbol of the South's doomed intransigence, see Potter, *Impending Crisis*, 98 (quoted); McPherson, *Battle Cry of Freedom*, 57–58, 71–72; and Allan Nevins, *Ordeal of the Union*, vol. 1, *Fruits of Manifest Destiny* (New York: Scribner, 1947), 278–83. For criticism, see Edward E. Baptist, *The Half Has Never Been Told: Slavery and the Making of American Capitalism* (New York: Basic Books, 2014), 300–301.

31. *CG Appendix*, 30th Cong., 1st Sess., 617 (May 10, 1848). On the potential Yucatán intervention, see Frederick Merk, *The Monroe Doctrine and American Expansionism, 1843–1849* (New York: Knopf, 1966), 194–232.

32. Sarah Myrtton Maury to Calhoun, August 15, 1848, *PJCC*, 26:4. On the negative evolution of British attitudes toward West Indian emancipation after 1833, see Williams, *Capitalism and Slavery*, 171–77, 188–95; Holt, *Problem of Freedom*, 278–309; Drescher, *Mighty Experiment*, 158–230; Catherine Hall, *Civilising Subjects: Metropole and Colony in the English Imagination, 1830–1867* (Cambridge, U.K.: Polity Press, 2002), 338–79; and Huzzey, *Freedom Burning*, 98–131.

33. See, for instance, "A Few Thoughts on Slavery," *SLM*, April 1854, 203; *Charleston Mercury*, October 24, 1854. In late 1857, four consecutive issues of *De Bow's Review*—from September to December in a solid bloc—prominently featured antiabolitionist quotations from the *London Times*.

34. Proslavery citations of Carlyle include [David Flavel Jamison], "British and American Slavery," *SQR*, October 1853, 369–409; and George Fitzhugh, "The Conservative Principle," *DBR*, May 1857, 454–55; see also Rugemer, *Problem of Emancipation*, 263–64. For proslavery citations of Trollope, especially his 1859 West Indian travelogue, see *Richmond Daily Dispatch*, February 9, 1860; and *Mobile Register*, February 24, 1860; see also Hall, *Civilising Subjects*, 209–21.

35. See Obadiah Jennings Wise to Henry Wise, August 21, 1853, Henry A. Wise Correspondence, Wise Family Papers, VHS; and David Moltke-Hansen, "A Beaufort Planter's Rhetorical World: The Contexts and Contents of William Henry Trescot's Orations," *Proceedings of the South Carolina Historical Association* (1981): 123, 130. On the continuing potency of cultural antislavery in Britain, see Huzzey, *Freedom Burning*, 21–39.

36. Randal William McGavock, *A Tennessean Abroad; or, Letters from Europe, Africa, and Asia* (New York: J. S. Redfield, 1854), 214; Jacob C. Levy to Calhoun, January 29, 1849, *PJCC*, 26:251. On slavery and elite southern travelers abroad, see Michael O'Brien, *Conjectures of Order: Intellectual Life in the Old South, 1810–1860* (Chapel Hill: University of North Carolina Press, 2004), 90–213; and Elizabeth Fox-Genovese and Eugene D. Genovese, *Slavery in White and Black: Class and Race in the Southern Slaveholders' New World Order* (New York: Cambridge University Press, 2008), 121–42.

37. James Gadsden to Jefferson Davis, July 19, 1854, *PJD*, 5:78–80; H [James Henry Hammond], "Maury on South America and Amazonia," *SQR*, October 1853, 445–47; emphasis in the original.

38. See, for example"The Cotton Trade of Great Britain," *DBR*, May 1855, 653; [Kettell], "Future of the South," 142. To be sure, southern triumphalists often wildly overstated their own power within this emerging international system. For more nuanced portraits, see Beckert, *Empire of Cotton*, 98–246; Harold T. Woodman, *King Cotton and His Retainers: Marketing the Cotton Crop of the South, 1800–1925* (Lexington, Ky.: University of Kentucky Press, 1968).

39. De Bow, *Industrial Resources*, 1:174–78; see also "The Growth and Consumption of Cotton," *SQR*, January 1848, 103–4.

40. De Bow, *Industrial Resources*, 1:178; emphasis in the original. For an account of antebellum southern politics that places this "cotton-centered commercial worldview" at the heart of proslavery confidence, see Schoen, *Fragile Fabric of Union*, esp. 161–74, 197–237.

41. David Christy, *Cotton Is King; or, Slavery in Light of Political Economy*, reprinted in E. N. Elliott, ed., *Cotton Is King, and Proslavery Arguments* . . . (Augusta, Ga.: Pritchard, Abbott and Loomis, 1860), 216; emphasis in the original.

42. W. G. Simms, "Literary Woolgatherings," *SQR*, January 1854, 193, 200–203. A "Flemish account" is an old Anglophone expression for a sum that was smaller than expected. On Lester, see Marcus Cunliffe, *Chattel Slavery and Wage Slavery* (Athens: University of Georgia Press, 1979), 69–103.

43. Simms, "Literary Woolgatherings," 204.

44. "The Black Race in North America, No. III," *DBR*, March 1856, 305. On slavery as the antebellum South's one true "king," see Manisha Sinha, *The Counterrevolution of Slavery: Politics and Ideology in Antebellum South Carolina* (Chapel Hill: University of North Carolina Press, 2000), 220.

45. *Charleston Mercury*, August 25, 1852.

46. *Cincinnati Weekly Herald and Philanthropist*, December 18, 1844.
47. George Fitzhugh, *Sociology for the South; or, The Failure of Free Society* (Richmond: A. Morris, 1854), 257–61; Fitzhugh, "The Counter Current, or Slavery Principle," *DBR*, July 1856, 90–95; Fitzhugh, *Cannibals All! or, Slaves without Masters* (Cambridge, Mass.: Belknap Press of Harvard University Press, 1960 [1856]), 162, 184–87. See also Nicholas Onuf and Peter Onuf, *Nations, Markets, and War: Modern History and the American Civil War* (Charlottesville: University of Virginia Press, 2006), 333–42. On Fitzhugh as a "bourgeois thinker" who saw slavery as part of a productive, progressive world order, see O'Brien, *Conjectures of Order*, 972–92. On the heterogeneity and elasticity of proslavery thought in general, see Schoen, *Fragile Fabric of Union*, 161.
48. George Frederick Holmes, "Slavery and Freedom," *SQR*, April 1856, 62–95.
49. On McCord, see Richard C. Lounsbury, ed., *Louisa S. McCord: Poems, Drama, Biography, Letters* (Charlottesville: University of Virginia Press, 1996), esp. 414–22 (quotations); Richard C. Lounsbury, ed., *Louisa S. McCord: Political and Social Essays* (Charlottesville: University of Virginia Press, 1995); Leigh Fought, *Southern Womanhood and Slavery: A Biography of Louisa McCord, 1810–1879* (Columbia, Mo.: University of Missouri Press, 2003).
50. McCord "Slavery and Political Economy," pts. 1 and 2, *DBR*, October 1856, 331–49, quoted 336, 338–39; November 1856, 443–67, quoted 452.
51. McCord, "Slavery and Political Economy," pt. 1, 338; McCord, "Slavery and Political Economy," pt. 2, 462–67; emphasis in the original.. On McCord's exchange with Holmes, see Bonner, *Mastering America*, 106–13. For the argument that Britain's political economists—and Britain's political leadership—did not actually abandon their faith in free labor, see Huzzey, *Freedom Burning*, 126–31.
52. Holmes, "Slavery and Freedom," 93–95.
53. On the *Standard*, see William L. King, *The Newspaper Press of Charleston, S.C.* (Charleston: Lucas and Richardson, 1882), 160–63; on Spratt, see Ronald G. Takaki, *A Proslavery Crusade: The Agitation to Reopen the African Slave Trade* (New York: Free Press, 1971), 1–9.
54. "Destiny of the Slave States," *DBR*, September 1854, 280–84.
55. "The Destiny of the Slave States," *Charleston Southern Standard*, June 25, 1853. Fragments of the editorial are quoted in Basil Rauch, *American Interest in Cuba: 1848–1855* (New York: Columbia University Press, 1948), 188–89; and Genovese, *The Political Economy of Slavery*, 248–49.
56. "The Destiny of the Slave States." For further southern musings on race, climate, and slavery, see Michael Dunning, "Manifest Destiny and the Trans-Mississippi South: Natural Laws and the Extension of Slavery into Mexico," *Journal of Popular Culture* 35, no. 2 (Fall 2001): 111–27.
57. See *Georgia Telegraph* (Macon, Ga.), August 2, 1853; Duff Green Papers, SHC-UNC. De Bow excerpted the piece from the *Richmond Enquirer*; *DBR*, September 1854, 280.

58. *New York Times*, May 16, 1854. For similar reactions, see the *National Era* (Washington, D.C.), June 1, 1854; "Slavery Extension," *Friends' Review* (Philadelphia, Pa.), June 10, 1854, 617–19; and "Exploration of the Valley of the Amazon," *New Englander* (New Haven, Conn.), August 1854, 362–83.

59. *Charleston Mercury*, November 8, 1854, and also October 24, 27, and 31 and November 4, 1854; Southern Commercial Convention minutes reported in the *Southern Recorder* (Milledgeville, Ga.), December 23, 1856. For an account of pro-slavery internationalism that puts the slave trade at its center, see Johnson, *River of Dark Dreams*, 303–420.

60. Matthew Fontaine Maury, "Southern Direct Foreign Trade," in De Bow, *Industrial Resources*, 3:5; empahsis in the original. Maury "put the ideologies and economies associated with slavery at the heart of his new mapping of the seas"; see Daniel Rood, "Plantation Technocrats: A Social History of Knowledge in the Slaveholding Atlantic World, 1830–1865" (PhD diss., University of California–Irvine, 2010), 155–71 (quoted 170); Johnson, *River of Dark Dreams*, 296–302; Chester G. Hearn, *Tracks in the Sea: Matthew Fontaine Maury and the Mapping of the Oceans* (New York: McGraw-Hill, 2002), 95–122; and D. Graham Burnett, "Matthew Fontaine Maury's 'Sea of Fire': Hydrography, Biogeography, and Providence in the Tropics," in Felix Driver and Luciana Martins, eds., *Tropical Visions in an Age of Empire* (Chicago: University of Chicago Press, 2005), 113–36.

61. Maury to Lieutenant William L. Herndon, April 20, 1850, enclosed in letter from Maury to Secretary of the Navy William Graham, October 8, 1850, in *The Papers of William Alexander Graham*, ed. J. G. de Roulhac Hamilton, 8 vols. (Raleigh: North Carolina Department of Cultural Resources, 1957–1992), 3:434–36. Maury's text mistakenly reads "Mediterranean Sea," a revealing and characteristic slip. See Matthew Pratt Guterl, *American Mediterranean: Southern Slaveholders in the Age of Emancipation* (Cambridge, Mass.: Harvard University Press, 2008), 12–46.

62. Matthew Fontaine Maury, "The Panama Rail-way and the Gulf of Mexico," *SLM*, August 1849, 441–57; Maury, "Southern Direct Foreign Trade," 3:6.

63. Maury, "Southern Direct Foreign Trade," 3:7; Maury, "Panama Rail-way and the Gulf of Mexico," 448; Gerald Horne, *The Deepest South: The United States, Brazil, and the African Slave Trade* (New York: New York University Press, 2007), 113–17.

64. Maury's major South American writings between 1849 and 1853 were published as a book: Matthew Fontaine Maury, *The Amazon, and the Atlantic Slopes of South America* (Washington, D.C.: Frank Taylor, 1853).

65. Maury instructed Herndon to query the citizens of Peru on "their feelings in regard to Slavery, and the slave trade." Maury to Herndon, April 20, 1850, in *Papers of William Alexander Graham*, 3:433–48; Maury, "Southern Direct Foreign Trade," 3:11; William Lewis Herndon and Lardner Gibbon, *Exploration of the Valley of the Amazon*, 2 vols. (Washington, D.C.: Robert Armstrong, Public Printer, 1853). See

also Horne, *Deepest South*, 107–27; and Whitfield J. Bell Jr., "The Relation of Herndon and Gibbon's Exploration of the Amazon to North American Slavery, 1850–1855," *Hispanic-AHR* 19, no. 4 (November 1939): 494–503.

66. Maury to Mrs. William Blackford, December 24, 1851, in Jacquelin Ambler Caskie, *Life and Letters of Matthew Fontaine Maury* (Richmond: Richmond Press, 1928), 131–32; Maury, "Southern Direct Foreign Trade," 3:11–13. On Maury and Virginia slavery, see Horne, *Deepest South*, 67–69, 108, 123–25.

67. Henry Wise to Nehemiah Adams, August 22, 1854, printed in the *New York Times*, September 15, 1854; *Charleston Mercury*, September 19 and October 4, 1854; see also the *Richmond Enquirer*, September 19 and October 2, 1854.

68. H [James Henry Hammond], "Maury on South America and Amazonia," *SQR*, October 1853, 412–49; emphasis in the original.

69. Ibid., 443–44; "The Destiny of the Slave States"; see also the *Richmond Enquirer's* notice of Herndon's travel narrative, February 10, 1854.

70. Herndon and Gibbon, *Exploration of the Valley of the Amazon*, 1:341; Jefferson Davis, speech in Senate, February 14, 1850, *JDC*, 1:289–90. For even more lavish southern praise for Brazilian slavery, see John C. Calhoun, speech in Senate, January 4, 1848, *PJCC*, 25:64; and C. G. Memminger, "Lecture Delivered before the Young Men's Association of Augusta, April 10th, 1851," reprinted in the *Federal Union* (Milledgeville, Ga.), July 1, 1851.

71. Richard Kidder Meade, speech to Dom Pedro II, reprinted in the *National Era*, February 18, 1858; Robert G. Scott, letter, reprinted in *DBR*, January 1858, 26.

72. "The Dred Scott Decision in Brazil," *New York Times*, February 16, 1858. In 1857 Brazil did agree to lower its tariff on wheat flour, which it largely imported from Virginia; see *Charleston Mercury*, June 19, 1857. On the deeper economic relationship between Virginia and Brazil across the antebellum decades, see Rood, "Plantation Technocrats," 174–254.

73. Charles Mercer Fenton Garnett to Muscoe Russell Hunter Garnett, May 13, 1858, Hunter-Garnett Papers, University of Virginia; Richard Morton Diary, Richard Morton Papers, VHS; emphases in the originals. On Richard Morton's journey to Brazil, see Rood, "Plantation Technocrats," 135–55.

74. James D. B. De Bow, "The Empire of Brazil," *DBR*, January 1858, 1–27; J. R. H., "Slavery in Brazil—The Past and Future," *Charleston Mercury*, January 24, 1860; reprinted in *DBR*, April 1860, 479–81.

75. Judah Benjamin, speech in Senate, *CG*, 35th Cong., 2nd Sess., 960 (February 11, 1859); *New-York Daily Tribune*, February 14, 1859.

7. Slaveholding Visions of Modernity

1. Frederick Porcher, "The Prospects and Policy of the South, as They Appear to a Planter," *SQR*, October 1854, 431–32.

2. For a sweeping overview of this historiography, see Frank Towers, "Partisans, New History, and Modernization: The Historiography of the Civil War's Causes, 1861–2011," *JCWE* 1, no. 2 (June 2011): 237–64.

3. George Fitzhugh, "Modern Civilization," *DBR*, July 1860, 67. Major works that embody different varieties of this perspective include W. E. B. Du Bois, *Black Reconstruction in America* (New York: Russell and Russell, 1935), 32–54; Eugene D. Genovese, *The Political Economy of Slavery: Studies in the Economy and Society of the Slave South* (New York: Pantheon, 1965), 155–239; Eugene D. Genovese, *The World the Slaveholders Made: Two Essays in Interpretation* (New York: Random House, 1969), 118–244. James M. McPherson, *Battle Cry of Freedom: The Civil War Era* (New York: Oxford University Press, 1988), 78–116; Stephanie McCurry, *Masters of Small Worlds: Yeoman Households, Gender Relations, and the Political Culture of the Antebellum South Carolina Low Country* (New York: Oxford University Press, 1995), 208–35; and John Ashworth, *Slavery, Capitalism, and Politics in the Antebellum Republic*, vol. 2, *The Coming of the Civil War, 1850–1861* (Cambridge: Cambridge University Press, 2007). Strikingly, McPherson, McCurry, and Ashworth all quote from Porcher's essay, although not the selection I have excerpted. Two important dissents came from Robert W. Fogel and Stanley L. Engerman, *Time on the Cross: The Economics of American Negro Slavery* (New York: W. W. Norton, 1974); and James Oakes, *The Ruling Race: A History of American Slaveholders* (New York: Random House, 1983).

4. See Frank Towers, "The Southern Path to Modern Cities: Urbanization in the Slave States," William G. Thomas, "'Swerve Me?': The South, Railroads, and the Rush to Modernity," and L. Diane Barnes, "Industry and Its Laborers, Free and Slave in Late-Antebellum Virginia," in L. Diane Barnes, Brian Schoen, and Frank Towers, eds., *The Old South's Modern Worlds: Slavery, Region, and Nation in the Age of Progress* (New York: Oxford University Press, 2011), 145–65, 166–88, 189–206.

5. For synthetic treatments see Robert W. Fogel, *Without Consent or Contract: The Rise and Fall of American Slavery* (New York: Norton, 1989), 81–113; Walter Johnson, *River of Dark Dreams: Slavery and Empire in the Cotton Kingdom* (Cambridge, Mass.: Harvard University Press, 2013); Edward E. Baptist, *The Half Has Never Been Told: Slavery and the Making of American Capitalism* (New York: Basic Books, 2014); and Sven Beckert, *Empire of Cotton: A Global History* (New York: Knopf, 2014), esp. 98–135. See also John Majewski, *Modernizing a Slave Economy: The Economic Vision of the Confederate Nation* (Chapel Hill: University of North Carolina Press, 2009); Aaron Marrs, *Railroads in the Old South: Pursuing Progress in a Slave Society* (Baltimore: Johns Hopkins University Press, 2009); Caitlin C. Rosenthal, "From Memory to Mastery: Accounting for Control in America, 1750–1880," PhD diss., University of California–Berkeley, 2012. Gavin Wright remains skeptical about overall southern development under slavery but notes that for slaveholders, at least, the institution allowed an accumulation of

wealth that surpassed that of their northern peers: *Slavery and American Economic Development* (Baton Rouge: Louisiana State University Press, 2006).

6. *Columbus (Ga.) Tri-Weekly Enquirer,* May 1, 1856. For wealth statistics, see Wright, *Slavery and American Economic Development,* 55–62; Adam Rothman, "The 'Slave Power' in the United States, 1783–1865," in Steve Fraser and Gary Gerstle, eds., *Ruling America: A History of Wealth and Power in a Democracy* (Cambridge, Mass.: Harvard University Press, 2005), 72; and James Huston, *Calculating the Value of the Union: Slavery, Property Rights, and the Economic Origins of the Civil War* (Chapel Hill: University of North Carolina Press, 2003), 27–30.

7. Judah Benjamin, speech in Senate, *CG,* 35th Cong., 2nd Sess., 960 (February 11, 1859); J. D. B. De Bow, *The Industrial Resources, etc., of the Southern and Western States. . . . . . ,* 3 vols. (New Orleans: Pudney and Russell, 1853); George Fitzhugh, "Southern Thought (Cont'd)," *DBR,* November 1857, 460. This usage was not limited to American slaveholders; in his landmark 1848 economics textbook John Stuart Mill generally used "industry" and "industrial" to refer to all forms of productive labor, rather than manufacturing in particular. John Stuart Mill, *Principles of Political Economy,* 5 vols. (London: John W. Parker, 1848).

8. C. A. Bayly, *The Birth of the Modern World: 1798–1914* (Malden, Mass.: Blackwell, 2003); Jürgen Osterhammel, *The Transformation of the World: A Global History of the Nineteenth Century* (Princeton, N.J.: Princeton University Press, 2014), esp. 904–5. "Modernity" has also been an important but seldom neatly defined concept for historians of slavery and the American South; see Paul Gilroy, *The Black Atlantic: Modernity and Double Consciousness* (London: Verso, 1993); Joyce E. Chaplin, *An Anxious Pursuit: Agricultural Innovation and Modernity in the Lower South, 1730–1815* (Chapel Hill: University of North Carolina Press, 1993); and Anthony E. Kaye, "The Second Slavery: Modernity in the Nineteenth-Century South and the Atlantic World," *JSH* 75, no. 3 (August 2009): 627–50.

9. S. N. Eisenstadt, "Multiple Modernities," *Daedalus* 129, no. 1(Winter 2000): 3–5. See also Michael Saler, "Modernity and Enchantment: A Historiographic Review," *AHR* 111, no. 3 (June 2006): 694.

10. This is the classic interpretation from the perspective of modern world history; see Barrington Moore, *Social Origins of Dictatorship and Democracy: Lord and Peasant in the Making of the Modern World* (Boston: Beacon Press, 1966), 111–56; Eric Hobsbawm, *The Age of Capital: 1848–1875* (New York: Charles Scribner's Sons, 1975), 141–43, 182–86; and Bayly, *Birth of the Modern World,* 161–65, 402–10.

11. For sensitive scholarship on proslavery thought, see Michael O'Brien, *Conjectures of Order: Intellectual Life in the Old South, 1810–1860* (Chapel Hill: University of North Carolina Press, 2004), esp. 938–94; Elizabeth Fox-Genovese and Eugene D. Genovese, *The Mind of the Master Class: History and Faith in the Southern Slaveholders' Worldview* (New York: Cambridge University Press, 2005); David Brion Davis, *Slavery and Human Progress* (New York: Oxford University Press, 1984), 231–45; Bertram Wyatt-Brown, "Modernizing Southern Slavery: The

Proslavery Argument Reinterpreted," in J. Morgan Kousser and James M. McPherson, eds., *Region, Race, and Reconstruction: Essays in Honor of C. Vann Woodward* (New York: Oxford University Press, 1982), 27–49; Drew Gilpin Faust, ed., *The Ideology of Slavery: Proslavery Thought in the Antebellum South, 1830–1860* (Baton Rouge: Louisiana State University Press, 1981); Faust, "A Southern Stewardship: The Intellectual and the Proslavery Argument," *American Quarterly* 31, no. 1 (Spring 1979): 63–80; and Manisha Sinha, *The Counterrevolution of Slavery: Politics and Ideology in Antebellum South Carolina* (Chapel Hill: University of North Carolina Press, 2000).

12. For further discussion, see Matthew Karp, "The World the Slaveholders Craved: Proslavery Internationalism in the 1850s," in Andrew Shankman, ed., *The World of the Revolutionary American Republic* (New York: Routledge, 2014), 414–32.

13. Eisenstadt, "Multiple Modernities," 5–8.

14. Frederick Cooper, *Colonialism in Question: Theory, Knowledge, History* (Berkeley: University of California Press, 2005), 113–15.

15. [Thomas P. Kettell], "The Future of the South," *DBR*, February 1851, 137; George Fitzhugh, "Acquisition of Mexico—Filibustering," *DBR*, December 1858, 618; Fitzhugh, "Southern Thought," *DBR*, October 1857, 337.

16. For scholarly discussions of nineteenth-century modernity that emphasize the centrality of slavery, see Gilroy, *Black Atlantic*, 46–58; Dale W. Tomich, *Through the Prism of Slavery: Labor, Capital, and World Economy* (Lanham, Md.: Rowman and Littlefield, 2004), xi–xv, 75–138; and Michael O'Brien, "Afterword," in Barnes, Schoen, and Towers, *Old South's Modern Worlds*, 298–308.

17. See James Oakes, *Freedom National: The Destruction of Slavery in the United States* (New York: W. W. Norton, 2012).

18. See Moon-Ho Jung, *Coolies and Cane: Race, Labor, and Sugar in the Age of Emancipation* (Baltimore: Johns Hopkins University Press, 2006); David Northrup, *Indentured Labor in the Age of Imperialism, 1834–1922* (New York: Cambridge University Press, 1995); and Stanley L. Engerman, "Contract Labor, Sugar, and Technology in the Nineteenth Century," *Journal of Economic History* 43, no. 3 (September 1983): 635–59.

19. James Henry Hammond, speech at Barnwell Court House, October 29, 1858, in Clyde N. Wilson, ed., *Selections from the Letters and Speeches of the Hon. James H. Hammond, of South Carolina* (Spartanburg, S.C.: Reprint Company, 1978), 346–48. For similar arguments from Senators Thomas Clingman and James M. Mason, see *CG*, 35th Cong., 1st Sess., 1974–76 (May 5, 1858); and *CG*, 36th Cong, 1st Sess., 3098–99 (June 18, 1860).

20. John Y. Mason to Lewis Cass, February 19, 1858, in *S. Ex. Doc. No. 49*, 35th Cong., 1st Sess. (1858), 55–57; Brian Schoen, *The Fragile Fabric of Union: Cotton, Federal Politics, and the Global Origins of the Civil War* (Baltimore: Johns Hopkins University Press, 2009), 220–21.

21. Historians have generally come to reject the notion that mid-nineteenth-century indentured-labor systems amounted to a "restoration of slavery"; see

Rachel Sturman, "Indian Indentured Labor and the History of International Rights Regimes," *AHR* 119, no. 5 (December 2014): 1439–65; and Elliott Young, *Alien Nation: Chinese Migration in the Americas from the Coolie Era through World War II* (Chapel Hill: University of North Carolina Press, 2014), 21–94.

22. Hammond, speech at Barnwell Court House, *Selections from the Letters and Speeches*, 347.

23. *Charleston Mercury*, October 4, 1854; see also W. W. Wright, "The Coolie Trade; or, The Excomienda System of the Nineteenth Century," *DBR*, September 1859, 296–321.

24. James B. Davis to Calhoun, July 22, 1848, *PJCC*, 25:613–15; *Washington Union*, reprinted in the *Georgia Telegraph*, December 16, 1856. On the failure of British cotton-planting experiments in India in the 1840s, see Beckert, *Empire of Cotton*, 125–27.

25. Daniel Lee, "Cotton and Uncle Tom," *Southern Cultivator*, June 1853, 161. On the importance of direct "supervision"—along with the threat and reality of physical violence—in extracting maximum productivity from slaves, see Johnson, *River of Dark Dreams*, 165–75, 199–208, 244–52; Baptist, *The Half Has Never Been Told*, esp. 111–44.

26. Green to Henry Carey, published in the *North American and US Gazette*, September 20, 1858; clipping saved in the Duff Green Papers, SHC-UNC. In fact, Britain's Colonial Office did consider a plan to grow cotton through "command of labor" in the Gold Coast; see Barrie M. Ratcliffe, "Cotton Imperialism: Manchester Merchants and Cotton Cultivation in West Africa in the Mid-Nineteenth Century," *African Economic History* 11 (1982): 87–113.

27. David Christy, *Cotton Is King; or, Slavery in Light of Political Economy*, reprinted in E. N. Elliott, ed., *Cotton Is King, and Proslavery Arguments . . .* (Augusta, Ga.: Pritchard, Abbott and Loomis, 1860), 113; Thomas Bocock, undated draft of essay or speech, Papers of the Thornhill Family and Thomas S. Bocock, University of Virginia.

28. Charles Sumner, speech in Senate, February 21, 1854, reprinted as *The Landmark of Freedom: Hon. Charles Sumner against the Repeal of the Missouri Prohibition of Slavery North of 36°30* (Boston: John P. Jewett and Company, 1854), 12–13.

29. "A Few Thoughts on Slavery," *SLM*, April 1854, 193–206.

30. In 1850 the Scottish economist John Ramsey McCulloch, a favorite source for George Fitzhugh, listed Brazil, Cuba, and Java as examples of the "indispensable" role of "compulsory labor" in "the production of sugar." John Ramsey McCulloch, *Dictionary, Practical, Theoretical, and Historical, of Commerce and Commercial Navigation* (London: Longman, Brown, Green, and Longmans, 1850), 1249–51.

31. Sumner, *Landmark of Freedom*, 13; "A Few Thoughts on Slavery," 204. On the persistence of bound labor and racial hierarchy in a wide range of modernizing societies in the mid-nineteenth century world, see Alison Frank, "The Children of the Desert and the Laws of the Sea: Austria, Great Britain, the Ottoman

Empire, and the Mediterranean Slave Trade in the Nineteenth Century," *AHR* 117, no. 2 (April 2012): 410–44; Richard B. Allen, "Satisfying the 'Want for Labouring People': European Slave Trading in the Indian Ocean, 1500–1850," *Journal of World History* 21, no. 1 (2010): 45–73; Daniel V. Botsman, "Freedom without Slavery? 'Coolies,' Prostitutes, and Outcastes in Meiji Japan's 'Emancipation Moment,'" *AHR* 116, no. 5 (December 2011): 1323–47; and Alessandro Stanziani, "Free Labor—Forced Labor: An Uncertain Boundary?," *Kritika: Explorations in Russian and Eurasian History* 9, no. 1 (Winter 2008): 27–52.

32. James D. B. De Bow et al., "The Memphis Convention," *DBR*, March 1850, 217–32.

33. Hobsbawm, *Age of Capital*, 135. On the renewed commitment to imperial expansion in midcentury Britain and France, in both ideology and practice, see John Gallagher and Ronald Robinson, "The Imperialism of Free Trade," *Economic History Review* 6, no. 1 (1953): 1–15; Jennifer Pitts, *A Turn to Empire: The Rise of Imperial Liberalism in Britain and France* (Princeton, N.J.: Princeton University Press, 2005); Linda Colley, *Captives: Britain, Empire, and the World* (New York: Anchor Books, 2004), 364–74; and David Todd, "A French Imperial Meridian, 1814–1870," *Past and Present* 210 (February 2011): esp. 173–83.

34. To the extent that historians of slavery have considered this question, they have usually stressed the connection between imperialism and abolitionism: see Davis, *Slavery and Human Progress*, xvii; and Richard Huzzey, *Freedom Burning: Antislavery and Empire in Victorian Britain* (Ithaca, N.Y.: Cornell University Press, 2012), 132–202. But long before the victory of antislavery was certain, American slaveholders developed their own aggressive ideas about the colonization and subjugation of the non-Euro-American world.

35. Robert E. May, *Manifest Destiny's Underworld: Filibustering in Antebellum America* (Chapel Hill: University of North Carolina Press, 2002), 60–64.

36. De Bow et al., "The Memphis Convention," *DBR*, March 1850, 217–32; William Harper, "Memoir on Slavery," *DBR*, March 1850, 232–43. On the role of racial thought in justifying the midcentury consolidation of the British Empire, see Catherine Hall, *Civilising Subjects: Metropole and Colony in the English Imagination, 1830–1867* (Cambridge, U.K.: Polity Press, 2002); and Karuna Mantena, "The Crisis of Imperial Liberalism," in Duncan Bell, ed., *Victorian Visions of Global Order: Empire and International Relations in Nineteenth-Century British Political Thought* (New York: Cambridge University Press, 2007), 113–35. On the filibuster invasions, see Chapter 8.

37. Edmund Ruffin diary entries, January 30, 1857, August 10, 1857, April 20, 1858, and April 26, 1858, in *The Diary of Edmund Ruffin*, ed. William K. Scarborough (Baton Rouge: Louisiana State University Press, 1972), 1:29, 96–97, 179, 182. To be sure, some southerners condemned British cruelty in Asia without qualification: Fox-Genovese and Genovese, *Mind of the Master Class*, 206–12, 215–18; Elizabeth Kelly Gray, "Whisper to Him the Word 'India': Trans-Atlantic Critics and American Slavery," *JER* 28, no. 3 (Fall 2008): 400–406.

38. George Frederick Holmes, "The Relations of the Old and the New Worlds," *DBR*, May 1856, 529; Louisa McCord, "Diversity of the Races: Its Bearing upon Negro Slavery," 1851, in Richard C. Lounsbury, ed., *Louisa S. McCord: Political and Social Essays* (Charlottesville: University of Virginia Press, 1995), 177–83. On the midcentury acceleration of white racism, see Reginald Horsman, *Race and Manifest Destiny: Origins of American Racial Anglo-Saxonism* (Cambridge, Mass.: Harvard University Press, 1981), 272–97; George M. Frederickson, *The Black Image in the White Mind: The Debate on Afro-American Character and Destiny, 1817–1914* (New York: Harper and Row, 1971), 43–129; and Douglas Lorimer, *Colour, Class, and the Victorians: English Attitudes to the Negro in the Mid-Nineteenth Century* (New York: Holmes and Meier, 1978).

39. *Charleston Mercury,* October 27, 1854; see also Fox-Genovese and Genovese, *Mind of the Master Class,* 188–94.

40. E. N. Elliott, "Slavery in the Light of International Law," in Elliott, *Cotton Is King,* 731–37; W. W. Wright, "Relations of the Negro Race to Civilization—Negroes as Aborigines," *DBR,* December 1860, 638–47.

41. Wright, "Relations of the Negro Race to Civilization," 640–47.

42. Elliott, "Slavery in the Light of International Law," 731–37.

43. Ibid. Elliott only offered a proslavery spin on the dominant nineteenth-century vision of international law that accepted fundamental distinctions "between barbarous and civilized societies"; see Jennifer Pitts, "Boundaries of Victorian International Law," in Bell, *Victorian Visions of Global Order,* 67–88.

44. For interpretations that stress the conservatism and pessimism of the religious defense of slavery, see Nicholas Guyatt, *Providence and the Invention of the United States, 1607–1876* (New York: Cambridge University Press, 2007), 230–46 (quoted 241); and Fox-Genovese and Genovse, *Mind of the Master Class,* 409–646.

45. Daniel Lee, "Agricultural Apprentices and Laborers," *Southern Cultivator,* June 1854, 169–70. See also E. Merton Coulter, *Daniel Lee, Agriculturalist: His Life North and South* (Athens: University of Georgia Press, 1972), 69–93. On the ideological compatibilities between paternalistic tutelage and capitalist exploitation within an imperial framework, see Jennifer Pitts, "Political Theory of Empire and Imperialism," *Annual Review of Political Science* 13 (2010): 216–18.

46. *Charleston Courier,* March 12, 1858; "Dr. Kilpatrick" [Andrew Roberts Kilpatrick], "The African El Dorado," *DBR,* May 1859, 503–13, and *DBR,* June 1859, 630–40.

47. *Charleston Courier,* December 31, 1857, and January 6, 1858. For further southern coverage of Livingstone's expedition, see the *Charleston Mercury,* October 27, 1854; *Columbus (Ga.) Enquirer,* June 3, 1858; "Dr. Livingstone's Discoveries," *SLM,* February 1858, 134–47; and *Richmond Whig,* May 28, 1859.

48. Maury to Herndon, April 20, 1850, in *The Papers of William Alexander Graham,* ed. J. G. de Roulhac Hamilton, 8 vols. (Raleigh: North Carolina Department of Cultural Resources, 1957–1992), 3:446–48; William Gilmore Simms, quoted in

Adam L. Tate, *Conservatism and Southern Intellectuals, 1789–1861: Liberty, Tradition, and the Good Society* (Colombia: University of Missouri Press, 2005), 229.

49. The theory of "internal colonialism," which identified the United States as an imperial nation-state with a racialized empire inside its borders, gained traction in sociology in the 1960s and 1970s but has made little impact on historical treatments of American slavery. See Bob Blauner, *Racial Oppression in America* (New York: Harper and Row, 1972); and Robert J. Hind, "The Internal Colonial Concept," *Comparative Studies in Society and History* 26, no. 3 (July 1984): 543–68.

50. James Holcombe, "Is Slavery Consistent with Natural Laws?," *SLM*, December 1858, 405; R. M. T. Hunter, speech in Senate, *CG Appendix*, 36th Cong., 1st Sess., 106 (January 31, 1860).

51. Daniel Lee, "Agricultural Apprentices and Laborers," *SQR*, June 1854, 169. Walter Johnson rightly terms the South's proslavery ideology "global whitemanism," and in fact, its conceptual boundaries stretched beyond the merely regional filibusterers and would-be slave traders he and other historians generally address. Johnson, *River of Dark Dreams*, 406–20.

52. On the relationship between European imperialism and scientific racism, see Cooper, *Colonialism in Question*, 178–82; and Mark Harrison, "'The Tender Frame of Man': Disease, Climate, and Racial Difference in India and the West Indies, 1760–1860," *Bulletin of the History of Medicine* 70, no. 1 (Spring 1996): 68–93.

53. George Fitzhugh, "The Atlantic Telegraph—Ancient Art and Modern Progress," *DBR*, November 1858, 507–11. For the classic treatment of this problem in mid-nineteenth-century America, see Leo Marx, *The Machine in the Garden: Technology and the Pastoral Ideal in America* (New York: Oxford University Press, 2000 [1964]).

54. Samuel A. Cartwright, "Slavery in Light of Ethnology," in Elliott, *Cotton Is King*, 691–728; Josiah C. Nott, *Two Lectures on the Natural History of the Caucasian and Negro Races*, reprinted in Faust, *Ideology of Slavery*, 206–38. On Cartwright, Nott, and the significance of racial science for southern politicians and intellectuals, see William W. Freehling, *The Road to Disunion*, vol. 2, *Secessionists Triumphant, 1854–1861* (New York: Oxford University Press, 2007), 39–44; O'Brien, *Conjectures of Order*, 215–52; James Denny Guillory, "The Proslavery Arguments of Dr. Samuel A. Cartwright," *Louisiana History* 9 (1968): 209–28; Reginald Horsman, *Josiah Nott of Mobile: Southerner, Physician, and Racial Theorist* (Baton Rouge: Louisiana State University Press, 1987); and William Stanton, *The Leopard's Spots: Scientific Attitudes toward Race in America, 1815–1859* (Chicago: University of Chicago Press, 1960).

55. See Samuel Cartwright, "Dr. Cartwright on the Caucasians and the Africans," *DBR*, July 1858, 45–56; Drew Gilpin Faust, *James Henry Hammond and the Old South: A Design for Mastery* (Baton Rouge: Louisiana State University Press, 1985), 278–82; Robert Toombs speech, *CG Appendix* 36th Cong., 1st Sess., 89 (January 24, 1860); and Jefferson Davis speech, *CG*, 36th Cong., 1 Sess., 1682 (April 13, 1860);

on the growing influence of racial science on proslavery thinkers in the 1850s, see Frederickson, *Black Image in the White Mind*, 76–90.

56. On the American school of ethnology, see Bruce Dain, *A Hideous Monster of the Mind: American Race Theory in the Early Republic* (Cambridge, Mass.: Harvard University Press, 2002), 197–263; Nell Irvin Painter, *The History of White People* (New York: Norton, 2011), 190–200. On Gliddon, Knox, and the "general Western movement toward racialist thinking," see Horsman, *Race and Manifest Destiny*, 62–78, 116–58; on Gobineau and his influence, see Hannah Arendt, *The Origins of Totalitarianism*, 2nd ed. (Cleveland: World Publishing Co., 1958), 170–75.

57. Josiah Nott and George Gliddon, *Types of Mankind* (Philadelphia: Lippincott, Grambo, and Co., 1854); Louis Menand, *The Metaphysical Club: A Story of Ideas in America* (New York: Octavo, 2001), 97–116.

58. Louisa McCord, "Negro-Mania," *DBR*, May 1852, 508; Lemuel Evans, speech in Congress, *CG*, 34th Cong., 3rd Sess. (February 4, 1857), 230; Horsman, *Race and Manifest Destiny*, 275–76. On scientific racism in Europe, see Nancy Stepan, *The Idea of Race in Science: Great Britain, 1800–1960* (London: Macmillan, 1982); and Seymour Drescher, "The Ending of the Slave Trade and the Evolution of European Scientific Racism," *Social Science History*, 14, no. 3 (Autumn 1990): 415–50. On the impact of scientific racism on Atlantic slave societies beyond the United States, see Robin Blackburn, *The American Crucible: Slavery, Emancipation and Human Rights* (London: Verso, 2011), 299–304.

59. McCord, "Negro-Mania," 524; J. L. M. Curry, *A Civil History of the Government of the Confederate States* . . . (Richmond: B. F. Johnson, 1901), 56–57. On Stephens, see Thomas E. Schott, *Alexander Stephens of Georgia: A Biography* (Baton Rouge: Louisana State University Press, 1996).

60. Alexander Stephens, speech at Augusta, Georgia, February 7, 1859, in Henry Cleveland, ed., *Alexander Stephens, in Public and Private, with Letters and Speeches, before, during, and since the War* (Philadelphia: National Publishing Co., 1866), 647–50.

61. Frederick Douglass, "Progress of Slavery," *Douglass' Monthly*, August 1859, 114.

62. "The Black Race in North America, Part IV," *DBR*, April 1856, 446–68; Dr. Ed. Barton, "Influence of Climate on Agricultural Productions, Health, etc.," copy of a paper read at the New Orleans Academy of Sciences, reprinted in *DBR*, June 1856, 715–39; Louisa McCord, "Slavery and Political Economy," pt. 1, *DBR*, October 1856, 339, 345; emphasis in the original.

63. George Fitzhugh, *Sociology for the South; or, The Failure of Free Society* (Richmond: A. Morris, 1854); Henry Hughes, *Treatise on Sociology, Theoretical and Practical* (Philadelphia: Lippincott, Grambo, and Co., 1854). On slavery and agricultural science, see Majewski, *Modernizing a Slave Economy*, 53–80; Alan L. Olmsted and Paul W. Rhode, *Journal of Economic History* 68, no. 4 (December 2008): 1123–71; Steven G. Collins, "System, Organization and Agricultural Reform in the Antebellum South, 1840–1860," *Agricultural History* 75, no. 1 (Winter 2001): 1–27; David F.

Allmendinger Jr., *Ruffin: Family and Reform in the Old South* (New York: Oxford University Press, 1990), 114–17, 126–51; Coulter, *Daniel Lee*, 69–93; Chester McArthur Destler, "David Dickson's 'System of Farming' and the Agricultural Revolution in the Deep South, 1850–1885," *Agricultural History* 31, no. 3 (July 1957): 30–34; and Weymouth T. Jordan, "Noah B. Cloud and the American Cotton Planter,'" *Agricultural History* 52 (July 1978): 394–406.

64. On John Bachman, see Peter McCandless, "The Political Evolution of John Bachman: From New York Yankee to South Carolina Secessionist," *South Carolina Historical Magazine* 108, no. 1 (January 2007): 6–31; and Lester D. Stephens, *Science, Race, and Religion in the American South: John Bachman and the Charleston Circle of Naturalists, 1815–1895* (Chapel Hill: University of North Carolina Press, 2000); on Maury as a proslavery scientist, see Daniel Rood, "Plantation Technocrats: A Social History of Knowledge in the Slaveholding Atlantic World, 1830–1865" (PhD diss., University of California–Irvine, 2010), 155–71.

65. Fitzhugh, "Southern Thought," 342; McCord, "Slavery and Political Economy," pt. 1, 340. On southern eagerness to refute British abolitionism with "the scientific method," see Matthew Mason, "A World Safe for Modernity: Antebellum Southern Proslavery Intellectuals Confront Great Britain," in Barnes, Schoen, and Towers, *Old South's Modern Worlds*, 56–59.

66. Elliott, "Slavery in the Light of International Law," 737; Cartwright, "Dr. Cartwright on the Caucasians and the Africans," 48–50. On the antebellum efforts at slave organization and the links among slavery, modernity, and management science, see Collins, "System, Organization and Agricultural Reform," 3–6; Oakes, *Ruling Race*, 153–91; R. Keith Aufhauser, "Slavery and Scientific Management," *Journal of Economic History* 33, no. 4 (December 1973): 811–24; and Elizabeth Esch and David Roediger, "One Symptom of Originality: Race and the Management of Labor in the United States," *Historical Materialism* 17, no. 4 (2009): 3–43.

67. *Charleston Mercury*, May 10, 1856. On the rhetoric of the "technological sublime" as a feature of midcentury culture, see Marx, *Machine in the Garden*, 194–224. On the importance of natural science metaphors for social and economic thought in the nineteenth century, see Philip Mirowski, *More Heat than Light: Economics as Social Physics, Physics as Nature's Economics* (Cambridge: Cambridge University Press, 1989).

68. Faust, "Southern Stewardship," 72–73; Eugene D. Genovese, *The Slaveholders' Dilemma: Freedom and Progress in Southern Conservative Thought, 1820–1860* (Columbia: University of South Carolina Press, 1992), 6–7; Michael O'Brien, "Conservative Thought in the Old South: A Review Article," *Comparative Studies in Society and History* 34, no. 3 (July 1992): 566–76.

69. J. C. [James Chesnut], "The Destinies of the South," SQR, January 1853, 192–93; Marshall Berman, *All That Is Solid Melts into Air: The Experience of Modernity* (New York: Penguin, 1982). If, as C. A. Bayly has argued, a conscious "aspiration . . . to

be modern" was a novel and significant feature of nineteenth-century modernity, then slaveholders' very desire to claim slavery as a progressive institution reflected their participation in this modern world. Bayly, *Birth of the Modern World*, 9–12.

70. Drew Gilpin Faust, "Rhetoric and Ritual of Agriculture in Antebellum South Carolina," *JSH* 45, no. 4 (November 1979): 552–54. See also O'Brien, *Conjectures of Order*, esp. 1–24; and Karp, "World the Slaveholders Craved."

71. Thomas Baring, speech in the House of Commons, February 4, 1848, quoted in Richard Huzzey, "Free Trade, Free Labour and Slave Sugar in Victorian Britain," *Historical Journal* 53 (2010): 359–79.

72. This southern conception has not loomed large in historical or theoretical discussions about global modernity, but it might well figure among the "multiple" and "alternative" modernities scholars have begun to identify inside and outside the Euro-American West in the nineteenth and twentieth centuries; Eisenstadt, "Multiple Modernities"; Dilip Parameshawar Gaonkar, ed., *Alternative Modernities* (Durham, N.C.: Duke University Press, 2001).

73. James D. B. De Bow, "The Origin, Progress, and Prospects of Slavery," *DBR*, July 1850, 13–14; De Bow, *Industrial Resources*, 2:313; Henry W. Hilliard, "Agricultural Science and Literature," address given to the Alabama State Agricultural Society, November 17, 1859, in *American Cotton Planter*, February 1860, 57–64. De Bow's most ambitious projection estimated a population of 20 to 27 million "negroes" in the South by 1950; "Southern Population—Its Destiny," *DBR*, July 1852, 13. On proslavery's "history of the future," especially as it related to the African slave trade, see Johnson, *River of Dark Dreams*, 413–20.

74. *New Orleans Daily Picayune*, June 24, 1857; Thomas Carlyle, "Occasional Discourse on the Negro Question," *Fraser's Magazine for Town and Country*, February 1849, 670–79; for southern quotation and reproduction, see "West India Emancipation," *DBR*, June 1850, 527–38; and [David Flavel Jamison], "British and American Slavery," *SQR*, October 1853, 406–8.

75. *Charleston Mercury*, May 15, 1857; "The Dual Form of Labor," *Russell's Magazine*, October 1859, 6–7. On the possibility of Caribbean reenslavement, see C. Stanley Urban, "Slaveocracy and Empire: New Orleans and the Attempted Expansion of Slavery, 1845–1861," unpublished manuscript, Northwestern University Library, 1976, 105–45; and Gale Kenny, "Manliness and Manifest Racial Destiny: Jamaica and African American Emigration in the 1850s," *JCWE* 2, no. 2 (June 2012): 151–78.

76. William Grayson, *The Hireling and the Slave, Chicora, and Other Poems* (Charleston: McCarter, 1856), 55. *De Bow's Review* carried excerpts from the poem in three issues: February, April, and August 1855. For varying interpretations of the poem, see Edmund Wilson, *Patriotic Gore: Studies in the Literature of the American Civil War* (New York: Farrar, Straus, and Giroux, 1962), 336–41; Eugene D. Genovese, foreword to Richard J. Calhoun, ed., *Witness to Sorrow: The Antebellum*

Autobiography of William J. Grayson (Columbia: University of South Carolina Press, 1991), x–xiv; and O'Brien, *Conjectures of Order*, 732–36.

77. William Grayson, "The Hireling and the Slave," *DBR*, August 1855, 214–15.

78. Ibid., 216.

79. Walt Whitman, "Thou Mother with Thy Equal Brood" (1872), in *The Complete Poems of Walt Whitman* (Ware, U.K.: Wordsworth Editions, 1995), 338.

80. The poem's marriage of willfully archaic form and uncompromisingly modern content offers an antebellum southern instance of the phenomenon noticed by Arno Mayer and others: forward-looking bourgeois elites becoming the nineteenth century's most "enthusiastic champions" of traditional and historicist art. Arno Mayer, *The Persistence of the Old Regime: Europe to the Great War* (London: Verso, 2010 [1981]), 189–92.

81. Grayson, "Hireling and the Slave," 216–18. The *Oxford English Dictionary* identifies Grayson's poem as the original source of the phrase "master-race." See "master, n.1 and adj.," OED Online, June 2013, Oxford University Press, http://www .oed.com.ezp-prod1.hul.harvard.edu/view/Entry/114751?rskey=9cSNa4&result =1&isAdvanced=false (accessed July 22, 2013).

8. Foreign Policy amid Domestic Crisis

1. Henry Harrison Simms, *Life of Robert M. T. Hunter: A Study in Sectionalism and Secession* (Richmond, Va.: William Byrd Press, 1935), 8; Hunter's son, quoted in John E. Fisher, "Statesman of the Lost Cause: R. M. T. Hunter and the Sectional Controversy, 1847–1887" (PhD diss., University of Virginia, 1968), 7; Mary Chesnut, *Mary Chesnut's Civil War*, ed. C. Vann Woodward (New Haven, Conn.: Yale University Press, 1993), 61.

2. The F Street Mess included Hunter's Virginia colleague James Murray Mason, chairman of the Senate Foreign Relations Committee; Andrew Pickens Butler of South Carolina, chairman of the Judiciary Committee; and David Atchison of Missouri, Senate president pro tempore. See Roy F. Nichols, *Franklin Pierce: Young Hickory of the Granite Hills* (Newtown, Conn.: American Political Biography Press, 2003 [1931]), 303–4; and Rachel A. Shelden, *Washington Brotherhood: Politics, Social Life, and the Coming of the Civil War* (Chapel Hill: University of North Carolina Press, 2013), 96–119.

3. Quoted in John Savage, *Our Living and Representative Men* (Philadelphia: Childs and Peterson, 1860), 346; James D. B. De Bow, "Presidential Candidates and Aspirants," *DBR*, July 1860, 100.

4. For a summary of Hunter's Nebraska speech that focuses on these domestic political arguments, see Fisher, "Statesman of the Lost Cause," 143–47. On the Kansas-Nebraska debate, see David M. Potter, *The Impending Crisis: America before the Civil War, 1848–1861* (New York: Harper and Row, 1976), 154–76; Sean Wilentz, *The Rise of American Democracy: Jefferson to Lincoln* (New York: W. W. Norton,

2005), 671–77; and Michael A. Morrison, *Slavery and the American West: The Eclipse of Manifest Destiny and the Coming of the Civil War* (Chapel Hill: University of North Carolina Press, 1997), 126–56.

5. Hunter's speech appears in full in the *CG Appendix*, 33rd Cong., 1st Sess., 221–26(February 24, 1854). It was widely reprinted in southern newspapers, including the *Charleston Courier*, February 28, 1854, and the *Richmond Enquirer*, March 7, 1854; the *Southern Quarterly Review* praised it as "one of the best efforts of the session." *SQR*, July 1854, 260.

6. D. W. Bartlett, *Presidential Candidates* (New York: A. R. Burdick, 1860), 244–45.

7. *CG Appendix*, 33rd Cong., 1st Sess., 225 (February 24, 1854).

8. For a summary of recent scholarship on the subject, see Michael E. Woods, "What Twenty-First-Century Historians Have Said about the Causes of Disunion: A Civil War Sesquicentennial Review of the Literature," *JAH* 99, no. 2 (September 2012): 415–39.

9. *CG Appendix*, 33rd Cong., 1st Sess., 225 (Feburary 24, 1854).

10. Ibid., For later and even more comprehensive proslavery vision of global imperialism, and the "four Powers which are now extending their dominion over inferior races" (Russia, France, Great Britain, and the United States), see Thomas Clingman, speech in House, *CG*, 35th Cong., 1st Sess., 1974–75 (May 5, 1858).

11. See Robert E. May, *The Southern Dream of a Caribbean Empire, 1854–1861* (Gainesville: University Press of Florida, 2002 [1973]); Amy S. Greenberg, *Manifest Manhood and the Antebellum American Empire* (New York: Cambridge University Press, 2005), esp. 1–53, 135–230; and Walter Johnson, *River of Dark Dreams: Slavery and Empire in the Cotton Kingdom* (Cambridge, Mass.: Harvard University Press, 2013), 330–94.

12. Jefferson Davis, speech at Jackson, September 23, 1848, *PJD*, 3:377. On the "dizzying outcome of the Mexican War" and its effect on proslavery thought, see Eugene D. Genovese, *The Slaveholders' Dilemma: Freedom and Progress in Southern Conservative Thought, 1820–1860* (Columbia: University of South Carolina Press, 1992), 20–22.

13. Potter, *Impending Crisis*, 90–120; Morrison, *Slavery and the American West*, 96–125.

14. Calhoun to Joseph H. Lesesne, February 21, 1846, *PJCC*, 22:612; Edward C. Cabell, speech in House, *CG Appendix*, 32nd Cong., 2nd Sess., 50 (December 21, 1852).

15. William Freehling contrasts the "southern mentality of the depressed 1840s—claustrophobic, cramped, craving a safety valve" with the buoyant and expansive mentality of "the prosperous 1850s." International politics, along with the domestic economy, helped achieve that transformation. William W. Freehling, *The Road to Disunion*, vol. 1, *Secessionists at Bay, 1789–1854* (New York: Oxford University Press, 1990), 430.

16. William Henry Trescot, *A Few Thoughts on the Foreign Policy of the United States* (Charleston: John Russell, 1849), 13–14. On Britain's reluctant but growing acceptance of U.S. continental supremacy after 1847, see Kenneth Bourne, *Britain and the Balance of Power in North America, 1815–1908* (London: Longmans, Green, 1967), 170–205.

17. On Trescot, see Michael O'Brien, *Conjectures of Order: Intellectual Life in the Old South, 1810–1860* (Chapel Hill: University of North Carolina Press, 2004), 1176–86; and Robert Nicholas Olsberg, "A Government of Class and Race: William Henry Trescot and the South Carolina Chivalry, 1860–1865" (PhD diss., University of South Carolina, 1972).

18. William Henry Trescot, *The Position and Course of the South* (Charleston: Walker and James, 1850), 6, 11–12. For contrasting interpretations of Trescot's secessionism, see Genovese, *Slaveholders' Dilemma,* 76–85; and Brian Schoen, *The Fragile Fabric of Union: Cotton, Federal Politics, and the Global Origins of the Civil War* (Baltimore: Johns Hopkins University Press, 2009), 197–201.

19. Trescot, *Few Thoughts,* 4–5.

20. Ibid., 12–15. Southern periodicals heaped praise on Trescot's prescriptions for a muscular U.S. foreign policy; see *Commercial Review of the South and West,* November 1849, 464; *SLM,* January 1850, 1–6; and *SQR,* October 1849, 252–53.

21. William Henry Trescot, "An American View of the Eastern Question," *DBR,* September 1854, 285–94, and October 1854, 327–50; W. H. T. [William Henry Trescot], "Mr. Everett and the Cuban Question," *SQR,* April 1854, 429–71; Trescot, *A Letter to A. P. Butler, on the Diplomatic System of the U. States* (Charleston: Walker and James, 1853).

22. Trescot, *Few Thoughts,* 23–24; Trescot, "Mr. Everett and the Cuban Question," 469; Trescot to Muscoe Russell Garnett Hunter, November 16, 1851, Hunter-Garnett Papers, University of Virginia.

23. On the Panama Railroad and the jumbled politics of Central American transit, see Robert R. Russel, *Improvement of Communication with the Pacific as an Issue in American Politics, 1763–1864* (Cedar Rapids, Ia.: Torch Press, 1948); and Aims McGuinness, *Path of Empire: Panama and the California Gold Rush* (Ithaca, N.Y.: Cornell University Press, 2009).

24. On the filibusters, see May, *Southern Dream;* and Robert E. May, *Manifest Destiny's Underworld: Filibustering in Antebellum America* (Chapel Hill: University of North Carolina Press, 2002).

25. For differing explanations of the filibusters' motives, see Robert E. May, "Epilogue to the Missouri Compromise: The South, the Balance of Power, and the Tropics in the 1850s," *Plantation Society* 1, no. 2 (June 1979): 201–25; and Richard Tansey, "Southern Expansionism: Urban Interests of the Cuban Filibusters," *Plantation Society* 1, no. 2 (June 1979), 227–51.

26. For an extremely thorough account, see Douglas A. Ley, "Expansionists All? Southern Senators and American Foreign Policy, 1841–60" (PhD diss., University

of Wisconsin–Madison, 1990). Interpretations that hew closely to this thesis include William W. Freehling, *The Road to Disunion*, vol. 2, *Secessionists Triumphant, 1854–1861* (New York: Oxford University Press, 2007), 145–67; and Joseph Fry, *Dixie Looks Abroad: The South and U.S. Foreign Relations, 1789–1973* (Baton Rouge: Louisiana State University Press, 2002), 66–70.

27. The fullest treatment of the elite South's belief in the interdependence of Caribbean slave societies in the 1850s is Matthew Pratt Guterl, *American Mediterranean: Southern Slaveholders in the Age of Emancipation* (Cambridge, Mass.: Harvard University Press, 2008), 1–6, 15–45.

28. Jefferson Davis, speech at Jackson, May 29, 1857, *PJD*, 6:121–22. On Walker and the South, see May, *Southern Dream*, 111–35.

29. James Murray Mason, speech in Senate, *CG*, 33rd Cong., 2nd Sess., 832 (February 20, 1855); Thomas Clingman, speech in House, February 5, 1857, in *Selections from the Speeches and Writings of Hon. Thomas L. Clingman* (Raleigh, N.C.: John Nichols, 1877), 403. On Mason, see Robert W. Young, *Senator James Murray Mason: Defender of the Old South* (Knoxville: University of Tennessee Press, 1998).

30. Even the southerners who defended the Clayton-Bulwer Treaty, an 1850 agreement between the United States and Britain that forbade either nation to claim exclusive rights over any part of Central America, most often argued that its terms actually facilitated the United States' peaceful rise to dominance in the region. See Ley, "Expansionists All?," 212–47.

31. James D. B. De Bow, *The Industrial Resources, etc., of the Southern and Western States . . .*, 3 vols. (New Orleans: Pudney and Russell, 1853), 1:26–30; emphasis in the original; M. F. M. [Matthew Fontaine Maury], "The Panama Rail-way and the Gulf of Mexico," *SLM*, August 1849, 456.

32. James Murray Mason, speech in Senate, *CG Appendix*, 32nd Cong., 2nd Sess., 134–38 (February 1, 1853).

33. For a strong southern argument on behalf of U.S. military intervention to seize Peruvian guano, see the *Richmond Enquirer*, March 9, 1854; on the politics of guano in the 1850s generally, see Jimmy M. Skaggs, *The Great Guano Rush: Entrepreneurs and U.S. Overseas Expansion* (New York: St. Martin's Press, 1995). On the *Water-Witch* incident in Paraguay and the naval expedition Buchanan sent to seek redress, see John H. Schroeder, *Shaping a Maritime Empire: The Commercial and Diplomatic Role of the American Navy, 1829–1861* (Westport, Conn.: Greenwood Press, 1985), 115–16, 133–35.

34. James Murray Mason, speech in Senate, *CG*, 35th Cong., 1st Sess., 1728 (April 21, 1858); Young, *Senator James Murray Mason*, 67–76.

35. Dr. Van Evne, "Slavery Extension," *DBR*, July 1853, 1–14.

36. Thomas Caute Reynolds to James Buchanan, July 27, 1847, *DCUS*, 8:410–12. On Cuban politics, the slave trade, and the sugar industry in the late 1840s and 1850s, see David R. Murray, *Odious Commerce: Britain, Spain, and the Abolition of the Cuban Slave Trade* (New York: Cambridge University Press, 1980); Arthur F.

Corwin, *Spain and the Abolition of Slavery in Cuba, 1817–1886* (Austin: University of Texas Press, 1967), 69–129; and Anton L. Allahar, "Sugar and the Politics of Slavery in Mid-Nineteenth-Century Cuba," in Bernard Moitt, ed., *Sugar, Slavery, and Society: Perspectives on the Caribbean, India, the Mascarenes, and the United States* (Gainesville: University Press of Florida, 2004), 110–34.

37. On Polk's abortive effort to purchase Cuba, see Basil Rauch, *American Interest in Cuba: 1848–1855* (New York: Columbia University Press, 1948), 55–101.

38. The most thorough account of López's expeditions is Tom Chaffin, *Fatal Glory: Narciso López and the First Clandestine U.S. War against Cuba* (Charlottesville: University Press of Virginia, 1996); but see also Greenberg, *Manifest Manhood*, 170–96; and Johnson, *River of Dark Dreams*, 303–66.

39. James Murray Mason, speech in Senate, *CG*, 32nd Cong., 2nd Sess., 139–41 (December 23, 1852); Albert Gallatin Brown, quoted in James M. Callahan, *Cuba and International Relations: A Historical Study in American Diplomacy* (Baltimore: The Johns Hopkins Press, 1899), 247. See also Ley, "Expansionists All?," 208–21.

40. Joshua Giddings, speech in House, *CG Appendix*, 32nd Cong., 2nd Sess., 38–40 (December 14, 1852).

41. Daniel Barringer to Everett, December 14, 1852, *DCUS*, 8:676–79; Hunter to Herschel V. Johnson, December 2, 1852, in Charles Henry Ambler, ed., "Correspondence of Robert M. T. Hunter, 1826–1876," *Annual Report of the American Historical Association for the Year 1916*, 2 vols. (Washington, D.C.: Government Printing Office, 1918), 2:154; Charles Faulkner, speech at public dinner, December 16, 1852, Faulkner Family Papers, VHS.

42. Abraham Venable, speech in House, *CG*, 32nd Cong., 2nd Sess., 189–92 (January 3, 1853); Trescot, *Few Thoughts*, 19–23. In 1853 *De Bow's Review* published two essays by the same author, both of which argued that U.S. and southern interests were best served by an independent slaveholding Cuba: W.J. Sykes, "Cuba and the United States," *DBR*, January 1853, 63–66; and W.J. Sykes, "Independence of Cuba," *DBR*, May 1853, 417–22. For summaries of the congressional debates of 1852 and 1853, see Callahan, *Cuba and International Relations*, 242–52; and Rauch, *American Interest in Cuba*, 240–55.

43. Pierce's diplomats included James Gadsden of South Carolina in Mexico, William Trousdale of Tennessee in Brazil, Solon Borland of Arkansas in Costa Rica, John Wheeler of North Carolina in Nicaragua, John Marling of Tennessee in Guatemala, and James Bowlin of Missouri in Colombia. The five Americans who served as consuls in Havana from 1853 to 1857 all hailed from Mississippi, Alabama, or Louisiana. See Walter B. Smith, *America's Diplomats and Consuls of 1776–1865* (Washington, D.C.: Government Printing Office, 1986). For Pierce's State Department offer to Hunter, see Allan Nevins, *Ordeal of the Union*, vol. 2, *A House Dividing, 1852–1857* (New York: Scribner, 1947), 47.

44. *Richmond Enquirer*, October 31, 1853; "Fairfax," writing in the *Richmond Enquirer*, January 10, 1854. See also "Our Representatives Abroad," *National Era*

(Washington, D.C.), October 26, 1854; "Slave-Breeding Diplomacy," *New-York Daily Tribune*, May 20, 1854; and Rauch, *American Interest in Cuba*, 259–61.

45. Franklin Pierce, Inaugural Address, March 4, 1853, James D. Richardson, ed., *A Compilation of the Messages and Papers of the Presidents*, 10 vols. (New York: Bureau of National Literature, 1897), 7:2731–32.

46. On the Young America movement and foreign policy, see Yonatan Eyal, *The Young America Movement and the Transformation of the Democratic Party, 1828–1861* (New York: Cambridge University Press, 2007). Tom Chaffin rightly notes that Latin American filibustering grew not out of southern separatism, but out of "an older U.S. nationalism that embraced both slavery and territorial expansion." That older tradition frequently maintained an interest in international slavery that actually transcended its desire for territorial growth. Tom Chaffin, "'Sons of Washington': Narciso López, Filibustering, and U.S. Nationalism, 1848–1851," *JER* 15, no. 1 (Spring 1995): 106–8.

47. Marcy to Buchanan, July 2, 1853, *DCUS*, 7:92–95; Marcy to Soulé, July 23, 1853, *DCUS*, 11:160–66. See also Buchanan to Marcy, November 1, 1853, *DCUS*, 7:508–9.

48. Marcy to Buchanan, July 2, 1853, *DCUS*, 7:92–95; Marcy to Soulé, July 23, 1853, *DCUS*, 11:160–66.

49. William H. Robertson to Marcy, November 27, 1853, in Despatches from U.S. Consuls in Havana, 1783–1906, Record Group 59, vol. 26, NA; hereinafter cited as Despatches from Havana. On Pezuela and the Spanish political context, see Corwin, *Spain and the Abolition of Slavery in Cuba*, 112–14

50. Soulé to Marcy, December 23, 1853, *DCUS*, 11:729–35 (quoted); William H. Robertson to Marcy, November 21, 1853, Despatches from Havana, vol. 26.

51. Robertson to Marcy, December 26, 1853, Despatches from Havana, vol. 26. For differing interpretations of Pezuela's governorship, see Rauch, *American Interest in Cuba*, 275–82; Corwin, *Spain and the Abolition of Cuban Slavery*, 113–21; and Murray, *Odious Commerce*, 233–37.

52. *Richmond Enquirer*, October 31, 1853; Hébert's proclamation, also quoted in the *Richmond Enquirer*, January 28, 1854; emphasis in the original.

53. Robertson to Marcy, December 21 and 26, 1853, and January 27, 1854, Despatches from Havana, vol. 26; Robertson to Marcy, February 14, March 1, and March 20, 1854, *DCUS*, 11:737, 740–42, 748–49. On Robertson's career, see his obituary in the *New York Times*, June 6, 1859.

54. Robertson to Marcy, May 7, 1854, *DCUS*, 11:772–73; Robertson to Marcy, February 27, 1854, Despatches from Havana, vol. 26.

55. Robertson to Marcy, April 21, Despatches from Havana, vol. 26; Robertson to Marcy, April 26, May 7, May 10, and May 14, 1854, *DCUS*, 11:764–66, 772–76, 782–83, 786–87; emphasis in the original. For Robertson, the example of Haiti made free black politics synonymous with white extermination. If Cuba had a "Toussant or a Dessalines," he noted on May 10, "ninety days would not elapse, I

think, before every white man, woman, or child, was sacrificed, including the General himself."

56. Marcy to Charles W. Davis, March 15, 1854, *DCUS*, 11:170–73; Henry M. Wriston, *Executive Agents in American Foreign Relations* (Baltimore: Johns Hopkins Press, 1929), 729–32. A sharp interest in the racial composition of Cuba's labor force had also marked the official dispatches from Havana in the fall of 1853; see Robertson to Marcy, November 23 and December 26, 1853; and Alexander M. Clayton to Marcy, November 30 and December 15, 1853, Despatches from Havana, vol. 26.

57. Davis to Marcy, May 22, 1854, *DCUS*, 11:788–96; Marcy to Soulé, April 3, 1854, *DCUS*, 11:175–77.

58. *CG*, 33rd Cong., 1st Sess., 1021–25 (May 1, 1854).

59. *New York Times*, July 2, 1853; *Richmond Enquirer*, February 17, 1854; *Charleston Mercury*, May 6, 1854. See also the *Georgia Telegraph*, May 9, 1854 ("emancipationist"); the *Southern Recorder* (Milledgeville, Ga.), March 28, 1854 (on Cuba's black army); and the *New Orleans Delta*, quoted in the *Texas State Gazette* (Austin), June 17, 1854 ("eight hundred thousand negroes").

60. See, for instance, the *Chicago Tribune*, November 2, 1853; and the *National Era*, May 11, 1854.

61. Georgia congressman Elijah Webb Chastain, speech in the House, reported in the *Federal Union* (Milledgeville, Ga.), June 20, 1854. For historical treatments of the phenomenon that emphasize slightly different motivations on the part of southern leaders, see C. Stanley Urban, "The Africanization of Cuba Scare, 1853–1855," *Hispanic American Historical Review* 37, no. 1 (February 1957): 29–45; May, *Southern Dream*, 31–45; and Murray, *Odious Commerce*, 231–40.

62. Robertson to Marcy, May 10, 1854, *DCUS*, 11:786; Quitman to Thomas Reed, August 24, 1854, in J. F. H. Claiborne, *Life and Correspondence of John A. Quitman*, 2 vols.(New York: Harper and Brothers, 1860), 2:207–8; Stephen Mallory, speech in Senate, *CG*, 33rd Cong., 1st Sess., 1260 (May 22, 1854). On Quitman's expedition and its supporters in Congress, see Robert E. May, *John A. Quitman: Old South Crusader* (Baton Rouge: University of Louisiana Press, 1985), 270–95; on the centrality of slavery and Africanization fears to Quitman's entire venture, see May, *Manifest Destiny's Underworld*, 254–59.

63. *Richmond Enquirer*, March 14, 1854; *Charleston Mercury*, May 6, 1854; for similar views, see the *Daily Dispatch* (Richmond, Va.), November 18, 1854. Soulé suggested that the United States treat Cuba as James Madison had treated Amelia Island in Florida in 1813—a direct naval landing that would trigger "the whole of Cuba . . . to rise in arms & assert its independence." Soulé to Marcy, May 3, 1854, *DCUS*, 11:771.

64. Faulkner, speech at public dinner, December 16, 1852; Trescot, "Mr. Everett and the Cuban Question," 462.

65. For the clearest distillation of this argument, see Potter, *Impending Crisis*, 198. See also May, *Southern Dream*, 59–76; and James M. McPherson, *Battle Cry of Freedom: The Civil War Era* (New York: Oxford University Press, 1988), 108–10.

66. James Dobbin, quoted in Rauch, *American Interest in Cuba*, 286–87; see also Louis M. Sears, "Slidell and Buchanan," *AHR* 27, No. 4 (July 1922): 720–22.

67. Robertson to Marcy, May 22, 1855, *DCUS*, 11:869. On the endgame for Quitman's expedition, largely doomed to failure after the administration's policy shift, see May, *John A. Quitman*, 285–95.

68. For optimistic coverage of Pezuela's about-face in the southern press, see *Mobile Daily Advertiser*, May 10, 1854; *Southern Recorder* (Milledgeville, Ga.), May 23, 1854; and *Richmond Enquirer*, June 19, 1854.

69. Thomas Savage to Marcy, August 29, 1854, Despatches from Havana, vol. 27; Gadsden to Jefferson Davis, July 19, 1854, *PJD*, 5:78–80; *Charleston Mercury*, December 4, 1854 (quotation); *Daily Dispatch*, April 5, 1855. On the retreat and recall of Pezuela, see Corwin, *Spain and the Abolition of Slavery in Cuba*, 120–23.

70. See Buchanan, Mason, and Soulé to Marcy, October 18, 1854, *DCUS*, 7:579–85; and Amos A. Ettinger, *The Mission to Spain of Pierre Soulé, 1853–1855: A Study in the Cuban Diplomacy of the United States* (New Haven, Conn.: Yale University Press, 1932), 357–68.

71. John Slidell, speech in Senate, *CG Appendix*, 35th Cong., 2nd Sess., , 90–92 (January 24, 1859). On the failure of Buchanan's Cuba bill in Congress, see May, *Caribbean Dream*, 163–89; and Callahan, *Cuba and International Relations*, 298–328. A significant reason that the South never mounted a serious filibuster effort after 1855 was the Spanish government's direct assurance that it would protect Cuban slave institutions; see the conversation between U.S. envoy Augustus Dodge and Spanish foreign minister Juan de Zavala, August 25, 1855, *DCUS*, 11:886–91; and Corwin, *Spain and the Abolition of Slavery in Cuba*, 124–26.

72. Stephens to W. W. Burwell, May 7, 1854, in Ulrich B. Phillips, ed., *The Correspondence of Robert Toombs, Alexander H. Stephens, and Howell Cobb*, 2 vols. (New York: Da Capo Press, 1970 [1913]), 1:344. On Stephens's vital role in the Kansas-Nebraska Act, see Potter, *Impending Crisis*, 145–76.

73. *Charleston Mercury*, May 6, 1854; Henry Wise to Muscoe Russell Hunter Garnett, June 19, 1855, Hunter-Garnett Papers, University of Virginia. Even private filibusters like Quitman relied implicitly on the power of the U.S. government as a deterrent against third-party interventions to stop their raids. Sometimes that reliance became explicit, as when Slidell and others moved for Congress to annul the Neutrality Acts on behalf of filibuster activity.

74. The Louisiana document was endorsed by Judah Benjamin on the Senate floor; *S. Misc. Doc. No. 63*, 33rd Cong., 1st Sess.(1854); *CG*, 33rd Cong., 1st Sess., 1298 (May 24, 1854).

9. The Military South

1. For debate over the South's "martial spirit," see John Hope Franklin, *The Militant South* (Cambridge, Mass.: Harvard University Press, 1956); Marcus Cunliffe, *Soldiers and Civilians: The Martial Spirit in America, 1775–1865* (Boston: Little, Brown, 1968),

335–84; James M. McPherson, "Antebellum Southern Exceptionalism: A New Look at an Old Question," *Civil War History* 29, no. 3 (September 1983): 230–44; and R. Don Higginbotham, "The Martial Spirit in the Antebellum South: Some Further Speculations in a National Context," *JSH* 58, no. 1 (February 1992): 3–26.

2. The eleven future Confederate states claimed 31.4 percent of the U.S. population in 1850 and 29.0 percent in 1860; their share of the free population in 1860 was 20.5 percent.

3. See Leonard L. Richards, *The Slave Power: The Free North and Southern Domination, 1780–1860* (Baton Rouge: Louisiana State University Press, 2000), esp. 177–216; and Michael Todd Landis, *Northern Men with Southern Loyalties: The Democratic Party and the Sectional Crisis* (Ithaca, N.Y.: Cornell University Press, 2014).

4. William Seward, *The Slaveholding Class Dominant in the Republic,* speech at Detroit, October 2, 1856 (Washington, D.C.: Buell and Blanchard, 1857). On the origins and evolution of this antislavery critique, see Richards, *Slave Power,* 1–28; and Corey M. Brooks, *Liberty Power: Antislavery Parties and the Transformation of American Politics* (Chicago: University of Chicago Press, 2016).

5. Seward, *Slaveholding Class Dominant in the Republic,* 8. Between 1847 and 1861 men from future Confederate states led the Treasury Department for six of fourteen years and the Post Office Department for just four of fourteen. Over the same period no secretary of state or attorney general hailed from a state south of Kentucky. Southern men did direct the new Department of the Interior, created in 1849, for seven of the twelve years before 1861. For committee chairmanships and cabinet offices, see U.S. Congress, *Congressional Directory* (Washington, D.C.: Government Printing Office, 1847–1861).

6. Don E. Fehrenbacher, *The Slaveholding Republic: An Account of the United States Government's Relations to Slavery* (New York: Oxford University Press, 2001), 231–94; David F. Ericson, *Slavery in the American Republic: Developing the Federal Government, 1791–1861* (Lawrence: University Press of Kansas, 2011).

7. Matthew Karp, "Slavery and American Sea Power: The Navalist Impulse in the Antebellum South," *JSH* 77, no. 2 (May 2011): 283–324.

8. David Todd, "A French Imperial Meridian, 1814–1870," *Past and Present* 210 (February 2011): 177. For the argument that the 1850s also witnessed a surge of modernizing, technocratic reform within European states, see Christopher Clark, "After 1848: The European Revolution in Government," *Transactions of the Royal Historical Society* 22 (December 2012): 171–97.

9. On the U.S. military as evidence that antebellum Americans did not fear a small but powerful centralized state, see Ira Katznelson, "Flexible Capacity: The Military and Early American Statebuilding," in Ira Katznelson and Martin Shefter, eds., *Shaped by War and Trade: International Influences on American Political Development* (Princeton, N.J.: Princeton University Press, 2003), 82–110; and Brian Balogh, *A Government out of Sight: The Mystery of National Authority in Nineteenth-Century America* (New York: Cambridge University Press, 2009), 151–218.

10. "Speech of Jefferson Davis before the State Democratic Convention in Jackson, Mississippi, January 3, 1844," *JDC*, 1:8–9.

11. *H. Rep. No. 448*, 29th Cong., 1st Sess.(1846), 1.

12. Thomas Butler King, speech in House, *CG Appendix*, 30th Cong., 1st Sess., 937–38 (July 19, 1848); emphasis in the original. On the long-standing southern desire for a convertible steam packet line, see Matthew F. Maury, "A Scheme for Rebuilding Southern Commerce," *SLM* (January 1839): 3–12; on King's 1847 plan, see John H. Schroeder, *Shaping a Maritime Empire: The Commercial and Diplomatic Role of the American Navy, 1829–1861* (Westport, Conn.: Greenwood Press, 1985), 88–90, 107–12; and Edward M. Steel, *T. Butler King of Georgia* (Athens: University of Georgia Press, 1964), 57–62.

13. Thomas Butler King, speech in House, *CG Appendix*, 30th Cong., 1st Sess., 938 (July 19, 1848); Matthew F. Maury, "Steam Navigation to China," *SLM*, April 1848, 246–54.

14. "Our Foreign Policy," *SLM* (January 1850), 1; Richard Kidder Meade, speech in House, *CG Appendix*, 31st Cong., 2nd Sess., 394–96 (February 28, 1851). On the ideological relationship between "manifest destiny" and the "maritime frontier," see Brian Rouleau, *With Sails Whitening Every Sea: Mariners and the Making of an American Empire* (Ithaca, N.Y.: Cornell University Press, 2014), 1–5, 74–101; for its impact on U.S. naval policy, see Schroeder, *Shaping a Maritime Empire*, 79–99; and Kurt Hackemer, *The U.S. Navy and the Origins of the Military-Industrial Complex, 1847–1883* (Annapolis, Md.: Naval Institute Press, 2001), 11–18.

15. King to Frederick Stanton, September 10, 1850, Thomas Butler King Papers, SHC-UNC. On the unsuccessful effort to win appropriations for a variant of this African steamer plan, see Frederick Stanton et al., *Colonization of the Western Coast of Africa, by Means of a Line of Mail Steam Ships* (New York: W. L. Burroughs, 1851); *CG Appendix*, 31th Cong., 2nd Sess., 200–204 (February 24, 1851); and Brainerd Dyer, "The Persistence of the Idea of Naval Colonization," *Pacific Historical Review* 12, no. 1 (March 1943): 57–58. On antiblack colonization in the antebellum South, see Eric Burin, *Slavery and the Peculiar Solution: A History of the American Colonization Society* (Gainesville: University Press of Florida, 2005), 126–30.

16. For Stanton's battleship plan, see *CG Appendix*, 32nd Cong., 1st Sess., 1051 (August 17, 1852); the Louisiana petition is reprinted in *DBR*, November 1852, 529–35. On Maury's influence with Graham, see Maury to Graham, October 7, 1850, in *The Papers of William Alexander Graham*, ed. J. G. de Roulhac Hamilton, 8 vols. (Raleigh: North Carolina Department of Cultural Resources, 1957–1992), 3:422; and Max R. Williams, "Secretary William A. Graham, Naval Administrator, 1850–1852," *North Carolina Historical Review* 48, no. 1 (1971): 53–72.

17. *Baltimore Sun*, March 8, 1853. Another friendly paper cobbled together all of three magnificently underwhelming sentences to describe the new naval chief: "James C. Dobbin was born in North Carolina in 1814.—He is the youngest man in the Cabinet, but not the man of the least talent. He has many qualifications

which fit him for the Navy." *Vermont Watchman and State Journal*, March 17, 1853. See also Harold D. Langley, "James Cochrane Dobbin," in Paolo E. Coletta, ed., *American Secretaries of the Navy*, 2 vols. (Annapolis, Md.: Naval Institute Press, 1980), 1:279–302.

18. Report of the Secretary of the Navy, *CG Appendix*, 33rd Cong., 1st Sess., 15–16 (December 5, 1853); emphasis in the original.

19. Ibid. Dobbin's report won a warm reception from the southern press; see the *Richmond Enquirer*, November 11, 1853; the *Baltimore Sun*, December 9, 1853; and *DBR*, February 1854, 182–84.

20. Bocock chaired the House Naval Affairs Committee from 1853 to 1855 and again from 1857 to 1859; Mallory chaired the Senate Naval Affairs Committee from 1855 to 1861. For Upshur's influence on Bocock, see Thomas Bocock, speech in House, *CG Appendix*, 33rd Cong., 1st Sess., 423 (March 28, 1854).

21. Thomas Bocock, speech in House, *CG Appendix*, 33rd Cong., 1st Sess., 422–25 (March 28, 1854); *Memphis Daily Appeal*, reprinted in *Charleston Mercury*, March 30, 1854; see also the *Richmond Enquirer*, March 22, 1854.

22. Thomas Bocock, Speech in House, *CG Appendix*, 33rd Cong., 1st Sess., 422–25 (March 28, 1854); emphasis in the original. See also Schroeder, *Shaping a Maritime Empire*, 122–24. For Bocock's opposition to interventionism, see T. H. Flood to Bocock, January 14, 1851; and Bocock to the editors of the *Richmond Enquirer*, February 10, 1852, both in Papers of the Thornhill Family and Thomas Bocock, University of Virginia.

23. Stephen Mallory, speech in Senate, *CG*, 33rd Cong., 1st Sess., 1456 (June 20, 1854); Report of the Secretary of the Navy, *CG Appendix*, 33rd Cong., 1st Sess., 15–16 (December 5, 1853).

24. Thomas Bocock, Speech in House, *CG Appendix*, 33rd Cong., 1st Sess., 422–25 (March 28, 1854). For similar comparative assessments of U.S. naval weakness, see *Charleston Mercury*, July 14, 1854; and William Henry Trescot, "An American View of the Eastern Question," *DBR*, October 1854, 327–50.

25. Report of the Secretary of the Navy, *CG Appendix*, 33rd Cong., 2nd Sess., 19–23 (December 4, 1854); Report of the Secretary of the Navy, *CG Appendix*, 34th Cong., 1st Sess., 21–26 (December 3, 1855); Report of the Secretary of the Navy, *CG Appendix*, 34th Cong., 2nd Sess., 27–31 (December 1, 1856).

26. Report of the Secretary of the Navy, *CG Appendix*, 33rd Cong., 2nd Sess., 20–21 (December 4, 1854); Report of the Secretary of the Navy, *CG Appendix*, 34th Cong., 2nd Sess., 28 (December 1, 1856).

27. Bocock in the House and Mallory and Hunter in the Senate led the struggle; see *CG*, 34th Cong., 3rd Sess., 989–91, 1085, 1103 (March 3, 1857).

28. *Charleston Mercury*, November 30, 1854.

29. Alfred Thayer Mahan, *From Sail to Steam: Recollections of Naval Life* (New York: Harper and Brothers, 1907), xiii–xviii, 34–36; see also Hackemer, *U.S. Navy*, 21–49.

30. *Richmond Enquirer*, November 22, 1853.

31. For Davis's early military and political career, see William J. Cooper Jr., *Jefferson Davis, American* (New York: Knopf, 2000), 9–122; on Davis's celebratory conflation of Jackson and Calhoun, see 112. On Davis as a "representative man" among the antebellum and Confederate slaveholding elite, see Stephanie McCurry, *Confederate Reckoning: Power and Politics in the Civil War South* (Cambridge, Mass.: Harvard University Press, 2012), 13–15.

32. Cooper, *Jefferson Davis*, 123–240. For examples of Davis's military advocacy even in the heat of the sectional crisis of 1850, see *CG*, 31th Cong., 1st Sess., 395 (February 20, 1850), 1179–81 (June 11, 1850).

33. James D. B. De Bow, "Presidential Candidates and Aspirants," *DBR*, July 1860, 96–97; "D. L. C.," "Selections," *Liberator*, December 28, 1855. On Davis's clout within the Pierce administration, see Cooper, *Jefferson Davis*, 264–76; William C. Davis, *Jefferson Davis: The Man and His Hour* (New York: HarperCollins, 1991), 223–25; and Roy F. Nichols, *Franklin Pierce: Young Hickory of the Granite Hills* (Newtown, Conn.: American Political Biography Press, 2003 [1931]), 248.

34. Report of the Secretary of War, *CG Appendix*, 33rd Cong., 1st Sess., 29–37 (December 1, 1853). The most complete overview of Davis's term in the War Department is John Muldowny, "The Administration of Jefferson Davis as Secretary of War" (PhD diss., Yale University, 1959). On army politics and army policy in the 1850s generally, see Robert M. Utley, *Frontiersmen in Blue: The United States Army and the Indian, 1848–1865* (New York: Macmillan, 1967), 1–58; Durwood Ball, *Army Regulars on the Western Frontier, 1848–1861* (Norman: University of Oklahoma Press, 2001), 13–86.

35. For careful recountings of events at the Sioux camp, see Paul N. Beck, *The First Sioux War: The Grattan Fight and Blue Water Creek, 1854–1856* (Lanham, Md.: University Press of America, 2004), 1–62; and R. Eli Paul, *Blue Water Creek and the First Sioux War, 1854–1856* (Norman: University of Oklahoma Press, 2004), 18–24.

36. See *Baltimore Sun*, September 13, 1854; and *Charleston Mercury*, October 20, 1854. On Harney's campaign, see Beck, *First Sioux War*, 83–134; Paul, *Blue Water Creek*, 27–128; and Jeffrey Ostler, *The Plains Sioux and U.S. Colonialism from Lewis and Clark to Wounded Knee* (New York: Cambridge University Press, 2004), 40–42.

37. *Washington Union*, October 28, 1854; Davis to A. O. P. Nicholson, October 28, 1854, *JDC*, 2:387; *Washington Union*, October 29, 1854; see also *New Orleans Commercial Bulletin*, February 1, 1855.

38. Report of the Secretary of War, *CG Appendix*, 33rd Cong., 2nd Sess., 13–19 (December 4, 1854)

39. Cooper to William Hoffman, August 20, 1855, in *S. Ex. Doc. No. 91*, 34th Cong., 1st Sess.,(1856); Beck, *First Sioux War*, 69–78.

40. Sam Houston, speech in Senate, *CG*, 33rd Cong., 2nd Sess., 437–41 (January 29, 1855); Beck, *First Sioux War*, 73–74.

41. Stephen Mallory and Augustus Dodge, speeches in Senate, *CG*, 33rd Cong., 2nd Sess., 499–501 (January 31, 1855).

42. On Davis and Faulkner's close cooperation, see Davis to Faulkner, January 25, 1855, *PJD*, 5:97–98. Faulkner authored the committee report that became the basis for the four-regiment bill: *H. Rep. No. 40*, 33rd Cong., 2nd Sess., *Increase and Better Organization of the Army* (1855), 1–59; Muldowny, "Administration of Jefferson Davis as Secretary of War," 134–38.

43. George Badger, speech in Senate, *CG*, 33rd Cong., 2nd Sess., 516 (February 1, 1855). For the full Senate debates, see *CG*, 33rd Cong., 2nd Sess., 393–99, 436–44, 457–70, 494–501, 510–25.

44. Sam Houston, speech in Senate, *CG*, 33rd Cong., 2nd Sess., 440 (January 29, 1855); John Bell, speech in Senate, *CG*, 33rd Cong., 2nd Sess., 396 (January 25, 1855).

45. Report of the Secretary of War, *CG Appendix*, 33rd Cong., 1st Sess., 30 (December 1, 1853). On army deployment in the 1850s, see Utley, *Frontiersmen in Blue*, 54–107; Ball, *Army Regulars on the Western Frontier*, 13–37.

46. Report of the Secretary of War, *CG Appendix*, 34th Cong., 3rd Sess., 22 (December 1, 1856); Muldowny, "Administration of Jefferson Davis as Secretary of War," 86–96 On the conquest of the Great Plains Indians as a consolidation of U.S. imperial rule, see Ostler, *Plains Sioux and U.S. Colonialism*, 1–108.

47. Report of the Secretary of War, *CG Appendix*, 33rd Cong., 2nd Sess., 16–17 (December 4, 1854). On the Crimea commission, see Muldowny, "Administration of Jefferson Davis as Secretary of War," 66–86; and Matthew Moten, "Mission to the Crimea: The American Military Commission to Europe and the Crimean War, 1855–1856" (PhD diss., Rice University, 1991).

48. James L. Morrison, *"The Best School": West Point, 1833–1866* (Kent, Ohio: Kent State University Press, 1998), 116. On the imperial inspirations for Davis's camel initiative, see Jefferson Davis, speech in Senate, March 5, 1851, *PJD*, 4:167–70; Davis to H. C. Wayne, May 10, 1855, *JDC*, 2:461; and Cooper, *Jefferson Davis*, 258–59.

49. For steamship figures, see *Register of the . . . Navy of the United States* (Washington, D.C., 1854), 104; *Register of the . . . Navy of the United States* (Washington, D.C., 1860), 105–6; and Donald L. Canney, *The Old Steam Navy*, vol. 1, *Frigates, Sloops, and Gunboats, 1815–1885* (Annapolis, Md.: Naval Institute Press, 1990), 45–70, 173–78.

50. In 1848 Britain stationed just over 14,500 troops in its colonies across the hemisphere, from Newfoundland to Guyana; see John Darwin, *The Empire Project: The Rise and Fall of the British World-System, 1830–1870* (New York: Cambridge University Press, 2009), 34.

51. Susan B. Carter et al., eds., *Historical Statistics of the United States, Earliest Times to the Present: Millennial Edition* (New York: Cambridge University Press, 2006),

Table Ed 26–47. Admittedly, "peacetime" is a problematic designation for a half century filled with U.S. military campaigns against Native Americans. Put another way, the troop expansion of 1853–1857 was larger than any other in pre–Civil War U.S. history except for the increases leading up to the War of 1812, the Second Seminole War, and the Mexican-American War.

52. William Seward, *Slaveholding Class Dominant in the Republic*, 11. On Davis's technological achievements as secretary of war, see Cooper, *Jefferson Davis*, 254–60.

53. Joseph L. Durkin, *Stephen R. Mallory: Confederate Naval Chief* (Chapel Hill: University of North Carolina Press, 1954), 70–83; Muldowny, "Administration of Jefferson Davis as Secretary of War," 144–54; Cooper, *Jefferson Davis*, 270–72.

54. See David M. Potter, *The Impending Crisis: America before the Civil War, 1848–1861* (New York: Harper and Row, 1976), 390–91, 418–20; Ariel Ron, "Developing the Country: 'Scientific Agriculture' and the Roots of the Republican Party" (PhD diss., University of California–Berkeley, 2011), esp. 159–220; and Robert W. Young, *James Murray Mason: Defender of the Old South* (Knoxville: University of Tennessee Press, 1998), 27–35.

55. Guy Gugliotta, *Freedom's Cap: The United States Capitol and the Coming of the Civil War* (New York: Hill and Wang, 2012).

56. H. Rep. No. 348, 33rd Cong., 1st Sess., No. 348: *Diplomatic and Consular System* (1854); John Perkins, speeches in Senate, CG Appendix, 33rd Cong., 2nd Sess., 356–66 (January 11, 1855; February 6, 1855); "The Consular System," DBR, January 1854, 1–16; "The New Diplomatic and Consular System of the United States," DBR, May 1855, 578–82. See also Wilbur J. Carr, "The American Consular Service," *American Journal of International Law* 1, no. 4 (October 1907): 891–913.

57. See Douglas A. Ley, "Expansionists All? Southern Senators and American Foreign Policy, 1841–60" (PhD diss., University of Wisconsin–Madison, 1990), 267–321; CG, 35th Cong., 3rd Sess., 2741–48 (June 7, 1858); and Brian Schoen, *The Fragile Fabric of Union: Cotton, Federal Politics, and the Global Origins of the Civil War* (Baltimore: Johns Hopkins University Press, 2009), 223–24.

58. Robert M. T. Hunter, speech in Senate, CG, 34th Cong., 1st Sess., 620 (March 10, 1856). On the distinction between domestic and overseas federal power, see Ron, "Developing the Country," 203–8.

59. Joshua Giddings, speech in House, CG Appendix, 33rd Cong., 1st Sess., 415–19 (March 16, 1854).

60. On the disruptive impact of the Republican arrival in Congress in late 1855, see Allan Nevins, *Ordeal of the Union*, vol. 2, *A House Dividing, 1852–1857* (New York: Scribner, 1947), 412–16; William E. Gienapp, *The Origins of the Republican Party, 1852–1856* (New York: Oxford University Press, 1987), 239–48; Jeffrey A. Jenkins and Charles Stewart III, *Fighting for the Speakership: The House and the Rise of Party Government* (Princeton: Princeton University Press, 2013), 177–208.

61. *CG Appendix*, 34th Cong., 1st Sess., 1790–92, 1089–95 (July 28, 1856; August 7, 1856); John Sherman, *Recollections of Forty Years in the House, Senate, and Cabinet* (New York: Werner, 1895), 101–3.

62. Andrew Butler, speech in Senate, *CG Appendix*, 34th Cong., 1st Sess., 1095 (August 7, 1856). On the tense summer of 1856, see Nevins, *Ordeal of the Union*, 2:416–50, 471–86; Potter, *Impending Crisis*, 199–214; and Nicole Etcheson, *Bleeding Kansas: Contested Liberty in the Civil War Era* (Lawrence: University Press of Kansas, 2004), 89–138.

63. Charles Faulkner, speech in House, *CG*, 34th Cong., 1st Sess., 2197 (August 18, 1856); *Louisiana Courier*, August 26, 1856 (quotation); *Charleston Courier*, August 27, 1856.

64. *CG Appendix*, 34th Cong., 1st Sess., 1095–1111 (August 7, 1856); *CG*, 34th Cong., 2nd Sess., 1–85 (August 21–30, 1856); Nichols, *Franklin Pierce*, 479–80.

65. On the Buchanan administration's commitment to slavery, see Landis, *Northern Men with Southern Loyalties*, 148–204; Potter, *Impending Crisis*, 297–327.

66. Report of the Secretary of War, *CG Appendix*, 35th Cong., 1st Sess., 32–36 (December 5, 1857); Hannibal Hamlin, speech in Senate, *CG*, 35th Cong., 1st Sess., 634 (February 9, 1858). On the Utah conflict, see Kenneth Stampp, *America in 1857: A Nation on the Brink* (New York: Oxford University Press, 1992), 196–208; and Richard D. Poll and William P. Mackinnon, "Causes of the Utah War Reconsidered," *Journal of Mormon History* 20, no. 2 (Fall 1994): 16–44.

67. Albert Gallatin Brown, speech in Senate, *CG*, 35th Cong., 1st Sess., 1432 (April 3, 1858). For the critical 1858 army debates, which stretched across the winter and spring, see *CG*, 35th Cong., 1st Sess., 406–18, 429–38, 492–97, 626–34, 667–77, 867–76, 969–72, 1425–32, 1474.

68. See William W. Freehling, *The Road to Disunion*, vol. 2, *Secessionists Triumphant, 1854–1861* (New York: Oxford University Press, 2007), 138–40; and Holt Merchant, *South Carolina Fire-Eater: The Life of Lawrence Massillon Keitt* (Columbia: University of South Carolina Press, 2014).

69. For the House naval appropriations debate, see *CG*, 35th Cong., 1st Sess., 2409–16, 2853–66. Proslavery legislative support for army and navy spending was not unanimous—Georgia's Robert Toombs, for instance, generally opposed military appropriations—but it was both pronounced and decisive.

70. *CG*, 35th Cong., 1st Sess., 1432, 1474, 2729–41, 2993, 3023; Canney, *Old Steam Navy*, 1:71–90.

71. On the economic boom of the 1850s and federal spending, see Stampp, *America in 1857*, 213–19; Freehling, *Secessionists Triumphant*, 19–24; Max Edling, *Hercules in the Cradle: War, Money, and the American State, 1783–1867* (Chicago: University of Chicago Press, 2015), 232–37; and Davis Rich Dewey, *Financial History of the United States* (New York: Longmans, Green, 1903), 248–70.

72. John Hale, speech in Senate, *CG*, 34th Cong., 1st Sess., 1003, 1013–14 (April 23–24, 1856); Owen Lovejoy, speech in House, *CG*, 35th Cong., 1st Sess., 2860 (June 9, 1858).

73. For the 1859 retrenchment debates, see *CG*, 35th Cong., 2nd Sess., 205–14, 708–11 (January 4, 1859; January 31, 1859); *CG Appendix*, 35th Cong., 2nd Sess., 184–90 (February 9, 1859); and James L. Huston, *The Panic of 1857 and the Coming of the Civil War* (Baton Rouge: Louisiana State University Press, 1987), 173–94.

74. James Henry Hammond, speech in Senate, *CG*, 35th Cong., 2nd Sess., 1524 (March 1, 1859); for Jefferson Davis's efforts to save military funding, see *PJD*, 6:231–36; and *JDC*, 3:536–40.

75. John C. Calhoun, speech in Senate, *CG*, 31st Cong., 1st Sess., 452 (March 4, 1850); Stampp, *America in 1857*, 330 See also Freehling, *Secessionists Triumphant*, 104–8.

76. The richest narrative interpretations of the sectional crisis, for all their myriad disagreements, generally fall within these basic lines; see Allan Nevins, *The Emergence of Lincoln*, vol. 1, *Douglas, Buchanan, and Party Chaos, 1857–59* (New York: Scribner, 1950), 60–249; Potter, *Impending Crisis*, 267–447; James M. McPherson, *Battle Cry of Freedom: The Civil War Era* (New York: Oxford University Press, 1988), 162–69, 188–89; Stampp, *America in 1857*, 321–31; Sean Wilentz, *The Rise of American Democracy: Jefferson to Lincoln* (New York: W. W. Norton, 2005), 707–34; and Freehling, *Secessionists Triumphant*, 59, 109–44.

77. Reprinted in J. M. Frederick, ed., *National Party Platforms of the United States* (Akron, Ohio: Werner, 1896), 28.

78. The metaphor of "cords" holding the Union together comes from Calhoun's final speech to Congress: *CG*, 31st Cong., 1st Sess., 451–55 (March 4, 1850); Potter, *Impending Crisis*, 100–101, 225.

10. American Slavery, Global Power

1. David M. Potter, *The Impending Crisis: America before the Civil War, 1848–1861* (New York: Harper and Row, 1976), 445–47; James M. McPherson, *Battle Cry of Freedom: The Civil War Era* (New York: Oxford University Press, 1988), 202–33; Don E. Fehrenbacher, *The Slaveholding Republic: An Account of the United States Government's Relations to Slavery* (New York: Oxford University Press, 2001), 295–308.

2. Taylor's cabinet also told the tale of southern clout over the chief executive: his secretaries of state, war, and the navy all hailed from slaveholding states.

3. Wise to Caleb Cushing, October 13, 1860, quoted in Craig M. Simpson, *A Good Southerner: The Life of Henry A. Wise of Virginia* (Chapel Hill: University of North Carolina Press, 1985), 236; Daniel to Peter Vivian Daniel, January 1, 1860, quoted in Peter Bridges, *Pen of Fire: John Moncure Daniel* (Kent, Ohio: Kent State University Press, 2002), 148. See also Michael E. Woods, *Emotional and Sectional Conflict in the Antebellum United States* (New York: Cambridge University Press, 2014), 206–31.

4. Steven Hahn, *The Political Worlds of Slavery and Freedom* (Cambridge, Mass.: Harvard University Press, 2009), 16; James Oakes, *Freedom National: The Destruction of Slavery in the United States* (New York: W. W. Norton, 2012), 69. See also Robert E. Bonner, *Mastering America: Southern Slaveholders and the Crisis of American Nationhood* (New York: Cambridge University Press, 2009), 32–40, 184–213.

5. The most detailed scholarship on secession has emphasized these internal anxieties, focusing especially on state rather than national politics; see Potter, *Impending Crisis*, 448–84; William W. Freehling, *The Road to Disunion*, vol. 2, *Secessionists Triumphant, 1854–1861* (New York: Oxford University Press, 2007), 343–534; William L. Barney, *The Secessionist Impulse: Alabama and Mississippi in 1860* (Princeton, N.J.: Princeton University Press, 1974); Michael P. Johnson, *Toward a Patriarchal Republic: The Secession of Georgia* (Baton Rouge: Louisiana State University Press, 1977); Stephanie McCurry, *Masters of Small Worlds: Yeoman Households, Gender Relations, and the Political Culture of the Antebellum South Carolina Low Country* (New York: Oxford University Press, 1995), 277–304; William A. Link, *Roots of Secession: Slavery and Politics in Antebellum Virginia* (Chapel Hill: University of North Carolina Press, 2003), 213–44; and Christopher J. Olsen, *Political Culture and Secession in Mississippi: Masculinity, Honor, and the Antiparty Tradition, 1830–1860* (New York: Oxford University Press, 2000), 169–96.

6. William H. Seward, *The Irrepressible Conflict*, speech at Rochester, October 25, 1858 (New York: New York Tribune, 1860), 1–2. Two valuable summaries of scholarship on the causes of disunion, both of which emphasize the importance of international affairs to the politics of secession, are Frank Towers, "Partisans, New History, and Modernization: The Historiography of the Civil War's Causes, 1861–2011," *JCWE* 1, no. 2 (June 2011): 237–64; and Michael E. Woods, "What Twenty-First-Century Historians Have Said about the Causes of Disunion: A Civil War Sesquicentennial Review of Recent Literature," *JAH* 99, no. 2 (September 2012): 415–39.

7. On Davis's reluctance to accept disunion, see William J. Cooper Jr., *Jefferson Davis and the Civil War Era* (Baton Rouge: Louisiana State University Press, 2008), 3–32. On Mallory and Hammond, see Joseph L. Durkin, *Stephen R. Mallory: Confederate Naval Chief* (Chapel Hill: University of North Carolina Press, 1954), 112–21; and Lawrence T. McDonnell, "Struggle against Suicide: James Henry Hammond and the Secession of South Carolina," *Southern Studies* 22 (Summer 1983): 109–37. On the Lower South's broad preference for cooperative rather than separate state action, see Freehling, *Secessionists Triumphant*, 375–94, 463–69. Other national leaders who later championed secession but initially opposed rash or independent action included Howell Cobb, William Trescot, and Albert Gallatin Brown.

8. William S. Hitchcock, "Southern Moderates and Secession: Senator Robert M. T. Hunter's Call for Union," *JAH* 59, no. 4 (March 1973): 871–84; Robert W. Young, *Senator James Murray Mason: Defender of the Old South* (Knoxville: University of Tennessee Press, 1998), 97–100; David Eugene Woodard, "Sectionalism, Politics, and Foreign Policy: Duff Green and Southern Economic and Political Expansion" (PhD diss., University of Minnesota, 1996), 199–214; Frances Leigh Williams, *Matthew Fontaine Maury: Scientist of the Sea* (New Brunswick, N.J.: Rutgers University Press, 1963), 348–64; Edward P. Crapol, *John Tyler: The Accidental President* (Chapel Hill: University of North Carolina Press, 2006), 257–65.

9. Henry Wise, public letter, December 1, 1860, quoted in Barton H. Wise, *The Life of Henry Wise of Virginia, 1806–1876* (New York: Macmillan, 1899), 267; Simpson, *Good Southerner*, 219–51.

10. Robert Toombs, speech in Senate, *CG*, 36th Cong., 2nd Sess., 270 (January 7, 1861). The fullest discussion of the importance of the "hereafter" clause is in Robert E. May, *The Southern Dream of a Caribbean Empire, 1854–1861* (Gainesville: University Press of Florida, 2002 [1973]), 206–35.

11. James Mason, speech in Senate, *CG*, 36th Cong., 2nd Sess., 403–4 (January 16, 1861); *H. Rep. No. 31*, 36th Cong., 2nd Sess. (1861), 20–21. See also Allan Nevins, *The Emergence of Lincoln*, vol. 2, *Prologue to Civil War* (New York: Scribner, 1950), 385–410; Potter, *Impending Crisis*, 522–34; and William J. Cooper Jr., *We Have the War upon Us: The Onset of the Civil War, November 1860–April 1861* (New York: Vintage, 2012), 96–112, 151–57.

12. For varying perspectives, see May, *Southern Dream*, 223–35; Freehling, *Secessionists Triumphant*, 469–75; and Cooper, *We Have the War upon Us*, 96–97.

13. Robert M. T. Hunter, speech in Senate, *CG*, 36th Cong., 2nd Sess., 332 (January 11, 1861); John E. Fisher, "Statesman of a Lost Cause: R. M. T. Hunter and the Sectional Controversy, 1847–1887" (PhD diss., University of Virginia, 1968), 200–214.

14. See James Oakes, *The Scorpion's Sting: Antislavery and the Coming of the Civil War* (New York: W. W. Norton, 2014), 22–50.

15. Abraham Lincoln, quoted in Nevins, *Emergence of Lincoln*, 2:394; Roscoe Conkling, speech in Congress, *CG*, 36th Cong., 2nd Sess., 651 (January 30, 1861). See also May, *Southern Dream*, 216–23; Eric Foner, *The Fiery Trial: Abraham Lincoln and American Slavery* (New York: W. W. Norton, 2010), 146–57; Kenneth Stampp, *And the War Came: The North and the Secession Crisis* (Baton Rouge: Louisiana State University Press, 1950), 166–70; and Sean Wilentz, *The Rise of American Democracy: Jefferson to Lincoln* (New York: W. W. Norton, 2005), 779–81.

16. On Davis in the secession crisis, see William J. Cooper Jr., *Jefferson Davis, American* (New York: Knopf, 2000), 313–24. For the argument that Davis and Toombs could have averted Lower South secession if the Republicans had accepted the Crittenden plan, see William J. Cooper Jr., "The Critical Signpost on the Journey toward Secession," *JSH* 57, no. 1 (February 2011): 3–16; for more skeptical views, see Nevins, *Emergence of Lincoln*, 2:385–401; McPherson, *Battle Cry of Freedom*, 252–57; and Freehling, *Secessionists Triumphant*, 474–75.

17. Matthew Maury, quoted in Crapol, *John Tyler*, 260–61; on the importance of African slavery within Maury's vision of hemispheric empire, see Chapter 6.

18. *CG*, 36th Cong., 2nd Sess., 850–53 (February 11, 1861).

19. Ibid.; Stampp, *And the War Came*, 114–16; Durkin, *Stephen R. Mallory*, 112–21.

20. On the dominance of mainstream politicians in the formation of the Confederacy, see Emory M. Thomas, *The Confederate Nation, 1861–1865* (New York: Harper Perennial, 2011 [1979]), 37–66; and E. Merton Coulter, *The Confederate States of America: 1861–1865* (Baton Rouge: Louisiana State University Press, 1950), 23–32.

21. For an overview of the secession crisis and the ideological roots of the Confederate experiment, which she identifies as a "gamble of world historical proportions," see Stephanie McCurry, *Confederate Reckoning: Power and Politics in the Civil War South* (Cambridge, Mass.: Harvard University Press, 2012), 1–84.

22. Charles B. Dew, *Apostles of Disunion: Southern Secession Commissioners and the Causes of the Civil War* (Charlottesville: University of Virginia Press, 2002).

23. Alexander Stephens, speech at Savannah, March 21, 1861, as transcribed in the Savannah *Republican* and reprinted in Henry Cleveland, ed., *Alexander Stephens, in Public and Private, with Letters and Speeches, before, during, and since the War* (Philadelphia: National Publishing Co., 1866), 717–29 (quoted 721).

24. Stephens, speech at Savannah, in Cleveland, *Alexander Stephens*, 721–23.

25. On King Cotton ideology and secession, see Brian Schoen, *The Fragile Fabric of Union: Cotton, Federal Politics, and the Global Origins of the Civil War* (Baltimore: Johns Hopkins University Press, 2009), 237–69. On the arrogance of early Confederate strategic thought, see Frank L. Owsley, *King Cotton Diplomacy: Foreign Relations of the Confederate States of America* (Chicago: University of Chicago Press, 1959 [1931]), 1–51; and Henry Blumenthal, "Confederate Diplomacy: Popular Notions and International Realities," *JSH* 32, no. 2 (May 1966): 151–71.

26. Jefferson Davis, Inaugural Address, February 18, 1861, *PJD*, 7:45–51.

27. See, for instance, Paul D. Escott, *After Secession: Jefferson Davis and the Failure of Confederate Nationalism* (Baton Rouge: Louisiana State University Press, 1978), 35–38; Shearer Davis Bowman, *At the Precipice: Americans North and South during the Secession Crisis* (Chapel Hill: University of North Carolina Press, 2010), 47–49; and Don H. Doyle, *The Cause of All Nations: An International History of the American Civil War* (New York: Basic Books, 2015), 32–37.

28. Jefferson Davis, message to the Confederate Congress, April 29, 1861, *JDC*, 5:70.

29. "A Declaration of the Immediate Causes Which Induce and Justify the Secession of the State of Mississippi from the Federal Union," in *Journal of the State Convention* (Jackson: E. Barksdale, 1861), 86–88.

30. Ibid. On Clayton's career and his likely authorship of the declaration, see *PJD*, 7:28; J. L. Power, *Proceedings of the Mississippi State Convention . . .* (Jackson: Power and Cadwallader, 1861), 40–43; and Timothy B. Smith, *The Mississippi Secession Convention: Delegates and Deliberations in Politics and War, 1861–1865* (Jackson: University Press of Mississippi, 2014), 144.

31. John Townsend, *The South Alone, Should Govern the South* (Charleston: Evans and Cogswell, 1860), 20–21, 56–59; John Townsend, *The Doom of Slavery in the Union: Its Safety out of It* (Charleston: Evans and Cogswell, 1860), 18–19. On Townsend's influence, see Freehling, *Secessionists Triumphant*, 389–94; and Schoen, *Fragile Fabric of Union*, 241–44.

32. Robert M. T. Hunter, speech at Charlottesville, reprinted in the *Boston Post*, August 30, 1860; see also "The Future of Our Confederation," *DBR*, July 1861, 39.

33. William H. Holcombe, *The Alternative: A Separate Nationality, or the Africanization of the South* (New Orleans: Delta Mammoth Job Office, 1860), 3–4; reprinted in *SLM*, February 1861, 81–88; Bowman, *At the Precipice*, 253.

34. Thomas Clingman, speech in Senate, February 4, 1861, in *Selections from the Speeches and Writings of Hon. Thomas L. Clingman* (Raleigh: John Nichols, 1877), 539.

35. Townsend, *South Alone*, 20; George Fitzhugh, "Blackwood," *DBR*, December 1860, 732; William Howard Russell, *My Diary North and South* (Boston: T. O. H. P. Burnham, 1863), 118; John Majewski, *Modernizing a Slave Economy: The Economic Vision of the Confederate Nation* (Chapel Hill: University of North Carolina Press, 2009), 116–19, 136–39; Robert E. Bonner, "Proslavery Calculations and the Value of Southern Disunion," in Don H. Doyle, ed., *Secession as an International Phenomenon: From America's Civil War to Contemporary Separatist Movements* (Athens: University of Georgia Press, 2010), 116–17. On "cool brains," see Michael O'Brien, *Conjectures of Order: Intellectual Life in the Old South, 1810–1860* (Chapel Hill: University of North Carolina Press, 2004), 11–12, 1161–1202.

36. On the actual shape of British opinion on slavery in the 1860s, see R. J. M. Blackett, *Divided Hearts: Britain and the American Civil War* (Baton Rouge: Louisiana State University Press, 2000); and Don H. Doyle, "Slavery or Independence: The Confederate Dilemma in Europe," in Cornelis A. van Minnen and Manfred Berg, eds., *The U.S. South and Europe: Transatlantic Relations in the Nineteenth and Twentieth Centuries* (Lexington: University Press of Kentucky, 2013), 105–24.

37. See also Schoen, *Fragile Fabric of Union*, 233–69; and Matthew Mason, "A World Safe for Modernity: Antebellum Southern Proslavery Intellectuals Confront Great Britain," in L. Diane Barnes, Brian Schoen, and Frank Towers, eds., *The Old South's Modern Worlds: Slavery, Region, and Nation in the Age of Progress* (New York: Oxford University Press, 2011), 47–65.

38. Mason to Nathaniel Tyler, November 23, 1860, in Virginia Mason, ed., *The Public Life and Diplomatic Correspondence of James M. Mason* (Roanoke, Va.: Stone Printing and Manufacturing Co., 1903), 156–57. See also Paul Quigley, "Secessionists in an Age of Secession: The Slave South in Transatlantic Perspective," in Doyle, *Secession as an International Phenomenon*, 151–73; and Andre Fleche, *The Revolution of 1861: The American Civil War in the Age of Nationalist Conflict* (Chapel Hill: University of North Carolina Press, 2012), 80–106.

39. On slaveholders as a ruling and governing class, see Fehrenbacher, *Slaveholding Republic;* Bonner, *Mastering America;* and Adam Rothman, "The 'Slave Power' in the United States, 1783–1865," in Steve Fraser and Gary Gerstle, eds., *Ruling America: A History of Wealth and Power in a Democracy* (Cambridge, Mass.: Harvard University Press, 2005), 64–91.

40. Edward Mayes, *Lucius Q. C. Lamar: His Life, Times, and Speeches* (Nashville: Methodist Episcopal Church, 1896), 637–38; Coulter, *Confederate States of America*, 19–21; Drew Gilpin Faust, *The Creation of Confederate Nationalism: Ideology and Identity in*

the Civil War South (Baton Rouge: Louisiana State University Press, 1988), 14; Paul Quigley, *Shifting Grounds: Nationalism and the American South, 1848–1865* (New York: Oxford University Press, 2011), 145–57.

41. Francis Bartow, quoted in Freehling, *Secessionists Triumphant*, 409.

42. [J. B. Gladney], "The South's Power of Self Protection," *DBR*, November 1860, 552, 672; Townsend, *South Alone*, 20 (emphasis in the original); Jabez L. Curry, speech at Talladega, Alabama, in Jon L. Wakelyn, ed., *Southern Pamphlets on Secession, November 1860–April 1861* (Chapel Hill: University of North Carolina Press, 1996), 51.

43. Stephens, speech at Savannah, in Cleveland, *Alexander Stephens*, 723–24; Richmond *Examiner*, June 1, 1861. See also Nicholas Onuf and Peter Onuf, *Nations, Markets, and War: Modern History and the American Civil War* (Charlottesville: University of Virginia Press, 2006), 308–11.

44. Trescot to Howell Cobb, January 14, 1861, in Ulrich B. Phillips, ed., *The Correspondence of Robert Toombs, Alexander H. Stephens, and Howell Cobb*, 2 vols. (New York: Da Capo Press, 1970 [1913]), 2:531; William Henry Trescot, *The Position and Course of the South* (Charleston: Walker and James, 1850), 24; Bonner, *Mastering America*, 217–23.

45. Gaillard Hunt, "Narrative and Letter of William Henry Trescot, Concerning the Negotiations between South Carolina and President Buchanan in December, 1860," *American Historical Review* 13, no. 3 (April 1908): 552; Schoen, *Fragile Fabric of Union*, 257.

46. On the Montgomery convention and its marginalization of fire-eating radicals and extreme states'-rights men, see William C. Davis, *"A Government of Our Own": The Making of the Confederacy* (New York: Free Press, 1994), 44–261.

47. J. L. M. Curry, *A Civil History of the Government of the Confederate States . . .* (Richmond: B. F. Johnson, 1901), 49. On the rapid and ambitious formation of the provisional government, see William C. Davis, *"Government of Our Own,"* 60–109; and Charles Robert Lee Jr., *The Confederate Constitutions* (Chapel Hill: University of North Carolina Press, 1963), 51–81.

48. David Yulee, quoted in Quigley, *Shifting Grounds*, 132. On the speed of the Confederacy's founding in 1861 compared to that of the United States in 1787, see McPherson, *Battle Cry of Freedom*, 234, 257–59.

49. R. M. T. Hunter, "The Border States—Their Position after Disunion," *DBR*, January 1861, 116. See also Bonner, *Mastering America*, 217–28.

50. For the text of both Confederate constitutions and a skeletal record of the (largely secret) convention debates surrounding them, see *Journal of the Congress of the Confederate States of America, 1861–1865*, 7 vols. (Washington, D.C.: Government Printing Office, 1904–1905), 1:25–39, 851–924. Both are also reprinted in Lee, *Confederate Constitutions*, 159–200. On the Confederate Constitution as the expression of a proslavery "Confederate Americanism," see Ian Binnington, *Confederate Visions: Nationalism, Symbolism, and the Imagined South in the Civil War* (Charlottesville: University of Virginia Press, 2003), 19–43.

51. Because the president was limited to a single six-year term, some scholars have concluded that Confederates sought to curtail executive power. But in view of the rest of the constitution and the explanations offered by leading Montgomery delegates, it seems more plausible that the denial of presidential reeligibility was intended to limit the influence of party politics rather than executive authority per se. See Robert H. Smith, *An Address to the Citizens of Alabama, on the Constitution and Laws of the Confederate States of America* (Mobile, Ala.: Mobile Daily Register Print, 1861), 7–14; Don E. Fehrenbacher, *Constitutions and Constitutionalism in the Slaveholding South* (Athens: University of Georgia Press, 1989), 57–81; David P. Currie, "Through the Looking-Glass: The Confederate Constitution in Congress, 1861–1865," *Virginia Law Review* 90, no. 5 (September 2004): 1257–71; and George Rable, *The Confederate Republic: A Revolution against Politics* (Chapel Hill: University of North Carolina Press, 1994), 56–59.

52. *Journal of the Congress of the Confederate States*, 1:909. On the dramatic failure of Confederate constitutional language to limit state and executive power in practice, see Richard Franklin Bensel, *Yankee Leviathan: The Origins of Central State Authority in America, 1859–1877* (New York: Cambridge University Press, 1990), 99–101; Majewski, *Modernizing a Slave Economy*, 143–51; and Thomas, *Confederate Nation*, 63–66.

53. On the constitution's expansions of federal power to strengthen slavery, see Robert H. Smith, *Address . . . on the Constitution*, 16–20; McCurry, *Confederate Reckoning*, 78–81; and Lee, *Confederate Constitutions*, 110–13.

54. Howell Cobb, quoted in William C. Davis, *"Government of Our Own,"* 135.

55. See Russell, *My Diary North and South*, 250–51; and May, *Southern Dream*, 235–44. For an argument that puts expansion at the heart of the Confederate project, see Adrian Brettle, "The Fortunes of War: Confederate Expansionist Ambitions during the American Civil War" (PhD diss., University of Virginia, 2014).

56. "Cuba: The March of Empire and the Course of Trade," *DBR*, January 1861, 33; Jefferson Davis, speech at Atlanta, February 16, *PJD*, 7:43–44.

57. See Robert Toombs to Charles J. Helm, July 22, 1861, in James D. Richardson, ed., *The Messages and Papers of Jefferson Davis and the Confederacy, Including Diplomatic Correspondence, 1861–1865*, 2 vols. (Nashville: United States Publishing Company, 1906), 2:46–48; R. M. T. Hunter to William Yancey, Pierre Rost, and A. Dudley Mann, August 24, 1861, ibid., 2;72–76. See also Matthew Pratt Guterl, *American Mediterranean: Southern Slaveholders in the Age of Emancipation* (Cambridge, Mass.: Harvard University Press, 2008), 50–59; and Wayne H. Bowen, *Spain and the American Civil War* (Columbia: University of Missouri Press, 2011), 55–83.

58. William Browne to J. A. Quintero, September 3, 1861, *Messages and Papers of Jefferson Davis*, 2:77–80; R. Curtis Tyler, "Santiago Vidaurri and the Confederacy," *Americas* 26 (July 1969): 66–76.

59. On the spectacular failure of early Confederate diplomacy in Mexico, see Thomas Schoonover, *Dollars over Dominion: The Triumph of Liberalism in Mexican–United*

States Relations, 1861–1867 (Baton Rouge: Louisiana State University Press, 1978), 13–47; and Owsley, *King Cotton Diplomacy,* 113–33.

60. George Fitzhugh, "Hayti and the Monroe Doctrine," *DBR,* August 1861, 131–36.

61. On the arrogance and negligence of early Confederate diplomacy, see Edwin De Leon, *Secret History of Confederate Diplomacy Abroad,* ed. William C. Davis (Lawrence: University Press of Kansas, 2005), 40–47; Charles M. Hubbard, *The Burden of Confederate Diplomacy* (Knoxville: University of Tennessee Press, 1998), 17–47; and Howard Jones, *Blue and Gray Diplomacy: A History of Union and Confederate Foreign Relations* (Chapel Hill: University of North Carolina Press, 2010), 11–20.

62. Richmond *Daily Dispatch,* May 6, 1861; Brettle, "Fortunes of War," 139.

63. John C. Calhoun, "Speech on the Treaty of Washington," in Senate, August 19, 1842, *PJCC,* 16:409; Jefferson Davis, Inaugural Address, February 18, 1861, *PJD,* 7:47. On the Confederate belief in slavery as an element of wartime strength, see McCurry, *Confederate Reckoning,* 218–33.

64. Stephens, speech at Savannah, in Cleveland, *Alexander Stephens,* 723–24; Robert H. Smith, *Address . . . on the Constitution,* 5–6. On the Davis administration's fixed purpose to force a U.S. evacuation of Fort Sumter even at the risk of starting a war, see Potter, *Impending Crisis,* 581–83; Richard N. Current, "The Confederates and the First Shot," *Civil War History* 7, no. 4 (December 1961): 357–69; and Ludwell Johnson, "Fort Sumter and Confederate Diplomacy," *JSH* 26, no. 4 (November 1960): 441–77.

65. Lawrence Keitt to Susan Sparks Keitt, February 19, 1861, in Elmer Don Herd Jr., "Lawrence Keitt's Letters from the Provisional Congress of the Confederacy, 1861," *South Carolina Historical Magazine* 61, no. 1 (January 1960): 22.

66. Sven Beckert, *Empire of Cotton: A Global History* (Knopf: New York, 2014), 242–73; Jay Sexton, *Debtor Diplomacy: Finance and American Foreign Relations in the Civil War Era, 1837–1873* (Oxford: Oxford University Press, 2005), 133–41; Blumenthal, "Confederate Diplomacy," 151–71.

67. On the enormous power and achievements of the wartime Confederate state, see Bensel, *Yankee Leviathan,* 94–237; Majewski, *Modernizing a Slave Economy,* 140–61; Chad Morgan, *Planters' Progress: Modernizing Confederate Georgia* (Gainesville: University Press of Florida, 2005); William Thomas, *The Iron Way: Railroads, the Civil War, and the Making of Modern America* (New Haven, Conn.: Yale University Press, 2011); Harold S. Wilson, *Confederate Industry: Manufacturers and Quartermasters in the Civil War* (Jackson: University Press of Mississippi, 2005); and Raimondo Luraghi, "The Civil War and the Modernization of American Society: Social Structure and Industrial Revolution in the Old South before and during the War," *Civil War History* 18, no. 3 (September 1972): 230–50.

68. On proslavery thinkers' ideological embrace of wartime statism, see Robert E. Bonner, "Proslavery Extremism Goes to War: The Counterrevolutionary Confederacy and Reactionary Militarism," *Modern Intellectual History* 6, no. 2 (August 2009): 261–85.

69. Jackson to Aaron V. Brown, February 9, 1843; Jackson to William B. Lewis, September 18, 1843, in John Spencer Bassett, ed., *The Correspondence of Andrew Jackson*, 6 vols. (Washington, D.C.: Carnegie Institute, 1926–1935), 6:201–2, 228–30.

70. On the failure of the Confederate project in wartime and the collapse of southern slavery, see W. E. B. Du Bois, *Black Reconstruction in America* (New York: Russell and Russell, 1935), 55–126; Armstead L. Robinson, *Bitter Fruits of Bondage* (Charlottesville: University of Virginia Press, 2005); McCurry, *Confederate Reckoning;* and Bruce Levine, *The Fall of the House of Dixie: The Civil War and the Social Revolution That Transformed the South* (New York: Random House, 2013).

71. In the Civil War, the planter aristocracy fell faster and harder than almost any other ruling class in modern history: see Steven Hahn, "Class and State in Postemancipation Societies: Southern Planters in Comparative Perspective," *AHR* 95, no. 1 (February 1990): 83–98.

Epilogue

1. For accounts of Harvard's 1890 commencement, see *Boston Herald*, June 26, 1890; *Boston Daily Journal*, June 26, 1890; and *Boston Courant*, quoted in *Indianapolis Freeman*, July 5, 1890.

2. *Nation*, July 3, 1890. On Du Bois at Harvard, see David Levering Lewis, *W. E. B. Du Bois, 1868–1919: The Biography of a Race* (New York: Henry Holt, 1993), 79–117; and Bruce A. Kimball, "'This Pitiable Rejection of a Great Opportunity': W. E. B. Du Bois, Clement G. Morgan, and the Harvard University Commencement of 1890," *Journal of African American History* 94 (2009): 5–20.

3. David Blight, *Race and Reunion: The Civil War in American Memory* (Cambridge, Mass.: Belknap Press of Harvard University Press, 2002), esp. 173–87, 255–72; Nina Silber, *The Romance of Reunion: Northerners and the South, 1865–1900* (Chapel Hill: University of North Carolina Press, 1997). Not every northerner was swayed; see also Caroline Janney, *Remembering the Civil War: Reunion and the Limits of Reconciliation* (Chapel Hill: University of North Carolina Press, 2013), esp. 181–85.

4. *Boston Herald*, December 12, 1889; *Boston Daily Journal*, December 12, 1889; *Springfield Republican*, December 12, 1889; *Boston Herald*, May 30, 1890; *Boston Daily Advertiser*, May 30, 1890.

5. *New-York Tribune*, June 26, 1890. On the transnational thought of contemporary black intellectuals, see Robin D. G. Kelley, "'But a Local Phase of a World Problem': Black History's Global Vision, 1883–1950," *JAH* 86, no. 3 (December 1999): 1045–77.

6. W. E. B. Du Bois, "Jefferson Davis as a Representative of Civilization," in David Levering Lewis, ed., *W. E. B. Du Bois: A Reader* (New York: Henry Holt, 1995), 17–19. For differing interpretations of the address, see Lewis, *W. E. B. Du Bois, 1868–1919*, 100–102; and David Blight, "W. E. B. Du Bois and the Struggle for American

Historical Memory," in David W. Blight, *Beyond the Battlefield: Race, Memory, and the American Civil War* (Amherst: University of Massachusetts Press, 2002), 228–29.

7. For overviews of this new global imperialism, see Eric Hobsbawm, *The Age of Empire: 1875–1914* (New York: Random House, 1987); C. A. Bayly, *The Birth of the Modern World: 1798–1914* (Malden, Mass.: Blackwell, 2003), 227–33; and Tony Ballantyne and Antoinette Burton, "Empires and the Reach of the Global," in Emily Rosenberg, ed., *A World Connecting, 1870–1945* (Cambridge, Mass.: Belknap Press of Harvard University Press, 2012), 285–431.

8. Theodore Roosevelt, *The Winning of the West*, vol. 3 (New York: G. P. Putnam's Sons, 1894), 45–46. For the similar views of British imperial strategists, see John Darwin, *The Empire Project: The Rise and Fall of the British World-System, 1830–1970* (New York: Cambridge University Press, 2009), 66–67.

9. Du Bois, "Jefferson Davis," 17–18. Du Bois also anticipated a criticism made by later historians: that Europeans unnaturally separated the rise of powerful "nations" from the rise of powerful "empires"; see Bayly, *Birth of the Modern World*, 227–28; Jürgen Osterhammel, *The Transformation of the World: A Global History of the Nineteenth Century* (Princeton, N.J.: Princeton University Press, 2014), 392–468; and Kelley, "'But a Local Phase,'" 1049–51.

10. Robert G. Athearn, *William Tecumseh Sherman and the Settlement of the West* (Norman: University of Oklahoma Press, 1956); Gordon H. Chang, "Whose 'Barbarism'? Whose 'Treachery'? Race and Civilization in the Unknown United States–Korea War of 1871," *JAH* 89, no. 4 (March 2003): 1331–65.

11. Hobsbawm, *Age of Empire*, 34–83; Darwin, *Empire Project*, 23–111; Marc William Palen, *The "Conspiracy" of Free Trade: The Anglo-American Struggle over Empire and Economic Globalisation, 1846–1896* (Cambridge: Cambridge University Press, 2016). On antislavery imperialism in Africa, see Richard Huzzey, *Freedom Burning: Antislavery and Empire in Victorian Britain* (Ithaca, N.Y.: Cornell University Press, 2012), 132–76.

12. Du Bois, "Jefferson Davis," 18. On the rise of imperial realpolitik in late nineteenth-century Europe and the simultaneous hardening of racial lines all across the globe, see Osterhammel, *Transformation of the World*, 493–99, 855–65; Gerrit W. Gong, *The Standard of "Civilization" in International Society* (New York: Oxford University Press, 1984); Marilyn Lake and Henry Reynolds, *Drawing the Global Colour Line: White Men's Countries and the Challenge of Racial Equality* (New York: Cambridge University Press, 2008), 54–238; and Robert Vitalis, *White World Order, Black Power Politics: The Birth of American International Relations* (Ithaca, N.Y.: Cornell University Press, 2015), 29–54.

13. Quotations all from Du Bois, "Jefferson Davis," 17–19. See also Robert E. Bonner, "Confederate Racialism and the Anticipation of Nazi Evil," in Steven Mintz and John Stauffer, eds., *The Problem of Evil: Slavery, Freedom, and the Ambiguities of American Reform* (Amherst: University of Massachusetts Press, 2007), 115–24; and more generally, Dominco Losurdo, *Liberalism: A Counter-History*, trans. Gregory Elliott (London: Verso, 2005), esp. 323–40.

14. Steven C. Topik and Allen Wells, "Commodity Chains in a Global Economy," in Rosenberg, *World Connecting*, 593–812; Sven Beckert, *Empire of Cotton: A Global History* (New York: Knopf, 2014), 274–378; Andrew Zimmerman, *Alabama in Africa: Booker T. Washington, the German Empire, and the Globalization of the New South* (Princeton, N.J.: Princeton University Press, 2010); Matthew Pratt Guterl, *American Mediterranean: Southern Slaveholders in the Age of Emancipation* (Cambridge, Mass.: Harvard University Press, 2008).

15. W. W. Wright, "The Coolie Trade; or, The Excomienda System of the Nineteenth Century," *DBR*, September 1859, 296; George Frederick Holmes, "Relations of the Old and New Worlds," *DBR*, May 1856, 529. On the Congo Free State, see Adam Hochschild, *King Leopold's Ghost: A Story of Greed, Terror, and Heroism in Colonial Africa* (Boston: Houghton Mifflin, 1999).

16. Eric Hobsbawm, *On Empire: America, War, and Global Supremacy* (New York: Pantheon, 2008), 75. Robert Bonner has suggested that the Confederacy's chief propaganda officer in London may have contributed to the evolution of the late nineteenth century's "international racist consensus"; Robert E. Bonner, "Slavery, Confederate Diplomacy, and the Racialist Mission of Henry Hotze," *Civil War History* 51, no. 3 (September 2005): 288–316.

17. W. E. Gladstone, "Memorials of a Southern Planter," *Nineteenth Century* 154 (December 1889): 984–86; Roland Quinault, "Gladstone and Slavery," *Historical Journal* 52, no. 2 (June 2009): 363–83.

18. Du Bois, "Jefferson Davis," 18; *Nation*, July 3, 1890. The same insight appeared in Du Bois's subsequent historical treatments of the antebellum South: W. E. B. Du Bois, *The Suppression of the African Slave Trade to the United States of America, 1638–1870* (New York: Russell and Russell, 1965 [1898]); and W. E. B. Du Bois, *John Brown* (Philadelphia: George W. Jacobs, 1909), 123–26.

Acknowledgments

To properly acknowledge all the people who made this book possible would take almost as long as it has taken me to write it. But it is a pleasure even to attempt a compressed version.

The origins of the project go back to my years as a student at Amherst College, where David Blight drew me to the Civil War era and Gordie Levin introduced me to the history of American foreign relations. At the University of Pennsylvania I began work on the dissertation that grew into this book. It is hard to imagine how any of it could have happened without my advisor, Steven Hahn, whose intellectual ambition and personal generosity gave the project both stimulus and shelter. My debts to Stephanie McCurry and Bruce Kuklick are nearly as large: in different ways they taught me how to read, think, and write like a historian.

Many teachers, friends, and colleagues at Penn deserve more acknowledgment than space allows: Richard Beeman, Andrew Berns, the late Deborah Broadnax, Greg Downs, the late Robert Engs, Ricardo Howell, John Kenney, Phoebe Kropp, Will Kuby, Jessica Lautin, Walter Licht, Andrew Lipman, Kathy Peiss, Peter Pihos, Joan Plonski, Brian Rouleau, Daniel Stedman-Jones, Cate Styer, Karen Tani, and Mike Zuckerman are a few of them. I am grateful to have been a part of Penn's legendary nineteenth-century reading group, which included founders Joanna Cohen and Erik Mathisen, Julie Davidow, Jack Dwiggins, Julia Gunn, Sarah Manekin, Sarah Rodriguez, and Nicole Myers Turner.

Much of the early research for this book was generously supported by the American Council of Learned Societies and the Virginia Historical Society. Research librarians at Penn, the Southern Historical Collection at the University of North Carolina, College of William and Mary, the Library of Virginia, the Virginia Historical Society, the Library of Congress, and the National Archives deserve my thanks. A special mention is owed to Amherst and Penn comrade Seth Bernard, and his parents, Shula and Steve Bernard, who opened their home to me for two separate research trips to Chapel Hill.

The McNeil Center of Early American Studies, led by the indefatigable Dan Richter, helped support my research and writing for two years. Within the large and lively McNeil community, I am grateful to Amy Baxter-Bellamy, Chris Bilodeau, Kate Gaudet, Michael Goode, Nicole Ivy, Barbara Natello, Laura Keenan Spero, and especially Whitney Martinko for making the MCEAS feel like an intellectual home. In 2011–2012, the History Department at Rowan University, and particularly Bill Carrigan, helped sustain the project in important ways.

At nearly a decade's worth of conferences, seminars, and colloquia, everything that did not kill this book made it stronger. I am grateful to Zara Anishanslin, Sven Beckert, Robin Blackburn, Ian Delahanty, Caitlin Fitz, Sam Haynes, Andrew Heath, Gerald Horne, Rafael Marquese, Kate Marshall, Michael McGandy, Christopher Nichols, Tâmis Parron, Dan Rood, Edward Rugemer, Brian Schoen, Jay Sexton, Andy Shankman, Dale Tomich, and Christopher Wilkins for questions and arguments that drove me forward.

My fellow visiting scholars at the American Academy of Arts and Sciences in Cambridge, where I spent the 2012–2013 year, were a remarkable group. The conversations and nachos I shared with Francesca Ammon, Melinda Baldwin, Hillary Chute, Christopher Loss, Nikki Skillman, Peter Wirzbicki, and also Mary Dunn and Patricia Meyer Spacks, all made this book better.

The Department of History at Princeton University gave this project vital support. My debt to the department chair, William Jordan, is imposing; I am also grateful to the department staff, including Jennifer Goldman, Judith Hanson, Pamela Long, Deborah Macy, and Etta Recke. Among many historians I met at Princeton, Jeremy Adelman, David Bell, Margot Canaday, Linda Colley, Angela Creager, Yaacob Dweck, Sheldon Garon, Joshua Guild, Dirk Hartog, Craig Hollander, Brandi Hughes, Tera Hunter, Kevin Kruse, Regina Kunzel, Michael Laffan, Ronny Regev, Teresa Shawcross, Keeanga-Yamahtta Taylor, and Sean Vanatta challenged me to think about my work in new and valuable ways.

Robert Bonner, Brian Distelberg, Katherine Hill, Jonathan Levy, Chris Loss, Robert May, James McPherson, Philip Nord, Martha Sandweiss, and Sean Wilentz read the entire manuscript and offered cogent feedback that shaped my revisions. Andrew Fagal, Whitney Martinko, Erik Mathisen, Dael Norwood, Ariel Ron, Caitlin Rosenthal, and Peter Wirzbicki read chapter drafts and helped me make them tangibly better. At Princeton, the writing group organized by Rosina Lozano and including Alec Dun, Caley Horan, Rob Karl, Jon Levy, Beth Lew-Williams, Rebecca Rix, and Wendy Warren was a dependable source of sharp insight and moral support. In the later stages of writing, Kar Min Lin offered shrewd and timely research assistance.

I have completed this book as an Andrew Mellon Fellow at the New-York Historical Society, and I thank Valerie Paley, Dirk Hartog, Cole Jones, Brendan O'Malley, Stephen Petrus, and Christine Walker (and also Aaron Jakes and Elspeth Martini) for helping me push the manuscript over the finish line.

At Harvard University Press, Brian Distelberg believed in the project from the beginning and guided it serenely through the choppy seas of submission and revision. In the last leg of the process, Joyce Seltzer assumed the helm and proved as vigorous a pilot as I could hope for. I am also grateful to Kate Blackmer for her beautiful maps, Charles Eberline for his incisive copy edits, Kate Mertes for her index, and Kathleen Drummy and Angela Piliouras for managing everything in the end.

Portions of this work have been published elsewhere in different forms. Chapter 2 is an abridged version of my article "Slavery and American Sea Power: The Navalist Impulse in the Antebellum South," in the *Journal of Southern History* 77, no. 2 (May 2011): 283–324. Reprinted by permission of the Southern Historical Association. Portions of the opening section of Chapter 6, "Free Trade, Bound Labor," first appeared in "King Cotton, Emperor Slavery: Proslavery Elites and the Global Argument over Labor," David T. Gleeson and Simon Lewis, eds., *The Civil War as Global Conflict: Transnational Meanings of the American Civil War* (Columbia: University of South Carolina Press, 2014), pp. 36–55. The opening pages of Chapter 8 and fragments throughout Chapter 9 first appeared in "Arsenal of Empire" in *Common-place: The Interactive Journal of Early American Life*, 12, no. 4 (July 2012). I am grateful to all of these publishers for allowing the material to be reproduced here.

My deepest and most inadequate expressions of gratitude go to my friends and my family. My grandparents, Harriet Karp and Martin Karp, did not live to see the conclusion of this project, but they live on with me every day. I dedicate this book to my mother, Freddi Karp, who has made everything in my life possible. And my final word of thanks goes to Katherine Hill, who has made everything in my life worthwhile.

Credits

Figures

John C. Calhoun. Engraving by Alexander Hay Ritchie (New York: A.H. Ritchie & Co., c1852). Library of Congress Prints and Photographs Division, LC-DIG-pga-02499   54

Henry A. Wise. Civil War Glass Negatives and Related Prints. Library of Congress Prints and Photographs Division, LC-DIG-cwpb-06502   73

The explosion aboard the USS *Princeton*, 1844. Lithograph by Currier & Ives (New York: N. Currier, 1844). Library of Congress Prints and Photographs Division, LC-USZ62-2526   94

Landing of the American forces under Genl. Scott, 1847. Lithograph by Currier & Ives (New York: N. Currier, c1847). Library of Congress Prints and Photographs Division, LC-USZ62-14216   117

Robert M. T. Hunter. Photograph by Brady National Photographic Art Gallery (Washington, D.C.). Civil War Glass Negatives and Related Prints. Library of Congress Prints and Photographs Division, LC-DIG-cwpb-05604   174

Jefferson Davis. Brady-Handy Photograph Collection. Library of Congress Prints and Photographs Division, LC-DIG-cwpbh-00879   210

The inauguration of President Jefferson Davis, 1861. Lithograph by A. Hoen & Co. (Baltimore: A. Hoen & Co., c1888). Library of Congress Prints and Photographs Division, LC-USZ62-2565   243

Index

Aberdeen, Lord, 93–94

abolitionism: American domestic politics and, 7–8, 22, 25, 138, 154; Atlantic slave trade and, 25, 28, 77–78, 80; Brazil and, 30, 70–71, 75–77, 80, 89; British attitudes toward, 1, 7–8, 15–17, 100, 127–40, 157, 234–36; British foreign policy and, 10–31, 34–46, 50–102, 127–28, 178–79, 190; Cuba and, 15, 59–65, 67–69, 190; European imperialism and, 163, 254; Texas and, 72, 83–88, 93–97, 128

Abreo, Antonio Paulino Limpio de, 79

Adams, Henry, 5

Adams, John Quincy, 110; on Cuba, 59; on Henry Wise, 72, 80; Monroe Doctrine and, 15; Panama Congress and, 13; on slavery and U.S. foreign policy, 25, 50, 231; on southern navalism, 34, 92; on Texas annexation, 7–8, 83–84, 99, 113

Afghanistan, British invasion of, 20, 21

Africa, 37, 204; "coolie" and apprentice labor systems in, 154–56, 237; European imperialism in, 3, 153, 156, 158–63, 172, 214–15, 253–55. See also Atlantic slave trade

African Americans, 13, 23, 86, 123, 160, 167, 171–72, 204, 251. See also racism; slaves

African slave trade. See Atlantic slave trade

Agassiz, Louis, 165

Algeria, French conquest of, 3, 113, 158, 170, 202, 214

Amazon River, 144–45, 185, 204

American Indians, 113, 171, 221, 253; Mexican-American War and, 114; in Nebraska, 210–13; in Texas, 97

American Revolution, 13, 113, 128, 177

Andersson, Charles John, 162

annexation of Texas. See Texas

Argaiz, Pedro Alcantara de, 62–64

Army, U.S.: annexation of Texas and, 92, 97, 99–100; antebellum southern efforts to expand, 9, 199–202, 208–25; Jefferson Davis and, 208–18, 220–25; states' rights and, 118–19, 201, 208–9, 212, 216–20; technology and, 201, 216; West Point, 33, 199, 209, 210, 215. See also Mexican-American War

Army and Navy Chronicle, 44

Aroostook War (1838–39), 19

Ashburton, Lord, 51, 53, 55

Atlantic slave trade: American participation in, 25–26, 52–53, 73–81; Brazil and, 73–81; British efforts to suppress, 28, 45, 51–52, 57, 60, 73–81; the Confederacy and, 245; Cuba and, 60, 186, 191–93; southern calls to revive, 141–48; U.S. Navy and, 37, 45. See also Navy, U.S.; right of search at sea

Atocha, A. J., 114

Bachman, John, 167

Badger, George, 214

Bagby, Arthur, 108

Bahamas, 23

Bancroft, George, 107, 111, 116

Bartow, Francis, 240, 241

Bayly, Thomas, 99

Bell, John, 213

Benjamin, Judah, 148, 151, 193, 233

Benton, Thomas Hart, 56, 98, 110, 115

Berlin Conference (1884–85), 253

Bermuda, 17, 82

Berrien, John, 14

Bismarck, Otto von, 253

Black Hawk War (1832), 209

blacks. See African Americans; racism; slaves

Black Warrior (U.S. steamer), 192
Blackwood's Magazine, 135
"bleeding Kansas," 176, 201, 219–21
Blight, David, 252
Blue Water Creek, slaughter of Sioux at, 211, 221
Bocock, Thomas, 157, 205–7, 221, 222, 225, 233
Bodichon, Eugène, 165
Bonaparte, Napoleon, 14, 68
Brazil, 70–81, 141–48; Amazon, international navigation of, 144–45, 185, 204; annexation of Texas and, 72, 75; Atlantic slave trade and, 73–81; Confederacy and, 246, 247; diplomatic relations with the U.S., 70–81, 96, 142, 144–47, 185; proslavery thinkers on, 57–59, 70, 138, 141–48, 188; slave economy of, 1, 4, 9, 70, 130; threats to slavery in, 8, 70–72, 78–81, 89
Breckinridge, John C., 238
Britain. *See* Great Britain
British Guiana, 81
British West Indies: apprentice and "coolie" labor in, 16, 18, 77, 154–55, 237; emancipation of slavery in, 1, 12, 15–17, 26–27, 29, 37; free black troops in, 22, 40, 42, 44–45, 62, 81, 85; post-emancipation economy of, 87, 127, 132–33, 135–36, 140, 142, 154–58, 180–81, 236; reenslavement, southern predictions of, 170–71, 184, 186. *See also* Great Britain; Jamaica
Brooks, Preston, 219
Brown, Albert Gallatin, 188, 213, 221
Brown, John, 176
Buchanan, James: on annexation of Texas and war with Mexico, 107–9, 110; Cuba and, 190, 197, 230; as minister to Great Britain, 189–90, 197; on Oregon, 106; as president, 181, 185, 220–22, 224
Butler, Andrew Pickens, 118, 119, 182, 219–20
Butler, Pierce, 97

Calhoun, John C., 6, 8, 11, 32, 54, 101, 104, 223–24, 244; Brazil and, 71–76, 78–79; British abolitionism and, 12, 20–24, 26–27, 30, 31, 50–53, 56, 60, 62, 66, 69, 128; Cuba and, 60, 62, 65–66; death, 134; Jefferson Davis and, 209; Mexican-American War and, 111–13, 118–23; on naval reform, 38–41, 43, 49, 205; on Oregon, 105, 106; as secretary of state, 65–66, 69, 71–76, 81, 92–99; on slavery and the world economy, 128, 129, 134–36, 148, 178–79; Texas and, 85–88, 90–91, 93–99, 101

California, 2, 111, 215; admission to union (1850), 125, 178–80, 223–24; "coolie" labor system in, 155; gold rush (1850), 183; international contest over slavery affecting, 2; Mexican-American War and, 110, 114, 118–21, 123; Monterey, U.S. seizure of, 44–45
camels, 215
Campbell, John A., 132
Campbell, Robert Blair, 63–66, 68
Canada: *Caroline* affair, 19, 20; Maine-New Brunswick border dispute, 19–20, 23, 51
Canning, George, 15
Capitol building, U.S., 217
Caribbean. *See* Latin America and Caribbean; West Indies; *and specific islands*
Carlyle, Thomas, 135, 138, 170
Caroline affair, 19, 20
Cartwright, Samuel, 164–65, 167–68
Cass, Lewis, 26, 120, 155
Central America. *See* Latin America and Caribbean; *and specific countries*
Century magazine, 252
Charleston Courier, 162
Charleston Mercury, 88, 138, 143, 145, 155, 160, 168, 170, 194, 195, 208, 211
Charleston *Southern Patriot*, 28
Charleston Southern Standard, 141
Chartism, 21
Chase, William Henry, 37, 38, 43, 100–101
Cherokee, 97, 213
Chesnut, James, 168–69, 238
Chesnut, Mary, 173, 238
China, 2, 23, 30, 37; Opium Wars, 20, 21, 237
Christy, David, 130, 137
Civil War, 5, 6, 9, 11, 151, 152, 199, 201, 225; Confederate defeat in, 248–50, 251–54; Confederate foreign policy and, 245–48; Mexican-American War and, 112–13, 123–24
Clarkson, Thomas, 135
Clay, Henry, 14, 40, 95, 97
Clayton, Alexander M., 236
Clemson, Thomas, 113
Clingman, Thomas, 184, 237
Cloud, Noah B., 167
Cobb, Howell, 232, 242, 245
coffee. *See* slavery
Colombia, 13, 15, 58, 246
colonialism. *See* imperialism
Colt, Samuel, 46
Colt revolvers, 216
Comanches, 97, 114
Comet (slave trade ship), 17–18

Compromise of 1850, 176, 178, 209

Comte, Auguste, 4

Confederate States of America: Civil War and, 248–50; Constitution, 242–45, 249; creation of, 232–33, 239–45; foreign policy of, 245–48; international confidence, 233–39

Conner, David, 107

Constitution, Confederate, 242–45, 249

Constitution, U.S., 48, 89; annexation of Texas and, 91–92, 95–96, 97–98, 99; Confederate Constitution compared, 244–45

"coolie" and apprentice labor systems, 9, 16, 18, 77, 193; global spread during 1850s, 148–49, 154–58, 171–72

Cooper, Frederick, 153

Cooper, Samuel, 212

"Cornerstone Address" (Alexander Stephens), 166, 234–35

Corn Laws, British abolition of, 128, 179

cotton, 41, 71, 181; annexation of Texas and, 100–101; British abolitionism and, 11–12, 14, 24–28, 30, 100–101; British tariffs, repeal of, 127–28; in proslavery arguments, 136–38, 156; secession and, 234–36, 239, 242. *See also* slavery

Creole slave revolt, 23, 41–42, 44

Crimean War, 175, 179, 181

Crittenden, John J., and Crittenden compromise, 229–31

Cuba, 57–69, 185–98; "Africanization" scare in, 191–96, 206; American offers to purchase, 186, 193; Atlantic slave trade and, 60, 186; British abolitionism and, 15, 59–69, 88, 190; Confederacy and, 246; European diplomacy and, 67–69, 182, 190; filibuster invasions of, 7, 159, 179, 183, 187–89, 194–96, 198, 217–18; Pierce administration and, 189–98; proslavery thinkers on, 57–59; slave economy of, 1, 4, 60, 138, 186; slave uprising (1844) in, 64–65; Tyler administration and, 59–69

Curry, Jabez, 240

Cushing, Caleb, 209

Daniel, John Moncure, 227

Davezac, Auguste, 123

Davis, Charles W., 193, 196

Davis, James Bolton, 156

Davis, Jefferson, 7–8, 9, 51, 136, 146, 164, 198, 202, 236; career and background, 209–10; Cuba and, 187, 196, 217–18; death of, 251–52; in Mexican-American War, 122, 178, 209, 253; as president of Confederacy, 235, 242,

246–49; secession and, 228–29, 231–33, 239; as secretary of war, 189, 196, 201, 209–18, 220–21; as Senate military affairs committee chairman, 201, 209, 221–23; subject of W. E. B. Du Bois lecture (1890), 251–56

De Bow, James Dunwoody Bronson, 129–30, 174, 209, 217; on imperialism, 158, 160, 254; *The Industrial Resources, etc., of the Southern and Western States* (1853), 135, 136–37, 151; on Latin America, 184; on Mexican-American War, 123; on modernity and slavery, 151–52, 169–71; on scientific racism, 164, 166; secession and, 228, 236; on slavery and the world economy, 129–30, 133, 135–37, 139–41, 143, 147

De Bow's Review, 129, 135, 139, 141, 158, 160, 164, 166, 217, 246, 255

Del Monte, Domingo, 61–62, 68, 78

Democratic Party: annexation of Texas and, 82, 89, 95; expansionism and, 121, 190, 197; Mexican-American War and, 119, 121; military reforms of 1850s and, 219–21; naval reform and, 39–40; on Oregon, 105–6; Polk administration and, 103–4; the second party system and, 14, 16

Dew, Thomas Roderick, 57, 60

Dickson, David, 167

diplomatic reform, 217–18

District of Columbia, abolition of slave trade in, 178

Dobbin, James Cochrane, 204–5; Cuba and, 196; Jefferson Davis and, 209; as secretary of the navy, 189, 198, 204–8, 215–16, 218, 220, 225, 228

Dodge, Augustus, 213

Dominican Republic, 81, 184

Dom Pedro II (emperor of Brazil), 79, 146

Donelson, Andrew Jackson, 106–7, 108

Douglas, Stephen, 218

Douglass, Frederick, 166

Dred Scott decision (1857), 19, 176, 224

Du Bois, W. E. B., 5, 9; lecture on Jefferson Davis (1890), 251–56

Dutch. *See* Netherlands

East India Company, 27

Economist, 135

elections: congressional election of 1854, 213, 219; presidential election of 1840, 22, 25; presidential election of 1844, 86, 95, 97, 103; presidential election of 1852, 189; presidential election of 1856, 220, 224; presidential election of 1860, 226–29, 238

Elliot, Charles, 107

Elliott, E. N., 160–61, 167

Emerson, Ralph Waldo, 100, 113, 123, 124

Encomium (slave trade ship), 17–18

England. *See* Great Britain

Enterprise (slave trade ship), 17–19

Espartero, Baldomero, 62–63

Europe: coolie and apprentice labor systems, embrace of, 154–58; empire, global scramble for, 158–63; free trade and consumption of slave-produced products in, 127–34, 236; seeming retreat from abolitionism, 134–41. *See also specific countries*

Evans, Lemuel, 165

Everett, Alexander Hill, 61–62

Everett, Edward, 25, 26–27, 90, 182

Faulkner, Charles James, 132–33, 187, 195, 213, 220

Faust, Drew, 168

Fessenden, William, 220, 232

Fillmore, Millard, 189, 204, 207

Fitzhugh, George, 138–39, 143; on modernity and slavery, 150, 152, 153, 164, 167, 168; secession and, 236, 238, 247

Florida: maroon settlements in, 13; U.S. acquisition of (1819), 37, 83; U.S. naval bases in, 37–39

Floyd, John, 14, 15, 221

Fontaine, C. R., 7–8

foreign policy, U.S., 2–9; before 1833, 12–16; Brazil and, 70–81, 146–47; British abolitionism and, 15–31; Cuba and, 59–69, 185–98; Mexican-American War and, 103–25; reform of the diplomatic service, 217–18; southern control of, 4–5, 50–51, 90–91, 189, 197–98, 224, 225–28; southern views of, during the 1850s, 173–86; Texas and, 82–102; U.S. Army and, 208–25; U.S. Navy and, 32–49, 202–8

Forsyth, John, 18–19, 22, 65, 66–67

Fort Sumter, 125, 183, 247–48

Fox, Henry S., 87

França, Ernesto F., 75–76, 78, 80

France: Algeria, conquest of, 3, 113, 158, 170, 202, 214; apprentice and "coolie" labor in, 154–55; British abolitionism and, 25–26, 28, 30, 41, 56, 69, 87, 90, 96–97, 101; Cuba and, 15, 182, 190, 192; the Dominican Republic and, 184; emancipation of French West Indies (1848), 132–33; Haiti and, 13, 60, 170; seeming retreat from abolitionism, 127,

155–57, 236–37; U.S. naval reform and, 37. *See also* French West Indies

free trade, 127–34, 135, 140, 148, 153, 178–79, 202

Frémont, John C., 220

French West Indies: apprentice and "coolie" labor in, 154–55, 237; emancipation of slavery (1848) in, 132–33; post-emancipation economy of, 127, 132–33, 142; slavery in, 69, 88–89. *See also* France; Martinique

fugitive slave law, 5, 6, 122, 178, 201, 225, 245

Gadsden, James, 96, 136, 183, 196, 322n43

gag rule, 5, 6

Garnett, Charles Fenton Mercer, 147

Garnett, Muscoe Russell Hunter, 147

Garrison, William Lloyd, 227

Giddings, Joshua, 99, 110, 188, 218–19

Gilder, Richard W., 252

Gilmer, Thomas W., 85, 92–93

Gladstone, William, 255

Gliddon, George, 165, 167, 215

Gobineau, Arthur, 165

Graham, William A., 144, 145, 204, 207

Grant, Ulysses S., 113

Grattan, John Lawrence, 211, 212, 221

Grayson, William J., 171–72

Great Britain: abolitionism, British foreign policy and, 10–31, 34–46, 50–102, 127–28, 176–79, 184, 190; Brazil and, 70–80; British West Indies, emancipation of, 15–17; "coolie" labor systems and, 154–58; Cuba and, 182, 190, 192; free trade embraced by, 127–28, 132–33, 178–79; imperial ambitions of, 158, 159, 176, 180–81; mail packets, 202; Mexico and, 44–45, 83–84, 111; Oregon and, 37, 104–6, 121; peace with, as proslavery policy, 51–57, 105–6; as possible ally for the South, 180–81, 238; seeming retreat from abolitionism, 134–39, 236–39; Texas and, 84–89, 93–100, 107; Webster-Ashburton Treaty (1842), 51–53, 55–56, 115. *See also* abolitionism; British West Indies; right of search at sea; Royal Navy

Greeley, Horace, 227

Green, Duff, 11–12, 55, 115, 129, 142; on Brazil, 70–71; British abolitionism and, 11–12, 24–28, 30, 40, 41, 51, 69, 76, 90; on British Guiana, 81; on European planters in Africa, 156; on free trade, 128; on Oregon, 105; on right of search at sea, 25–26, 52; secession and, 228; on Texas, 86, 93, 101; as Tyler administration agent overseas, 25–27, 30, 52, 56, 115

Grinnell, Josiah, 4–5
Guadalupe Hidalgo, Treaty of (1848), 120–21, 178, 183
guano, Peruvian, 185

Hahn, Steven, 227
Haiti: Cuba and, 58, 60, 63, 186; Dominican Republic and, 81; France and, 13, 60, 170; Great Britain and, 23, 27; possible reenslavement of, 170–72, 247; revolution in, 13–14; Texas and, 86; Venezuela and, 82
Hale, John, 222, 232
Hamilton, Hamilton, 77
Hamilton, James, 15
Hamlin, Hannibal, 118, 221
Hammond, James Henry: on annexation of Texas, 98; army reform and, 223; British abolitionism and, 20, 30; on "coolie" labor systems, 154–55; naval reform, 41; scientific racism and, 164; secession and, 228; on slavery and the world economy, 127, 145–46
Harney, William S., 211
Harper, William, 53–55, 57–58, 60, 158–59
Harper's Ferry, John Brown's raid on, 176
Harrison, Robert Monroe, 22, 63, 87
Harrison, William Henry, 25, 40
Harvey, William, 234
Hébert, Paul, 191–92
Hegel, Georg Wilhelm Friedrich, 4
Herndon, William Lewis, 144–46
Herrera, José Joaquín, 109
Hilliard, Henry W., 170
Hobsbawm, Eric, 2, 3, 133, 158, 255
Hogan, John, 81
Holcombe, James, 163
Holcombe, William H., 237
Holland. *See* Netherlands
Holmes, George Frederick, 139, 140, 255
Holmes, Oliver Wendell, 251
Home Squadron, 40–41, 43, 107
Honduras, 184
Horne, Gerald, 74, 145
Houston, Sam, 92, 213, 214, 222
Hughes, Henry, 167
Hunt, Memucan, 85, 101–2
Hunter, Robert Mercer Taliaferro, 173–75, 179, 209; army reform and, 212, 213, 218, 219, 220; Capitol extension plan and, 217; on Cuba, 187, 188, 197, 230; on imperialism and slavery, 163; on Mexican-American War, 114, 120; Pierce administration and, 189; secession and, 228, 230, 231, 233, 237, 239, 242–47, 249; on slavery

and the world economy, 126–27, 175–77; speech on Kansas-Nebraska bill, 173–77

imperialism: abolitionism and, 163, 254; Confederate foreign policy and, 245–48; Cuba and, 176, 180–81; European scramble for empire, 158–63, 251–54; racism and, 159–60, 162, 163, 180–81, 255; secession and, 229–33
Indian rebellion (1857), 159, 169
Indians. *See* American Indians
internal colonialism, 214
international law, British abolitionism and, 17–19, 23. *See also* right of search at sea
Irving, Washington, 64–65, 69

Jackson, Andrew, 7, 51; British abolitionism and, 12, 31; Democratic Party and, 14; Florida, conquest of, 13; Jefferson Davis and, 209; Maine-New Brunswick border dispute and, 52; presidential campaign of 1828 and, 11; on southern political power, 91; on Texas, 85–86, 97, 249
Jamaica, 22, 42, 61–63, 87, 132, 157, 186. *See also* British West Indies
Japan, 159, 161, 207
Jefferson, Thomas: on Cuba, 59; on Great Britain, 14, 15; Louisiana Purchase and, 95; naval reform and, 34; on Texas, 82–83
Johnson, Andrew, 222
Jollivet, Thomas Marie Adolphe, 69, 101
Jones, Anson, 107
Jones, Thomas ap Catesby, 44–45

Kansas: "bleeding Kansas," 176, 201, 219, 220, 221; Lecompton Constitution, 224
Kansas-Nebraska debates: army reform and, 206, 212, 213, 217; "coolie" labor systems and, 157; Cuba and, 195, 197; Democratic Party, turn against, 219; Hunter on, 173–78
Kearney, Stephen W., 114
Keitt, Lawrence, 221–22, 248
Kettell, Thomas, 130, 132, 133
Kilpatrick, A. R., 162
King, Thomas Butler, 40–41, 47, 60, 202–4
King, William R., 90, 96–97, 101, 123, 132, 134
Kiowas, 97
Know-Nothing Party, 219, 220
Knox, Robert, 165

Lakota Sioux, 210–12, 221
Latham, R. G., 165

Latin America and Caribbean, 6; Confederate foreign policy and, 246; Crittenden compromise and, 229–31; filibuster invasions of, 7, 159, 179, 183, 187–89, 194–96, 198, 217–18; Monroe Doctrine and, 14–15, 67–68; proslavery views of, 57–59, 139–40, 141–48, 162; revolutions against Spain, 13; U.S. diplomacy in the 1850s and, 182–86. *See also specific countries*

Lecompton Constitution (Kansas), 224

Lee, Daniel, 161, 163, 167

Lee, Robert E., 187, 252

Legaré, Hugh Swinton, 16, 17, 87

Lenin, Vladimir Illich, 114

Leopold (king of Belgium), 255

Lester, Charles Edwards, 137

Levy, Jacob, 136

Lincoln, Abraham, 126, 176, 226–29, 231, 240–42, 251

Lincoln, Robert Todd, 252

Livingstone, David, 162, 254

London Cotton Supply Reporter, 236

London Times, 135, 236

López, Narciso, 187, 189

Louisiana Purchase, 95, 240

Lovejoy, Owen, 222

MacArthur, Douglas, 116

Macaulay, Thomas B., 100, 163

Mackenzie, Alexander Slidell, 115

Madison, Dolly, 93

Madison, James, 13, 15

Madisonian, 27, 42, 51, 56, 85, 88

Magnolia; or, Southern Monthly, 49

Mahan, Alfred Thayer, 208

mail steamers, 202–4

Mallory, Stephen: army reform and, 205, 207, 213, 216, 218, 224, 225; on Cuba, 193, 194; secession and, 228, 231–33

Malte-Brun, Conrad, 165

manifest destiny, 82, 104, 159, 179, 183, 206

Mann, Ambrose Dudley, 189

Marcy, William: Cuba and, 190, 192–93, 196; Jefferson Davis and, 209; Mexican-American War and, 111, 116, 117; in Pierce administration, 189

Martinique, 69, 132. *See also* French West Indies

Marx, Karl, 7, 150, 260

Mason, James Murray: on Cuba, 184, 185, 187; secession and, 228, 230–33, 239; on slavery and the world economy, 134

Mason, John Y., 155, 189, 196, 197

Maury, Matthew Fontaine: on naval reform, 35–38, 40, 42–43, 46–48, 203–4, 207, 216; on right of search at sea, 42, 52; scientific racism and, 167; secession and, 228, 231; on slavery and Latin America, 143–46, 162, 182, 185, 254

Maximilian (emperor of Mexico), 36

McCord, Louisa, 139–40; on imperialism, 159, 161; on scientific racism, 165–67; on slavery and the world economy, 139–40

McCulloch, John Ramsay, 138–39

McGavock, Randal, 135–36

McLane, Louis, 106

Meade, Richard Kidder, 146–47, 203–4

Memphis Daily Appeal, 206

Mexican-American War (1846–1848), 8, 103–24; American responses to victory in, 122–24, 178, 182–83; annexation of Texas and, 106–9; Calhoun and, 111–12, 113, 118–23; causes of, 107–11; European diplomacy and, 111, 122–23, 178–79; Guadalupe Hidalgo, Treaty of (1848), 120–21, 178, 183; as imperial episode, 112–14, 122–24; Mexico City, U.S. occupation of, 84, 115–7, 120; Polk and, 104, 107–12, 114–23; slavery and, 7, 110–11, 117, 119–24; U.S. Army and, 113, 115–16, 117, 118–19; Veracruz, U.S. capture of, 115–16, 120, 183; as war of conquest and expropriation, 112–17

Mexico: Confederate foreign policy and, 246–47; Cuban slavery, as threat to, 58; ex-Confederate migration to, 36; rumored alliance with Great Britain, 44–45, 83–84; Sonora, U.S. purchase of, 183; Tehuantepec, claims of American right of access to, 185. *See also* Mexican-American War; New Mexico; Texas

Mill, John Stuart, 139, 140

Milton, John, 142

Mississippi declaration of secession, 235–36

Missouri Compromise (1819–1821), 13, 229

modernity, slaveholding visions of, 9, 150–72; antimodern defenses of slavery, 150, 152, 168; "coolie" labor systems and, 154–58; imperialism and slavery, 158–63; science, 163–69; slavery and progress, 152–54, 157–58, 169–72

Molinari, Gustave de, 140

Monroe, James, 13, 15, 83

Monroe Doctrine, 14–15, 67–68

Monterey, California, U.S. seizure of, 44–45

Montgomery Convention, 242–45, 249

Mormons, 221
Morton, Richard, 147
Morton, Samuel George, 165
Murphy, William S., 87–88, 92

Napoleon Bonaparte, 14, 68
Napoleon III (emperor of France), 155
Nation, 251, 255
Native Americans. *See* American Indians
Navigation Acts, British abolition of, 128, 179
Navy, British. *See* Royal Navy
Navy, U.S., 8; antebellum southern efforts to
    expand, 32–49, 181, 202–8; Atlantic slave
    trade and, 37, 45; Brazil and, 76, 79; British
    abolitionism and, 34–35, 37–38, 41–45, 49,
    203; bureaucratic structure, 46–48; Cuba
    and, 63–64, 66–68, 187, 195–96, 206, 218;
    Home Squadron and, 40–41, 43, 107;
    Mexican-American War and, 107; Pacific
    Ocean and, 20, 37, 44–46, 112, 114, 203, 208;
    states' rights and, 32, 47, 48–49; technology
    and, 40, 46, 93, 204–5, 216; Venezuela and, 82
Nebraska, "Fort Laramie massacre," debate
    over, 210–13. *See also* Kansas-Nebraska
    debates
Netherlands: British abolitionism and, 30, 81;
    "coolie" labor systems and, 4, 154; Dutch
    Guiana, 81; free trade in, 129; as imperial
    power, 158, 253
New Mexico: army education in Spanish and,
    215; Compromise of 1850, 178; Mexican-
    American War and, 114, 118–21, 123;
    secession and, 230
New Orleans, Battle of (1815), 37
New Orleans Commercial Bulletin, 45–46, 53,
    59–60, 67–68, 69
New Orleans Daily Picayune, 170
New York Times, 142, 147, 193
New Zealand, 20, 158
Nicaragua, 7, 159, 183–85
northern states, growth of, 125, 179–80,
    223–24
Northup, Solomon, 123
Nott, Josiah, 164–65, 167
nullification crisis, 40

Oakes, James, 227
O'Donnell, Leopoldo, 64
Opium Wars, 20, 21, 237
Oregon, 37, 104–6; Calhoun on, 105–6;
    Mexican-American War and, 109–10, 123;
    Polk on, 104–6, 109, 110, 121; Tyler on, 106

Ostend Manifesto, 197
Ottoman Empire, 2, 20, 156, 157, 175, 228

Pakenham, Richard, 93–95, 99
Palmerston, Lord, 17, 18, 19, 26, 254
Panama Congress (1826), 13–14
Panic of 1837, 28, 129
Panic of 1857, 222
Paraguay, 185
Paredes y Arrillaga, Mariano, 109, 115
Parker, Theodore, 2
The Partisan Leader (Tucker, 1836), 10–12, 24, 27,
    32, 91
Pedro II (emperor of Brazil), 79, 146
Peel, Sir Robert, 86–87, 128
Pensacola Gazette, 38
Perkins, John, 217
Perry, Matthew C., 37, 207
Peru, 1, 44–45, 146, 185
Pezuela, Juan de, 191–96
Pickens, Francis, 20, 22–24, 55, 105
Pierce, Franklin: army reform and, 198, 204–5,
    208–11, 216, 218–20, 222, 227; Cuba and,
    189–90, 192, 193, 195, 196, 198; free trade and,
    129; as president, 156, 184, 189–90, 209
Poe, Edgar Allan, 10
Poinsett, Joel, 58
Polk, James K., 6; annexation of Texas and, 89,
    95, 97–98, 106–10; British abolitionism and,
    31; Cuba, offer to purchase, 186; executive
    power, use of, 115–16; Mexican-American
    War and, 104, 107–12, 114–23; naval
    development under, 204; Oregon and,
    104–6, 109, 110, 121; Tyler administration
    compared, 103–4, 111–12, 115
Porcher, Frederick, 150, 152
Potter, David, 121
Powell, Levin M., 43
Princeton (ship): explosion of gun on, 92–93; in
    Mexican-American War, 107
Prussian general staff, 202, 215
Puerto Rico, 14, 191

Quintuple Treaty (1841), 25–26, 30, 42, 49, 56
Quitman, John, 194–96, 197–98

racism: annexation of Texas and, 83–86,
    96–97; army reform and, 206, 213;
    European imperialism and, 159–63, 180–81,
    253–55; free African Americans and, 94–95,
    171–72, 204; Mexican-American War and,
    113–14; scientific racism, 164–68, 234; in

racism *(continued)*
    southern attitudes toward Cuba, 66, 190–94,
      197; in southern attitudes toward Latin
      America, 13–14, 16–17, 79–82, 96–97, 140–48,
      159, 175–79, 206
Randolph, John, 13–14, 15
Rathbun, George, 98
republicanism, 32–34, 51, 180, 208–9
Republican Party: antislavery principles of,
    125–26; army reform resisted by, 219–23,
    224; Cuban annexation and, 197; secession
    and, 226–32
Revolutionary War, 13, 113, 128, 177
Revolutions of 1848, 123, 125
Rhett, Robert Barnwell, 173, 297n69
rice. *See* slavery
Richmond Daily Dispatch, 130
Richmond Enquirer, 7, 20, 22, 191, 193–94, 208–9
Richmond Examiner, 227, 241
Richmond Whig, 36
right of search at sea, 25–26; Brazil and, 77;
    naval reform and, 42, 44; Quintuple Treaty
    (1841), 25–26, 30, 42, 49, 56; Webster-
    Ashburton Treaty (1842), 51–53, 55–56
Robertson, William H., 192, 196
Roosevelt, Theodore, 253, 254, 255
Royal Navy: Atlantic slave trade and, 28, 45,
    51–52, 57, 60, 73–81; U.S. naval reform and,
    33–34, 37–39, 41–46, 202, 203
Ruffin, Edmund, 159, 167
Russell, John, 128
Russell, William Howard, 238
Russell's Magazine, 170
Russia, serfs in, 138, 157

Saint Domingue, 13, 66
Santa Anna, Antonio López de, 83, 114–15, 116
Schlesinger, Arthur, 5
scientific racism, 163–69, 234, 237
Scott, Robert G., 147
Scott, Winfield, 116–17, 120, 124, 216
secession, southern, 9, 226–45; compared to
    other world secessionist movements,
    239–41; Crittenden compromise and,
    229–31; early advocates for, 10–12, 178,
    180–81; election of 1860 and, 226–29;
    empire, southern concern with, 229–33;
    international status of slavery and, 234–39;
    states' rights and, 244–45, 249
second party system, 16, 22, 40, 125
secret service, 96, 107, 115
Sevier, Ambrose, 117

Seward, William, 155, 200, 213, 216, 220, 228, 254
Sherman, John, 219
Simms, William Gilmore, 123–24, 137–38, 162
Simpson, Craig M., 74
slavery, 1–9; American domestic politics and,
    16, 22, 40, 49, 90–91, 94–95, 117, 120, 125–26,
    134, 148, 173–78, 201, 216–25, 226–33; Brazil
    and, 8, 70–81, 141–48; British abolitionism
    and, 8, 10–31; Confederacy and, 233–50;
    "coolie" labor systems and, 154–58; Cuba
    and, 57–69, 185–98; European imperialism
    and, 158–63; free trade and, 127–34, 135, 140,
    148, 153, 178–79; future of, 169–72, 235–38;
    historical interpretations of, 2–3, 150–53;
    industrial development and, 129, 136;
    international legacy of, 251–56; Mexico and,
    8, 103–24; modernity and, 9, 150–72;
    paternalist arguments for, 139–40, 160–63;
    reestablishment of in the West Indies,
    170–72, 179, 184, 186, 247; science and,
    163–69; secession and, 9, 226–39; staple
    agriculture and, 9, 125–49; Texas and, 8,
    82–102; U.S. military reform and, 8–9,
    32–49, 199–225; the world economy and, 9,
    125–49
slaves: in Brazil, 57–58, 73–81, 145; in Cuba,
    57–66, 186–96, 206; fugitives, 110, 122, 178;
    revolts, real and imagined, 13, 16–17, 23, 41,
    64–65, 78, 87, 163, 186, 206, 249–50; in
    Texas, 83–86, 110; in the United States, 13,
    16–17, 23, 110, 122–23, 160, 167–68, 171–72,
    204, 251
Slidell, John: on Cuba, 193, 194, 196, 197;
    Mexican-American War and, 109–10;
    secession and, 231, 233
Sloat, John, 114
Smith, Adam, 234
Soulé, Pierre: Cuba and, 190–91, 193, 195–97,
    218; in Pierce administration, 189
Southern Cultivator, 156
Southern Literary Messenger, 36, 70, 124, 157, 163,
    203, 291n92
Southern Quarterly Review, 27, 30, 70, 113, 132, 139,
    145, 181–82
southern states, power in American politics,
    4–8, 16, 90–91, 189, 197–98, 224, 226–29, 239
Spain: attitude toward slavery, 68–69, 188, 196,
    246; British abolitionism and, 28, 59–60,
    89, 186; Confederacy and, 246; diplomatic
    relations with the U.S., 62–69, 83, 96, 186,
    188, 196–97; Latin American revolutions
    and, 13–14. *See also* Cuba

Spratt, Leonidas W., 141–45

Stanton, Frederick, 204

states' rights, 5–6; army reform and, 201, 208–10, 216–20; Confederacy and, 240, 244–45, 249; Mexican-American War and, 104, 112, 118–19, 122; naval reform and, 32–35, 47, 48–49, 203–4; slavery and, 50–51, 174–76, 201; Texas and, 89, 99–100

steam power, 40, 60, 202–4, 205

Stephen, Leslie, 251

Stephens, Alexander: "Cornerstone Address," 166, 234, 235; Cuba and, 197; memoirs of, 256; scientific racism and, 166, 234; secession and, 231, 233–35, 239, 241–42, 248; on slavery and foreign policy, 7, 239

Stevenson, Andrew, 18–20, 25

Stockton, Robert F., 37, 92–93, 107–8

Story, Joseph, 48

Stowe, Harriet Beecher, 135

sugar: British tariffs, repeal of, 127–28, 132; Cuba, slave economy of, 60, 138, 186; French West Indies, emancipation of, 132. *See also* slavery: the world economy and

Sumner, Charles, 157, 176, 213, 219

Syria, British involvement in, 20, 23

Taylor, Zachary, 108–13, 178, 204, 226

technology: science, proslavery interest in, 163–69, 234; steam power, 40, 60, 202–4, 205; U.S. Army and, 201, 216; U.S. Navy and, 40, 46, 93, 204–5, 216

Texas, 7–8, 82–102; American annexation of, 90–100, 106–9; Brazil and, 72, 75; British abolitionism and, 72, 83–88, 93–97, 107, 128; cotton trade and, 100–101; independence from Mexico, 82–83; Polk administration and, 89, 95, 97–98, 106–10; threats to slavery in, 83–89; Tyler administration and, 50, 84–89, 91–93, 95–99, 101

Thompson, Waddy, 61, 89

Thornwell, James Henley, 161

tobacco. *See* slavery: the world economy and

Toombs, Robert, 229, 231, 233, 242, 246–47

Townsend, John, 238, 240

Trescot, William Henry: army reform and, 205; on Cuba, 188–89, 197; foreign policy views of, 179–82; *The Position and Course of the South* (1850), 179–81; secession and, 241–42, 249

Trist, Nicholas, 120–21

Trollope, Anthony, 135, 236

Trotsky, Leon, 114

Tucker, Nathaniel Beverley: Abel Upshur, correspondence with, 55; *George Balcombe* (1836), 10, 12; naval reform and, 48; *The Partisan Leader* (1836), 10–12, 24, 27, 32, 91; Texas and, 88, 91–92

Turkey, 2, 20, 156, 157, 175, 228

Turnbull, David, 63

Turner, Nat, 16

Tyler, John: annexation of Texas and, 50, 84–89, 91, 92, 93, 95–99, 101, 106, 108; Brazil and, 70, 71, 72–73, 75, 77–78, 81; British abolitionism and, 24, 25–27, 31, 50–51; Cuba and, 58, 61–67; on Mexican-American War, 124; on naval reform, 32, 40, 44, 47, 48, 204; on Oregon, 106; Polk administration compared, 103–4, 111, 112, 115; secession and, 228, 230–31; succeeding Harrison as president, 25, 40

Uncle Tom's Cabin (Stowe, 1852), 135

United Kingdom. *See* Great Britain

United States Telegraph, 11

Upshur, Abel Parker: Brazil and, 71; British abolitionism and, 25, 26, 31, 52, 55–56; Cuba and, 62–65; death in *Princeton* explosion, 93; review of Story's *Commentaries on the Constitution* (1840), 48; as secretary of state, 50–51, 62–65, 85, 87–94, 97; as secretary of the navy, 6, 32–35, 36, 41, 42–49, 202, 205, 207, 254

Uruguay, civil war in, 75–76

U.S. Constitution. *See* Constitution, U.S.

Utah, 178, 221

Van Buren, Martin: British abolitionism and, 19, 22; Cuba and, 58; Maine-New Brunswick border dispute and, 52; naval reform and, 40; Texas and, 95; in Tucker's *The Partisan Leader*, 10, 11

Van Zandt, Isaac, 93

Venable, Abraham, 188

Venezuela, 82, 159, 189

Vesey, Denmark, 16–17

Wade, Benjamin, 219

Walker, Robert J., 83

Walker, William, 183, 184

War of 1812, 13, 113

Washington, George, 65, 116

Washington Union, 156, 211

Webster, Daniel: British abolitionism and, 22, 26; as secretary of state, 51–53, 56, 62, 65–66, 87, 115, 190

Webster-Ashburton Treaty (Treaty of
   Washington: 1842), 51–53, 55–56, 115
Westcott, James, 134–35
West Indies. *See* British West Indies; French
   West Indies
West Point, 33, 199, 209, 210, 215
Whig Party (American): annexation of Texas
   and, 89, 95; British abolitionism and, 16,
   22, 25, 26; Mexican-American War and,
   111, 118–19, 121; naval reform and, 38–40
Wickliffe, Charles, 107, 108
Wilberforce, William, 135
Wilmot, David, 117, 119, 120

Wise, Henry Alexander, 72–73; Atlantic
   slave trade and, 73–80; British abolitionism and, 20, 96; on election of 1860,
   227; as minister to Brazil, 73–81; on naval
   reform, 47; secession and, 228–29; on
   slavery in Brazil, 145; on Texas, 84, 96,
   100
Woolf, Virginia, 251
Wurdemann, J. G. F., 61, 68, 79

Yancey, William Lowndes, 101, 173
Yell, Archibald, 107
Young America movement, 190